Honomichl on Marketing Research

Jack J. Honomichl

This limited special edition has been published exclusively for the friends of Survey Sampling, Inc. in appreciation of their continued support.

NTC Business Books
a division of National Textbook Company • Lincolnwood Illinois U.S.A.

Published by Crain Books, an imprint of National
Textbook Company, 4255 West Touhy Avenue,
Lincolnwood, Illinois 60646-1975
© 1986 by Jack J. Honomichl. All rights reserved. No
part of this book may be reproduced, stored in a retrieval system, or transmitted in any form, or by any
means, electronic, mechanical, photocopying or
otherwise, without the prior written permission of
National Textbook Company

Library of Congress Catalog Card Number: 85-062994
International Standard Book Number: 0-8442-3092-8

Manufactured in the United States of America.

5 6 7 8 9 0 IS 9 8 7 6 5 4 3 2 1

To Rance Crain for opening the pages of *Advertising Age* to the world of research, and to F.A.H. in memory of *The Analyst.*

Contents

Part 1   Marketing Case Histories
  Preface to Part 1

  Chapter 1   Ore-Ida: Mom, Flag—and a French Fry   1
    Part I   1
      Growing Pains   2   •   Young Turks Take Over   4
      Sales vs. Marketing   6
    Part II   8
      Now We Are National   9   •   Food Service Market   12
      Breezing into the '80s   14
    Interview with Paul Corddry   16

  Chapter 2   President Reagan's Marketing Plan, 1980   27
    The Development of Reagan's Marketing Plan   28
      The Black Book   30   •   The Issues   32
      Reagan Approves   34
    The Final Predictions   35
      Modeling   36   •   13 States to Carter   38
      An 11-Point Spread   38
    Postelection Analysis   39
      The Undecided Vote   41

  Chapter 3   The Big Four of Political Research   43
    The Background of Political Polling   43
      Marketing Orientation   44
    The Big Four   46
      Robert M. Teeter   46   •   Richard B. Wirthlin   47
      Peter D. Hart   48   •   Patrick H. Caddell   49
    What It All Means   49
    Postscript (August 1985)   51

  Chapter 4   Election '84: Inside Reagan's Research   53
    "I Listen to America Speak"   53
      Long-Range Plans   54   •   Listening In   55
      Copy Testing   55   •   Hands Across the Sea   57
    Postelection Interviews with Richard Wirthlin and Peter Hart   58
      Interview with Richard Wirthlin   58
      Interview with Peter Hart   65

Chapter 5   "Catch the Spirit": Selling the United States   73
   The Assignment   73
   Solicitation No. 50-SATS-4-00017   74
   Ms. Tuttle??   77
   The A Team   78
   Catch the Spirit   81
   Budget Cuts   82
   Why Germany?   84
   Donna Tuttle - Effective Leader   85
   Interview with Donna Tuttle   85

Chapter 6   The Marketing of Cycle Dog Food   91
   Setting the Stage   91
      The Topeka Plant 92 • Enter Cycle 93
      First Test Market 94
   The Magic Number   94
      Heavy Expenditures 95 • Signs of Weakness 96
   Cycle Dry   97
      Changes in 1981 98 • Cycle 2 Revisited 99
   Full Circle   99
   Postscript (August 1985)   100

Chapter 7   Marketing a Marketing Information Service   101
   The Launch   101
   Market Study   102
   IRI Leads the Way   103
   Staffing Up   105
   New Offices   106
   The Missing Link   106
   Going Public   108
   D-Day   110
   Interview with Arthur Nielsen, Jr.   110

Chapter 8   The Marketing of Arm & Hammer   117
   The Marketing Story—The Product as Hero   117
      Cool Sales Spur 118 • Behind the Campaign 120

Previous Expansion Efforts 122 • Research Guidance 123
The Bottom Line 124 • The Current Situation 125

Baking Soda: What Is It? How Does It Work? 125

Bob Davies Looks Back: "If I Had It to Do Over Again" 127

Postscript (August 1985) 133

Chapter 9 How Detroit Reacted to the Imported Car Threat 135

Early Background - The Compacts 135
The Dinosaur 136 • Charlie Brown's Falcon 137
U.S. News Story 139

The Middle Years—Monza, and Others 140
Unsafe at Any Speed 140 • Half-Hearted Response 141

The Foreign Approach 142

The OPEC Impact 144

The Government's Role 146

Postscript (August 1985) 149

Chapter 10 Launching Renault's Alliance 151

The Alliance Story 151
Born of Necessity 152 • Need to Sell Dealers 153
The X-42 153 • Naming the Baby 154
The Advertising Battle—Grey vs. Compton 156
Robots in Kenosha 158 • Task Force 159
Announcement Day 160 • Aftermath 161

W. Paul Tippett, Jr., Talks about the Alliance 162

Postscript (August 1985) 167

Part 2 The U.S. Marketing Research Industry 169

Preface to Part 2 171

Chapter 11 The U.S. Research Industry 173

The Early History 173

Chapter 12 A.C. Neilsen, Sr.: Obituary Traces History 177

A.C. Nielsen, Sr. 177
The Dark Days 178 • Into Broadcast 179

Chapter 13 Alfred Politz: A German-American Original 183
Overview of Politz's Life 183
Alfred Politz Research, Inc. 185
 Politz U. 185
The Legend 190
 Early Years in New York 191 • Cumulative Audience 193
 The Heyday '50's 195 • Perpetual Motion 198
 Fighting the Establishment 200 • Retirement in 1967 201
 November 8, 1982 202

Chapter 14 Princeton: U.S. Research Capital 203
What Princeton is Like 203
 Gallup Organization 208 • Opinion Research Corporation
 (ORC) 209 • Benson & Benson 209 • Gallup &
 Robinson 210 • Schrader Research & Rating Service
 (SRRS) 210 • Response Analysis Corporation (RAC) 211
 Total Research Corporation (TRC) 211 • Research 100 212
 Spencer Bruno Research Associates (SBRA) 212 • Mapes &
 Ross 212 • Frank Reeder Marketing Research 212
 R L Associates (RLA) 213 • Mathematica Policy Research
 (MPR) 213 • J. Ross Associates (RA) 214 • Hase -
 Schannen Research Associates (HSR) 214 • Kenneth Hollander
 Associates 214 • Princeton Research & Consulting Center
 (PRCC) 214 • Audits & Surveys (Government Research
 Division) 215

Chapter 15 Top Forty U.S. Research Firms 217
U.S. Research Industry Grows 13.7% in 1984 218
The Urge of Merge 222
Size of U.S. Market 223
Individual Company Profiles 224
 A.C. Nielsen Company 224 • IMS International 225
 Selling Areas - Marketing, Inc. (SAMI) 226 • Arbitron Ratings
 Company 226 • Burke Marketing Services, Inc. (BMSI) 227
 M/A/R/C, Inc. 228 • Market Facts, Inc. 229
 Information Resources, Inc. 229 • NFO Research, Inc. 230
 The NPD Group 231 • Maritz Market Research, Inc. 232
 Westat, Inc. 232 • Elrick and Lavidge, Inc. 233
 Walker Research, Inc. 233 • YSW Group 234
 Chilton Research Services 234 • ASI Market Research 235
 Louis Harris and Associates, Inc. 235 • Opinion Research
 Corporation 236 • The Ehrhart-Babic Group, Inc. 236
 Winona Research, Inc. 237 • Simmons Market Research Bureau
 (SMRB) 237 • Data Development Corporation (DDC) 238
 Decisions Center, Inc. (DCI) 238 • Harte-Hanks Marketing
 Services Group 239 • McCollum/Spielman & Co., Inc. 239

Admar Research Company, Inc. 240 • Custom Research, Inc. 240 • National Analysts 241 • Decision/Making/Information 241 • Consumer Research Division, Management Decision Systems, Inc. 242 • The Gallup Organization 242 Starch INRA Hooper, Inc. 243 • Mediamark Research, Inc. 243 Market Opinion Research 244 • Kapuler Marketing Research, Inc. 244 • Ad Factors Marketing Research 245 Response Analysis 245 • Decision Research Corporation 246 Oxtoby-Smith, Inc. 246

Marketing Information Service Firms Grow Rapidly During 1984   **247**

Marketing Information Service Firm Profiles   **248**
Claritas, L.P. 248 • EPSILON 248 Interactive Market Systems (IMS) 249 • Majers Corporation 250 Management Decision Systems, Inc. 250 • SPAR, Inc. 251

Chapter 16   Top Fifteen World Research Organizations   253

The World of Research   253

Company Profiles   255
A.C. Nielsen Company 255 • IMS International 255 Selling Areas—Marketing, Inc. (SAMI) 256 Arbitron Ratings Company 256 • AGB Research PLC 256 Burke Marketing Services, Inc. (BMSI) 257 • Information Resources, Inc. (IRI) 257 • Research International (RI) 258 M/A/R/C, Inc. 258 • Market Facts, Inc. 258 • Infratest 259 GFK 259 • The NPD Group 259 • Maritz Market Research 259 • Westat, Inc. 260

Postscript (August 1985)   260

Chapter 17   How Much Is Spent on Research in the U.S.?   261

Adding Up the Numbers   261

The Nonprofits   264

Chapter 18   TV Copy Testing Flap   267

TV Copy Testing Flap: What to Do About It   267
Improvement Is Possible 268 • 32,500 Commercial Exposures a Year 269 • Those Who Have the Gold, Rule 269 Why Blame Copy Testing? 270 • Multi-Faceted Inquiry 271 Fighting the Curve 272 • Ten Ways to Improve the Situation 273

Copy Testing Techniques   274
Day-After Recall 274 • Persuasion Testing 276 Physiological Testing 277

Top Creatives - What They Say   279

Chapter 19   The Research Function in Top
              U.S. Advertising Agencies   281
  An Overview   281
      Agencies, Clients Differ 284
  Agency Research Profiles   286
      Young & Rubicam 286 • BBDO 287 • Leo Burnett USA 288
      Foote, Cone & Belding Communications 289 • J. Walter
      Thompson USA 290 • Ted Bates & Company 291 • Doyle
      Dane Bernbach, Inc. 292 • Grey Advertising, Inc. 293
      Needham, Harper & Steers Advertising, Inc. 294 • D'Arcy-
      MacManus & Masius 295

Part 3   The Future of Marketing   297

Chapter 20   Turmoil in the U.S. Research Industry:
              What Will the New Order Bring?   299
  The Speech   299
      Exhibit 1 300 • Exhibit 2 302 • Exhibit 3 305
      Exhibit 4 307 • Exhibit 5 307

Chapter 21   A Final Word   309

Name Index   313

Company/Product/Service Index   321

Foreword

If someone were to ask me to read a history of the market research business, I would probably tell them to stick it in their ear. Business histories have a way of turning people off. But, I would be wrong in this case.

One of the gifts that enriches our lives is the ability to make factual information interesting, even exciting. Jack Honomichl has this gift in spades. He has written a real "page turner." If there ever was to be a story of the world of market research, it would have to have been written by Jack—and here it is. He has created an exciting case book and history.

The science of marketing research is not a science at all. It is a mysterious combination of art and scientific method with some statistics and psychology thrown in. It is really the efforts of some fascinating people —some good, some not so good, some of them quite brilliant, and some of them just very lucky. They have developed a tool which permits businesses and politicians to predict with accuracy what will happen in the future.

In a sense, *Honomichl on Marketing Research* is two books which achieve very different effects. Part One, "Marketing Case Histories," takes us through the process of finding out how marketers' predictions take place and how they work out. It looks at the use of marketing research to answer questions like, how did we keep our car industry alive when it was attacked by a powerfully skilled opponent from Japan? How did Arm & Hammer manage to take a prosaic commodity like baking soda and turn it into a very successful new type of air freshener? How do our presidents get elected today?

Then in Part Two, "The U.S. Marketing Research Industry," the author takes us into the lives of some really fascinating people who made it happen. People like A.C. Nielsen, Sr. and Alfred Politz are truly legendary figures. They are as important to this industry as Jefferson and Adams were to this country. How did they do it?

I remember in my early days being fascinated with Alfred Politz's insistence that he talk only to top management who were in a decision-making mode. He took marketing research out of some of the horrible errors they were making like trying to predict elections in the 30's from telephone interviews when phone ownership was a sign of affluence and probably Republicanism. The industry has come a long say since then and Jack shows clearly how it happens and where it is today.

Marketing research is an important business and it's a big industry. It's a treat to have the major facts about this field presented in such an appealing way. Jack has given us a history with feelings and humanity. It's all here—the controversies and the agreements, the successes and the failures, the breakthroughs and the breakdowns.

David Hardin
Chairman, Market Facts, Inc.

Part 1
Marketing Case Histories

Preface to Part 1

As of 1984, about $88.8 billion is spent annually on advertising in measured media in the United States, including direct mail, according to estimates prepared for *Advertising Age* by Robert J. Coen, senior vp, McCann-Erickson, New York. Another $83 billion is spent on sales promotion each year, a large portion of which is in the package goods field, according to estimates by Russell D. Bowman of Westfield Marketing. I calculate that about $1.6 billion is spent in the U.S. each year on advertising/marketing/public opinion research, most of which is marketing related. Lord knows how much more is spent on other implementers of the marketing process—product publicity, new product development, trade shows, package design, etc. But beyond the awesome boxcar expenditures, marketing efforts are a drive spring for our national economy—the font of new, improved products and services that power growth, make jobs, and ultimately create prosperity.

This is my personal point of view, and everything in this book finds its roots in my conviction that marketing—and its integral ally, marketing research—is one of the most important, engaging, and intrinsically interesting fields of commercial endeavor.

Yet, given its importance, unfortunately little is written on the subject—and lots of what is comes from outsiders looking in. What these people report is often illuminating and worthwhile, but—somehow—it seldom does justice to the raw endeavor as viewed and experienced from the inside. That insider's point of view, I hope, is what I have accurately reflected, appreciated, and documented in the articles that comprise this book.

One reason that insiders do not often tell their tales is, of course, confidentiality. Much of the behind-the-scenes work done in marketing and marketing research is considered proprietary; after all, it's been done at considerable expense with the intent of getting the edge on competitors. This is especially true of marketing, advertising, and new product developmental research that is done to develop and perfect marketing plans that, one hopes, are attuned to the wants and needs of some segment of American society. These studies are considered secret, and seldom do the detailed findings get aired in public.

So, much of what is written in this book would not have been possible without the full cooperation of those top executives who, for the first time, provided a writer access to their private marketing files and studies. Their candor, plus insights from innumerable marketing functionaries who were hands-on participants in the stories being told, have made possible the revelatory writing, which, unfortunately, is quite rare.

Aldous Huxley is quoted as saying, "Experience is not what happens to you; it is what you do with what happens to you." I subscribe to that. You will find a bit of marketing philosophy in this book, but more important, some helpful tips and insights from marketers who have been there—the hard way, with profit and loss responsibility sitting on their shoulders like a big grizzly bear with an abscessed tooth. This is their story; I am merely the spokesman. Mostly, it's the workaday, grind-it-out story of marketing professionals, human to the core, doing their jobs, making almost accidental discoveries that seem brilliant in retrospect, perpetuating mistakes, taking gambles, making end runs around stronger competitors, and—just generally—working in the exciting world of marketing.

1 Ore-Ida: Mom, Flag—and a French Fry

In marketing, a common term is "product enhancement." It refers to taking a basic product and, through either production or marketing skills, turning it into something of considerably more allure to the consumer and—ideally—into something that is considerably more profitable to the manufacturer. It's Cinderella and the glass slipper.

Imagination is a key ingredient in the successful marketing of "enhanced products"—and a beautiful example is what the potato-processing industry in general, and Ore-Ida Foods subsidiary of H. J. Heinz in particular, have done with the lowly spud.

Although Advertising Age *ran part of my Ore-Ida story and the interview with CEO Paul I. Corddry in two installments (November 12 and 15, 1984), over 60% of the story was not published due to space limitations. Here's the full, unabridged version—and I think you'll find it fascinating, especially if you like to eat french fries.*

Part I

Campbell built its empire by giving the consumer easy-to-prepare soups and variety. General Mills did the same with cake mixes. And, indeed, many of the most successful brands in America's grocery stores are based on exploiting—and expanding the usage of—what originally were huge homemade product markets.

And so it is with Ore-Ida Foods, Inc., the hero of this story. This Boise-based subsidiary of H. J. Heinz now holds about a 51% share (in pounds) of the U.S. frozen potato market at retail and about 61% of that market in dollars. The lion's share is under the Ore-Ida name, but one strong regional item, Deep Fries, is marketed under the Heinz name. Put another way, in 1983 the *Ore-Ida brand alone* ranked 10th among all food brands in dollar sales at retail (Campbell's condensed soups were first) and third among all frozen brands (after Stouffer's single dishes and Minute Maid's orange juice).

Equally important to Ore-Ida is its 12% share of the huge food service market for frozen potatoes, which is estimated at 3.7 billion pounds (about four times the size of the retail market). It's this food service market, driven by the fast-food giants like McDonald's and Burger King, and the vast sums they've spent to glamorize the french fry and to convince a generation of kids that a hot serving of fun fries is a God-given right, that has made Ore-Ida's development of the home market different—and easier—than, say, Campbell with soups or Betty Crocker with cake mixes. Between them, the fast-food giants and Ore-Ida have rewritten America's credo "Mom, Flag and Apple Pie." Now, probably, it should read "Mom, Flag—and a French Fry."

These USDA statistics tell the story: per capita consumption of frozen potatoes—almost all of which are fried—in the U.S. went from 2.7 pounds in 1960 to 11.7 pounds in 1970 to 16.9 pounds in 1980. In 1983, it is estimated, it went up to 19.8 pounds. And, ironically, this was going on while many food processors were rushing in to ride the low-cal-nutritional-health food crest, which they saw sweeping the country. (In fact, Ore-Ida hedged its bets too; in 1978 it acquired Foodways National, Inc., packers of the frozen Weight Watchers' brand.)

In a given month, according to Ore-Ida research, 65% of U.S. households will prepare fried potatoes, either from scratch or from a commercial frozen product. And as for away-from-home consumption, the CREST service of NPD Research shows that french fries are served as part of 23% of all restaurant meals. (The only item that tops that penetration is total soft drinks with 29%.) McDonald's alone, it is estimated, serves up 650 million pounds of frozen fried potatoes a year; Burger King, to whom Ore-Ida is a major supplier, fries between 280 and 300 million pounds.

The following text tells the story of how Ore-Ida, which started as a nearly defunct frozen vegetable processor, grew to dominate the in-home frozen potato industry. And a rich story it is, spanning the purchase by Heinz, the complete overhaul of Ore-Ida's top management led by a band of young Turks, the painful—sometimes acrimonious—transition from a sales-driven to a marketing-driven organization, the push into national distribution, inept competition, the role of Doyle Dane's "All-Righta" campaign, which has been on-air since 1975, the very successful launch of numerous flanker items, each calculatingly designed to fill one of the nooks and crannies of in-home market segmentation, and Ore-Ida's latest expansion move: opening up the in-home fried potato market in Japan.

Growing Pains

The story starts in 1951 in Ontario, Ore., a small town on the Idaho border about 55 miles northwest of Boise, and smack in the middle of America's most fertile potato-growing region.

Russet-Burbank—King of the Fries

Whenever you savor a quality, commercial french fry, odds are that it was processed from a Russet-Burbank, the white potato species that is preferred, overwhelmingly, for frozen potato products. About 93% of the potatoes grown in Idaho are Russet-Burbanks.

Russet-Burbanks are oblong in shape, and that means more yield of long cuts, which are valued aesthetically and monetarily by the upscale food service market. Long strips create the illusion that more volume is being served vis-à-vis the same weight of short cuts. The eyes, or growth defects, tend to be relatively few and shallow, making for a higher yield. Perhaps most important, Russet-Burbanks have—relatively—a high solid content (i.e., less water) than most potatoes, and this results in a fry interior that is fluffy and mealy.

Russet-Burbanks thrive in the semiarid climate of southern Idaho and eastern Oregon. In addition to the right soil (volcanic loam), the days are hot and the nights are cool—thanks to altitude: the potato-growing areas in southern Idaho range from 2,400 to 4,500 feet above sea level. A steady supply of water comes from irrigation, with the dammed up Snake River and its tributaries being the main source. Steady watering means steady tuber growth over the season.

Ore-Ida contracts with local growers for their Russet-Burbank crops, paying a premium for #1 quality (i.e., relatively large tubers with few blemishes).

After the Russet-Burbanks are harvested in September and October, they are stored in piles over 20 feet deep in huge climate-controlled warehouses; each is as large as a football field and holds about 15,000 tons of potatoes. Warehouse temperature is held at 40 to 42 degrees throughout the year, and humidity is constant at 95%. The objective is to reduce weight shrinkage (most potatoes are about 80% water) and to slow the natural conversion of potato starch into sugar. Since much of the Russet-Burbank crop is stored for nearly a year, any technical improvement in storage facilities (i.e., shrinkage control) can result in millions of dollars in savings—and this subject gets lots of attention at Ore-Ida.

When the potatoes are taken from storage for processing, they are blanched, which removes much of the natural sugar content that has been building up. Later in processing, the french fry cuts are passed through a "sugar drag," which restores the original sugar level in an even coating. This makes for a uniform, and highly desirable, even browning during frying because, primarily, the golden color an eater sees is carmelization of the sugar coating.

Processing is highly mechanized and fast; from the time a Russet-Burbank is dumped into a processing plant bin to the time the finished product is in cold storage, about 105 minutes have passed. In that time span, the potato has been washed, sorted to size, deskinned (in a steam peeler), blanched, cut to size, visually inspected in "specking" lines, sugar-coated, deep fried, dried, quick frozen, bagged, boxed, and moved into storage.

About 10% of the total U.S. Russet-Burbank crop is so processed in Ore-Ida plants each year.

Two brothers, Nephi and Golden Grigg, bought a small freezing factory that was going under and organized Oregon Frozen Foods, Inc. At first, the emphasis was on corn, but in 1952 they started processing frozen french fried potatoes—becoming a pioneer in that business. A major breakthrough came in 1958 when the company developed Tater Tots, an extruded product which still is a mainstay in Ore-Ida's retail line. The cutting of long french fries takes the heart of a potato, but leaves plenty of scraps that can be used to make formed products—like Tater Tots and Hash Browns—thereby greatly increasing overall efficiency and profitability of processing. (Other manufacturers may discard this waste, turn it into cattle feed, or make dry potato flakes that are used in boxed products, like instant potato mix.)

Oregon Frozen Foods prospered. In 1961, it changed its name to Ore-Ida Foods, Inc., went public, and opened a second potato processing plant, this one in Burley, Idaho, about 135 miles southeast of Boise on the Snake River. (Yet another plant in Burley was purchased in 1964.)

A master broker, D. B. Berelson & Co. of San Francisco, had purchased the sales rights to Ore-Ida brands at retail, and through a growing network of frozen food brokers, a line of frozen potatoes, corn on the cob, onion rings, and chopped onions was being pushed into national distribution—but it was still weak and spotty in the Northeast, a particularly strong area for fried potato consumption and the bastion of the Birds Eye division of General Foods, Ore-Ida's main competitor at the time. Ore-Ida opened another processing plant in Greenville, Michigan, to reduce distribution costs; theretofore, product from Ontario and Burley was shipped via refrigerated trucks into the eastern U.S.

Packaging for the retail line of frozen potatoes was paper carton with a prominent Idaho-shaped logo—the better to identify with that state's growing reputation for quality potatoes. Consumer awareness of the Ore-Ida brand name was 20%.

That was the marketing state of affairs at Ore-Ida when Frank B. Armour, then vice chairman of Heinz, fingered it for acquisition, just about a year after he had engineered the purchase of Star-Kist Foods (home of Charlie the Tuna and the famous cat Morris).

Ore-Ida had annual sales of $30.8 million and about a 23% share of the U.S. frozen potato market at retail when, in 1965, it was sold to Heinz for stock valued at $29.7 million. McKinsey & Co. was brought in to study efficiency possibilities, and things seemed to be proceeding normally until 22 months later. Then all hell broke loose.

Young Turks Take Over

"A lot of things were chaotic when we came into this company," recalls Robert K. Pedersen, who was brought in by Frank Armour from Star-Kist where he was vp-operations, to head Ore-Ida. "On a Monday in August,

1967—it's called Black Monday by some of the people who are still around—the Heinz board and Burt Gookin [at the time, CEO of Heinz] particularly, decided it had to change management. So they came out here and summarily fired the top seven people," he reminisced in a recent interview. "Then they said to Frank [Armour], 'Now you run the company.'" Three days later, the call went out to Pedersen who came with the understanding that in a short while he would become president and CEO of Ore-Ida, a post he held until he retired in 1977.

There were two main problems. McKinsey's study had uncovered possible conflicts of interest in that top executives of the old management were also potato farmers contracting their crops to Ore-Ida. Also, a year earlier, with the idea that Ore-Ida should raise its own raw material, they had purchased a 10,000-acre plot called Skyline Farms near Ontario. "Skyline never did make it because it was poor soil," says Pedersen, "and we were losing a million and a half bucks a year on it." Even worse, the Skyline move had aggrieved local farmers and, recalls Pedersen, "We sucked hind tit when it came to contracting."

The other main problem was that Ore-Ida's plants were run down. "They [the previous management] had set the company up to sell," says Pedersen. "They had capitalized pencils. But they had spent very little money expense-wise on repair or maintenance for two or three years. We had a few problems on quality too," he adds, and "things were sloppy." Each of the three plants was being run as a "personal fiefdom," and there was little cooperation. "They'd run the things that ran best, which gave us inventory imbalance."

To solve these and other problems, Armour recruited a new Ore-Ida management board, which met every morning. All board members, except Pedersen (who was in his mid-40s at the time) were in their early 30s. (One, J. Wray Connolly, a 32-year-old lawyer from Heinz brought in to clean up procurement, is today president of Heinz U.S.A.)

"Frank Armour realized we needed marketing skills," says Pedersen, "and he had a fellow he liked in Pittsburgh called Paul Corddry, the brand manager on ketchup." Corddry, who was 32 at the time, joined Ore-Ida's sales operation (which was still in San Francisco) as general manager, product marketing; he became vp-marketing a year later. (Today, Corddry is president of Ore-Ida, a post he assumed in 1977. An interview with him follows at the end of Part II of this chapter.) In 1968, the new management bought D. B. Berelson's rights to sell Ore-Ida products and brought in an ex-Berelson executive, William Moseley, to be vp-sales.

Attracting and holding the bright new team of young executives to Ontario, Ore., was proving to be a real problem, and the decision was made to move corporate headquarters to Boise.

In mid-1969, near disaster struck; Ore-Ida's main plant in Ontario was totaled by fire. This did, however, give Gerald D. Herrick, the new vp-operations, the opportunity to build a modern, efficient plant from scratch—a job he finished in six months. This set the stage to standardize equipment and procedures in all plants and was a big step toward a key Ore-Ida goal: low-cost production and high-quality control. "Our yield was below 45% then," recalls Pedersen in discussing the amount of salable product derived from raw potatoes on the dock, "and Gerry [Herrick] was able to get it well above 50%."

Perhaps a more important effect of the new plant was the capital expenditure authorization it represented from Heinz; it helped quell rumors that Heinz was sick of the mess at Ore-Ida and thinking divestiture.

Sales vs. Marketing

With operational problems on the mend, attention at Ore-Ida increasingly turned to marketing expansion—increased distribution and new products—and this threw the spotlight on Corddry. "Heinz—Burt Gookin especially—dictated that Ore-Ida was to be a consumer-driven company, marketing-directed," says Pedersen, "and I've always felt it was smart to do what your boss wants."

Corddry had started the marketing ball rolling in 1967, when he joined the company in San Francisco, by retaining Glendinning Associates, a Westport, Conn.-based marketing consulting firm. (Joel Smilow, the Glendinning contact man, is now president of International Playtex.) Then Corddry retained Doyle Dane Bernbach, Los Angeles, Ore-Ida's first agency of record.

The next step was to recruit a marketing staff. Five young assistant product manager-level people were hired; none had package goods experience, so a training program was instigated. (One of the five, Dietmar Kluth, who came from Kennecott Copper, is today vp-sales and marketing at Ore-Ida. Another, Pamela Beaumont, is now vp-marketing for Albertson's Inc., the seventh largest U.S. supermarket chain, which is headquartered in Boise in a building next door to Ore-Ida. "She might have been the first woman vp at Ore-Ida if she'd hung on," opines Pedersen.)

In 1969, a crucial decision in the marketing history of Ore-Ida was made: "We followed the dictates of Heinz," says Pedersen: "Give the profit responsibility to marketing, the volume responsibility to sales. So, marketing controlled the budget—and if you don't think that didn't lead to problems! In the past, sales managers out in the field could make some expenditures on their own, trade deals; now marketing had to approve trade deals."

Concurrent with this was marketing's need to educate Ore-Ida's new management board, none of whom (except Corddry) had marketing backgrounds or really knew what to expect from a consumer-driven orientation.

Pedersen, basically an operations man, said this recently about his own limitations at the time: "My conception of marketing was that it was advertising-driven, and there were a lot of Mickey Mouse gimmicks that go with it. I saw the glamour side; I had no idea of the analytical side. I found out that in marketng you need to crunch a lot of numbers; you don't wing anything. Paul wanted to see the numbers; what are the cost–value relationships? Paul started marketing research, wanted to find out what the consumer wanted. He was looking for product segments, so we got a research guy in."

As for client–agency relations, Pedersen felt, "You need marketing decisions in-house; you don't want them forced on you by guys who surely have an interest in what they can earn on you. I admit, I got some damned good lessons on where marketing ought to be going from these younger guys, and I could see that the agency didn't like to lose that handle on you."

In 1969, in what was then a momentous move, Corddry—marketing—recommended that Ore-Ida change its retail packaging and, inferentially, its corporate image. Landor Associates in San Francisco was retained to come up with a new design.

One reason for the change was to get out from under the Idaho state shape logo on existing packaging that implied that all Ore-Ida products were made from potatoes grown in Idaho (which was not the fact). Also, there was a desire to have packaging that would create a dramatic billboard effect in retail freezers and to get away from the "commodity look" marketing believed to be associated with existing packaging.

Consumer research done as part of this project indicated that there was not even a consistency in the way people pronounced the word "Ore-Ida," particularly on the East Coast, and only one third of the respondents associated the word with potatoes. (This started thinking about radio and/or tv advertising.) In any case, Landor came up with a bold design and a new double-leaf logo printed in orange and brown to depict the company's earthy primary product—potatoes.

This recommendation led to what Corddry now recalls as "major battles." For one, sales of Ore-Ida products were growing, and, said the traditionalists, "Why fix something that isn't broken?" Second, the cost to switch over to polyethylene bagging would be $300,000, and "that was $300,000 we didn't have," recalls Pedersen.

More important, sales opposed the move, and that focused the hostility. "It got to the point where they [sales and marketing] weren't talking," says Pedersen. "Bill Moseley was a traditionalist, one hell of a salesman—a volume salesman—but I finally had to make a decision—one of the toughest decisions I had to make there—to let Moseley go."

So, in 1971, sales and marketing at Ore-Ida were combined into one division under the direction of Paul Corddry. "You gotta make marketing predominant in that they control the budget, but you gotta make sure you have salespeople who appreciate that. Fortunately, we did that early on," says Pedersen, who emphasizes that then it is incumbent to recruit field sales managers "who understand marketing, who use the tools marketing gives them." But, to make it work harmoniously, he adds, sales must be given a lot of input into the marketing decision-making process.

With internal operations shaping up and the marketing-sales friction put to rest, Ore-Ida was finally ready to think and act like a national marketer, with the emphasis on developing their retail business. Things start popping in Part II of our story.

Part II

In the early 1970s—with its procurement, manufacturing, and top management problems on the mend, and the acrimonious sales/marketing squabble settled—Ore-Ida's attention was focusing more on the outside world, and its actions were becoming more like those of an important national marketer with its hand on the consumer's pulse. But while the rocky road traveled since the Heinz acquisition in 1965 had smoothed a lot, there was still a long, uphill road ahead before Ore-Ida would achieve the dominance it enjoys today, and two potentially formidable competitors—Birds Eye and Carnation—would try to block the way.

New, modern packaging, with the new leafy logo, had impacted Ore-Ida's visibility (and sales too, tests showed) in supermarket freezers by 1970, and there was an extensive potato product line in production: French Fries, Crinkle Cuts, Shoestrings, Pixie Crinkles, Country Style Dinner Fries, Cottage Fries, Southern Hash Browns, O'Briens, Small Whole Peeled, and Tater Tots (an extruded product originally developed by the Grigg brothers back in 1958 and available in regular, with onions, or with bacon).

But an important distribution weakness had to be rectified before large-scale national advertising would make sense. That was in the Northwest where Ore-Ida's strongest competitor at the time, Birds Eye french fries, was dominant.

General Foods had, in the late 1960s, apparently decided there wasn't a profitable future in having fried potato items in its Birds Eye frozen vegetable line. So it sold that part of the business to some ex-employees who formed a company called American Kitchen Foods, which was bad news for Ore-Ida; AKF proved to be a lot more aggressive than General Foods had been. For one, AKF marketed an extruded product called Tasty Fries, and in the important Northeast where consumption of fried potatoes is relatively high, the Birds Eye products outsold Ore-Ida, whose strength was centered in the Midwest and the West Coast.

What to do? The answer, according to Dietmar Kluth, vp-sales and marketing at Ore-Ida today, was an Eastern Market Development Program that featured Ore-Ida products not provided by Birds Eye. "We said," recalls Kluth, "let's go after the specialty products—Tater Tots, Hash

Browns, Dinner Fries—and say to the trade, 'There's a demand for these products, and Birds Eye doesn't have them.'"

"So," says Kluth, "we brought all the eastern brokers into a meeting in New York and had a slide show; there was a strong trade plan."

As things worked out, the Birds Eye competition faded away. The American Kitchen Foods operation was eventually sold to a company called Potato Services, which had a licensing agreement with General Foods to use the Birds Eye name, and that firm eventually went Chapter 11. (Today the production facilities are owned by Simplot Corp.)

General Foods, with all its resources, could have fought Ore-Ida for dominance in the frozen potato market, but it gave up by default. Ore-Ida has been lucky this way (as we'll see later when Carnation decided to compete with Ore-Ida at the retail level). In fact, in retrospect, inept competition is one of the main reasons Ore-Ida has been so successful. (But that certainly hasn't been true in the huge food service market.)

Now We Are National

With East Coast distribution beefed up, Paul Corddry—vp-sales and marketing at the time—was finally ready in 1972 to make a proud announcement: after years of local market tv and newspaper advertising, Ore-Ida would have its first national campaign—a seven-page schedule in each of six consumer magazines, including *Family Circle, Good Housekeeping,* and *Reader's Digest.* Six different potato items would be featured.

"The purpose of the new campaign," wrote Corddry at the time, "is to build awareness of the Ore-Ida brand name and link our name with quality. We hope to accomplish this by clearly establishing the company and its people as potato people who really know their business."

Earlier—in February 1970, to be exact—Ore-Ida marketing had started on another project that had considerable potential to expand in-home consumption of frozen fried potatoes. But, in retrospect, it proved to be a long, drawn out project that was never completely successful—a move that Paul Corddry today considers the company's worst marketing mistake. (See interview with Corddry at the end of this chapter for more details.)

It was commonplace at the time for people at home to cook up frozen french fries in a skillet with hot grease. The way around this messy, sales-inhibiting procedure, Ore-Ida figured, was a line of products that could be cooked in an oven without grease, but that would still have the attributes, basically, of a product that had been deep fried. Research showed that some consumers would be willing to pay a premium price for such a product.

Such a product was easier described than made, but a new technology was developed to create a line of fried potatoes which had been oil-sprayed so that, when reconstituted in a high-temperature oven, the end result would be a darker, apparently deep fried appearance and texture. The name: Deep Fries. The slogan: The frozen french fries that actually fry.

Deep Fries went into test market under that name with no Ore-Ida identification and at a premium price over regular Ore-Ida fries. This was done to minimize cannibalization of existing Ore-Ida products, a continuing concern as Ore-Ida's line extensions and flanker items grew. (Because of this concern, Ore-Ida has through time been a heavy user of consumer panel purchase date which would show the degree to which a new item was building market, attracting new users to the Ore-Ida line, or taking business from existing products.) Deep Fries was tested in three markets, one of which was AdTel's Charleston system.

Deep Fries did well enough in test to justify a rollout, but that fell flat because, says Kluth, "We didn't provide enough ad support." One consequence of that, according to Stephen J. Encarnacao, who was product manager on the line, was that brand name recall was low. So, they went back to the old drawing board.

In 1974, Ore-Ida tried again, but with a much different approach. This time Deep Fries went into seven test markets with a new name: Heinz Deep Fries, the first time an Ore-Ida product had leaned on its parent's name for consumer recognition. Advertising had been shifted from Doyle Dane to Foote, Cone & Belding/Honig, Los Angeles, and there was a new "self-sizzling" slogan.

The end result is that today Heinz Deep Fries distribution is limited to a few Northeastern markets, but it is still a major brand—with 7 or 8% share—in New York and Boston. And the experience had another impact: the Ore-Ida account was moved from the San Francisco office of Doyle Dane Bernbach (DDB) to the New York office (where it's been ever since), and the development of Ore-Ida's first national tv advertising program was in the works. (Later, in 1979, DDB got the Deep Fries billing back.)

By 1973, Anthony J. F. "Tony" O'Reilly had taken over as president at Heinz, and when he came along, recalls Robert Pedersen, president of Ore-Ida at the time, "One of his first comments was, 'Is that thing ever going to make money?' "—referring to the 10,000-acre Skyline Farms potato-growing venture in which the previous management had involved Ore-Ida. "I said, 'No,' " says Pedersen, "and he said, 'Let's get rid of it.' That opened up heaven for me." Skyline was sold for $2 million, and Ore-Ida took an $8 million tax write-off. But, much more important, a $1.5 million a year drain on Ore-Ida's bottom line had been eliminated, and that made it easier to get marketing money for expansion.

While Ore-Ida had made some regional tv buys a year earlier, 1975 saw the advent of its first network buy ($3 million) and the debut of DDB's "All Righta" campaign, versions of which have been on the air ever since. "Unaided awareness of the Ore-Ida name went from 35 to 63% in two years, and I give copy most of the credit," says Kluth. In addition, there were coupon ads in *Reader's Digest*.

In the 1970s Ore-Ida was on a roll, gathering momentum. Specifically, from 1972 to 1980, the frozen potato market—pound volume at retail—in the U.S. grew from 771 million pounds to 867 million, and Ore-Ida's share of that market went from 26.7 to 48.4%. Unaided brand awareness had gone from 23 to about 80%. During that span, there were several new product launches, including CRISPERS! in 1976, which was described as "the most successful we've ever had," by Richard Blott, an executive recruited from International Playtex to be vp-sales and marketing at Ore-Ida from 1976 to 1980. (He went on to become president of Gagliardi Bros., an Ore-Ida subsidiary, and is now senior vp-domestic marketing for Brown and Williamson Tobacco Company.)

This appraisal by Kidder, Peabody (circa 1977) pretty well sums it up: "Ore-Ida has had four years of super growth in sales averaging 12% per year and earnings (15%). Its after-tax margins are between 4.5 and 5%, whereas most frozen-foods companies may get 5% pre-tax."

This is not to say that there weren't some bumps along the way. In 1974, for instance, there was an industry-wide shortage of potatoes, and Ore-Ida, like most others, was forced to short ship. Sales fell and the company took six price increases within eight months.

In 1977, the year Paul Corddry assumed the presidency at Ore-Ida, Carnation, which was already established in the food service end of the frozen business and at retail with a price brand called Lynden Farms, decided to attack Ore-Ida head-on at retail. The reason, as estimated by a financial analyst at the time, was that "the grocery trade is suddenly realizing that they are competing with the fast-food outlet down the street. Frozen foods can offer the housewife the means to prepare good meals conveniently without going out to a restaurant."

In any case, Carnation started test marketing a line of 12 frozen potato items in five markets under the Carnation name, and priced head-on with Ore-Ida. The introduction plan was estimated at from $10 to $15 million, annualized and nationalized, and included a one-free-with-four trade sell-in offer.

The management of Ore-Ida was aghast. Not only did the Carnation packaging closely resemble Ore-Ida's, but the names were close too. For instance, Ore-Ida had a Tater Tots and Carnation came out with a Tater Pops. And so on with slogans like "Deep Fried Taste Without Deep Frying."

Ore-Ida sued in federal court in Houston and won; Carnation was issued a cease and desist order. After a sell-through of existing inventory, Carnation changed the product name and packaging—but for all practical purposes, their competitive threat was stunted. Looking back today, Kluth appraises the Carnation misfire to marketing mistakes. "They had a me-too product and a limited line. They spent a lot up front, but then backed off; they quit too soon. And while they were able to get decent distribution, the clout Carnation has with the trade didn't carry over to the frozen end of the business." (In 1981, Carnation announced its final withdrawal from the retail market.)

As Ore-Ida's luck would have it, 1977 was also the year that the largest power in frozen potato processing, Simplot Corp., decided to withdraw its brand from the retail market. Nationally, Ore-Ida now stood alone.

Food Service Market

The food service market for frozen potatoes is estimated at 3.7 billion pounds, about four times the size of the retail market. It is dominated by the Boise-based Simplot Corp., a conglomerate founded by Jack R. Simplot who was fortunate enough to know Ray Kroc, founder of McDonald's, way back when. Kroc, of course, elevated the french fry to an art form. It is estimated that today Simplot fills about 80% of McDonald's potato needs. In addition to that golden brown gold mine, Simplot is also a supplier to Wendy's and the Marriott Hotel chain, among others, and is estimated to hold about a 30% share of the total U.S. food service potato market. The second-largest food service supplier, with about 20% of the market, is a Portland, Ore.-based firm, Lamb-Weston, which is a division of AMFAC. The third-largest food service supplier, with about 12% share (which is roughly equivalent to its retail business in pound volume), is Ore-Ida which includes as its customers: Burger King, Hardees, Jack in the Box, and Roy Rogers. Carnation is fourth largest, with about a 10% share, and Chef-Reddy is fifth with an 8% share. The remaining 20% of food service fried potato sales is divided among 12 or more potato processors.

Boise—Potato Capital Of The World

About 25% of the U.S. potato crop is grown in southern Idaho, and eastern Oregon accounts for another 6%. The commercial hub of this fertile agricultural region is Boise, a very pleasant city (pop. 102,000) that nestles in a green belt—there are 3,000 acres of public parks in Boise—along the Boise River. From executive office windows in Ore-Ida's modern headquarters building, located on the river bank, it is commonplace to see people fishing or just drifting downstream in innertube rafts.

Within 200 miles of Boise—which was a boom town in the 1860s due to gold and silver strikes—there are now eight frozen potato processing plants. Two are owned by Ore-Ida. Three plants—including the largest—are owned by Simplot Corp., and one each is owned by Carnation, Lamb-Weston, and Idaho Frozen Foods.

The emphasis on potatoes sometimes overshadows the fact that, in addition to Ore-Ida and Simplot, Boise is headquarters town for Albertson's (a retail grocery chain), Boise-Cascade (a lumber and packaging conglomerate), and Morrison-Knudsen (a worldwide heavy construction organization). Hewlett Packard also has a large plant there. And, of course, Boise is the capital of Idaho with all that implies

—as well as being the cultural oasis in what the Boise Chamber of Commerce calls "Treasure Valley." Recreation is an important industry, too. The Bogus Basin ski area in the Salmon Mountains is just 45 minutes from Boise, and Sun Valley is 150 miles away. White water rafting on the middle fork of the Salmon River, north of Boise, brings thousands of tourists into the area too.

Still, the commercial vibrations of Boise pivot around the annual potato crop. This interest is institutionalized in the Idaho Potato Commission, which spends about $3.5 million a year for public relations and advertising (through the D'Arcy MacManus Masius office in San Francisco) to promote the superiority of Idaho-grown potatoes. There is an Idaho potato logo limited to use on packaging of potatoes that were grown in Idaho.

This presents a dilemma of sorts: while it obviously is to Ore-Ida's advantage to support the Potato Commission and to have a public perception that Idaho potatoes are indeed superior, the fact is that Ore-Ida packs Russet-Burbanks that are grown in Oregon, Washington, Wisconsin, and Michigan, in addition to Idaho—and only one of Ore-Ida's four potato processing plants is located in Idaho. Reluctantly, one Ore-Ida executive concedes, "The production from all our plants is uniform in quality."

No comment about the Boise area would be complete without mention of its most famous resident, Jack R. Simplot, 75, the colorful founder of Simplot Corp., a huge potato-growing, potato-processing, mining, cattle, and electronic equipment conglomerate. J. R.—rustic farmer with an eighth-grade education—is generally conceded to be the founder of Idaho's potato processing industry and one of the richest men in the U.S. *Forbes* estimates his personal fortune to be over $500 million and quotes J. R. as saying, "It makes me feel good to know I can walk into a bank and get $80 million just on my name."

J. R. often spends his afternoons playing cribbage at the exclusive Arid Club, which is headquarters for Boise's business elite (no women allowed before 5 p.m.).

Quick insight into what the fast-food giants have done for frozen —mostly fried—potato consumption comes from these USDA statistics: in 1971, the per capita consumption of frozen potatoes eaten away from home was 8.9 pounds; for 1983, it is estimated at 16.0 pounds. Put another way, the 3.7-billion-pound food service market in 1983 had an average wholesale price of about 30 cents a pound, and that works out to be about $1.1 billion. It's a bitterly competitive market, mostly because currently the frozen potato manufacturing industry is operating at only an estimated 65 to 70% of its capacity.

Ore-Ida's strategy has been to concentrate on quality, the high end of the food service market. This is most evident when you view the slick, humorous sales/product use training films made for Ore-Ida to promote its food service brand, Premium House. One features sleuth Sam Spud, who solves "the case of the perfect fry." All the emphasis is on quality product, careful preparation (e.g., oil quality and temperature), and an end-result product which has visual appeal on the plate. Good eating experiences make for repeat business.

According to Christopher C. Howard, manager of food service marketing at Ore-Ida, the food service market in recent years has become much more consumer-driven. "There's a demand for new forms and shapes," he says, "and it's more adult-oriented."

Consequently, according to Martin V. Thomas, now general manager, sales and marketing services at Ore-Ida, a considerable amount of the marketing research budget is focused on developing new potato products that can be presented to the food service clients as menu alternatives. "But," says Thomas, "it's a long, drawn out process. From the time there's an idea, and it's been consumer-tested, and the product has been formalized for mass production, and a prospective customer has field tested it in a few outlets, and it's finally accepted for chain-wide use, three or five years may go by. It takes patience."

Breezing into the '80s

Ore-Ida breezed into the current decade with more strength than ever. A new plant in Plover, Wis., which is touted by Lloyd Cox (general manager, manufacturing at Ore-Ida) as the most technologically advanced and efficient in the industry, had come on line. A band of brand managers and marketing staffers recruited from consumer product giants like General Mills, Scott Paper, S. C. Johnson, Kellogg, General Foods, Campbell Soup, and Clorox was settled in, and attracting such people to Boise was getting much easier as word of Ore-Ida's marketing successes spread. It also helped when, in 1979, Ore-Ida moved into a beautiful new headquarters building located along the banks of the Boise River.

Testing of Hispanic tv showed sales gains of 20%, and Ore-Ida name awareness among target groups jumped 16 points to 48% within one year; in 1981 Ore-Ida expanded into Hispanic network advertising.

Ore-Ida's field sales force had been beefed up, and broker relations were good (there are 85 in the retail network). "We do a very, very good job in staying in touch with our brokers," Kluth told me recently, "and we have a generally respected position—we're a profitable account." (Ore-Ida pays less than 3% brokerage, compared to an industry norm of 3 to 4% on frozen products. "I say to them," says Kluth, " 'Don't look at percentages. Are you happy with what you take to the bank? Are you happy with the increases year to year?' ")

Backing up this broker network is an Ore-Ida distribution system of common carrier trucks (with about 300 on the road at any given time). Heavy use is made of computer modeling and operational research techniques to optimize low-cost delivery schedules.

From 1980 to mid-1984, the retail market for frozen potatoes went from 867 million to 905 million pounds, and the Ore-Ida share of that went from 48.4 to 49.5%. (If you include Deep Fries and the "B" Grade price brands packed by Ore-Ida, their total share is now 55%.) The annual advertising budget on potatoes is over $10 million. About 60% of the total marketing budget goes to advertising and consumer deals, 40% to trade deals.

If anything, with the 1980s Ore-Ida is even more aggressive in testing and rolling out new retail items. Five new products have been introduced so far—Home Style, Crispy Whips!, Cheddar Browns, Crispy Crowns! (a bite-size product in plain, bacon, and sour cream and chives), and Golden Patties (an oven-prepared hash brown). The newest and most exciting addition is a whole new line of low-cal fried potatoes called "Lites," which have 100 calories per serving versus 160 calories for a normal cut.

A key element of this new product program—the main goal of which is to design products which will, basically, expand consumer use of frozen potatoes by catering to additional in-home applications, or segments of the market where normal usage now is nil or very low—is consumer research.

For test markets, the preferred procedure at Ore-Ida is Yankelovich, Skelly and White's LTM (Laboratory Test Market) simulated test market system, which is used for an early read on copy and price variables. Then, if a new product has large capital investment implications at the plant level, it probably will go into a full-blown test market in three locations for six to eight months. (Adds Kluth, "We sometimes use LTM on competitive products too.")

Up front, the research emphasis is on identifying key niches in the market which open the door for other specialty line extensions. Since 1973, Ore-Ida has been a regular subscriber to MRCA's (Market Research Corporation of America) Menu Census to study the size of the homemade potato market and in-home preparation methods, and attitudinal segmentation studies have been conducted by BAI (Behavioral Analysis, Inc.), a survey research firm in Irvington, N.Y. Ongoing awareness tracking studies are conducted by Marylander Market Research, Inc., (Sherman Oaks, Calif.), which also handles some in-home product placement tests. "These present some special problems," says Thomas, "because the products are frozen. They have to be packed in Styrofoam with dry ice and shipped by air, and then the field people have to use door-to-door placement or contact people in malls."

Ore-Ida contracts for its own TV copy tests, and the usual supplier is Mapes and Ross, Inc., in Princeton, N.J.

Including retail performance and distribution measures, such as Ore-Ida purchases from SAMI, Majers, and Burgoyne, the total annual research expenditure for potatoes alone at Ore-Ida is about $2 million, according to Thomas, who says, "More important than the amount is the consistency; we've been investing in research at a steady level all through the years."

Little is left to chance at Ore-Ida, it seems, and they take a long research look before they jump.

Frying Japan

The latest fried potato expansion at Ore-Ida, after a year-long study by McKinsey & Co.–Japan, is the opening of a new subsidiary in Japan to capitalize on the growing popularity of American fast-food tastes, as cultivated by McDonald's and Kentucky Fried Chicken. (In Japan, Kentucky Fried Chicken sells french fries—made by Ore-Ida in Ontario, Ore., and shipped in—instead of mashed potatoes, as it does in the U.S.)

"That market is at the stage now," says Paul Corddry, "where the U.S. was in the early '60s. They have about half the population of the U.S., but only 1/30th the consumption of potatoes." Ovens are rare in Japan, and home cooking is usually done in frying pans, which is messy, and the locally produced frozen potatoes available at retail are deemed inferior to french fries produced in the U.S. "We adapted our products for heating in toaster ovens—86% of Japanese homes have them," says Corddry, "and we plan to play up that Ore-Ida potatoes are from Idaho." Introductory advertising started last August through the Japanese agency Dai-Ichi Kitaku.

As for the rigors of entering the Japanese market, Corddry says, "In consumer goods, the reasons for American failure are not because Japan puts up any artificial barriers, or anything like that. It's because those that failed weren't willing to go in and persevere for a while. It's a fiercely competitive market, and if you have a good thing, there will be two or three competitors coming in fast. We probably won't see any black for two or more years."

Paul Corddry, Ore-Ida President

Paul I. Corddry, 48, has been president and CEO of Ore-Ida Foods, Inc. since May 1977.

After receiving an M.B.A. from the University of Chicago, Corddry started his marketing career with Procter & Gamble, where he was a brand manager when he left to join H. J. Heinz (Ore-Ida's parent) as a product manager in 1964. He was general manager, product marketing, at Heinz when, in 1967, he was appointed general manager, product marketing at Ore-Ida's sales/marketing operation (located in San Francisco at the time). He was named vp-marketing in 1968 and assumed responsibillity for all sales functions in 1971. He became executive vp of Ore-Ida in 1975.

The following interview took place in New York City on August 30, 1984, as Corddry reminisced about the trials and tribulations of building a company's marketing department from scratch—and the future course of Ore-Ida's marketing thrust.

HONOMICHL: What's it like to set up a marketing department from scratch in a company which, at the time, probably didn't know what marketing is all about?

CORDDRY: We had the blessing from Pittsburgh, but it was not something like, "You've got X years to do it." Instead, it was more like, "Assuming you can turn a buck out there, fellas, let's get more market-oriented." I think that was the message that Bob [Pedersen, president of Ore-Ida at the time] got.

When I first went to San Francisco in 1967 and started to put everything together, I tell you, it was scary. There was literally one guy to help me; he was part of the old Berelson [master broker] group. So, I used Glendinning; the guy I used was Joel Smilow, now president of International Playtex. Joel and I went out and started to do the first work; we got some market research in, got our first hint of what our shares were like, what the attitudes were.

After we culled all that—it was a pretty rugged summer; we were basically burning the midnight oil—Joel and I were walking down California Street one night, and he said, "The best piece of advice I can give you is send your resume out as fast as you can." So, there were times in the early going when things looked pretty bleak.

If you ask what it takes to start something up like that from scratch, it's perseverance—because what we had to do was educate the whole management team. At that time, Ore-Ida was not making any money and people couldn't see why—with all the other problems we were having—we would go and spend money we had not spent in the past. That was a constant ongoing dialogue; sometimes "dialogue" was not strong enough a word. We really had to hang in for a while.

HONOMICHL: You usually win by proving something. What was the first thing you did that got those people to say, "Ah, I see what marketing can do for us"?

CORDDRY: I'm not sure there was any one thing; there was a sequence, and there were more converts over time; it took a lot of time and lots of results.

The first thing we did that was really consumer-driven was a test; it was all we could afford. We were in three markets where we had tv for the first time—and those markets did better. That started people saying, "There might be something here." A second thing: I decided we really had to change our packaging. We had some major battles over that internally because people said, "Hey, we're doing fine. We've got a 25% share. We're the brand leader. Why would we want to do that?" And, second, it cost $300,000, and that was $300,000 we didn't have.

But we made the change, and the change was so striking that business picked up again, and people started saying, "Hey, maybe that guy is not totally crazy!"

The kicker was that by then business was getting a little better, and all sorts of things were going on simultaneously. We were operating on three precepts, even in the late '60s. The first was get your costs down—be the low-cost producer. We were coming along with all sorts of ways to automate our plants, and our costs were coming down—which gave us some margins. Second, let's make absolutely sure we have consistent high quality—consistency is very important to the Ore-Ida image; we see that in a lot of the attitudinal stuff we have. Third, with that money we're getting from low-cost production, let's put some of it back towards the consumer.

Those things were starting to work in the early '70s at the time O'Reilly [Anthony J. E. O'Reilly, now president, CEO of Heinz] came in. He smelled the thing had turned around, and he gave a lot of blessing from Pittsburgh, which probably allowed us to move faster.

I don't think I really sat back and took a deep breath and said, "The [marketing] thing is sold," until probably 1972 or '73.

HONOMICHL: But you won the shootout between marketing and sales. That must have been a morale booster.

CORDDRY: Around 1971; that was a turning point from the standpoint that the two of us had different philosophies about the business, and, after all, the sales guys really built the business; they had done a lot of things right. But it was a question of "Is now the time to go from push to pull?"

HONOMICHL: Once you got the marketing concept in place, you recruited a few young people who were learning on the job, almost. It must have been tough to recruit good marketing people into Boise. In fact, you didn't want to move from San Francisco...

CORDDRY: No, I didn't at all.

HONOMICHL: And they had to move the operation over from Ontario to even start to make it attractive...

CORDDRY: That's right. The move was made in 1968. They boiled it down to three cities: Portland, San Francisco, or Boise. Almost everybody was on the West Coast, and that seemed to make some sense.

They finally opted for Boise because it was a lot less hassle for the people in Ontario, being only 60 miles away. It turned out to be a good choice.

When I heard that we were moving to Boise, I told Frank Armour [Franklin R. Armour, vice chairman of the board, Heinz, at the time]—who was really running Ore-Ida at the time—"I don't think that Paul Corddry and Boise are made for each other."

He replied, essentially, "Well, help us through the next few months and I'll alert Pittsburgh, and we'll get you out of there before too long." Funny part, I don't think I was in Boise more than a month and the whole family just fell in love with the place. Very friendly people, and just a no-hassle style of living. So, that corrected itself pretty soon.

HONOMICHL: Is it relatively easy to recruit people into Boise now?

CORDDRY: Yes, but we don't get them all. A lot of people turn us down automatically when they hear it's Boise. I had a Boise-Cascade recruiting guy tell me the first year I was in Boise, "You're going to find out one thing: It's pretty doggone hard recruiting in here, but it's a heckuva lot harder transferring out." With most people we've brought in, that's been a fact.

We don't have any problem recruiting in the other business functions, but we still have some problems with marketing. I think it becomes less and less as more people become interested in the nonurban lifestyle—fishing, hunting, skiing. Of course, we have all those things to offer. But it's still got to be put on the problem list we have.

HONOMICHL: There was a crossroads; early on, the choice was to go against Simplot and the food service market, or to go retail. In retrospect, seeing how the food service market has grown, do you wish you'd gone the other way?

CORDDRY: That was far more of an evolutionary thing than revolutionary; there wasn't a day when we sat around and said, "Let's go retail." In fact, by the time I arrived on the scene, the die had been cast to some degree that it was the retail way the company was going to go.

HONOMICHL: There are better margins at retail?

CORDDRY: Better margins, and the retail business actually spins off a more profitable food service business. Basically, what we do—unlike any other competitor—is put out essentially one sort of class product for food service....

HONOMICHL: You go for the upper end of the food service market?

CORDDRY: Right. Our retail can take off the rest, and that's the most profitable part of the food service business. The other part of the retail thing that makes it so attractive is the much heavier use of by-products—the Tater Tots and Hash Browns of the world—which means that we can really do more with that potato going through our plant. We have far less waste, far less offal. Some other manufacturers just put some of that down the drain.

HONOMICHL: Cattle feed?

CORDDRY: Cattle feed, and others put it into flake products, which has never been a particularly strong market.

HONOMICHL: Yield—the percent of potato weight that hits the dock that's converted to salable product—you are getting 55% or something close to that?

CORDDRY: It's good; it's relatively high for this industry.

HONOMICHL: Processors that went the food service route—they don't get that kind of yield?

CORDDRY: They probably don't, unless they have a large amount going into dehydrators. But it's not as profitable a mix. That's what retail has really done for us; it has given us a much more profitable end product mix.

HONOMICHL: Are margins on your flanker items higher than those on the basic french fries?

CORDDRY: They're the same. This has been an ongoing discussion with us for years, and it depends a lot on what your cost accounting system is. But the way ours is, we've got basically everything priced out to give about the same margins, right across the board, with very few exceptions.

HONOMICHL: You've been Mr. Marketing at Ore-Ida since 1967, the architect of their success. Looking back, in retrospect, if you had it to do all over again, what would you do differently?

CORDDRY: Going back, I probably would have spent more time in the early years totally focusing in on the frozen potato business instead of looking for other ways to grow the company.

We spent quite a bit of time in the first years saying, "What else ought we to do in frozen foods?" Looking back over it now, if we had spent more time and focused more energy on potatoes, things might even have happened faster. I'd say that's the biggest regret.

HONOMICHL: What's the biggest mistake you made—from a marketing point of view, just potatoes?

CORDDRY: Probably the way we handled the Deep Fries product line. Are you familiar with that?

It was an interesting idea. We decided to actually put a premium niche even on Ore-Ida. And in those days, Ore-Ida had less of a premium price than it has now. We came out with a product that is darker and —more important—we sprayed it with oil which gave it different properties in the oven.

We introduced it in the early 1970s, and it did really well in test markets. There was not a lot of cannibalization of other Ore-Ida products, which we liked to see. We were in three markets—and we used an AdTel panel in Charleston.

HONOMICHL: Ore-Ida was one of the very early users of AdTel....

CORDDRY: Yes. I knew Adler because he was involved in an early piece of work Booz Allen did for us, and we were one of the first guys that used that setup.

It was still before we had really turned the company around, and we weren't playing with a lot of spare money. We took [Deep Fries] out of test market, and we made the classical marketing mistake. You'd think you'd learn once, but people continue to do it. We came in with a plan that was underspent compared with what we had in our first group. We went into the Northeast, did pretty well—but not as well as in the original test markets—and then we started to roll it out with even less spending back of it.

Deep Fries are still a factor in New York and Boston—we have from a 7 to 8% share of market there—but they really never took off anywhere else. What we should have done—if we didn't have the money to do it right—is gone slower.

HONOMICHL: How much of Ore-Ida's success is due to the fact that the competition hasn't really put up an honest dog fight for the retail business? Birds Eye sold out, Carnation's entry was inept....

CORDDRY: I think there's something to that. The flip side is that I think we were the first to smell that we had a gem here. Back when we really started to put some marketing effort against the company, we had a share in the mid-20s. Birds Eye was below us, but there were a lot of brands in there slugging it out. But they were all doing what most frozen brands were doing in those days; they were really under-merchandising and doing everything by the push method and nothing against the consumer. And we just smelled that we might be able to do something with that. It was a right judgment to go ahead with it, but there is no question that by the time the rest of the world realized this was a pretty good category, it was pretty tough to stop us; we really had the momentum by then.

You're looking at a business that has to have a lot of varieties and sizes, private label will always be a factor, and there's really not room there for a second brand unless they've really got some reason for being.

There's no question that competition hasn't been terribly strong, but I have a strong feeling that once we got things started, it would have been a very tough go for anybody, regardless of how well they executed. The other thing we've got going is that it's a terribly capital-intensive business. So anybody who wants to make a commitment, take a run at us—unless they are one of the existing guys—is talking about some massive capital.

HONOMICHL: I have the impression that when frozen french fries first came on the market they were a dog product.

CORDDRY: Yeah, they weren't too good.

HONOMICHL: It seems to me, a layman looking in from the outside, that a good part of Ore-Ida's success has been technical, in the sense that you have improved your product tremendously.

CORDDRY: No question about it. It's another example of something that should be obvious to all of us in this business over the years: you've got to have quality to win.

Look at the frozen category right now. Finally people woke up in several of these categories and started putting out really good quality stuff, and they are the brands that are successful. Price value, not all price. It's what you put on the plate.

We're bears on that now. We spend more time with our operations guys—they know they have their cost goals—but, guys, don't denigrate that quality.

HONOMICHL: Palatability, eye appeal—is there some way you can quantify the difference between the Ore-Ida french fry that is marketed today versus the one of years ago?

CORDDRY: The biggest difference is that we're more consistent. With the systems and processes we have in there now, we can chug out quantity upon quantity of french fries, and they're all basically alike.

The feedback you get from customers is not particularly good in our business in that we don't have any real branded competition. So, we don't get a lot of complaints. We don't have any other gold standard to compare with; we are the gold standard, at retail.

Where we do get a lot of feedback is with our food service customers. By and large, they will tell us that in their independent cuttings, we usually win because we outyield the competition. There's a complex series of things that happen in our processing, but one of them results in consistent length. Another is that we probably fry a little more than a lot of other companies.

HONOMICHL: How much further can you go with new products?

CORDDRY: It's amazing; people were asking me that same question 10 years ago!

What we've found out, basically, in scanner panels with our new products—and it's not always true, but it usually works out this way—new products cannibalize a third, share build for us for a third, and market build for a third. That's essentially what BehaviorScan and the other scanner panels tell us.

Then I think there are some really big hit opportunities out there that don't just come in as nice little 15–20-million-pound businesses, which most of our flankers are. And they're fine; I'd like to have 10 more.

I think we've got a couple of big hits that might be emerging in the coming years, not the least of which is Lites, which we have in test market now.

HONOMICHL: What about microwave? Do you have a product coming? Wouldn't that give you a major breakthrough?

CORDDRY: Sure would. We have probably developed in the past 10 years—and in recent years with more intensity as microwave penetration goes up—seven or eight prototypes, but we can't get anything that will come out consistently. It has a lot to do with the inconsistency between microwave ovens.

We're not going to put anything out there until we have something that we feel comfortable putting the Ore-Ida name on. But it's still right up there at the top of our priority list.

HONOMICHL: Is it a conscious decision, or just happenstance, that the great trade name Ore-Ida, and its identification in the potato business, hasn't been put on dry products?

CORDDRY: We had one. We had an Ore-Ida potato flake product, and we pulled it from market in the early '70s because, by that time, we were seeing our imagery improve and the brand name was getting much, much more recognition. Quite frankly, because we use so much of the potato other places, what was left for those flakes gave us an inferior product, and we said, "We're not going to play that game."

Second thing, the flake business has its ups and downs; you don't get rich quick in the potato flake business.

HONOMICHL: Are the margins on dry products relatively low compared to frozen?

CORDDRY: I haven't looked at them for quite a while, but they certainly were.

HONOMICHL: What about potato chips, or anything related to potatoes?

CORDDRY: We are, right now, doing a lot of brand name work, in terms of "What does Ore-Ida really mean?" And what it means is a lot of good things; it is stronger than I thought it was, and I was pretty biased.

As a result, we are now—on a fairly vigorous basis—looking at how we can extend that brand name. It's mostly frozen, but we've also said, "The sky's the limit. We can look at nonfrozen too."

Really part of our strategic charter has been, "Hey, we're going to focus on frozen; that's the business we know; we have a distribution system second to none; and that's where we really have our strengths." But I have to say there are a couple of nonfrozen items on our extension list. Whether we franchise them out, or whatever, I don't know at this point.

HONOMICHL: So, you think there's still a lot of growth doing basically what you're doing, but more of it?

CORDDRY: Yes, and there's also potential in extending the Ore-Ida name out of potatoes.

I'm really hoping that something like Lites does something to the market because I'd like to see the market on a little stronger growth wicket.

HONOMICHL: Lites is a low-cal french fry?

CORDDRY: A reduced calorie line; we have four items, with a couple of others we are developing. There are 100 calories per serving—a normal, full three-ounce serving; that's a big plate of fries. For the normal cut, it's 160 calories. So it's a pretty sizable reduction.

We LTM'd [Laboratory Test Market Service of Yankelovich, Skelly and White] that, and we've found out that cannibalization isn't very high, and there is market expansion.

HONOMICHL: You're reaching a new user?

CORDDRY: Yes. That's what we're hoping.

HONOMICHL: You must get schizophrenic at Ore-Ida. One minute you're doing the Weight Watchers thing, and the next you're watching the USDA figures show fried potato consumption going up year after year, albeit it's mostly food service. It strikes me as amusing.

CORDDRY: Yes; we're on both sides of the fence. Actually, it's one of the things that led us to Foodways [Foodways National, Inc., acquired in 1978] at first. During our business planning exercises, which are almost ongoing now, you tend to map out, "Okay, what are the down sides we are looking at in the future?"

And one thing we had to worry about is, "Are eating habits going to change—move away from potatoes?" It didn't take a genius to see that there's a move towards nutrition and weight consciousness, so that was one of the reasons why we got really excited about Foodways and pushed it hard. But, when you look at our total portfolio, we've got some strange bedfellows.

HONOMICHL: Looking back over quite a history, of all the new items you took to test market, what was your hit rate? What percent made your expectations?

CORDDRY: Two thirds, at least. That may be low; I'd have to go back and tote them up.

We have two things going. We research things pretty well before we take them to market. Second, we've got an inherent feel about what's going to work in that line, and the line carries it.

We usually have either a hit or a miss; we don't have anything that sorta falls in the middle, and we'll pull them out after test market.

HONOMICHL: A lot of companies won't let the Glendinnings or the MCAs in. But as far as I can see, they've been a permanent fixture at Ore-Ida. From a marketing executive's point of view, what do you look for from such consulting firms?

CORDDRY: A couple of things. First of all, Heinz as a company, and Ore-Ida certainly as well, has a style that says, "Keep your management group pretty lean." And I think that's absolutely right. We don't have a lot of assistant product managers running around out here. The theory is that I would rather periodically go to the outside—to the MCAs or Glendinnings—and get another independent point of view, rather than loading up on fixed cost and building up an organization inside, and have them do some of the work you would have done internally if you had a larger group. I think it's really good for all of us to periodically get another group of people to look at a problem.

HONOMICHL: I get the impression that at Ore-Ida, you haven't turned to Doyle Dane [Doyle Dane Bernbach–New York, Ore-Ida's agency since 1975] for marketing counsel as much as some companies use their agencies for that.

CORDDRY: We use Doyle Dane the way, by and large, I've always used agencies—we certainly encourage them to help in new product development areas and promotions. Fair to say that the bulk of the work that comes out of most agencies really helps the client in the creative area. But there have been numerous occasions where Doyle Dane has provided valuable insights into our business other than creative and media.

I think the reason we do use outside people is the theory that the more people you've got really interested in your business, and coming from various places and various mind sets, the better you probably impact, surround, and analyze the problems.

HONOMICHL: I've been very impressed with the stable of market research services you use. Do you let them speak up and make recommendations?

CORDDRY: My personal philosophy is that we should listen to everybody we can. We can sort out ourselves, hopefully, the good from the bad.

There's an ongoing philosophy in the company—it's certainly true internally—one of the things we hear often when we have a consultant in on a problem is that the thing they see at Ore-Ida that is a little different is communications, which tend to be very open.

We tend to be open with outsiders, very open inside. What I've heard from outsiders who look at our organization is great peer group communications—marketing guys talk to operations, talk to R&D, talk to quality control—and they don't go up the line. This is something we've really tried to work hard on. We've really tried to make it a nice place to work because we think we are a heckuva lot more effective that way.

So, we try to decentralize as much as we can; we want to get good people in, and we want to give them something important to do. We try to keep down the level of bureaucracy to a bare minimum, put the emphasis on oral communications, and try to do away with as much paper work as we can. We absolutely emphasize, "Don't go up the line" with your problem. If you've got something over there in production, Mr. Product Manager, call up the production guy. We've got that set in. Another thing, we have an absolute rule that we do not practice politics. I just will not hear one division guy coming in and giving the rap on another division; they have to work it out. We're not going to play that game. As a result, I think there's something special out here in terms of how people are. By and large, the mood is upbeat; people like to come to work, and that's helped us.

HONOMICHL: I hear that brand managers have more responsibility at Ore-Ida.

CORDDRY: One thing we do that some companies don't—our marketing people have full access to profit data. They are often goaled on profit return as opposed to volume or something else. They are absolutely expected to know the impact on the bottom line of their actions, and so we have full brand P&Ls—and they have access to the total company P&L.

HONOMICHL: Brand managers—do they have the kind of clout where they can kill copy?

CORDDRY: Yeah, probably. I think from the standpoint—and I don't know if this is a plus or a minus, and this is an ongoing battle in this business—product managers can certainly kill alternative campaigns. They may see five or six alternatives, and by the time it sifts up the organization, two or three or four are gone. From that standpoint, they have.

Copy is such a critical thing and such a judgmental thing I would like to think we give it sort of a team approach. But I don't think it works that way, in all honesty. Normally, our copy meetings are attended by at least a general manager as well as a brand manager.

HONOMICHL: How would you summarize the Ore-Ida experience?

CORDDRY: One of the interesting things that's happened, since we turned the corner, is that there is a lot of continuity out there; we have very little turnover.

A large percentage of the people in our company went through the thin before it got to be good, and I think that's helpful. It brings you down to the floor every now and then; they remember when. The top managers, mostly, are really good friends—they've got a "go-through-it-together" sort of feeling. The young Turks are greying a little now because we've been going through it together since the late '60s.

Marvelous thing what momentum will do for you. Once we turned the corner, and the numbers started to come in pretty fast in our favor—to watch us go from what was really a band-aid operation where we were fighting fires to a company now that I think is pretty much on the leading edge of planning—how we relate to our people—it just seems to carry over everywhere.

2 President Reagan's Marketing Plan, 1980

I first became interested in the use of survey research—what media often call "political polling"—and its application in developing the marketing plan for aspirants to high political office during the Nixon-Humphrey campaign of 1968.

Since then, every four years, it has become increasingly evident that the "marketing" of political personalities has come to be every bit as well financed and sophisticated as the marketing of nonhuman goods and services; maybe more so, in some cases. This development reached a new high during the presidential campaign of Ronald Reagan in 1979; no other consumer-research program in the political sector has come close to being so well funded or sophisticated.

I had been in touch with his advisors in this area at the time, one being Vincent J. Breglio (executive vice president of Decision/ Making/ Information, the California-based survey research firm that masterminded the program) from the Republican nominating convention on. But, immediately after the election, when I asked Breglio for more details, I was overwhelmed by his offer: I could come to their headquarters in Washington, D.C., and review the now famous Black Book (a campaign marketing plan written by Richard B. Wirthlin, president of DMI, and deputy campaign director for strategy and planning in the Committee to Elect), and then review all the survey data that had been done, state by state, in the closing phases of the campaign. This was unprecedented; never before had the planners of a presidential campaign made such a detailed revelation to any publication exclusively. In effect, Advertising Age *(in which the chapters in this book were originally published) had come into possession of instant history, in awesome detail, of what was going on behind the scenes and the information candidate Reagan and his political advisors had at their disposal at various stages of the campaign.*

Rance Crain, editor of Advertising Age, *was quick to recognize the significance of this, and the* Advertising Age *issue of December 15, 1980, carried in its main news pages one of the longest stories* in the history of the publication; it ran four full pages, with tables and charts.

As a by-product of all this, Richard B. Wirthlin was named by the editors of Advertising Age as Advertising Man of the Year for 1980, a tribute to his key role in planning Ronald Reagan's stunning success. Wirthlin is the only researcher who has been so honored.

The Development of Reagan's Marketing Plan

Having full access to internal memoranda and the now-renowned campaign strategy Black Book makes it possible to look back over history's shoulder and see how campaign problems and challenges were perceived by then-Govenor Reagan's planners seven months before the general election.

A confidential memo authored by Richard B. Wirthlin, who was to become the campaign's deputy director for strategy and planning, stated on March 28, 1980: "With over a third of the 998 delegate votes needed to nominate now locked into the governor's column, and with his best primary states now starting to come up on the primary calendar, the general election campaign, from our point of view, starts today."

The basic points Wirthlin made in that memo could be considered a preamble to the strategy Black Book, which he wrote two months later:

- Never before has the electorate been as volatile in switching support from one candidate to another; the loyalty of voters runs thin indeed.
- The primaries [to date] have clearly revealed Carter's basic vulnerability.
- In the process of walking through and beyond the hot coals of the Iowa setback, we learned once again that our most effective asset is providing the electorate with in-depth exposure to Ronald Reagan.
- Care must be exercised so that the govenor's criticism of Carter does not come off as too shrill or too personal. We *can* hammer the president too hard, which will spawn blacklash.
- While ideology does not cut strongly in the primary contests, it will be a major vote determinant in November. We have no opportunity to win the general election unless we pull substantial numbers of moderate ticket splitters into our column.

Confidential surveys conducted by Wirthlin through his company, Decision/Making/Information (DMI), showed the Reagan base position with various segments of the electorate as of May 1979 (see table 2.1).

Table 2.1. Voter Types, as Predictor of Reagan-Carter Vote

% of Electorate*	Voter Type	% Reagan	% Carter	% Undecided
22	Conservative Republican	85	12	4
7	Moderate/liberal Republicans	69	25	6
13	Conservative ticket splitters	50	41	9
17	Moderate ticket splitters	50	40	10
14	Conservative Democrats	37	58	5
22	Liberal Democrats	25	68	7
6	Hispanics	17	78	5

*Note: Adds to more than 100% because of rounding.

Additional benchmark information came from a psychographic study conducted in June 1979 for the Reagan for President Committee. Entitled "A Survey of Voter Values and Attitudes," this study was based on extensive, in-depth personal interviews with 220 registered voters in 20 large cities. The purpose: "to seek to explain some of the motives underlying people's attitudes and opinions. Psychographic variables reflect psychological traits and personal stands, and they reflect a person's general outlook on life." The project director on this study was Vincent J. Breglio, Wirthlin's partner and executive vp of DMI.

One of the study's main conclusions was that "Reagan voters obtain high scores on the following scales: respect for authority, individualism, and authoritarianism—and a low score on egalitarianism." The study then pointed out that Democrats over age 55 tend to follow the same pattern and, hence, were a prime target for conversation.

This point was later refined to Eastern European ethnic groups living in large cities and explains why—especially at the start of the campaign—Reagan made highly visible visits to such neighborhoods. "He was not comfortable doing it, but he did it," recalls Breglio. Later Reagan decided to stop the practice because "he considered it exploitative."

Out of the psychographic study, three groups of special interest to the campaign were identified:

1. Democrats, head of household employed, 35 years and older, earning less than $15,000.

2. Voters who switch toward Kennedy. [The reasoning was that people who vacillated between Carter and Kennedy must not have strong ideological underpinnings since the two men are so disparate.]

3. Voters who prefer Reagan over both Carter and Kennedy.

Logistically, the lay of the land—as it appeared to Reagan's planners in the spring of 1980—was that basically states west of the Missouri River were in the governor's bag, and there was a good chance of carrying Iowa, Texas, and Florida, too. That suggested, then, a concentration of campaign efforts (and public opinion research measures) in the nine big-electoral vote states that could swing the election. These were Illinois, Ohio, Pennsylvania, Texas, Michigan, California, New Jersey, Florida, and New York.

New York was considered a special case; the cost of turning the state around was considered exorbitant, and there were three big "ifs": (1) if the upstate Republican organization did an outstanding job of turning out the vote, (2) if Representative John Anderson's position did not fall below 13%, and (3) if the very important Jewish vote was more fractured than normal. Consequently, after the early campaign period, the Reagan forces stopped doing their own opinion tracking studies in New York and relied on studies from other sources to stay in touch. As things worked out, Reagan carried the state.

Another key memorandum addressed to Reagan, William J. Casey, and Edwin Meese III was written by Wirthlin on May 26. Entitled "Strategy for the Doldrums," it advised on the short-term strategy for the six-week period between the end of the primaries and the start of the Republican National Convention. The basic tone was cautious—"Stay away from unnecessary predictions, specifics, and arguable statements."

The Black Book

Pivotal in campaign planning was a 176-page strategy statement by Wirthlin and his associates Vincent J. Breglio and Richard S. Beal (a consultant to DMI). "This was the campaign Bible," notes Breglio, "and about one-half was based on surveys Richard [Wirthlin] had done for Governor Reagan before and during the primaries [research expenditures in the primaries were about $400,000]; about one-fourth was based on historical voting behavior data, and the balance on practical judgment."

As to the public opinion surveys during the campaign, a budget of $1.4 million was earmarked for four major national studies on continuous tracking studies in nine pivotal states. Part of the statewide survey fieldwork would be handled through DMI directly, and the balance would be via piggy-backing on state-level studies being done for local candidates by another major Republican political survey firm, Market Opinion Research (MOR) in Detroit.

The Black Book, which was finished in June, starts off with 19 "Conditions of Victory," a listing of important "ifs" on which success would depend. Here are some of the more noteworthy:

- The conservative Republican Reagan base can be expanded to include a sufficient number of Moderates, Independents, soft Republicans, and

soft Democrats to offset Carter's natural Democratic base and his incumbency advantage.
- The impact of John Anderson on the race stabilizes, and he ends up cutting more into Carter's electoral vote base than into Reagan's.
- The campaign projects the image of Governor Reagan as embodying the values that a majority of Americans currently think are important in their president—namely, strength, maturity, decisiveness, resolve, determination, compassion, trustworthiness, and steadiness.
- The candidate and/or campaign avoid fatal, self-inflicted blunders.
- The attack strategy against President Carter reinforces his perceived weaknesses as an ineffective and error-prone leader, incapable of implementing policies, and not respected by our allies or enemies.
- Inoculate the voters against Carter's personal attacks by pointing out in the early stages of the campaign through surrogates that Carter has in the past, and will in the future, practice piranha politics.
- We can neutralize Carter's "October Surprise." [Because of the 7 a.m. press conference Carter called on the morning of the Wisconsin primary to hint at a hostage solution, the Reagan planners fully believed another such caper would be forthcoming toward the end of the national campaign.]
- The governor does not personally answer the Carter attacks; that will be the job of the vice presidential candidate and other surrogates.
- He can win the easiest and least expensive minimum of 270 electoral votes with victories in California, Illinois, Texas, Ohio, Pennsylvania, Indiana, Virginia, Tennessee, Florida, Maryland, Idaho, South Dakota, Wyoming, Vermont, Utah, Nebraska, North Dakota, New Hampshire, Kansas, Montana, New Mexico, Nevada, Arizona, Oregon, Alaska, Iowa, Colorado, Washington, and Maine (320 electoral votes).

At this stage, the Reagan planners were looking forward to a tough, close race and were well aware that, historically, whenever an elected incumbent was challenged in a reelection bid, two-thirds of the time the challenger lost. "Thus," concluded the Black Book, "unseating Jimmy Carter will be extremely difficult, even unlikely."

There followed a recap of some prevailing political wisdom on which the planners reckoned, to wit: "Older voters are almost twice as likely to vote as are the younger . . . the highly educated are two to three times as likely to turn out as the poorly educated. . .the numerous groups of 'Born Again' Protestants and 'high church' Protestants are very likely to vote, and vote Republican . . . voters in the Mountain, Pacific, Farm Belt, and Great Lakes regions constitute almost one-half of the population, and also have the highest turnout probability."

As to target groups—the prime source of Democratic shifters—"The campaign must convert into Reagan votes the disappointment felt by

- southern white Protestants,
- blue collar workers in industrial states,
- urban ethnics, and
- rural voters, especially in upstate New York, Ohio, and Pennsylvania."

To this portion of the brief, Wirthlin added this philosophism: "There is a tendency in our increasingly complex and highly technological society to forget that American Democracy is less a form of government than a romantic preference for a particular value structure." Indeed, although the Black Book didn't belabor the point, the election of Carter in 1976 was dramatic evidence of that point of view.

The Issues

A large national survey conducted by DMI in early June cataloged the issues that would probably most influence the American electorate. For instance, table 2.2 shows the main issues as of June 1980.

Table 2.2 Main Issues Influencing the Electorate as of June 1980

	% Electorate "Very Interested"
Reduce government spending	75
National defense	72
Federal income tax policy	62
Draft registration	56
Abortion	48
Women's rights movement	33
Ownership of Panama Canal	31

Special attention was paid to the so-called single-issue voter, that segment of the electorate that was so predisposed to just one issue that it might determine voting behavior despite political affiliation and the candidate's position on other issues.

As of June 1980, 28% of the electorate were broadly categorized as single-issue voters. Table 2.3 shows the reigning issues among this group. With a tighter definition of single-issue voters, people who would be activists, write letters, give money, etc., they were estimated at about 10% of the electorate. For these people, ERA, gun control, and abortion were all prime issues.

Table 2.3 Percentage Breakdown of Single-Issue Voters on Key Issues as of June 1980

National defense	27%
Reduce government spending	25
Draft registration	11
Abortion	11
Federal income tax policy	10
Women's rights	7
Ownership of Panama Canal	1
Other	8
	100%

Another way to view issue voting was to ask (as was done in the DMI June study) the electorate's perception of the "most pressing national problems" (see table 2.4).

Table 2.4 Percentages of Voter Opinion on Most Pressing National Problem(s)

Improve the economy—general	22%*
Cut inflation	20
Reduce unemployment/poverty	17
Reduce Government spending	11
Improve Government leadership	11
Improve immigration policy	10
Secure release of hostages	10
Improve general social conditions	9
Solve energy crisis	8
Reduce welfare	8
Reduce taxes	8
Improve national defense	6

*Total exceeds 100% because of multiple answers.

Out of all this, obviously, reduction of government influence dominated the issue list, no matter how the subject was approached, with national defense running a close second. And these were, of course, the themes Reagan hammered on endlessly throughout the campaign.

In terms of awareness, as of June 1980, DMI showed that about 90% of the electorate were familiar with the Reagan name; however, about 40% felt they knew very little about what he stood for politically. Clearly, there was a mass education job necessary, especially east of the Mississippi.

The most important thing—"the key to the election" in the opinion of Breglio—was the June study findings in relation to voter expectations.

When asked to name "something good" that would happen if Reagan were elected, 67% of those interviewed could state something positive, from their personal point of view. In the case of Carter, only 55% could name "something good." In other words, about half of the electorate could not imagine even one good thing resulting from the reelection of Carter.

On the negative side, when voters were asked to name "something bad" that would happen if Reagan were elected, 72% could name something. For Carter's reelection, it was 83%. "This was very encouraging at the time," recalls Breglio, "because it indicated that if people voted their expectations of the future, we would win."

"The only chance Carter had to win," in the opinion of Breglio, "was to change the electorate's perceptions of the future, to provide a positive vision. When he chose to make Govenor Reagan the main issue, he was lost."

The same questions were asked in three DMI national studies done after the Black Book was written. Table 2.5 shows how the data from all four studies looked together.

In the end, Reagan had a significant lead over Carter in both the large number of voters who perceived at least something good coming from his election and the smaller number who perceived something bad.

Table 2.5 Voter Expectations of the Future

	Something "Good" % Naming	Something "Bad" % Naming
If Reagan elected		
June 1980	67	72
July 1980	70	85
August 1980	66	64
September 1980	66	67
If Carter Reelected		
June 1980	55	83
July 1980	39	85
August 1980	52	77
September 1980	50	78

Reagan Approves

Immediately after the Republican National Convention in Detroit, key Reagan advisors met to read and approve the Black Book strategies. "They went through it page by page," recalls Breglio, "with Governor Reagan attending."

At this point, structure of the Reagan–Bush organization was firm, too, with deputy directors as follows: William Timmons, organization;

Richard Wirthlin, strategy and planning; Edwin Meese, policy and issue research; Peter H. Dailey, advertising/media; and Vernon Orr, comptroller. These deputies reported to campaign director William J. Casey. (Later, Stuart Spencer, a political consultant from California who had handled Reagan's gubernatorial campaigns, joined this group.) "The Black Book pertained to strategy only," Wirthlin told me recently, "and it was up to the deputy directors to devise tactics; if the Black Book had tried to dictate tactics, the campaign would have failed."

Having a plan is one thing, but adhering to it is another, as any marketing manager knows. For instance, "The activists were putting tremendous pressure on Pete Dailey to make and run negative commercials. They wanted to crucify Carter one fingernail at a time," says Breglio. But the plan called for not attacking Carter's record until after establishing Reagan's credibility as presidential timber, even though Reagan was "champing at the bit" to go on the offensive. The Reagan–Bush Committee didn't start to air negative tv commercials until October 10.

"The Black Book plan helped Pete Dailey stand his ground," says Breglio. "There was an accepted rationale for holding off. Timmons, Spencer, Meese, and Wirthlin were particularly adamant about sticking to the plan. And, in the end, it worked."

In the four months between the Republican convention and November 4, the Reagan–Bush Committee alone spent $29.4 million on the campaign effort, and there were additional expenditures by the Republican National Committee, which aided the Reagan cause. Annualized, then, this effort would equal a marketing budget of over $100 million. It was spent by a group of men who were basically strangers at the start. They had to learn to work together in a hurry, under pressure, and to manage a part-time staff of over 300. Everyone seems to agree—it was Richard Wirthlin's Black Book plan that held things together.

The Final Predictions

Table 2.6 shows the actual computer output from DMI's simulation model as it was finally run in Santa Ana, California, at 5:09 p.m., Pacific time, on Monday, November 3, 1980. Using "worst case" assumptions, it predicted that Reagan would have a minimum of 395 electoral votes, Carter a maximum of 140. (The "best case" assumptions run later in the evening predicted a maximum of 480 electoral votes for Reagan.)

"These data were never shown to Governor Reagan or his advisors because we were too conservative," according to Breglio. "It was too good to be true; we kept checking for errors."

"The first time we used the word 'landslide' out loud was Monday afternoon," recalls Richard S. Beal, a consultant to DMI and director of political information systems for the Reagan–Bush Committee. "We were looking over the latest runs in our hotel room in California, and it was very exciting. Two Spanish-speaking maids came in to clean the room, and we told them it was going to be a runaway election. They couldn't understand, and probably thought we were crazy."

Modeling

A computer base in DMI's Santa Ana office was the home of survey research studies being conducted by Republican candidates in most key states. In some states, there were continuous telephone surveys being conducted by the Reagan–Bush Committee, either through DMI directly or through Market Opinion Research in Detroit. In some states where the Reagan–Bush Committee did not have its own poll data, those of Republican candidates running in statewide elections were used as available, as well as studies conducted by other third parties, such as local media, etc. (Each source was examined for research standards before its data were admitted to the system.)

Through a voter simulation model, DMI was to manipulate these data, asking the computer to calculate the changing impact of key assumption variables, such as how the undecided vote, or the Anderson vote, might distribute at the last minute, or the effect of an especially light or heavy voter turnout.

In the "worst case" data shown in table 2.6, for instance, the going-in assumption was that more of the undecided vote and the last minute switches away from Anderson would go to Carter than Reagan. (In fact, a postelection study based on just people who actually voted showed that the last-minute undecided vote went 43% Carter, 42% Reagan, and 5% Anderson.)

Table 2.6 Final Simulation Model "Worst Case" Predictions

State	EV	Reagan Margin	Reagan EV	Carter EV	Toss Up	Reagan %	Carter %	Anderson %
Large Electoral States								
California	45	9.1	45	0	0	49.6	40.5	9.9
Illinois	26	14.6	71	0	0	53.0	38.4	8.6
Michigan	21	8.8	92	0	0	50.4	41.6	8.0
New York	41	−13.5	92	41	0	40.4	53.9	5.7
Ohio	25	6.6	117	41	0	49.8	43.2	7.0
Pennsylvania	27	6.8	144	41	0	50.3	43.5	6.2
Texas	26	17.1	170	41	0	57.3	40.1	2.6

President Reagan's Marketing Plan, 1980

State	EV	Reagan Margin	Reagan EV	Carter EV	Toss Up	Reagan %	Carter %	Anderson %
Medium Electoral States								
Florida	17	8.1	187	41	0	51.8	43.7	4.5
Georgia	12	-23.8	187	53	0	35.4	59.2	5.3
Indiana	13	20.5	200	53	0	58.2	37.7	4.2
Louisiana	10	9.0	210	53	0	53.3	44.3	2.4
Maryland	10	-2.6	210	63	0	43.8	46.5	9.7
Massachusetts	14	-0.6	210	77	0	42.3	42.9	14.7
Minnesota	10	-4.1	210	87	0	42.5	46.6	-10.9
Missouri	12	7.4	222	87	0	51.2	43.8	5.0
New Jersey	17	20.9	239	87	0	55.2	34.3	10.6
North Carolina	13	-12.9	239	100	0	42.0	54.9	3.1
Tennessee	10	-2.1	239	110	0	47.8	49.9	2.3
Virginia	12	17.7	251	110	0	55.8	38.0	6.2
Wisconsin	11	4.5	262	110	0	49.6	45.0	5.4
Small Electoral States								
Alabama	9	1.8	271	110	0	49.8	47.9	2.3
Alaska	3	30.2	274	110	0	62.8	32.6	4.6
Arizona	6	23.9	280	110	0	59.9	35.9	4.2
Arkansas	6	5.0	286	110	0	51.0	46.0	3.1
Colorado	7	22.3	293	110	0	56.9	34.7	8.4
Connecticut	8	12.6	301	110	0	51.0	38.4	10.6
Delaware	3	-1.5	301	113	0	43.7	45.2	11.1
Hawaii	4	-1.8	301	117	0	45.1	46.9	8.0
Idaho	4	45.2	305	117	0	70.1	24.9	5.0
Iowa	8	10.1	313	117	0	51.8	41.6	6.6
Kansas	7	20.7	320	117	0	56.9	36.2	6.9
Kentucky	9	-13.4	320	126	0	42.2	55.6	2.3
Maine	4	-1.2	320	130	0	42.9	44.1	13.1
Mississippi	7	9.3	327	130	0	54.2	45.0	0.8
Montana	4	15.9	331	130	0	54.2	38.2	7.6
Nebraska	5	21.9	336	130	0	57.3	35.4	7.3
Nevada	3	39.4	339	130	0	65.0	25.6	9.4
New Hampshire	4	27.5	343	130	0	57.8	30.3	12.0
New Mexico	4	9.4	347	130	0	50.2	40.8	9.1
North Dakota	3	25.4	350	130	0	55.1	29.7	15.2
Oklahoma	8	19.8	358	130	0	58.0	38.2	3.9
Oregon	6	5.6	364	130	0	48.3	42.7	9.0
Rhode Island	4	-9.4	364	134	0	36.4	45.8	17.7
South Carolina	8	7.6	372	134	0	52.1	44.6	3.3
South Dakota	4	18.4	376	134	0	56.2	37.7	6.1
Utah	4	53.9	380	134	0	73.5	19.6	7.0
Vermont	3	0.1	383	134	0	44.1	44.0	11.9
Washington	9	9.8	392	134	0	50.4	40.6	9.0
West Virginia	6	-9.3	392	140	0	43.2	52.5	4.3
Wyoming	3	32.8	395	140	0	61.9	29.2	8.9

13 States to Carter

The "worst case" prediction showed 13 states with 140 electoral votes going to Carter—New York, Georgia, Maryland, Massachusetts, Minnesota, North Carolina, Tennessee, Kentucky, Maine, Rhode Island, Delaware, Hawaii, and West Virginia. (In fact, just six of those states—Georgia, Minnesota, Maryland, West Virginia, Hawaii, and Rhode Island—plus the District of Columbia, for a total of 49 electoral votes, went to Carter.)

The most important of these, New York with its 41 electoral votes, was a special case. The campaign planners had decided that the cost of campaigning in New York was exorbitant, as related to the chances of success, so after the early campaign stages, no money was spent doing continuous telephone tracking studies there. The research data in DMI's model came from other sources, including studies done by public polling operations, such as Gallup and Harris. Also, the decision was made not to spend advertising money in New York except as necessary to reach Connecticut and New Jersey.

For Reagan to win New York, the planners felt, three things had to happen: (1) the upstate organization had to do an especially good job in turning out the vote, (2) Anderson's share of the popular vote could not drop below 13%, and (3) the Jewish vote had to fracture, not be as monolithic as normal. A postelection study showed that nationwide about 30% of the Jewish vote did go for Reagan, the largest share a Republican presidential candidate has ever received. Presumably, something like that happened in New York State, too. Reagan ended up carrying the state.

An 11-Point Spread

For 18 days before the November 4 vote, DMI was conducting 500 telephone interviews a day nationally; this was increased to 1,000 a day over the final three days, November 1–3. Both the November 2 and the November 3 readings predicted Reagan would have an 11-point spread over Jimmy Carter in the popular vote (see figure 2.1).

In fact, Reagan won with 51% of the popular vote, compared to Carter's 41%—a 10-point spread. Of all national polls for which data are publicly available, the closest was the ABC/Harris Poll, conducted by Louis Harris, which at the last predicted Reagan winning with a 5-point margin.

More important, in postelection agonizing, public pollsters have tended to claim that their final predictions, which widely missed the mark, were thrown off by a massive, last-minute voter shift to Reagan. The DMI data refute this; they show that Reagan was holding a consistent 5- to 7-point lead over Carter during the period October 17–October 19, and that then started to open up, day by day, to the ultimate 10-point margin.

The undecided vote, shown at about 12% of the electorate on election eve, eventually split 43% Carter, 42% Reagan, and 5% Anderson, according to a postelection survey of actual voters. There was a surprise in the

Jewish vote; about 30 percent voted for Reagan, the best penetration ever achieved by a Republican presidential candidate. The black vote gave Reagan about 7–8% which is about normal for Republican candidates.

Figure 2.1 How the Reagan Polling Went: Oct. 17–Nov. 3 Final Projection

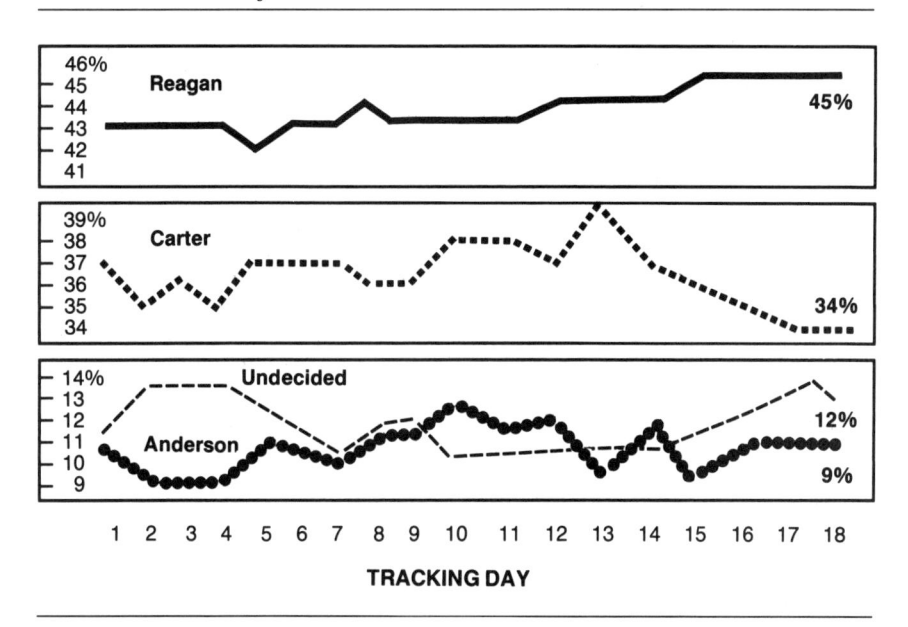

TRACKING DAYS: 1–Oct. 17, 2–Oct. 18, 3–Oct. 19, 4–Oct. 20, 5–Oct. 21, 6–Oct. 22, 7–Oct. 23, 8–Oct. 24, 9–Oct. 25, 10–Oct. 26, 11–Oct. 27, 12–Oct. 28, 13–Oct. 29, 14–Oct. 30, 15–Oct. 31, 16–Nov. 1, 17–Nov. 2, 18–Nov. 3.

Postelection Analysis

Within a five-day period after the November 4 election, DMI did a telephone survey of 3,000 people who had actually voted in the election. The results of this study, which became available in early December 1980, make possible a comparison with data gathered from prospective voters in three previous surveys conducted by DMI (1,500 interviews each) in June, September, and mid-October.

These data show how Reagan stood with various segments of the electorate at the beginning, and how these perceptions changed as a result of massive advertising, public appearance, and Carter–Reagan debate exposure. And, finally, they capture the impressions (from the postelection study) of what the electorate's perceptions were as they actually voted.

The data in table 2.7 show that Reagan's strength with self-avowed Democrats changed little over the five-month span, but there was considerable shift in his favor by both avowed Republicans and registered voters who considered themselves independent. Among voters of various political ideologies, the most dramatic shifts toward Reagan came from voters labeled very conservative and moderate. The postelection analysis showed that of voters considered somewhat liberal, 28% in fact voted for Reagan, and for very liberal voters the number was 20%.

These data also show steadily increasing support for Reagan from union members, starting with 30% in June, and ending with 43% of that group actually voting for him on November 4. In the area of religious identification, Reagan started in June with less than 40% support from both Catholics and the "born-again" Protestants; this had increased to 50% of both groups by election time.

Reagan's stand on ERA, which supposedly would cost him dearly with female voters, apparently was not a serious impediment; 48% of women voters supported him on November 4, according to the DMI postelection survey. These data also show that Reagan started with strong support (49%) with voters in Jimmy Carter's Deep South, and that changed little over the next five months. In the border states—Tennessee, Kentucky, West Virginia et al.—the situation was much different; Reagan started off in that region with only 36% support, but that increased to 50% by election time.

Table 2.7 Reagan's Position within Voter Segments

Voter Groups	% Registered Voters June	Sept.	Oct.	% Actual Voters Postelection
Republican	73	70	77	87
Democrat	21	23	22	25
Independent	38	40	44	53
Very conservative	55	64	61	71
Somewhat conservative	52	48	53	64
Moderate	29	39	38	41
Somewhat liberal	23	24	27	28
Very liberal	21	22	19	20
Union members	30	34	35	43
Born-again Protestant	38	44	NA*	50
Catholic	36	42	NA	50
Male	37	42	48	55
Female	35	39	39	48
Deep South	49	49	43	51
Border States	36	42	46	50

*Not asked.

Throughout the interviewing, prospective voters were asked their impressions of Reagan, Carter, and Anderson on a battery of traits relevant to a position of presidential leadership. Table 2.8 shows the data, from all four national studies, on how the public perceptions of Reagan were changing over a five-month period.

Most notable is registered voter perception of Reagan as a strong leader, which had stayed in the 42% range prior to the election; however, of people who voted, 61% attributed this quality to Reagan at voting time. Another dramatic shift came on the "reduce inflation" issue—with about half the voters giving him that credit prior to the election and 71% at election time. The specter of Reagan as a potential warmonger apparently remained constant—41% of registered voters in September thought he "would be likely to start an unnecessary war" and then again in October. In the voting booth, it dropped to 39% of actual voters.

Table 2.8 Voter Perception of Reagan on Leadership Traits

Perceived Traits	% Registered Voters			% Actual Voters
	June	Aug.	Oct.	Postelection
Strong leader	42	45	42	61
Trustworthy	NA	29	39	33
Reduce inflation	46	53	NA	71
Likely to start unnecessary war	NA	41	41	39
Cares about elderly/poor	27	26	—	26

*Not asked.

The Undecided Vote

Of special interest in the postelection survey of actual voters was the size of the last-minute undecided vote and how that vote distributed among Reagan, Carter, and Anderson. Since DMI had conducted similar surveys after the presidential elections of 1976 and 1972, it was possible to make that further comparison.

As the data in figure 2.2 show, 46% of people who actually voted had decided for whom they would vote nine weeks before Labor Day (which fell on September 1 in 1980). At the time of the election on November 4, 13% were still undecided (as compared to 11% in 1976 in the Carter-Ford election).

This 13% last-minute undecided vote split 43% to Carter, 42% to Reagan, and 5% to Anderson. The balance (10%) was distributed among a variety of splinter party candidates.

These data, of course, go counter to the so-called big bang thesis held by Carter's research expert, Patrick Caddell, and others, saying that there was a massive last-minute shift of this vote to Reagan. Caddell has been quoted as saying his data showed that 8 million voters shifted to Reagan during the last two days of the campaign, a thesis also held by Warren Mitofsky, the director of the polling effort run by CBS News and shared by the *New York Times*.

Figure 2.2

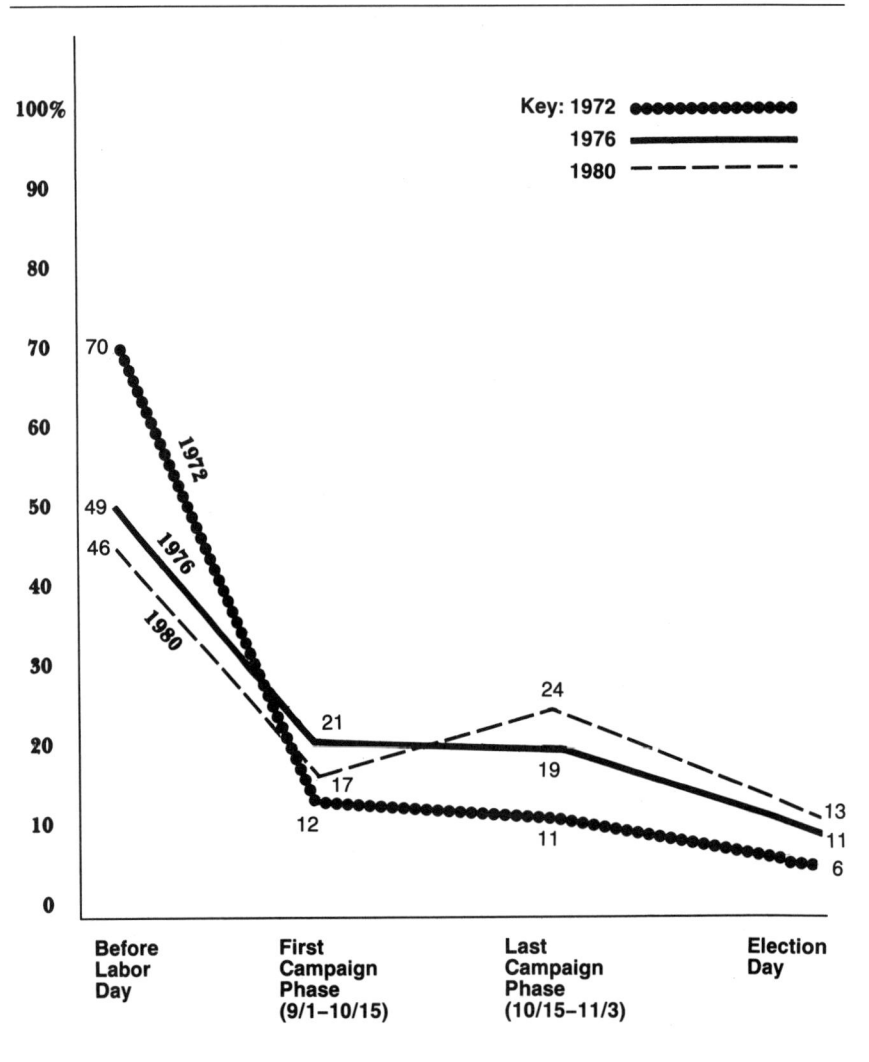

When Did the Electorate Make Up Its Mind to Vote for Presidential Candidates?
1972 – 1976 – 1980 Compared

Key: 1972 ●●●●●●●●●●●●●
1976 ─────────
1980 ─ ─ ─ ─ ─

	Before Labor Day	First Campaign Phase (9/1–10/15)	Last Campaign Phase (10/15–11/3)	Election Day
1972	70	12	11	6
1976	49	21	19	11
1980	46	17	24	13

3 The Big Four of Political Research

Just four men—Richard B. Wirthlin, Robert M. Teeter, Peter D. Hart, and Patrick H. Caddell—dominate political survey research, or "polling," in the U.S. For instance, during the mid-term elections of 1981-82, these four and the organizations behind them, worked for 50 senatorial, 163 congressional, and 44 gubernatorial aspirants. In total, these campaigns accounted for about $13 million in political survey research.

It should come as no surprise, then, that these four have come to be media personalities in their own right; they are constantly being interviewed by tv commentators and news magazine reporters about the mind-set of vox populi *in the United States.*

Yet, to marketers away from the political arena, these four men are relatively unknown. Hence, this article from Advertising Age *of February 28, 1983. Among other things, it included a historic photograph—the first time these four men had been photographed together. Quite appropriately, the photo was taken on a cool, windy day on the west lawn of the White House, where all four wish they had a client in residence—but only Richard Wirthlin does.*

The Background of Political Polling

Before, during, and after the 1982 elections they seemed omnipresent. *Time, U.S. News & World Report,* the *New York Times*—and especially the *Washington Post*—quoted them at length. The tv public affairs talk shows sought them as guests, and NBC's *Today* show and ABC's *Good Morning America* brought them into your breakfast nook. They were queried as political gurus and asked to explain *vox populi,* and reporters listened carefully. After all, if these guys couldn't explain the American voter's psyche, hopes, and frustrations, who the hell could?

"These guys" are an increasingly prominent genus of survey researchers, or "political pollsters," as the media label them. There aren't many—

maybe a dozen or so operating in the political big leagues. But some—especially Richard B. Wirthlin and Robert M. Teeter on the Republican side of the aisle, and Peter D. Hart and Patrick H. Caddell on the Democratic side—have become media personalities. At first, this was basically fame rub-off from their clients: the congressional, senatorial, gubernatorial, and, above all, presidential candidates. But now, these four have come to have, it seems, a public presence that transcends their association with one or more prominent politicians or the vicissitudes of a specific election wave.

A recent example: right after President Reagan's State of the Union address to Congress on January 25, Tom Brokaw and Roger Mudd of NBC-TV News interviewed a panel of political pollsters—Wirthlin, Hart, and Teeter—on their personal reactions to the political impact of the president's message.

One reason, I suggest, is that more editors and tv producers now realize that, as the cost and sophistication of politicking in the United States escalates, these pollsters have huge survey budgets at their disposal to study American society, the undercurrents, the attitudes, and the predispositions that drive trends over and beyond immediate election results.

For instance, just the Big Four—Wirthlin, Teeter, Hart, and Caddell—collectively, in the 1981–82 election campaigns (including primaries) fielded public opinion surveys for 50 senatorial, 163 congressional, and 44 gubernatorial aspirants. These candidates spent about $13 million on research, and this is estimated to be 60–65% of the total spent by all major political candidates.

One extraordinary case in point was the unsuccessful gubernatorial campaign of Lewis E. Lehrman (R) in New York State in 1982 which, according to him, cost $14 million. In excess of $300,000 of that was spent on survey research through Wirthlin's firm, Decision/Making/Information. Obviously, after such an exercise, the researcher involved becomes extraordinarily knowledgeable about the public mood in New York State—region by region, ethnic group by ethnic group.

So, the likes of Wirthlin, Teeter, Hart, and Caddell have probably become the best-financed social scientists in the United States or, perhaps more accurately, the best-informed marketers in the sense of relating effective appeals to target market segments.

Marketing Orientation

"Winning elections today is a science, not an art form, and I believe that 10% of any campaign budget should be spent up front on public opinion studies—to make sure the other 90% is not wasted," opines Richard Richards, past chairman of the Republic National Committee. Teeter estimates that, on average, it ran about 5% in the campaigns he was involved with in 1982.

The "big four" of political research (left to right): Peter Hart, Patrick Caddell, Richard Wirthlin, and Robert Teeter.

Square that with *Time* magazine estimates that, in 1981–82, U.S. Senate and House candidates alone spent roughly $300 million on their campaign efforts, and that was an increase of about 25% over 1980. *Time* went on to say, "When races for governor and state legislative posts are added in, the grand total may hit half a billion dollars."

Hugh Sidey, one of the most respected observers of the presidency, added this prediction in one of his recent *Time* essays: "The upcoming [1984] presidential race will be the longest, most televised, most computerized, most numbing electoral spectacle in history. It could also be the most expensive, exceeding the record $275 million spent in 1980, if Ronald Reagan does not run and the Republican field crowds up with free-spending long shots."

That 1984 race has already started; as of January 1, 1983, stated candidates for the presidency became eligible for federal matching funds. Political operatives are already in place in Iowa, where the first caucuses are tentatively scheduled for February 27, 1984.

Ted Kennedy has bowed out. Walter F. Mondale, Alan Cranston, John Glenn, Gary Hart, and Reubin Askew have announced officially. And, believe it, the campaign managers who "handle" these candidates have basically the same mentality as high-powered marketers of detergents, cigarettes, or beer. Their "product" is a personality who represents a point of view. As for the political pollsters who support these campaigns with data, and in some cases, intimate counsel, they may well spend between $25 and $30 million on political surveys, modeling, and analysis of past voting behavior on behalf of their clients, state committees, and political action groups between now and the '84 election.

The Big Four

As things steamed up with the first 1984 primary (New Hampshire on March 6, 1984), the Big Four were there—Wirthlin, Teeter, Hart, and Caddell—pontificating on the ebbs and flows of public opinion. Who are these men?

Robert M. Teeter

Robert M. Teeter, 46, has been in the political arena since the mid-1960s when, as a young instructor in political science at Albion College in Michigan, he put in two summers of volunteer work for George W. Romney, the former president of American Motors who became Republican governor of Michigan.

In 1966, Teeter joined the Detroit-based survey research firm of Market Opinion Research (MOR) and devoted most of his time to Governor Romney's unsuccessful bid for the presidential nomination. This work led to the staffing of a Political Division of MOR which, in 1972, hit the jackpot—management of the survey research program for a president of the United States, Richard Nixon, who was running for reelection. (In the 1968 election, Nixon's work was done primarily by Thomas W. Benham at Opinion Research Corporation (ORC), Princeton, N.J. In 1972, ORC and Decision/Making/Information did some of the Nixon work.)

"Most of our presentations were made to Bob Haldeman or John Mitchell at the Committee to Re-Elect," says Teeter, "but some of the meetings were with Nixon personally." For political pollsters, that's the ultimate ego trip—interface with a sitting president.

The election of 1976 found Teeter and MOR doing all the polling and research for Gerald R. Ford, another sitting President. By now Teeter was a familiar face at the southwest gate, where most staffers enter the White House.

Concurrently, Teeter and MOR were building a base in Canadian politics, having done survey research for the Conservative party in the federal elections of 1972, 1974, and 1979. And in the United States, MOR has worked for hundreds of Republican political aspirants over the years; in 1982 alone, they were involved in 97 gubernatorial, senatorial, and congressional races.

Today, Teeter, a stalwart in Republican party affairs, is most closely associated with Vice President George Bush. "We became friends back in the '70s when he was chairman of the Republican National Committee," says Teeter, who handled all the survey research for Bush in the presidential primaries of 1980.

Teeter, who became president of MOR in 1979, lives in Ann Arbor, Michigan, with his wife Betsy and their two children. He received his M.A. degree in political science from Michigan State University.

Richard B. Wirthlin

Richard B. Wirthlin, 54, is a soft-spoken, cherubic man with an academic demeanor who currently reigns as the *paterfamilias* of the political research coterie because, bluntly, he has a client—and personal friend—sitting as president of the United States. With that come all sorts of political status symbols, such as flights on Air Force One and data presentations at the Reagan ranch outside Santa Barbara.

Dr. Wirthlin (Ph.D. in economics from the University of California at Berkeley) was chairman of the department of economics at Brigham Young University and director of BYU's Survey Research Center when, in 1968, he first met and did a survey for Ronald Reagan who was serving his first term as governor of California. The go-between was Richard Richards, at the time head of the Republican Committee in Utah (and on Reagan's election as president, chairman of the Republican National Committee).

Wirthlin left academe in 1969 to form a survey research firm, Decision/Making/Information (DMI), in Santa Ana, Calif., along with Paul Newman (now a political consultant in Seattle), Vincent J. Breglio (until recently, executive director, National Republican Senatorial Committee; now president of Research/Strategy/Management, a Washington-based political survey firm), and Vincent Barabba, who has served twice as director, Bureau of the Census, and now director, marketing intelligence at Eastman Kodak Company.

Through the years, Wirthlin's firm, DMI, has handled the survey research for literally dozens of Republican biggies, including Senators Barry Goldwater, Paul Laxalt, Robert Dole, John Tower, and Peter Domenici—and Governor Nelson Rockefeller.

During Reagan's presidency, DMI has gotten the lion's share of public opinion survey work that, while paid for by the Republican National Committee, is really designed and destined for political strategists (and the president) within the White House. (Teeter's firm, MOR, does work for the committee, too.)

This continuous tracking of public opinion is, without doubt, the most extensive ever utilized by an administration. But the scope and detail are played down lest, fear President Reagan's advisors, he appear to be reacting to whims in public opinion instead of imposing his own political leadership. Be that as it may, this part of DMI's work causes Wirthlin to make the short walk from his personal office in the District over to the White House almost daily to confer with James A. Baker III, Edwin Meese III, Michael K. Deaver, and other presidential advisors.

"Since I've been involved in politics—and that's less than 20 years—there's been a revolution in the way politicians go about running for public office. Some of the changes are good for society, and the country; some concern me," Wirthlin told me in a recent interview. "On the positive side, I think it's healthy for a democracy when elected officials must listen to their constituencies with an open ear. And political polling is the vehicle that makes it possible. That's healthy."

But, on the negative side, notes Wirthlin: "I'm concerned about the rising power of tv, and how that's weakened the political parties. Also, the cost of running for office has become forbidding. We must find a way to keep the channels to elective office as open as possible."

Because of his work as deputy campaign director of strategy and planning for the Reagan campaign of 1979–80, Wirthlin was named Advertising Man of the Year by *Advertising Age*, the first researcher so honored.

Wirthlin, his wife Jeralie, and the youngest of their eight children live in McLean, Va.

Peter D. Hart

Peter D. Hart, 43, is the only one of the Big Four who hasn't grabbed the White House brass ring—yet. The son of an English professor at the University of California at Berkeley, Hart went east to attend college (Colby College in Maine; B.A. in history) and stayed to start his political apprenticeship in 1964 with Louis Harris, the pollster who became famous working for John F. Kennedy in 1960, the first presidential campaign where survey research was an important planning tool. Hart served Harris as a $75-a-week coder.

In 1968, Hart had his first client: John J. Gilligan in an Ohio senate race. Then he did off-year surveys for the Democratic National Committee and, in 1970, joined the political polling firm run by the late Oliver Quayle. He returned briefly to Louis Harris and Associates as a vice president before founding his own firm, Peter D. Hart Research Associates, Inc., in the District.

In the years since, Hart has worked for numerous Democratic politicians, including Edward Kennedy (1980), Henry "Scoop" Jackson, John Stennis, and Illinois Congressman Abner Mikva. In the 1982 elections, Hart's firm worked on 35 senatorial, congressional, and gubernatorial campaigns. Hart also handled the 1984 Mondale–Ferraro campaign. (See chapter 4 for details.)

"In recent elections the Republicans have outspent the Democrats about 2½ to 3 to 1 for political polling," says Hart, "but I don't view that as seriously as some people. It really comes down to understanding the dynamics of a campaign—public perception of the candidate, the key issues, and the qualities voters are looking for in a particular public office. The role of survey research is to understand those dynamics, and in that respect, I don't think the amount of money spent is all that important. I look for 'windows of opportunity' for the candidates we work for, and that may well come from one benchmark survey."

Hart lives in Washington, D.C., with his wife Florence and their two children.

Patrick H. Caddell

Patrick H. Caddell, 34, the most flamboyant of the Big Four, was named by *Time* magazine in 1974 as one of its 200 "future leaders of the United States," in part for his survey work for George McGovern in his ill-fated campaign of 1972. Now, of course, he is best known as the survey researcher who served President Carter.

Caddell got started early. As a high school student in Jacksonville, Fla., he worked on an analysis of election returns in the state of Florida as a math project. Notoriety from this work got him an appointment as a special assistant to the Speaker of the Florida House of Representatives, while still a high school student.

At age 21 and still an undergraduate at Harvard University, Caddell —along with some student friends—founded a firm called Cambridge Survey Research, worked in the McGovern campaign, and first met an obscure politician from Georgia by the name of Jimmy Carter. In 1974, he founded a second research firm, Cambridge Reports, to conduct omnibus national surveys for commercial clients.

In 1975, when Carter faced a showdown primary battle in Florida against Governor George Wallace of Alabama, he called on Caddell, whose knowledge of Florida was well known (his senior thesis at Harvard was on changing trends in southern politics). Carter won, and Caddell became part of the young, relatively inexperienced team that swept into the White House on Carter's surprise victory. As a young bachelor with a Rolls-Royce and a townhouse in the District's posh Georgetown section, Caddell became well known as a nightlife buddy of Jody, Ham, and Stu. (When Hamilton Jordan broke up with his wife, he moved into Mr. Caddell's home.)

Today Caddell heads Cambridge Survey Research and—in addition to political work—is striving to build up a commercial clientele. (He is no longer involved in the other firm, Cambridge Reports.)

In the 1982 elections, he worked for Democratic senatorial, congressional, and gubernatorial aspirants, including Senator Edward Kennedy's reelection campaign in Massachusetts.

What It All Means

The world political researchers work in is, in many respects, much different than that of most market or social researchers, and that carries over to the people, too. Here are some observations, for the record.

The political pollsters are very political animals—articulate and skilled at dealing with the press. Generally, they have more of a marketing orientation than many researchers who work in package goods companies. One reason for that is that they are closer to the action, the decision making, and the splattering of blood if something goes wrong. Also, they tend to get more personally involved with their clients and the issues at stake.

Political researchers work horrendously long hours and, especially during the political season, against very short deadlines. Compared to most market researchers, theirs is a strict winner-takes-all mentality. A marketer, for instance, might launch a new product that has a goal of 5% share of market. It might fall short to, say, a 3.5% share, but still be worthwhile and profitable. No such gray area exists in political campaigns; only winning counts.

The ultimate ego trip for a political researcher is to latch onto a rising political star and coattail him (or her) into the White House—with all that implies with press attention, the attraction of business to the firm, the percs, invitations to speak, and—perhaps—a personal relationship with the president that make the researchers feel that, to some degree, they're players on the world's stage. But such a win is a long shot, and, day to day, a political polling business is built on continuous relationships with state political party committees or national political action [read: funding] groups like the National Republican Senatorial Committtee. These groups often select the local slates, advise the candidates, and are in the position to urge the use of (or approve) a particular campaign manager or pollster. This is bread-and-butter—the over-the-transom work from literally hundreds of aspiring congressional candidates new to politics who are being coached on how to run a successful campaign.

The increasing clout political survey research plays in this process was summarized by Howell Raines, a political writer for the *New York Times:* "In the new campaign weaponry, polls have become enormously important for novel reasons. For example, to gain entrance to political action committees, which are the 'fat cats' of today's political order, a candidate needs a survey, or at least an encouraging letter, from a big-name polltaker."

Like any good commercial market researcher who cringes when a client ignores or misuses research data—and heads over the cliff—political researchers have the same frustrations. Campaign managers can cut them off from the candidate or read their own personal interpretations into the data. Advertising advisors—often volunteers—can screw up a campaign thrust. And, to a political pollster who has worked on literally hundreds of campaigns and seen every mistake and screw-up in the book, it can be very frustrating not to have a dominant voice in campaign operating decisions.

Political researchers tend to be myopic; theirs is a tight, cliquish community. For instance, the impressive sounding National Association of Political Pollsters, which was founded in 1975 to represent the interests of political pollsters with the Federal Election Commission, has just four members—Wirthlin, Teeter, Hart, and Caddell. The by laws are written in such a way that maybe two other prominent pollsters are qualified to join, assuming they come up with the $2,500 annual fee.

Savvy, a mite world-weary, hard-working, inveterate name droppers—the political researchers drive a growing, prominent segment of the survey research industry. And the press attention has elevated them to research superstar status.

Postscript (August 1985)

Jockeying for position in the 1984 campaigns was well underway at the time this article appeared in *Advertising Age*, and as it worked out, Reagan ran again and Richard Wirthlin resumed his function as chief pollster and a key strategy planner. His title in the Reagan–Bush '84 Campaign staff: campaign director, polling and planning. A considerable amount of the actual polling work was handled through Teeter's firm, MOR, and Teeter personally was a consultant to the Reagan–Bush '84 staff.

The Democratic camp effort was not nearly as clear-cut because of the various factions vying for leadershhip and the nomination. Patrick Caddell, the gadfly of Democratic politics, was quite outspoken about what he believed to be a lackluster field of candidates, and reportedly he spent considerable effort trying to convince the senator from Delaware, Joe Biden, that he should enter the race. Also, Caddell was involved in the election efforts of Harold Washington, the first black mayor of Chicago.

Out of the blue, Gary Hart made a race of it, and his pollster was Dorothy J. Lynch, president of Lynch Research in Washington and a former employee of Caddell's firm. Lynch became the first woman pollster to be involved in a serious run for the presidency. She was touted as an expert on the so-called gender gap. Right along, Peter Hart was Mondale's chief pollster.

After Mondale had won the nomination and his campaign effort was sputtering, Caddell surfaced within the Mondale staff as a consultant, and a very vocal one. He was given the funds to do some special studies, and, of course, this set the stage for an awkward, point-counterpoint relationship with Peter Hart. This, if anything, added to the apparent lack of direction in Mondale's campaign, which is covered more thoroughly in chapter 4.

4 Election '84: Inside Reagan's Research

The way American presidential politics work today, one election is no sooner over than planning for the next one starts. This was certainly the case with the people/apparatus supporting Ronald Reagan. The cast in 1984 was well organized—and certainly well funded.

I was one of two journalists allowed into the backroom of the Reagan survey research operation in 1984, and the article I wrote appeared in Advertising Age *on November 5, the day before the election. As you'll see, I tried to introduce the key people in the planning operation and to describe their functions.*

It was agreed that I would return after the election and do a postelection interview, and excerpts from that article—in the form of interviews with Richard Wirthlin (President Reagan's head pollster) and Peter Hart (Walter Mondale's counterpart) that took place in their respective offices in Washington on November 26— appeared in Advertising Age *on December 10, 1984.*

After the interviews, the two agreed over the phone to allow me to put down side by side the top-line data they were showing their respective clients at the same points in time during the campaign. I do not believe this revealing match-up has appeared in print elsewhere, and it's a rich addition to our nation's political lore.

"I Listen to America Speak"

MCLEAN, VA—One night last week I listened to America speak—and it sure sounded like "four more years."

This listening was done in the inner sanctum of the Reagan–Bush '84 polling operation where, night after night, starting back on June 1—about six weeks before the Democrats nominated Walter Mondale—American public opinion on a variety of election-related issues was monitored via a massive telephone survey research program, which measures at both the national and state levels. The survey cost the Republicans an estimated $2 million.

Reports—some totaling 300 tables of data—were produced by 6 a.m. the morning after interviewing and made available to Reagan strategists for decisions related to scheduling of campaign trips and the issues to be stressed. So, for instance, if the subject of President Reagan's age started to increase as a negative factor, the system picked it up and identified what segments of the voting population were most concerned.

The planning, execution and analysis of data from this tracking program, and other communications research related to the campaign, including tv copy testing, was headed by Richard B. Wirthlin, director of polling and planning, Reagan–Bush '84—and a long-time friend and confidant of President Reagan.

Wirthlin and his 23-person staff, ironically, are located in campaign headquarters at 440 First Street, NW, in the District of Columbia—right in the middle of the only political turf the Republicans are willing to concede to Mondale. (Minnesota was considered a toss-up and was finally the only state that Mondale won.)

Long-Range Plans

Reagan's research program started a long time ago. For the large-scale survey work contemplated, one of the first steps was to purchase 770,000 household names with phone numbers from Donnelley Marketing Information Services, a Dun & Bradstreet unit located in Stamford, Conn. This then became the sampling frame from which samples for individual surveys were drawn as needed.

Coordination of the survey program was headed by Charles F. Rund (director of survey research) and his staff. They started in the summer of 1984 with 250 interviews nightly for the national study, with four waves cummed for reports. In early October, the pace increased to 500 interviews a night; in mid-October, it went up to 1,000 a night, and that continued right up to November 5. Individual surveys were done in all 48 contiguous states back in the beginning, but toward the end of the campaign, the focus shifted to tracking studies in 20 to 25 key states specified by Wirthlin and Rund. Young political scientists on Rund's staff reviewed these data daily, wrote brief analyses, and made action recommendations, as required, which immediately went to campaign managers.

It takes a big machine to handle such interviewing traffic. It was divided among three telephone interviewing centers (Provo, Utah; Santa Ana, Calif.; and McLean, Va.) operated by Wirthlin's firm, Decision/Making/Information, Inc. (DMI), and one each operated by Market Opinion Research, Inc. (MOR), in Detroit and Lance Tarrance & Associates in Houston—firms long associated with political work for Republican candidates. (MOR, for instance, is headed by Robert M. Teeter, the pollster who has long been an advisor to George Bush.)

In total, these five phone centers had about 520 interviewing stations, many of which were equipped for computer-assisted telephone interviewing (CATI). At the McLean center, for instance, most of the interviewers had work stations with their own **IBM PC, Jr.** computers which manage their interviewing paces and data collection. These units were then networked into a master computer for data tabulations. All five centers were linked by phone lines for data transmission. (This system, working full blast, could do about 7,800 interviews each evening, if required.)

The national tracking study questionnaire had about 30 questions, mostly closed-end, and execution took about 15 minutes—after the respondent had been identified as a registered voter. Only about 10% of people contacted refused to be interviewed, according to Tom McNiven (vp-operations at DMI). Questioning covered a variety of subjects ranging from political party affiliation (and the degree of that commitment) to the concern about problems facing the U.S. today, to questions about Reagan's age and the growing and/or declining opinion of Geraldine Ferraro (which interviewers were instructed to pronounce "Fur-RAH-row"). And, of course, there was a battery of questions—such as, "Who is effective in getting things done?"—where respondents, by naming either Reagan or Mondale, end up painting a profile of the candidates' perceived image or identification with prominent issues.

Listening In

It was on the national tracking study interviewing from the McLean center that I listened in—using a supervisor's booth which enabled me to cut in on any interview at any time without the interviewer or respondent knowing. And a fascinating earful it is listening to your fellow citizens react to the campaign—a young black man very Democratic, who nevertheless gives Reagan high marks on leadership (but his vote to Mondale); a woman, apparently bored, bored by the whole thing—and Mondale right down the line with no reservations; a 60-year-old blue collar factory foreman, a lifetime Democrat who is all the way with Reagan this time around; a retired worker who labels himself independent but who answers pure Republican; and a monumental coincidence—an elderly man who says that way back when Ronald Reagan was a young man, he (Reagan) stopped to help him get a motor started, a helpful hand from a stranger. "I doubt he remembers me," said the man, "but I'm sure going to vote for him." And so on through the night. Interviewing starts at 5:30 p.m. in McLean and follows the sun west, ending up at 12:30 a.m. in McLean (9:30 p.m. in California). In mid-evening, when I was there, interviewing switched off the national study to a survey in Oregon, one of the key states singled out for special attention.

Copy Testing

Two of the key men on Wirthlin's staff are former executives at Ted Bates Advertising—John D. Moss, who was an executive vp, client services, and

John A. Fiedler, who was senior vp/executive research director. Not surprisingly, these two were involved, starting in July, in up-front research on issue development (strongest unique selling proposition) and tv copy research.

"We went after it as if we didn't know anything," says Fiedler, "and we weren't trapped by conventional wisdom." There were four studies, part qualitative, part quantitative—and over 50 focus groups, most of which were conducted in 15 states by the New York-based firm, the Qualitative Consultancy, Inc. The focus groups pertaining to strategy development were handled by Lesley A. Bahner, who was with Ted Bates Research before joining Qualitative Consultancy as a vice president two years ago.

The "it" they were seeking was a unique, credible, sum-it-all-up theme for the Reagan advertising campaign. The source: extensive, in-depth interviews regarding the imagery of Reagan and Mondale and the relative importance of key issues.

"We finally got it down to something like 'strong leadership for the future, it works,'" said Fiedler, "and that's the way a researcher would say it. The advertising people got it down to 'leadership that's working.'"

Part of this exercise involved Moss and Fiedler developing what they call "attack themes" for both Reagan and Mondale; that is, the issues on which each was most vulnerable to attack and which could impact voting behavior. "At the time," says Fiedler, "I think we had a better sense of that than they [the Mondale camp] did, but it looks as if they had some pretty good research," referring to the subsequent strategies developed by the Mondale campaign.

All of this, of course, was folded into tv commercial development, the most successful of which has proven to be "Bear." It is a strikingly different type of political commercial which starts off showing a great big bear rambling through the woods—and the question is, "Will this bear turn vicious and attack or just amble on its way?" But, if it proves to be mean, best to be prepared to defend yourself—and Reagan is the personification of preparedness.

Of the many copy boards tested by Fiedler, this one proved to score relatively high on what is called the Viewer Response Profile, a copy theme testing methodology created by Mary Jane Schlinger, professor of marketing at the University of Illinois–Chicago for Leo Burnett Co., and widely used by other agencies, including Ted Bates. In May 1984, Bear was tested on-air in three small markets. It finally was put on network tv on October 18.

During the Reagan–Mondale debates, the Reagan–Bush research team used the TRACE copy testing equipment/methodology of Market Facts, Inc. to monitor, second by second, audience reaction to statements made by the candidates. This was accomplished by having people in the audience register their gut reaction to what was being said concurrently via a small hand-held dial device. The point is that one of the biggest negatives registered was Mondale's reaction to the president's comments about making a theoretical missile defense system available to the USSR in return for some sort of disarmament agreement. As luck would have it, the Mondale advertising people (not, of course, privy to the same research) took clips of that exchange and built a tv commercial around it. So, from the Reagan researcher's point of view, the Democrats were spending precious advertising money to air what was, from the audience's point of view, one of the most positive segments for Reagan and one of the most negative for Mondale.

Hands Across the Sea

One of the most interesting aspects of the Reagan reelection planning function is the public relations monitoring system set up by Raymond E. Beckham, professor of communications at Brigham Young University, who was on leave to work with Wirthlin's group.

Among other things, a campaign trick or two had been learned from the campaign leading to Margaret Thatcher's landslide reelection in 1983. Before that election in Great Britain, Sir Christopher Lawson was named director of marketing for the Conservative party. This had caused a stir because Lawson had previously headed the Mars, Inc. operations in the U.K., and he was dubbed "the man from Mars" who sold Thatcher like candy bars. (The Mars advertising agency in the U.S. is Ted Bates.)

Lawson came to the U.S. to study the Reagan campaign of 1980, and in turn the Reagan–Bush '84 group studied Thatcher's 1983 campaign.

One program, managed by Dr. Beckham, involved setting up the "Voices for Victory" program which calls for a Republican party spokesperson to be located in each of the 208 ADIs. That person monitored what was written in the local newspapers and what appeared on tv about the election. The gist of this was funneled into the Reagan–Bush '84 headquarters nightly via a network of computers and phone lines, so there was two-way communication.

Input for the day was distilled, and, as necessary, rebuttals to what was being said by the Democratic politicians were fed back to the local spokespeople who then made them available to the local press. For instance, say Mondale made a speech saying something of particular interest. The Reagan–Bush '84 group computerized everything Mondale has said in public or written dating back to 1961. They could access this file, show how Mondale's current statement perhaps conflicted with something he had said in the past, and then feed it out to the Voices for Victory network the next day in memos called Rapid Response. This local public relations network concept was adapted from the Thatcher campaign, where it was deemed very successful in getting local press attention for what were considered political points to be scored.

Postelection Interviews with Richard Wirthlin and Peter Hart

Both Wirthlin and Hart were interviewed in their offices—Wirthlin in McLean, Va., and Hart in Washington D.C.—on November 26, 1984. Each interview lasted longer than an hour, and both were taped.

Interview with Richard Wirthlin

HONOMICHL: What is President Reagan like when you make presentations to him? Is he a numbers mavin? Does he get involved?

WIRTHLIN: I wouldn't call this president a numbers mavin as such although he is extremely interested in numbers, and he frequently asks questions that I sometimes have to do further research to answer. But he is a good user of survey research; he understands its weaknesses, and he also understands its value. He does not get involved in the detail of the numbers; he has not felt like interfacing with our computers, nor has he asked to see any of our tabulations. I work from the general charts and graphs.

HONOMICHL: How long will he devote to listening to data presentations?

WIRTHLIN: Generally, those presentations run between 30 and 45 minutes. On occasions, they have run an hour.

HONOMICHL: Does Nancy come and listen?

WIRTHLIN: Not in the Oval Office. She frequently asks me to give her private briefings, which I do on somewhat a regular basis, and those presentations are made in the residence.

HONOMICHL: Are those formal? Do you use graphics?

WIRTHLIN: Those are much more informal; they don't go into the depth that I go into with the president. Frequently, they are just an overview of what's happening.

HONOMICHL: I gather from what you've said, the president is not a detail type person...but I wonder, how much of what you say is strictly communication of findings versus interpretation of data with recommendations on the way to go?

WIRTHLIN: The presentations are a combination of both. He's interested in understanding what the numbers mean as well as what they are, and he doesn't always agree with my conclusions. But, more frequently he appreciates the analysis we've done. Facts don't explain themselves, and the president takes an active role in reviewing the implications of that data I present to him.

The thing I learned very early was that the president was perhaps the best audience of one I've ever had in this sense: he listens carefully and intently to what is being said. He has tremendous skill in absorbing information—and complex information—in a verbal briefing. But beyond that, when I have had to take him bad news—and over the past 16 years I have not always been the bearer of good news—I have found him to accept bad news with a calmness that, again, has made it very easy not to be overly concerned about his reaction to the data. The president is basically an optimistic individual, but he is also sufficiently self-confident that he's the kind of person you can take very bad news to without getting a strong emotional reaction.

HONOMICHL: Other than the president, who in the White House was being kept abreast of the survey work that was being done for the campaign?

WIRTHLIN: The chief of staff, James Baker, and Mike Deaver and Ed Meese. But also I was asked by the White House to make several presentations to the cabinet about the status of the campaign. And I have also given full reviews of public attitudes to some of the assistant secretaries and the major presidential surrogates.

HONOMICHL: What was the last presentation you made to the president before the vote?

WIRTHLIN: I reviewed the results of our surveys with the president on Air Force One as we were flying from Chicago back to Sacramento. We reviewed where we stood on a state-by-state basis. I told him I was very confident that he would win the election, that it would be an electoral vote landslide and a very strong popular vote.

HONOMICHL: Did he believe it?

WIRTHLIN: The president has always—and this goes back through every campaign I've been involved with—while the president has confidence in the technique, been very reluctant to believe he's won until the day after the election, and he was pretty much in that same mood on Sunday evening—except I believe that he was quite confident that he was going to win then, but he never said, in essence, for all intents and purposes it is over.

HONOMICHL: Did Rollins believe?

WIRTHLIN: Oh, Rollins believed.

HONOMICHL: Did Baker believe?

WIRTHLIN: Yes. I think all the key staffers were pretty well convinced.

HONOMICHL: Was there a pool? Do politicians bet on elections like other people bet on football games?

WIRTHLIN: There was a pool. With the exception of the *Washington Post* crystal ball, I don't get into such pools. But I did feel strongly enough to wager a dinner with two other key staffers that Reagan would get at least 59% of the vote. So, I'll collect on that later.

HONOMICHL: Who won the pool?

WIRTHLIN: I don't know.

HONOMICHL: A postelection survey by the New York Times/CBS News shows that 66% of the people who didn't vote in the recent election would have voted for Reagan; 25% said they preferred Mondale. Does your postelection survey substantiate this?

WIRTHLIN: The CBS result was almost precisely the same as our own. We showed that of registered voters who did not vote, 67% said they would vote for Reagan and only 26% said they'd vote for Mondale.

HONOMICHL: Wouldn't that finding be the single most important news story coming out of the last election? His popular support is even more overwhelming than the vote showed.

WIRTHLIN: There is no question about it. If all Americans who were registered had gone to the polls, Reagan would have won by a larger popular vote than any previous president.

HONOMICHL: The people who didn't vote—was it because they felt the outcome was predetermined, or was it procedural—absentee ballots required, etc.?

WIRTHLIN: We were watching closely the number of people who agreed with the statement, "Reagan is so far ahead that my vote really won't count for anything," and we found that 12% of his vote believed that the margin was so large that a vote didn't matter. So it is possible. But almost the same proportion of individuals who supported Mondale felt that he was so far behind, it didn't matter. But, on the net, as the two postelection studies reflect, if there had been a bigger turnout, Reagan would have enjoyed a bigger margin.

HONOMICHL: Does he know that?

WIRTHLIN: This result we learned just recently. I'm going to give a postelection wrap-up for him probably within the next 10 days, [by December 6, 1984] and he'll surely know it then.

HONOMICHL: When will you complete your postelection study and analysis?

WIRTHLIN: That analysis will probably take another 30 to 60 days. We have made a quick review of what happened—why people voted as they did—but I've got almost 1,000 pages of computer output in the next office waiting for my perusal, and we will be working on a variety of questions that this election generated for several months.

HONOMICHL: Have you discovered anything so far that seems to be a startling revelation—beyond how the nonvoters would have voted?

WIRTHLIN: I think that those of us who worked in this election are very fortunate in being active in our professions at this particular time. Without question, the 1984 election was an historical election in a number of ways.

To begin with, we're seeing the strong signals of party realignment, and that realignment is occurring in part because the Republican party is drawing into its voter pool large blocks of first-time voters. Specifically, only 44% of voters under 24 cast their ballots for Ronald Reagan in 1980. In 1984 that ballooned to a full 64%. Additionally, in 1980 there was a 17-point gap between Republican and Democrat identifiers. And today, our own data—and some of the public data that are beginning to surface—show that the Republican party is no longer a minority party; it's a parity party.

The other thing that fascinates me is the reasons why people say they voted for Reagan. There were those political pundits—and some of our opponents—who said it was simply his style, but one of the most important questions that we dealt with in the postelection study was "Why did you vote for...?" or, "Why didn't you vote for...?" It is very clear that Reagan's major support came from the belief that he was effective in getting things done. Over four out of ten of his voters said they voted for him because of his job performance. Three out of ten supported him because of his position on some specific issues, and another 12% voted for him because of his strength of leadership. Only 8 out of 100 said they voted for him because they liked his style or personality.

HONOMICHL: Do you think people can really speak accurately about their motivations in the voting booth? You make it sound pretty glib...too simplistic.

WIRTHLIN: Well, I'm summarizing 30 to 40 different reasons that people gave, and one of the things we do to avoid oversimplifying the response as given is record the verbatims in each of the categories, so those are the generalized categories we used. But, it was also clear to us that people, even before the campaign, were able to articulate in very specific terms why they favored Reagan, and why they didn't favor him. And why they didn't favor Mondale.

HONOMICHL: One of the impressions I get is that the Reagan administration is one of the most survey-oriented in history, both in terms of amount of money they are spending and the attention they give to the data. How much of that is also influencing public policy? The between election surveys?

WIRTHLIN: I'm not sure this administration uses research more extensively than others.

HONOMICHL: What administration would have used more? Nixon?

WIRTHLIN: Yes, probably. Understanding what attitudes the general population has is one dimension that is considered in forming public policy, and probably not the most important. But it is considered, and it would be impossible to trace through what impact such insight might have on a specific policy.

HONOMICHL: You could argue that a president's researcher is an ombudsman, and the man who takes public opinion into the White House is representing the American populace. Have you ever thought of it that way?

WIRTHLIN: I've not thought of it as an ombudsman. But I have thought of my role as being one of providing the president with an ear to what the average American would tell the president if he could sit down with the president and express his hopes and fears and his opinions on a wide variety of issues. That is one of the most valuable and healthy aspects of having a president well informed about public attitudes, namely that almost everyone who walks into his office has a particular cause to plead, and I think the president appreciates—and I think it clearly is a help—to be able to tap the attitudes of Americans on a wide variety of topics.

HONOMICHL: Does he see numbers, or does he hear *vox populi*?

WIRTHLIN: He does both. He sees numbers, but frequently I'll read some of the verbatims that I think are particularly revealing.

HONOMICHL: Does he give any indication that he looks at you as a spokesperson for *vox populi*?

WIRTHLIN: I'm not sure he looks at me in that role, but I think that's the role to a larger extent I do perform.

HONOMICHL: Some of the more calculating and sophisticated people around him—what is their reaction to survey research?

WIRTHLIN: I think every person has a little different impression of survey research. I think some of them are every bit as interested as the president, and some are less.

HONOMICHL: Are any of them really knowledgeable about what makes for good survey research? The key advisors around Reagan?

WIRTHLIN: One of the tasks I've tried to fulfill during the past 16 years is not only providing the numbers but also in acquainting those who use research what the weakness and strength of the tool might be. And some of those people I've been working with for 16 years.

One of the reasons I am thoroughly convinced that what I do is beneficial comes from an experience I had when I was about 19. When I was 19, I went to Switzerland and I was able to observe their system. The Swiss go to polls and vote almost every week on things of both small and major dimension. That doesn't happen in the United States directly, but by carefully and scientifically drawing a tight sample we are, in essence, able to poll the entire American electorate—and beyond that, even those not registered to vote—and find out how they feel on a variety of attitudes. I found out that to be extremely healthy and beneficial to an administration as complex as ours.

HONOMICHL: The special *Newsweek* edition—The Untold Story of Campaign '84—says that the media and creative people working on the campaign tried to force you out—that is, rebuff your data input. Was that the conventional creative versus research friction, or something else?

WIRTHLIN: Well, if there was friction, it was never readily apparent during the campaign—that is, there were never any knock-down-drag-out controversies about what the thrust or themes of the campaign should be. I think there is always a need to close the gap between research and creative execution. In this campaign, those who were on the creative side were somewhat more independent of the research results than in 1980. But I felt that our working relationship with the creative team was very satisfactory.

HONOMICHL: Will you ever work for another presidential candidate?

WIRTHLIN: Oh, I think the possibilities are fairly good that I will sometime, but my major commitment now, and for the next several years, is to do everything I can to help this incumbent president.

HONOMICHL: That includes doing surveys continuously? Public opinion...?

WIRTHLIN: We will be doing surveys for the White House on a very regular basis.

HONOMICHL: And who is the client? Who pays for all that?

WIRTHLIN: The Republican National Committee has paid for the survey research that has been done for the White House for the last four years.

HONOMICHL: Can you give me an idea of the scope of that? How much money is spent to do survey research to keep the president in touch with *vox populi*?

WIRTHLIN: Well, the studies we do are not done solely for the White House, but the cost of doing surveys for the White House and the Republican committees will probably range between $600,000 and $900,000 next year.

HONOMICHL: So, you're going to stay in public opinion polling for the Republicans?

WIRTHLIN: I'd say that about a third of my time.

HONOMICHL: What will you do with the other two-thirds?

WIRTHLIN: We'll be serving the other kinds of clients that Decision/Making/Information has. As a matter of fact, we estimate that only about 30% of our business next year will be for political clients. And the White House and RNC are only two of many we will be dealing with next year. The other 60–70% of our revenues are generated from public affairs clients and marketing research clients.

HONOMICHL: Do you personally get involved with the commercial clients?

WIRTHLIN: Yes, to some extent—but that responsibility is primarily with Tom Hughes, who heads our marketing.

HONOMICHL: The total Reagan campaign research program, that cost about $2 million?

WIRTHLIN: It was a little less than that.

HONOMICHL: Well, is that the standard now—should any future aspirant to that office expect to spend that much on research?

WIRTHLIN: The amount of research needed in a presidential campaign is very dependent on the type of candidate, the type of environment you run in—but the amount that we spent on research and analysis is, as a matter of fact, a little less than it was in 1980 and about the same as it was in 1976. So, if there is a standard established, I think that standard was set in 1972 or '76.

HONOMICHL: Well, your firm—DMI—worked in several highly contested senatorial campaigns—Jepsen in Iowa, Boschwitz in Minnesota, Pressler in South Dakota, Domenici in New Mexico. What is the standard there? How much are these campaigns spending on research?

WIRTHLIN: I think it can range from 8 to 14% of the total budget, but again that is somewhat variable. When you get into spending $20 or $30 million in total, that percentage can fall below 8%.

HONOMICHL: Is that escalating? Are they tending to spend more?

WIRTHLIN: I don't think as a proportion of total budget it is. I think that we're able to provide much more sophisticated analysis much more quickly because of our access to computers, and, of course, the cost of using computers is falling. So, I don't believe the amount of spending is stabilizing. In some cases—for instance, I was involved in an environmental bond issue race several years ago, and in that case over half the budget went into research.

HONOMICHL: And in important congressional districts?

WIRTHLIN: I think probably more money was spent in the congressional races. We did 35 races, and we won every incumbent race and all the open seats, and there were nine seats that were Democratic and we won six out of the nine challenge races. And in those races, I believe that in fact more research dollars were spent.

HONOMICHL: What would you estimate, on average, over those 35 races?

WIRTHLIN: My guess would be about $30,000, on average.

HONOMICHL: And for a gubernatorial race?

WIRTHLIN: A gubernatorial race can be a very research-intensive kind of race. In those kinds of races, you're looking at $50,000—and in the very big states, such as New York and California, those races can absorb up to $300,000 to $350,000 in research.

HONOMICHL: Your company, DMI, is one of the few specializing in political research that also does a lot of commercial research. Which is learning from which?

WIRTHLIN: Well, it's turned out for us to be a great advantage in doing both commercial and political work, and it's hard to say who draws more from the other. During this past year, we used perception mapping techniques in the political area with great impact, and on the other hand, the speed and accuracy political research requires—the need to get into drawing strategic conclusions—I think gives us an edge in working with some of our commercial clients.

HONOMICHL: In an interview on BBC television, Patrick Caddell was quoted as saying, "We [political consultants, strategists, pollsters] have preempted the political system. We decide who are the best and more likely people to be successful, and so we have contributed to the decline of political parties. I'm not sure it's healthy at all, and it's a question that bothers me."

Do you agree?

WIRTHLIN: No, I don't agree with Patrick that we've preempted the political system at all. I think that we do provide a degree of insights into the system that wasn't there ten years ago, but I don't believe that we are the king makers of the system. I do believe that what we learn may make or break some candidates, but I'm not at all as convinced as he is that we have the power to go around the political parties or the candidates themselves. The limitation of what we do is one of time, namely: we have a very good understanding of what attitudes are at a point in time, but a political system not only has to rely on a quick and accurate measure of what is happening now, but also—in putting its agenda together, whether it be a political party or candidate—do so with an eye to the future. And no one has a magic crystal ball.

Interview with Peter Hart

HONOMICHL: Please describe Mondale's survey research program from the time he became the Democratic candidate. From the primaries on...

HART: We did no general election polling until after the primary season, which means post June 5. At that stage, we undertook a major national public opinion poll which was done with 1,500 respondents door to door, and the interview took 90 minutes, so it was very intensive and far-reaching in scope. So that was done in the middle of June with the information available to the client by the beginning of July.

We did a series of short interviews related to the vice presidential election in the beginning part of July, and in a few selected states. Then we did a series of what we call tracking length polls from Sunday night through Thursday night.

HONOMICHL: This was telephone?

HART: Telephone; in fact, everything we did after the initial survey was telephone. Tracking length polls were done during the convention week to test the themes, to test the reaction to the selection of Ferraro, to everything that was going on at the convention—and those data were available overnight to Mr. Mondale. So, we did the interviewing starting at about 9 p.m., tabulated over the night, and had the information available first thing in the morning, which helped to guide some of the things we were doing through the convention.

We did a series of selected state polls during the month of August, probably about a dozen states. And then we started national tracking polls right after the Republican convention, August 29–30, and we continued those up to election day.

At the beginning we were concentrating solely on Democrats and Independents, and from early October on, we were looking at the total electorate. We changed our sampling methodology because of changes in party alignment that were going on. We probably did in the neighborhood of 35,000 interviews from the beginning of the general election, from Labor Day to November 5.

We were doing mainly tracking length polls, but it should be noted that we did two or three special studies that were related to the debates. One study we did prior to the first debate, which was an integral part of the strategy that was just talking to possible Reagan defectors and undecided voters to be able to see exactly what they were looking for, what they cared about, etc. And then, on the night of the first debate, we did an overnight after the debate and we did the same thing after the second debate.

HONOMICHL: Where were you doing your interviewing for Mondale?

HART: Right here in Washington. We have a phone bank with 175 stations right in the District, and we could do 450 interviews an hour.

HONOMICHL: Did you subcontract any of the work?

HART: No. We did all the work with our own office, our own staff.

HONOMICHL: What would you estimate was spent on survey research and related things—from the time Mondale became the known candidate?

HART: My guess is in the neighborhood of about $1.3 million.

HONOMICHL: And the client was the committee, Mondale for President?

HART: Yes.

HONOMICHL: Does that sum include the studies Caddell was doing?

HART: That's correct. That includes Caddell, and it includes the focus group work done which I was relating to, but not in charge of.

HONOMICHL: Let's talk about presentations to Mondale. Did you make them personally?

HART: Only in certain instances, only for a few of the major polls. Most of it was either written or other oral communications.

HONOMICHL: What's Mondale like as a relater to survey work? Is he a number mavin; does he understand surveys?

HART: I would tell you Mondale is a person who understands public opinion surveys and certainly has no difficulty grasping concepts or the data implications. At the same time, as he said all the way along, he was not a person who was a numbers mavin, or who was guided by all this. He certainly wanted it as part of the campaign, but he was not a person who would phone you at 11:30 at night and say, "What did you find out?" Generally, the information went directly to the campaign chairman, Jim Johnson, and then it was relayed to Mondale.

HONOMICHL: Does Johnson savvy survey research?

HART: There are two ways in which I judge a person's understanding the knowledge of survey research. One, how much input and how much insight can he bring to you in terms of questionnaire design? And Jim, I always found, had good suggestions and good ways of approaching problems. And the second thing, the ability to grasp and deal with the numbers. I would say of all the people I've dealt with, Jim was somebody who looked at the numbers and understood them—and probably knew the details even better than the pollsters involved.

HONOMICHL: Did Mondale get involved to the degree that he asked that specific questions be added to the surveys?

HART: Well, I don't think directly. Sometimes he would say this is an area he's interested in, or he wanted to find out how the public was feeling in such or such area.

HONOMICHL: The special *Newsweek* edition—The Untold Story of Campaign '84—says that when Pat Caddell got his nose under the Mondale campaign tent, he, too, was doing surveys that were showing significantly different numbers than those you were doing. And it looks as if you two were more or less running at odds there for a while just prior to the debates. What was he doing that was so different?

HART: I guess what I would tell you is that I don't think *Newsweek* got the entire story, or even got everything correctly aligned. Pat was doing a series of special projects for the campaign, of which I was informed exactly what was happening. And, I would tell you, probably about 95% of the work we did was pretty parallel, and the findings and recommendations were headed in the same direction. By and large, the numbers tended to be pretty much the same.

HONOMICHL: What was the final report you made to Mondale?

HART: The last one we did was from November 2 through 4, and we showed 56% for Reagan, 38% for Mondale. [The 6% undecided was unallocated.]

To us, the critical period—and here's an instance where Pat [Caddell] and I came up with a little different result—we did a poll the night of the second debate and called people directly after the debate, and what we had is an 11-point spread that night, and that was approximately in the range of the 53–40 margin we had going into the debate.

Pat polled the same night, and he came up with a 16-point spread. So, we had it a little closer, and he had it a little wider. The following night, we polled and we came up with 57–37, Wirthlin came up with 55–38, and Pat had it down to 12 points, so he had it closing. Then we polled the following two nights and found the same thing held, and so did Wirthlin; he had 57–36; we had 56–37.

HONOMICHL: You weren't allocating the undecided.

HART: That's right.

HONOMICHL: From the time of the Democratic convention, the undecided held that firm?

HART: Throughout that whole period, we were running 5, 6, 7, or 8% undecided. It never got into double digits.

HONOMICHL: One gets the impression that Republican candidates for the presidency have direct face-to-face exposure to their pollsters and their data, while the Democrats don't—the data are screened through intermediaries. Again this seems true with Mondale. Why is that?

HART: I don't think it is a pattern. I think it comes down to the style of each individual candidate. I have some candidates who are terribly interested in each number and all the nuances, and other candidates who are less interested. The fact that Ronald Reagan was more interested in the numbers may say one thing about him. Jimmy Carter was another person who was terribly interested in the individual numbers, and the personal presentation. Walter Mondale reacted differently, and I'm not sure we get better leaders if they are deeply involved in survey research and all the data or people who are less involved. If I had a choice, I would opt for the person who would be guided more in terms of policy implications and other factors than numerous pieces of data.

HONOMICHL: *The New York Times*/CBS News postelection poll shows that 66% of those who did not vote would have voted for Reagan. Do you have any postelection analysis to confirm that?

HART: The answer is no. But the one thing we noted in our surveys—going into the last week—we say 90 million as sort of the floor.

HONOMICHL: You mean a voter turnout of 90 million?

HART: Yes, a minimum turnout. At that point, we had about a 20-point gap between the two candidates, with that group. When it increased to 92 million, we saw the 2 million coming in as heavily Reagan. We saw the last 3 million that might come in being split about 50–50. So, when the vote came in at 92 million, it was an ideal situation for Reagan, and not so ideal for us. So, that is why you had the 18-point gap that you did instead of something in the neighborhood of 16. But, either way, it was a decisive advantage for the president.

As for nonvoters, we have not studied those groups, but obviously you get a certain halo effect any time the election process takes place. To suggest those voters were more on one side than the other, I think, would be a mistake.

HONOMICHL: Then you don't see it as another manifestation of what some people are calling a revolution, a major shift in party alignment?

HART: Well, I think clearly, the days of where the Democrats have a 20-point registration advantage over the Republican party are gone. The question is "Where do we go from here?" I think we're into a competitive, two-party situation. To me, those who predicted realignment in 1980 were premature, and I would tell you at this stage of the game we're moving into a new era of politics, and I think it's open for both parties. The Republicans get a half-step advantage out of this election, certainly, with younger white voters, and the Democratic party needs to address that group.

HONOMICHL: I realize that when you made public appearances, you had to keep up the brave front, but the numbers you were showing Mondale were consistently discouraging. Did Mondale get it through his head way back when that he was not about to win that election?

HART: No. I think any individual running for the presidency of the United States is not about to throw in the towel and say he is not going to win an election. We knew the cards we were dealt; we knew the difficulty and odds against us right from the beginning. At the same time, I will tell you that given that, we basically were trying to come up with a strategy to deal with the situation, which was difficult.

We had these factors: first of all, the mood of the nation was basically positive; the voters thought things were moving in the right direction, and that worked for the president. And it got better and better as the election cycle went on. Two, they personally liked the president, and we knew that. And three, they basically saw the economy as working instead of being in trouble. So, it was a situation where we needed to draw a strategy which worked to our advantage, and in part that meant concentrating on the future, and second, working on policy questions that worked to a Democratic advantage—war and peace, the question of fairness, and fair trade. We had to put that together. The final part is that voters did not perceive Walter Mondale as a strong leader going into the general election. And, obviously, we were trying to build up his credentials on that front. And probably the high point was the first debate when voters really had a chance to see him for 90 minutes answering tough questions and, indeed, as someone who knew where he wanted to take this country.

HONOMICHL: If you had to do it over again, in retrospect, what would you have urged the Mondale campaign to do differently?

HART: When you lose an election, there's a lot you'd do differently. Simply put, I think what I would have done is stress the ability to stay on course.

HONOMICHL: There is a wonderful quote attributed to you in the *Newsweek* report, something like, "Don't pull the plant up by the roots to see if it's still growing." But, there was a lot of shifting of emphasis in the Mondale campaign.

HART: I think there is a basic problem with any campaign that's behind. That is, "Let's try something new." And again it's the ability to understand your basic objectives and what you're trying to achieve, and to keep a campaign following that path. In this campaign, as with any that's behind, there is tendency to say, "Maybe this will move us, maybe this will help." And so you take detours and go into cul de sacs, and them come back onto the basic path.

I give the Reagan campaign great credit in understanding their basic objectives and not getting detoured. I think in the Mondale campaign we tended to go on too many detours. Any time you're facing a popular incumbent president, you have to do everything right—and have a little bit of luck. We didn't do everything right, and we didn't have a lot of luck, and, therefore, we lost.

HONOMICHL: Do you think that these people who have made a career of becoming political pollsters, or survey experts, should deal with candidates at arm's length—feed them facts and let it go at that—or should they become consultants?

HART: Well, I think that obviously people want a translation of the data.

HONOMICHL: Yes, but that's a bit different than becoming an advocate.

HART: Well, I would simply say it is terribly important to be able to translate the data. I've never been in favor...

HONOMICHL: Let me say it another way. It seems as if Caddell wanted to be Mondale's campaign manager. In that sense, he ceased to be a neutral, objective interpreter of data. Do you think that's an appropriate role for pollsters?

HART: The important thing is that a campaign needs to hire an outside pollster in order to give them objective outlooks on what is happening. At the same time, they need insights on how you translate that. If a pollster attempts to become both a campaign manager as well as the pollster, in that respect he starts to lose some of the objectivity that the campaign looks for when they hire a pollster. So, my theory has always been, "Present the data, present the path—the suggestions of where it is to go." But there is an invisible—but important—fine line between running the campaign and being the counsel to the campaign. I've always tried to be the counsel to the campaign, and I think that's the way a Dick Wirthlin or a Bob Teeter approaches it also.

HONOMICHL: You worked in some of the more highly contested senatorial campaigns, like Hunt in North Carolina, Harkin in Iowa, Doggett in Texas, Jay Rockefeller in West Virginia. What is the going thing today? What would you advise a senatorial client to budget for research?

HART: I would tell you that most clients budget in the neighborhood of 5% of their total budgets for polling. So, as the cost of campaigns have gone up, you're looking at $100,000 to $200,000.

HONOMICHL: And for major congressional races?

HART: Again, I'd say in the neighborhood of 5 to 8%. They will spend in the neighborhood of $30,000 in an individual campaign.

HONOMICHL: Is that still escalating, or is it starting to top off?

HART: Well, since I got into the business in 1972, where an average campaign might spend $25,000, I would say an average campaign now spends in excess of $75,000 for survey research—senatorial and gubernatorial levels. The big thing here is tracking surveys. We happen to do them at a relatively modest cost, but when you're interviewing 100 to 200 people every night for 30 days, those costs mount up.

HONOMICHL: What's next for Peter Hart? More of the same—working for Democratic aspirants?

HART: I believe in never predicting the future, especially three weeks after an election. Let's just say that win, lose or draw—having worked for Walter Mondale and his presidential campaign, there's probably no finer public servant in terms of representing decency and the best, never blaming, never whining about his fate in this campaign. So I tell you I sort of wear the Mondale label, and I look at it as the red badge of courage and one I am proud to have served with.

The polls tell us where people are today; polls don't predict the future. This pollster won't predict his own personal future.

HONOMICHL: What percent of your total business is political?

HART: About 50% is political and 50% is nonpolitical.

HONOMICHL: Do you get personally involved in the nonpolitical end of your business?

HART: Very much so. We do a lot of media research, institutional research, and special kinds of market research. And that can be exciting—and a lot less strenuous than the political, which all winds up on one day.

HONOMICHL: Patrick Caddell, in a BBC Television interview, is quoted as saying, "We [political consultants, strategists, pollsters] have preempted the political system. We decide who are the best and more likely people to be successful, and so we have contributed to the decline of political parties. I'm not sure it's healthy at all, and it's a question that bothers me."

Do you agree?

HART: The answer is, not really. I think obviously pollsters have a way to get direct input from the people who are the most important, and that is the voters. And so, instead of dealing with hearsay evidence, you now have at least a semiscientific way to find out. I would tell you that I think, in part, both of the parties may have declined, but I do not think it is directly due to the pollsters. Obviously, it's a changing society, and the way we communicate is very different than the way we communicated 40 years ago. There is now a way to communicate with every voter—either through the mass media or through direct voter contact, either by mail or telephone.

Table 4.1 1984 Presidential Election National Tracking Studies Results

Date	What Wirthlin was Showing Reagan			What Hart was Showing Mondale		
	Reagan	Mondale	Undecided	Reagan	Mondale	Undecided
Sept. 1	55%	37%	8%	53%	39%	8%
Sept. 20	55	37	8	54	39	7
Oct. 2	54	38	8	53	40	7
Oct. 7	54	38	8	53	40	7
Oct. 9–12	52	40	8	54	38	8
Oct. 13–15	–	–	–	53	40	7
Oct. 16–17	–	–	–	52	42	6
Oct. 17–19	54	37	9	53	40	7
Oct. 21	–	–	–	52	41	7
Oct. 22	55	38	7	57	37	6
Oct. 23–24	57	36	7	56	37	7
Oct. 25–26	57	36	7	56	38	6
Oct. 27–28	55	38	7	55	38	7
Oct. 29–30	55	38	7	57	37	6
Oct. 31–Nov. 1	55	37	8	55	38	7
Nov. 2	56	36	8	57	37	6
Nov. 2–4	55	38	7	56	38	6
Nov. 5	56	37	7	–	–	–

5 Catch the Spirit!: Selling the United States

American business, and the public in general, were shocked into the realization, going into the 1980s, that the U.S. was in an economic war of sorts with the rest of the world. Major industries, like steel and automotive, had been severely damaged, and the recession of 1980–82 plus the mounting concern over the federal deficits being run up in Washington had American business at an even greater disadvantage: the hard (vis-à-vis foreign currencies) U.S. dollar made U.S. products and services even more expensive in world markets.

The more trade deficits mounted, the more government realized that a service industry, international tourism and travel, was contributing to those deficits. Washington started to stir—but no one could have predicted that the leader in tourism's cause would turn out to be a young woman from California who had no previous experience in the travel industry—and little other business experience, for that matter.

This, basically, is that woman's story. Excerpts from it ran in the Advertising Age *of August 19, 1985.*

The Assignment

"I want you to handle this as if it were a $20 million account," Louis T. Hagopian, CEO of N. W. Ayer, told his troops. And that was quite a mandate since the billings, at first, would be only $662,925, a mere droplet by big agency standards, and the gross profit, as stipulated by U.S. government regulations, was limited to $56,349. But, symbolically, the account was—potentially—as big as the whole outdoors. The mission, no less—as stated in bureaucratese—was to "Develop and Test a Thematic Concept for the U.S. Travel and Tourism Administration" (USTTA), a division of the U.S. Department of Commerce.

Translated into Madison Avenue language, this meant the feds wanted a theme or concept line akin to "Reach Out and Touch Someone," or "Be

All You Can Be," or "Diamonds Are Forever," that would provide a conceptual umbrella and rallying cry for the U.S. travel/tourism industry in its worldwide battle for a larger share of the travel market. So, if successful, the result would be a big red, white, and blue feather in Ayer's creative cap—as well as a big come-on for private sector travel accounts, a point not lost on Ayer, who had (from 1978 to 1981) the Pan American World Airways account, which billed about $45 million.

Ironically, the campaign to be developed for Uncle Sam would never be seen in the United States, for the USTTA marketing plan called for a test market in West Germany, starting in the fall of 1985, and if all went as well as hoped/expected, country-by-country execution in major foreign countries with the explicit goal of increasing pleasure travel to the U.S.—that is, assuming Congress continued to fund USTTA.

There follows the story of how this campaign was instigated in Washington, D.C., how Ayer got the assignment, the extensive research program that was done around the world prior to creative development, some of the vagaries of government budget-making procedures, and the potential impact such a campaign could have on the U.S. economy—especially on our international balance of trade deficit—over the years to come. And, in the process, you'll come to know some of the major players—Donna F. Tuttle, President Reagan's political pal who, at age 36, became the Under Secretary of Commerce for Travel and Tourism in 1983; Agi Clark, a senior vp, executive creative director at Ayer (New York), who—as a girl—escaped from Hungary during the uprising of 1956; J. Desmond "Des" Slattery, an affable Irishman who, as a senior vp at Ayer, shepherds the USTTA account; and Henry Riegner, who has held the USTTA regional office network together through the years despite budget ups and downs.

Solicitation No. 50-SATS-4-00017

Officially, our behind-the-scenes story starts with an RFP (Request For Proposal) issued by the U.S. Travel and Tourism Administration on March 29, 1984. Governmental agencies usually are required by law to advertise their proposed programs, their intent and budget parameters, and then to entertain responses from qualified bidders.

USTTAs RFP (technically, Solicitation No. 50-SATS-4-00017) was, like most government RFPs, a dry, technical project outline written in bureaucratese. But this one glittered in that it was, in effect, an open invitation to advertising agencies with international experience/connections to become something akin to the official U.S. agency.

Thomas F. Maxey, an executive vp at N. W. Ayer in New York saw the RFP ad, as did many other agency executives, and realized what a showcase project this would be to the $194 billion U.S. travel and tourism industry. As Maxey told me later, "It doesn't hurt to have Ayer creative shown to the USTTA advisory board." Indeed! That board includes top executives from Hilton Hotels, Sheraton, American Express, Holiday Inns, Harrah's Hotel and Casino, and the New York Convention and Visitors Bureau, to name a few.

No surprise either that other major agencies responding to the USTTA RFP included Ogilvy & Mather, McCann Erickson, Ted Bates, and Young & Rubicam—plus "some little agencies." But Ayer's response was particularly determined; it is estimated they spent about $15,000 preparing for what proved to be the winning presentation. It didn't hurt that years before, when Maxey was handling the Pan American World Airways account at Ayer, he—along with other industry leaders—testified before Congress on the need to set up an aggressive USTTA-type government agency to help the U.S. travel industry capture a larger share of the huge world travel market, a special concern now because of our negative foreign trade deficit. (Currently, the number of Americans traveling abroad each year exceeds the number of foreign tourists to the U.S. by about 3 million.)

Also, it didn't hurt that another Ayer executive, J. Desmond "Des" Slattery, in addition to overseeing Ayer accounts like the Bahamas Government Ministry of Tourism and the Australian Tourist Commission, was at the time president-elect of the Travel Tourism Research Association and well known in travel industry conclaves. And it didn't hurt that the five-person team Maxey led to Washington to make Ayer's presentation to USTTA included, as the creative spokesperson, Agi Clark who had, prior to joining Ayer, worked on accounts like Air Jamaica, BOAC, and the India Government Tourist Office.

Because of their experience, the Ayer group probably was more conscious than most agencies of just how big a force USTTA could be, and should be, in driving a sell-America campaign budget through Congress.

The stakes are high. Statistics compiled by USTTA and the World Tourism Organization, headquartered in Madrid, say that in 1984 world foreign tourist expenditures exceeded $100 billion, excluding international fare receipts, and the U.S. share of that market was 11.4%, down from 11.9% in 1983. Nearly 21 million foreign tourists visited the U.S. in 1984, and that was about 6.9% of total world arrivals, down from 7.4% in 1983 and 7.6% in 1982.

In local market terms, USTTA calculates that in 1983, 3.72 million international tourists visited Florida and dropped $2.65 billion into the local economy. The numbers for New York State were 4.78 million tourists and $1.57 billion—and so on through the most visited states: Hawaii, California, Nevada, Illinois, Arizona, Texas, Massachusetts, and the District of Columbia. About 313,000 Americans are employed as the result of foreign visitor spending, USTTA calculates.

The point is that foreign tourism is big business, right down to the mayoral level, and the U.S. has been losing position over recent years. Part of the problem currently is the hard American dollar, which makes U.S.

travel relatively expensive. Another reason, long holding, is that many other countries have had concerted and well-financed tourism promotion programs. In contrast, U.S. efforts to lure visitors have been wimpish; the so-called private sector has had to shoulder the promotional load.

For 1981, for instance, World Tourism Organization data (the latest available) show that government promotion budgets to foster tourism in Belgium, Korea, Jamaica, and Bermuda exceeded those of the U.S. Turkey and Greece each spent twice as much as the U.S. And countries like Canada, Spain, the U.K., and the Bahamas spent over three times as much. Hong Kong, specifically, spent $7.7 million in 1981 versus the U.S. expenditure of $5.8 million. "We [the U.S.] are so far behind, it's embarrassing to talk about it," says William H. Edwards, president of the Hotels Division of Hilton Corporation.

Leaders of the U.S. travel industry, of course, are very much aware of these statistics, and many had long been urging Washington to take the lead in developing a well-funded, continuous program to attract tourists. In fact, the Travel Industry Association of America, a group of airline, hotel, etc., member firms, had launched in August 1983, at a cost of $1 million, a study, the purpose of which was to present the Reagan administration with an international travel marketing plan. "The private sector felt a recommendation would be helpful," says Edwards. It was in that context that industry leaders viewed USTTA's Solicitation No. 50-SATS-4-00017. Was help from Washington finally on the way? Or was this just so much smoke that would blow away?

You can't blame them for being skeptical; Washington's support of the international travel industry had theretofore been—at best—uninspired. The Eisenhower administration, for instance, had gotten Congress to sponsor some overseas advertising, but that was mostly to foster a people-to-people exchange program. The Kennedy administration, in much the same vein, got legislation passed in 1961 to establish the U.S. Travel Service, a unit of the Department of Commerce, but USTS appropriations never exceeded $3 million a year up through 1968, when they started to increase. The high point was 1977 when the USTS budget was $14.5 million. The Carter administration practically cut USTS funding in half, and during his last days in office, President Carter pocket-vetoed a bill to continue USTS funding.

Through these years, the main activity of USTS was the operation of regional offices (in London, Paris, Frankfurt, Mexico City, Toronto, and Tokyo) which coordinated activities with major international air carriers, distributed literature, attended travel conferences, etc. This regional network reports to Henry G. Riegner, 67, managing director, marketing and field operations, who has been with USTS/USTTA since 1973, one of the few constants in that operation. Directors of USTS (and USTTA) are political appointees, and over the 10-year period ending in 1983, nine directors had come and gone, with long periods when no director was on hand. Through these years, recalls Riegner, "Morale was good and people were doing their best with the resources they had," but repeated threats to cut budgets were "frustrating."

One of the first acts of the Reagan administration was to pass the National Tourism Policy Act of 1981, which converted USTS to USTTA and, inferentially, recognized international tourism as a major industry. Longtime congressional friends of tourism, such as Senators Inouye (Hawaii) and Pressler (South Dakota), were making the obvious point that the negative balance of trade would be helped by increasing tourist travel to the U.S., and congressional support was warming up to making a sizable increase in the USTTA budget (in 1980, it was $8 million).

Ms. Tuttle??

Not much happened until late 1983 when, in a surprise move, President Reagan appointed Donna F. Tuttle, then 36, as Under Secretary of Commerce for Travel and Tourism, the director of USTTA. Even travel industry leaders, long used to purely political appointments, were stunned. Tuttle's previous experience consisted of teaching in a junior high school in Los Angeles and founding an interior design firm.

But, if you looked beyond that to what it takes to get something done in Washington, Tuttle had sterling credentials. Her father-in-law was Holmes Tuttle, a self-made millionaire and charter member of the so-called Kitchen Cabinet which nurtured Ronald Reagan through his political infancy. One close Reagan advisor is quoted by the *Wall Street Journal* as saying, "Ronald Reagan cannot say no to Holmes Tuttle." Mr. Tuttle's son, Robert, Donna's husband, is director of the Office of Presidential Personnel in the White House. Also, it turned out, Ms. Tuttle had been very, very active in fundraising and Republican campaign activities in California. So, here, out of the blue, was the new champion of tourism in Washington and, in short order, instigator of the advertising program that surfaced in Solicitation No. 50-SATS-4-00017.

Tuttle hit the ground running. In the weeks between being nominated and being sworn in, she started contacting—at her expense—key travel/tourism industry leaders. What needed to be done? How could USTTA help? And, as she is quick to acknowledge, she was selling Donna Tuttle too. They learned quickly that if she did not do a job at USTTA, it wouldn't be for lack of energy, determination, or forceful personality. (To help out, cram courses on administration/management, conducted by Harvard Business School faculty, were offered in the White House for key administration appointees. Tuttle attended.)

After the swearing in, it seems as if Tuttle did five things at once. One was to line up strong congressional allies, such as Senator Laxalt (Nevada). (One key argument: a government study that showed for every $1 spent to promote foreign tourism, the U.S. could expect $18.60 back in tourist expenditures.)

Then she rejuvenated and restaffed the Travel and Tourism Board, a group of industry leaders who counsel USTTA. She jacked up the USTTA office and field staff, put the accent on the positive, and hired a pr person (Vivian Deuschl). Then she found funding for market research, a long-neglected item in USTTA budgeting. ("How," she asked during an interview, "can you put together a good marketing plan without good information? You can't.")

And, finally, convinced that the USTTA should take the lead in stimulating foreign tourism, she instigated the search for an advertising agency to develop a campaign and test it in Germany. All of that was embodied in the project described in Solicitation No. 50-SATS-4-00017. The people at Ayer understood and dug in.

On May 31, 1984, a committee consisting of Tuttle, Martin J. Darity (at the time assistant secretary, tourism marketing at USTTA), and Riegner, met to evaluate the written responses to USTTA's RFP. Joining them were two industry representatives: Brian D. Smith, vp-marketing, Busch Entertainment Corp., and Terry L. Underwood, vp-marketing, Greyhound Lines, Inc. (Another, T. J. Koors, vp-transportation services, Northwest Orient Airlines, disqualified himself when he learned who the finalists were; it presented a conflict.)

Out of this review, says Tuttle, there was a "preliminary designation" of Ayer as the winning agency, and Ayer was invited down to make a presentation "as a final check." No other agency was invited to present.

The A Team

On June 26, 1984, a five-person team from Ayer, led by Maxey, flew into Washington and went to the Commerce headquarters for an audiovisual presentation to Tuttle, Riegner, and Lee Wells, Riegner's deputy. It started promptly at 2 p.m.

The Ayer presentation included this: Tom Maxey started by discussing Ayer's credentials. Agi Clark, the creative spokesperson, talked about "human contact" and showed the inevitable reel (De Beers, Bahamas Tourism, AT&T, Pan Am, and the U.S. Army Recruiting Command). Jerry N. Jordan, president of Ayer's International Division, then talked about Ayer's world network of subsidiaries and affiliates and showed a Pan Am case history. He was followed by Des Slattery who talked of Ayer's knowledge of the travel business—and showed two case histories: the Bahamas and AT&T. Also, he stressed Ayer's experience with co-op advertising in the travel industry, a key point as far as USTTA was concerned.

After Slattery, Joe Dinslage—at the time with Copartner Ayer, Ayer's subsidiary in Germany—talked about test marketing the USTTA campaign in Germany. Then Clark and Slattery came back on to talk about how Ayer goes about concept development and the coordination they could expect from their German subsidiary. Finally, Maxey came back on to wrap up—and stress how Ayer could help USTTA with co-op development and the preparation of collateral materials (pamphlets, etc.). The whole presentation took only two hours.

Tuttle was ebullient. As she told me later, "Ayer had the most comprehensive marketing plan. They were absolutely the best in terms of Germany. They segmented the market and looked at who was traveling and who wasn't. Their presentation was the most professional, the most well done—and the bottom line—you could tell they, unbelievably, wanted this account." The A team had done its job.

But, time was a problem; the USTTA schedule was tight in that the test market in Germany was to start yet in 1985. USTTA had already contracted with Gallup International for a survey of potential vacation travelers to the U.S., with interviews in Britain, West Germany, and France. Ayer was to proceed concurrently with its extensive research program, knowing that Gallup's results wouldn't be available until after the Ayer creative task was almost complete.

The Gallup survey (fielded from October through December 1984) started with 2,000 interviews in each country to identify characteristics of international air travelers, and then in stage two, personal interviews of 45-minutes duration were conducted with international travelers. The goals of the survey were (1) to determine the U.S. market share; (2) to identify sources of information about travel destinations and media exposure; (3) to measure level of awareness of specific U.S. tourists' destinations; (4) to measure the relative importance of various touristic attributes; and, finally, (5) to determine the relative ratings of the U.S. against competing destinations. The findings, reasoned USTTA, would be helpful to all American firms involved in tourism.

The need for market-by-market planning is dramatized by the Gallup study results. For instance, on the vacation attribute statement, "Food is an important part of a good vacation," international travelers in the U.K. made it number one. But with West Germans, it was number five, and "Sunshine is an important part of a good vacation" topped the list. In France, the attribute, "One of the best parts of traveling is to visit new cultures and new ways of living," scored highest; the food item dropped off the chart.

As for preferred U.S. destinations, overseas travelers scored the Grand Canyon first, but that was fifth with the West Germans, who preferred Hawaii most. The French put Southern California/Los Angeles first, the Grand Canyon seventh. (Overall, however, the Grand Canyon is one of the most alluring tourist attractions in the U.S., and that's why it is featured so often in travel ads.)

To get the creative juices flowing, Ayer's USTTA team in New York contacted their affiliates/subsidiaries in major foreign countries and said, in effect, "Based on your perceptions of the U.S., what kind of campaign—off the top of the head—would you prepare for USTTA for [name of the country]?" The results, which included thorough memos, some storyboards, and dummies of print ads, are fascinating.

From Connaghan & May Ayer (Australia) came the tag line, "How Come You've Never Visited When You Know Us So Well?" From Reklame-Adviesburo BV Marketwinning-Ayer Wierden (Holland), no suggested copy, but a memo explaining, "The constant rise of the U.S. dollar causes a negative effect on traveling to the U.S.—and so does the cost of living in the U.S., which is 1½ times the rate of The Netherlands." From McKim Advertising (Canada): "Your Holiday Goes a Long Way in the U.S.A." From Japan, a consideration: "When thinking about advertising the USA as a Japanese tourist destination, always keep in mind that the Japanese know almost as much about America as Americans do. On any night of the week, on any commercial tv channel, you will see at least a dozen images of America. And that's not counting the news."

And so on, all grist for the Ayer creative mill, which—as far as USTTA was concerned—was Agi Clark and her team: Morleen Novitt and Delores Hanan, writers, and Marguerita Breen and George Fastbinder, art directors. Clark has worked on the J. C. Penney, AT&T, Australian Tourist, and Bahamas Tourism accounts at Ayer, and as noted earlier, on accounts like Air Jamaica and BOAC before joining Ayer. But, when I asked Clark why she had been singled out to handle USTTA creative, she turned her head slightly, looked up, and said simply, "Because I'm the best." Do not be mislead: Clark simply has a lot of confidence in her ability to handle image advertising, and as Maxey puts it, "What the U.S. is selling is a big fat intangible."

Moving ahead on this front was an extensive research program headed by Richard Golden, head of Ayer's Developmental Lab operation. Meant to be a bridge between research and creative, the lab takes on assignments like the U.S.A. theme and provides guidance to creative people like Clark who are involved in the process as much as they care to be.

According to Golden, who had been senior creative director at AT&T before joining Ayer in 1966, the lab's procedures are modeled after the so-called synectics groups, and the goal is to make the creative process less random. The lab's staff includes five professionals and internally reports to Fred Posner, senior vp and executive director of marketing and research at Ayer.

Over the years, according to Golden, the lab has contributed directly or indirectly to the development of such themes as "Never run out of things to do" (Bahamas); "Reach out and touch someone" (AT&T); "Be all you can be" and "This is the Army" (Army Recruiting Command); all of the 7-Up campaigns; and some positioning problems of J. C. Penney. Quite an impressive collection, indeed.

The exact procedures used by Golden and his staff are considered proprietary, and I've been asked not to describe them. Let it suffice that Golden and two of his staff conducted 42 sessions with international travelers over a five-week period in Japan, Australia, Germany, The Netherlands, France, Italy, England, Mexico, and Canada. "I don't think I'd ever try to do that again," sighs Golden.

Agi Clark sat in on some of these sessions in Canada, but more important, perhaps, the lab presented her (and USTTA) with a one-inch thick report that synthesized the findings, some of which were quantified.

The goal of this research, which cost USTTA about $100,000 (out of all overall budget of about $700,000 for theme development), "was to determine the position for the United States most likely to motivate tourism to the U.S." Several copy themes with illustrations were presented to respondents, including "Only in America," "America. Share the feeling," and "America, face to face."

To give you a feeling for what comes out of such quantitative/qualitative research, consider verbatims from a respondent reacting to a picture of one of America's deserts: "...attractive because of its size and wild aspect. The picture of the desert is very appealing to me; it gives me a feeling of great open spaces; it makes you think of the vastness that is America, the gigantic dimensions of America."

Deserts, of course, are a novelty to Europeans, and the size of the U.S. is extraordinary by their standards. Such themes are recurring.

Catch the Spirit

Agi Clark's spacious office on the 42nd floor of 1345 Avenue of the Americas building is glassed all along one side and offers a splendid view of Central Park. Clark sits at one of those tiny round tables, as agency executives are wont to do, and when I talked with her after the "America. Catch the Spirit" theme had been made public, she explained the thinking that went into its development.

"We were looking for a unique position. What's unique about America?" she recalled, adding, "I think we were influenced by an incredible love of this country; we wanted to show its best, most wonderful light." (Clark, nee Solti, doesn't bring it up, but as a girl of 15 she escaped from Budapest with her family during the Hungarian uprising of 1956.)

"I would have bet my life on the 'Only in America'—with a bit of smile in that line," said Clark, referring to one of the themes tested by Golden in his lab sessions. The illustrations accompanying the copy picture average Americans in amusing situations. "But we didn't execute with extravagance, and I learned that humor didn't translate; it came across as bragging. What the reader brings to an ad is so important. Also, it just wasn't exciting enough. The U.S. is exciting, and this theme seemed to play to the negative; Europe is a more cynical culture.

"But the U.S. is exciting—it's where things are happening, there are vast vistas. 'Spirit' seemed to embody all things American—and we wanted to catch that spirit, the vitality." (Recall the patriotic furor that was sweeping the U.S. in the summer/fall of 1984 due to the Olympic Games in Los Angeles.)

Music, from the start, was meant to be an important communications medium, partly because tv exposure is so limited in many countries but radio is available almost everywhere. "We wanted a three-minute song—not a jingle—that could be made into a record," says Clark. "Lyrically, we were looking for a song that expressed experience, not a travelogue." Also, ideally, it should be contemporary—and adaptable to various music forms, a la jazz, blues, country, etc. And, added Clark, "We even thought about using a famous singer—like Frank Sinatra."

Ayer creative invited bids from three music companies, and the winner was Jon Silbermann Music, which wrote both music and lyrics (see sidebar for lyrics). Musically, this piece—entitled "America. Catch the Spirit"—is reminiscent of the Anheuser-Busch corporate commercial, "Here's to you, America."

Budget Cuts

The big unveiling of the "Spirit" campaign took place at a press conference in Ayer's New York offices on February 4, 1985. Donna Tuttle made a little speech; so did Tom Maxey, who showed some "Spirit" posters. Gordon Heald, director of Gallup International, flew in from London to reveal that their study showed America was the number one vacation destination for potential travelers from Germany, France, and Great Britain.

But, questions posed by the 15 or so reporters in the audience focused on a sour note. Recent revelations from the Reagan administration's budget-cutting plans indicated that David Stockman wanted to "zero out" USTTA. Tuttle was on the defensive; she had to explain that the USTTA advertising program, including the test market in Germany, was funded through completion. Even so, press reaction to the program was dampened. *Advertising Age*, for instance, only ran a short story on page 66 of its February 11, 1985 issue.

Undaunted, Tuttle took to the speaker's circuit to sell her campaign—satellite press conference beamed to European journalists, meetings with Travel Industry Association of America leaders, speeches to governors' conferences on tourism, etc. Concurrently, being the good soldier she is in the Reagan administration, Tuttle was preparing her testimony before Congess explaining the special budget required to close down USTTA, if, in fact, it should come to that.

Catch The Spirit

Music and Lyrics by Jon Silbermann

THERE IS A LADY WHO'S BEEN CALLING YOU
SHE'S REACHING TO THE VERY HEART OF YOU
THAT PART OF YOU THAT MAKES YOU FEEL YOUNG
MAKES YOU FEEL ALIVE
THE PART OF YOU THAT WANTS TO SPREAD YOUR WINGS AND FLY

Chorus:
AMERICA...CATCH THE SPIRIT
CATCH THE THRILL
GET THE FEELING OF IT ALL
CATCH THE BEAUTY
OF AMERICA
LET YOUR SPIRIT SOAR.

LOOKING OUT TO THE CITY BELOW
CATCH THE RHYTHM AS THE PEOPLE COME AND GO
PEOPLE JUST LIKE YOU
PEOPLE FILLED WITH LIFE
AMERICA WILL CAPTURE YOU
AMERICA WILL MAKE YOU SMILE

(REPEAT CHORUS)

THE QUIET OF THE CANYONS
THE RUSH OF THE SURF
THIS IS A VERY SPECIAL PART OF THE EARTH
THE SPIRIT'S EVERYWHERE
TOUCHING YOU AND ME
THE WONDER AND THE MAGIC
WILL SET YOUR SPIRIT FREE
AMERICA CATCH THE SPIRIT...*(Instrumental)*

(REPEAT CHORUS)

THERE IS A LADY WHO'S BEEN CALLING YOU.

©Copyright 1985 by Elliot Music Co. Inc.
International Copyright Secured
Made in U.S.A. All rights reserved.
Used by permission.

Why Germany?

Meanwhile, things moved apace. USTTA was finishing plans to open new regional offices in Italy, The Netherlands, and Australia. A new assistant secretary with a strong marketing perspective, Richard L. Seely, joined USTTA. Tuttle continued to lobby.

At Ayer, plans proceeded to start the test market advertising in December 1985. Germany had been chosen by USTTA because they wanted a foreign language country, but one where tourism to the U.S. was large enough for test purposes. In 1984, 540,000 West Germans visited the U.S., accounting for about 2.6% of total visitors, but 4.8% of total travel receipts. This was down 4% from 1983.

"Spirit" advertising, designed to influence tourism to the U.S. in the spring/summer of 1986, breaks in the German travel trade press *(Geo, Merian, Abenteuer & Reisen* and *Traveller's World)* in December, according to Seely. Also in December, consumer advertising starts—a color spread or page per month through May—in magazines like *Der Spiegel* and *Stern.* Then there are special supplements planned for some consumer magazines, like *Bunte,* in January and March 1986.

Beyond that, says Seely, USTTA and Ayer are working with American travel interests—rent-a-car companies, airlines, hotel chains, etc.—to develop a co-op supporting campaign that would overlap USTTA advertising.

So, how will the test market results be measured? First, two groups of known international travelers will be studied. One consists of West Germans who have visited the U.S. heretofore. Previous studies show that there is a 0.76 probability such travelers will repeat-visit. The real increases are expected from the other group, international travelers who have yet to vacation in the U.S. A reasonable goal, according to Don Wynegar, director of the USTTA Office of Research, is a 10% growth in German tourism over two years, but he's quick to note that a lot depends on the relationship between the U.S. dollar and the German mark.

But, measure they will. One device is in-flight tourist interviews, in cooperation with 29 overseas airlines. People flying back to Germany from the U.S. will be asked about their previous visits, what they did in the States, etc. (USTTA started in-flight surveys in 1982, and they are a valuable source of such information.)

Next, says Wynegar, there will be coupon conversion studies. Print ads run in consumer publications will include coupons, through which interested parties can send for literature about travel to the U.S. Follow-up interviews can determine the conversion rate; i.e., how many actually came to the U.S.

Further, says Wynegar, there will be pre- and post-surveys done in Germany to determine awareness of USTTA advertising and changes in attitudes towards U.S. travel. Finally, there will be an ongoing count of the number of Germans who, somehow, request travel information about the U.S.

All of this, of course, takes time—and even then the data must be interpreted in light of changes in the world economy, general increases/decreases in tourism, etc. If all goes well, USTTA hopes to have in due course the documentation to take to Congress and say, "See, if you spend so much to promote international tourism, here's what you'll get back—and we proved that in Germany. Give us the money to do the same in several key countries." Time will tell.

Donna Tuttle—Effective Leader

A high-visibility Tuttle, of course, gets considerable credit for pushing the USTTA program so far so fast. "She's done an excellent job so far," says Bill Edwards of Hilton. "This woman came in and studied, learned, worked, and stimulated—she's one hell of a woman," says Des Slattery of Ayer, who adds, "She's won over hard-bitten professionals, and she's done a hell of a job." From Wynegar, "It was very clear from the first that she was a determined leader and was going to devote a tremendous amount of time and energy to the job."

And, this final word from Vivian Deuschl: "I came [to USTTA] from the industry, and people respected it [USTTA] for what it was trying to do, but always with a concern because there was a feeling that the potential was there to do something good, but it didn't have the continuity of leadership, and it was beset by uncertainty. Mrs. Tuttle has done a lot to change that."

Interview with Donna Tuttle

Donna Frame Tuttle was sworn in as Under Secretary of Commerce for Travel and Tourism on December 13, 1983, at the age of 36, making her what is believed to be the youngest under secretary in the department's history (and one of the highest ranking women in the Reagan administration; there are but three under secretaries in the Department of Commerce).

Tuttle had a lot to prove. Her previous work experience consisted of a teaching post in a junior high school in Los Angeles and founding an interior design firm. But Tuttle's political credentials were sterling. She had served as either chairman or finance director [read: fundraiser] in several local, state, and national campaigns in Southern California, and her husband, Robert Tuttle, is director of the Office of Presidential Personnel in the White House. More important, her father-in-law is Holmes Paul Tuttle, 79, one of the famous Kitchen Cabinet claque of business tycoons who launched Ronald Reagan into big-time politics.

On a table behind her big desk at the Department of Commerce, there are 13 framed photographs, plus several on the walls; they picture Tuttle in the most prestigious of Republican company.

I interviewed Tuttle in her office on February 22, 1985, just as she was preparing her budget testimony for hearings on the Hill. The night before, she had hosted at her home in the District a social gathering for the 25 top-ranking women in the Reagan administration.

HONOMICHL: Were you given any sort of mandate when you were given this job? Did someone say, "Go in there and shake up that operation"?

TUTTLE: A mandate from the administration? No. I'll tell you what; I came in, I think, at a little bit of a lucky time. For the first time, the agency got some real money that it hadn't gotten in a long time; it came exactly when I showed up. We found that they [Congress] had argued back and forth up on the Hill and had voted $12 million.

I think there was a lot of new life. For once, we had a great deal of money to do a good program. Everyone felt good, and we all knew we needed to do some dramatic things.

HONOMICHL: Did you increase the USTTA staff?

TUTTLE: No; we kept it the same, 79. We've kept it that way because we want to keep a small Washington staff and really keep the workload in offices overseas.

HONOMICHL: How did you start the new program?

TUTTLE: I had done a great deal of studying of the agency and I knew some of the problems, and I knew what they had been facing, and came and looked at marketing plans, looked at the fact that Don [Wynegar, director, Office of Research] hadn't had any money to do any research—and if you don't have statistics, it's very difficult to really do a good marketing plan—and we talked about the kind of things we needed to do, and took that $12 million....

HONOMICHL: Did leaders of the travel industry come in and sit down at your desk and say, "Can you get something going for us?" Did they push you?

TUTTLE: No. Number one, there was a little bit of a change on the board [industry advisory board to USTTA]. In fact, it had been a long time since the board had had a meeting—probably had been eight months before the time I got there.

There was some controversy on my appointment because I was not from the industry, so I immediately went out—and one by one—invited each one of the leaders out and sat and talked about what they thought about the agency. [Mrs. Tuttle visited with between 35 and 50 leaders, mostly in the Southern California and Washington, D. C. areas.]

HONOMICHL: You did that out of your own pocket?

TUTTLE: Absolutely. And I spent three or four months.

HONOMICHL: So you got the industry's point of view—and you were selling Donna Tuttle....

TUTTLE: That's right. I wanted to calm their fears that it was going to work out, and that I did have the background. But again, by that time, I had done enough studying of the agency—I had gone back and read all the transcripts [of USTTA budget testimony on the Hill] so I knew what the problems were, and I knew what I thought needed to be done. One of the main problems was turnover in leadership; that has hurt the agency. [Over the past 10 years, the USTTA has had nine directors, including Tuttle, and there were periods when no director or an interim acting director was on the job.]

HONOMICHL: Will you be here for the balance of the Reagan administration?

TUTTLE: Ah, you know...yes; my intent is to be here.

HONOMICHL: So, what you've done in a year and one-half—blessed by the $12 million—is extraordinary in the recent history of the agency?

TUTTLE: Well, it's worked out very well. I think it's a combination of things; there's no doubt about it. Obviously, a lot comes from the leadership [i.e., Reagan administration]. Obviously, I like to move quickly and accomplish a lot, and there was a lot to be done. And, as I said, I think I came in at just the right time to do just that.

HONOMICHL: You have a personal relationship with President Reagan....

TUTTLE: Yes.

HONOMICHL: Have you discussed the agency's problems with him?

TUTTLE: No. All the communications have been through channels. The personal relationships really have been through families; my husband's family [and the Reagans] are very close.

HONOMICHL: What did you want to do with the USTTA?

TUTTLE: I think there was a swelling also in the industry on the outside—I think there was a very growing movement of, "Hey, we need to identify ourselves with the travel/tourism industry. We need to pull everyone in, combine together, and we need to do something about this agency." What the problem was—this agency cannot do a marketing plan based on funds it doesn't have—and right before I came in, they asked up on the Hill, "What would you do if you had $12 million?" and [her predecesor] said, "I can't give you the plans because I don't have the $12 million."

I really think in the summer before I came in that prompted the industry to say, "The agency can't do it. Let's put together our own marketing plan for the U.S. government to compete." That's when they all agreed that they would forget their competition, forget their egos, share their statistics, and really come together and form this committee.

HONOMICHL: And they wanted USTTA to become the focal point....

TUTTLE: That's right. The industry came together. But, I might say, I wasn't aware of all this. I came in and we did our own thing, and the two just jelled. I think it was obvious what this agency needed, but it was nice that there was industry support at the same time. One of the weaknesses of the agency was that no one took travel/tourism seriously....

HONOMICHL: The Congress?

TUTTLE: No one. The press, the public, the Congress. But there have been a few people on the Hill who have been stars. One of the best was Senator Inouye [Daniel K. Inouye, D-Hawaii]. Pressler [Larry Pressler, R-South Dakota] came on in '80. Laxalt [Paul Laxalt, R-Nevada] now is wonderful.

I understand that 20 years ago, Senator Inouye was walking the halls talking tourism, and people said, "Oh, come on; you're just talking Hawaii. It's a frivolous activity."

Now people are saying, "It's an export. It does create revenues. It does make a difference in the balance of payments."

HONOMICHL: Have you talked to people on the Hill about what to expect from a good USTTA program? That is, for every dollar spent to promote tourism they can expect so many dollars in extra revenues?

TUTTLE: Well, there was a study several years ago. That study proved that for a dollar invested there was a return of $18.60.

HONOMICHL: Why did USTTA select Ayer?

TUTTLE: Ayer had, first of all, the most comprehensive marketing plan. They were absolutely the best in terms of Germany. We had asked for a prototype of what would you do in Germany, and they segmented the market, they looked at who was traveling and who wasn't. They told you whom you could possibly go after, and they went into all kinds of different ideas of how you could go after them.

We had asked for examples of co-op advertising, and they had experience in that area. There are a lot of good agencies who have never done cooperative advertising, and that scared us.

Their presentation was the most professional—the most well done. And the bottom line—you could tell they put more into it than I had ever seen. It was by far....

HONOMICHL: Had you ever seen an agency presentation before?

TUTTLE: No. But I'm even talking about the written ones [agency responses to the USTTA RFP]. I mean, you could tell, you could tell from the way they wrote up their plans. You can tell a stock plan compared to someone who has really investigated this agency and what we're trying to do.

They [Ayer] were really excellent; someone clearly researched it and spent a lot of time on it.

HONOMICHL: What is it you want people to remember about your directorship at USTTA?

TUTTLE: It's funny. I was told when I got here, just think of one thing you want to do; don't try to do a lot of things.

I've tried to put a mechanism in place—a marketing plan. It's logical management, but it wasn't happening.

6 The Marketing of Cycle Dog Food

Behind the facade of slick advertising, huge promotional budgets, and what appears to be the sound positioning of a consumer product, there is often a much less estimable story. Obviously, these are the stories that seldom become public.

In my opinion, Cycle dog food from the Pet Foods Division of General Foods Corporation is a classic example of such behind-the-scenes revelations. Despite the glitter and gold that General Foods and its advertising agencies could bring to the product, well—it just never really paid off.

The story, which appeared in Advertising Age *on July 19, 1982, was edited considerably, and, of more concern, a full page of typed text was inadvertently left out in the middle of the story. Here's the full story, as originally written. I think it contains some sobering lessons for marketing management too eager to push a new product into the marketplace.*

Setting the Stage

The Pet Foods Division of General Foods Corp. had an operating profit of $35 million on established brands in fiscal year 1974, I've been told by a former top-level GF executive who was there at the time. In fiscal 1981, the division had an operating loss of $12 million, as estimated by a prominent financial analyst in Chicago. Lots of things, of course, contributed to that dramatic reversal, but the most conspicuous—and probably most important—was Cycle dog food.

This is an insider's story of Cycle's development, marketing strategy, and the going-in miscalculations that haunt GF's marketing management to this day. The moral: having an enormous amount of money to spend doesn't mean you can buy marketing happiness in the pet food industry, or—from an advertising agency's point of view—"The client can hand you a dandy, built-in copy platform and huge budgets, but that doesn't necessarily mean you can advertise him out of a hole he dug for himself [in Topeka, Kans.]."

Let's start by positioning Cycle canned dog food, which has been in national distribution since spring 1976. (A dry, bagged version was rolled out two years later.) The concept of the product is that a dog's diet should be adjusted according to its position in the life cycle. So, there were four Cycle products: Cycle 1, "specially balanced for puppies up to 18 months of age"; Cycle 2 for adult dogs between 1 and 7 years of age; Cycle 3 for less active [read: overweight] dogs; and Cycle 4 for older dogs (over 7 years).

The original Cycle canned line, which was taken national, had two varieties, beef and chicken, so for the concept to be fully expressed on the shelf, a store had to stock a minimum of 8 items. Two facings on each meant 16 items, and so on. And if one of the items (or Cycles) was delisted because of slow movement, the whole concept started to unravel. (We'll come back to that.)

The canned Cycle product is a formed product, common in the dog food packing industry; it's meant to convey the impression of a meatball, such as humans might eat, say, on spaghetti. These balls are packed in a gravy-like sauce, and through time such products have been promoted as "the dog food that doesn't look like dog food."

It should be noted that, historically, other packers who have gone the meatball route have had, at best, lackluster success in the marketplace, and many died aborning. It's a long list, but here are some prominent examples: the original Recipe Balanced Dinners line from Campbell Soups Champion Valley Divison, Rival Tasty Chunk Dinners from Nabisco, the original Skippy Premium line from National Pet Food, and—ironically—Gaines Supreme, a GF brand test marketed before Cycle. Neither Alpo nor Kal Kan, the leading brands in the canned dog food market, carries a meatball item in its extensive line. The reason: slow movement.

And, finally, Cycle canned from the beginning was priced significantly higher than Alpo's Beef Chunks, the leading premium-priced canned item, then and now.

The Topeka Plant

One of the main characters in Cycle's passion play is a 150,000-square-foot canned dog food plant GF's Post Division started to build in Topeka, Kans., in November 1971, adjoining a plant GF had built two years earlier on a 110-acre plot to produce dry dog food.

This canned plant, which came on-line in May 1973, is a classic example of putting the cart before the horse. At the time the Topeka investment was authorized—circa summer 1971—GF's Pet Foods Division did not have a proven canned product for the plant to produce. What it had instead was a product concept in test and, in retrospect, a lot of wishful thinking.

The original hope was a meatball line called Gaines Supreme, which GF put into test market in Buffalo and Albany in March 1970, with Ogilvy & Mather as the agency. For those not familiar with this product class, Gaines is an old and esteemed name in the dog food world. GF has it via the 1943 acquisition of a regional dry packer in Sherburn, N.Y., and GF still markets a line of dry products under the Gaines name.

Gaines Supreme didn't do well in Buffalo/Albany, so two years later two new test markets (Miami and Denver) were opened.

No doubt, GF had grandiose plans for Gaines Supreme. At first, they used Arlene Francis as a product spokesperson, but later they reportedly cut a deal with singer/actress Doris Day, "a well-known dog fancier," that called for $1 million over five years to tout Gaines Supreme.

There was a hang-up, however: Gaines Supreme died in test market (with less than a 5% share of canned pounds), and that left a big capital investment in the prairies of eastern Kansas gathering dust.

Enter Cycle

But, across the plains of Kansas and the White Plains in Westchester County, N.Y., another concept came barking: Cycle, "every day, for the life of your dog."

The name and concept originated with a small advertising agency, John Rockwell & Associates, which was brought into GF by William E. Rawlings. Rawlings was president of the Pet Foods Division from 1971 to January 1974 (at which time he left after a much-publicized wrangle with the president of GF, James L. Ferguson). Rawlings reportedly was pushing for a faster expansion of GF's pet food business and felt top management was sluggish in approving new moves.

Rockwell, who had been executive vp of Needham, Harper & Steers before setting up his own shop, specialized in ginning up new products. He was on retainer to GF from October 1969 to April 1971.

The Cycle concept, according to research, showed that "dog owners are highly anthropomorphic—quick to attribute human traits to their pets—and would respond to a canned line that delivered nutrition specially formulated to the dog's age and 'life style.'" If it succeeded, it would be a good market segmentation and differentiate the Cycle brand from competition—and it was something agency creatives could really get their teeth into. Rockwell recently told me he envisioned the concept executed in all three product forms—canned, dry, and semi-moist.

(The deliberations GF marketing people were going through in early 1970 trying to decide how best to approach the canned dog food market are documented, apparently factually, in a case study used at the Harvard Business School and The Wharton School, University of Pennsylvania. Included in this 37-page manuscript are the findings of a large-scale GF market segmentation study of dog owners, which sets the framework for execution of the Cycle concept.)

First Test Market

GF took its first version of Cycle canned into test market in Grand Rapids and Sacramento in early 1973, and the product was assigned to Grey Advertising, which was the agency of record until 1982 when the product (both canned and dry) was moved to Benton & Bowles.

The first test had four Cycle products, but no flavors. "That's what we learned," says Richard O'Brien, who was the Cycle account executive at Grey from the beginning; "you have to give the consumer flavor variety." They also learned that test results projected about a 4.5% share of the canned market, not enough volume to provide a reasonable payout on the brand.

Back to the drawing board. An expanded Cycle line—this time with beef and chicken varieties—was put into a new test area (Syracuse, N.Y.) in April 1974, and later that year it was expanded to a GF sales region that encompassed Boston; Providence, R.I.; Hartford, Conn.; and Portland, Maine. There it sat until April 1976, when the national rollout started.

I've been told by a GF executive who was deeply involved that between $2 and $3 million was spent on marketing research alone in those test markets. One reason was the length of the test, and another was the low incidence level of target populations—households with puppies, with overweight dogs, etc. Since continuous, diary-type purchase panels were set up to track trial and repeat purchase rates, the screening costs alone were astronomical.

The Magic Number

The "magic number" several GF executives have told me was 6%; that was the share of canned pound market that seemed necessary to jell the payout plan on Cycle. I've been told that, in fact, the Syracuse test market did project out to a 6% national share. I have also seen data that suggest that in the larger New England region, Cycle only got a 4.7% share in the first year. Also, I've been told that the Pet Foods Division's market research department (MRD) felt that test market results were "minimally acceptable," and even after making liberal estimates of the volume to expect, MRD felt that the brand would only achieve in national distribution about 50% of the volume the Pet Foods marketing people anticipated. MRD's conclusion: "Don't go national." ("I doubt that," one ex-GF pet food executive told me; "the system would have flagged such a recommendation from MRD, and I didn't know about it.")

Trial in New England seemed good—about 40% of the dog-owning households had tried at least one can of Cycle in the first year. And, indeed, much money had been spent to induce trial—about $500,000 annually in spot tv alone in the New England markets. (The same effort now would probably cost over $1 million.)

Was it that MRD was especially conscious of how much Cycle was sold as deal merchandise, and the extraordinary amount of money that was spent to achieve those levels? Or was it, as one GF executive has suggested, a fear of rolling out in a recession economy? In whatever case, going natural was what an ex-marketing manager for the Pet Foods Division recently termed "a difficult and somewhat contentious decision."

It all seems to boil down to this: "Why, in a high-velocity product class like canned dog food, did it take two years of testing to determine if Cycle canned was go or no-go?" It certainly didn't take the Topeka plant that long to pack the required shelf-stocking quantities.

And the really key question is this: "If it was a borderline decision, how much was it influenced by that under-utilized plant in Topeka?"—then nearly three years old, which one ex-GFer recently characterized as "that magnificent monument to futility."

"Phil Smith [Philip L. Smith, president of GF's Pet Foods Division at the time] was too hard-headed a guy to let a factory influence such a spending recommendation," says one GF executive who was in on the decision making. But another says flat out, "I doubt Cycle would have been taken national except for that plant."

In any case, the go-national decisions was made by GF's Management Committee, which included GF's president at the time, James L. Ferguson.

Heavy Expenditures

The national launch was in April 1976, at the start of a new GF fiscal year. The Maxwell House Division, GF's traditional cash cow, was particularly flush due to a run-up in inventory and futures values caused by a severe frost in Brazil, which damaged coffee trees and the yet-to-be-harvested crop. The economy was improving, and it seemed an advantageous time to go out and buy a sizable share of the canned dog food market.

The much-heralded Cycle introduction was estimated at $18 million, with $12 million in advertising and the balance in promotions. It is estimated that 200 million coupons were dropped, and waves of Donnelley's Carol Wright co-op were used, with some coupons having values as high as "one free with one." The cost of goods, laydown, and redemption on such an effort is awesome, especially in the context of the canned dog food business, 1976.

Alpo, which had been the most heavily advertised canned dog food, spent $9 million in measured media in 1976. In just nine months (April–December), Cycle spent $13 million, giving it a 26% share of voice in the category for the year.

In 1977, the heavy spending continued—$9.7 million in measured media—making it the most heavily advertised canned brand. This translated into a 23% share of voice in the category, compared to a share of pound volume of about 5%. Put another way, Cycle canned sales at retail were about $43.2 million in 1977. With an ad expenditure of $9.7 million, that gave Cycle an advertising/sales ratio of 22.4%. The other leading premium priced canned brands were running at an advertising/sales ratio from 4 to 7%.

I asked a top executive at Grey Advertising if GF had a share of voice goal. "No," he replied, "they pooh-poohed share of voice at GF; we looked at the absolute expenditures needed to achieve goals [i.e., trial and awareness]. We wanted to burn the concept in, whatever the cost." (An ex-marketing manager at GF refutes this: "We did too pay attention to share of voice," he told me recently.)

But it was the Cycle deal levels that were most impressive, especially to established canned dog food packers. Right from the start and on through 1977, month after month, over 35% of Cycle canned was sold as consumer-recognized deal merchandise, meaning that a coupon, or off-label price, or advertised store special price was influencing the transaction. Now, that may not seem high compared to some other product classes, but in the canned dog food business in 1976–77, the category average was about 16% and would have been lower if Cycle weren't included.

GF's direct sales force did a good job; Cycle was quickly pushed into national distribution. (In fact, the Pet Foods Division was an outgrowth of the Post Division at GF, and it was Post's sales force that took Cycle out.)

Signs of Weakness

This spending/selling binge really did a job. In one 28-day period in the summer of 1976, 2.9 million dog-owning households bought at least one can of Cycle (which translates into 25% of all households that bought any canned product at all). In contrast, 2.3 million households bought some Alpo, the best-selling brand. That pace tapered off, and toward the end of 1976, about 1.5 million households were buying some Cycle in a 28-day period. Another thing that Pet Foods management learned about then was that Cycle ingredient costs were running much higher than predicted.

Beneath the surface, a disturbing signal started to flash—at least to those who were watching closely. The average household that purchased Cycle bought about 5 pounds in a 28-day period; the comparable figure for Alpo was 9 pounds, and for Kal Kan, 12 pounds. What this suggested, of course, was that the huge expenditures to induce trial were getting fine penetration for Cycle, but the brand was either reaching relatively light users of canned dog food or people who were not too committed to the brand and/or concept but who were simply reacting to juicy trial offers. (By 1978, the figure had moved up to about 7.5 pounds as the number of households purchasing dropped down to a 1.4 million level every 28 days, but it was still way lower than Alpo or Kal Kan.) Also, it turned out that Cycle had a better penetration of households owning one dog than it did of households owning two or more dogs.

In any case, Cycle share of the total canned pound market progressed as follows: 4.9% in 1977; 5.4% in 1978; 6.1% in 1979; 5.9% in 1980; and 6.5% in 1981.

Advertising pressure on Cycle canned dropped off to $6.1 million in 1978 and $6.9 in 1979, but the advertising/sales ratio was still at 12%, way above the category average of about 3%.

Cycle Dry

Buoyed by what on the surface appeared to be a successful launch of Cycle canned, the Pet Foods Division put a Cycle dry version into test market in Syracuse in April 1976 (again, at the start of a GF fiscal year). Since Cycle canned also had been tested in Syracuse, this enabled Pet Foods MRD to measure the cross-purchasing between the canned and dry products.

The dry Cycle was rolled into national distribution in the spring of 1978, and GF was talking about a total budget of $34 million to support the line.

Going into dry form presented a concern. Most nationally promoted, premium-priced, dry dog food brands are packed in four sizes: 5, 10, 25, and 50 pounds. Now, if the Cycle concept was fully expressed in the dry dog food section of a supermarket, that would mean stocking at least 16 items just to get one shelf facing on each. This would have been a very tough sell, indeed. (I should add, many supermarkets—especially in the East—do not stock 50-pound bags.)

GF backed off; in the beginning Cycle dry was available in just two pack sizes, 5 and 25 pounds. While this curtailed the brand's reach, at least it left the sales force with something other than an impossible mission. (Later, Cycle dry was made available in a 10-pound pack in western markets.)

In any case, the introduction of a dry line highlighted one of the problems with the Cycle concept: you had to get and hold shelf space on a lot of items to make it fully effective. This is no problem if the brand and individual items have a sizable share or fast turnover. But, with a low share and a sluggish turnover, individual items are always running the risk of being delisted, and—poof!—there goes the concept.

I asked an ex-GF executive if there had been any worry about this in Pet Foods marketing. "Yes," he said, "we talked about it, but we thought we could overcome the problem." Was the GF sales force consulted, I wondered? "Not until we were well down the road," was the answer; "marketing made those decisions." Another executive added, "It was rare that marketing consulted sales, but the shelf-space problem was well recognized."

All of this is of special concern because during the general time period Cycle dry was going national, all hell was breaking loose in the dry dog food market. Ralston Purina was introducing Fit 'n Trim, Kal Kan was taking out Mealtime, Allen Products was introducing Alpo Beef Flavored Dinners, and Quaker was introducing its innovative new product, Tender Chunks, with a campaign estimated at $29 million. In a word, the fight for new listings and shelf space was intense, and in that context the GF sales force had to get more space than their products' sales might justify. Tough.

Great credit to that sales force, however; they did a good job. But I doubt the Cycle concept had as much charm for them as it did to marketing management back at the Plains, or to Mr. Rockwell.

Anyway, as Cycle dry continued to build share of market in the summer and fall of 1978, the amount of goods moving as consumer-recognized deal merchandise was extremely high: about 50%, as compared to a category average of about 26%. By the late fall, 1.7 million households were buying at least one package of Cycle dry in a 28-day period (about 13% of all dry buyers), but as with Cycle canned, they did not buy nearly as much Cycle pounds per period as, say, a Purina Chow buyer would buy of Chow. Again, the data suggested that Cycle was not, relatively, getting to the heavy user.

Changes in 1981

All sorts of doctoring was done on Cycle canned in 1981. The can was downsized. A new flavor, liver, was added to the line. The label was redesigned—for the fourth time in five years—and a little Gaines logo was added, as if that might make a difference. Originally, Cycle was labeled "chunk." This was changed to "dinner of beefy chunks and beef gravy." To use the word "dinner" on a dog food label, a product must have 25% or more meat content. Later label designs dropped "dinner" and went to "flavor," which can be used with less than 25% meat.

Also, at this stage of its development, it was becoming more and more difficult to find grocery buyers who paid list price for Cycle canned (or dry). The trade deals were so staggered a retail chain could buy discounted merchandise almost continuously.

In early 1982, there was considerably more change. Ralph L. Cobb, a group vice president at GF, was brought in as president of the Pet Foods Division, replacing Robert Sansone. The Cycle account was switched from Grey Advertising to Benton & Bowles as part of a "consolidation," but that didn't seem to matter much since the advertising budget for Cycle had been cut back to nearly nothing. The marketing staff in the Pet Foods Division was drastically reduced, down to about one-fourth its previous size.

Cycle 2 Revisited

To confound matters, GF started to launch in January 1982 a new canned "meatball" line called Gravy Train, which has "all the appeal of a homemade meal." The GF promotional literature says the initial six months' advertising and promotional package will be $17 million.

If you look closely at the ingredient statement and the guaranteed analysis on the new Gravy Train beef-flavor item and compare it with the same on Cycle 2 ("specially balanced for adult dogs 1–7 years") beef flavor, you'll see that they are, for all practical purposes, identical. Cut the cans and you'll see they look alike.

Full Circle

If you'd like to know who was responsible for the Cycle situation at GF, it's interesting to note that since 1971, when the Pet Foods Division was set up separate from the Post Division, there have been five presidents: William E. Rawlings, Philip L. Smith, Edward Fuhrman, Robert Sansone, and, as of February 1982, Ralph L. Cobb. (Cobb, ironically, was president of the Post Division—of which pet foods was part—in the late 1960s when John Rockwell sold the Cycle concept to GF.)

Two of those division presidents (Rawlings and Fuhrman) are no longer with General Foods. David Hurwitt, who was marketing manager of the Pet Foods Division when Cycle canned went national, is now in France with GF International. Irving M. Saslaw, who was marketing and development manager for pet foods at the time and who was most directly involved in managing the development of the Cycle product, is now with GF's Technical Center in Tarrytown, New York, as group director/strategic technical planning. Smith, who was division president when Cycle went national, is now president and chief operating officer at GF; James L. Ferguson, president of GF through the Cycle era, is now chairman and chief executive officer. And Rockwell, Cycle's inventor, is with Booz Allen & Hamilton, the consulting firm, in New York.

I spoke with Cobb immediately after an annual meeting of Pet Foods Division executives in Chicago the week of June 21, 1982, and he emphasized that, "We still have confidence in the Cycle concept; it has lots of vitality that we have not obtained." He says that Pet Foods marketing management is in the process of "re-staging" the Cycle business, and, toward that end, a new piece of advertising copy is now being market tested. "We might start advertising again by the end of this year," he adds.

Go into almost any supermarket in the U.S. today, and you'll probably find numerous shelf facings of Cycle products, well positioned. But, if you dig beneath that superficial appearance of success, you'll find an inherently weak brand that got off on the wrong foot years ago and survives now more from marketing push than consumer pull. Over that time, GF's Pet Foods Division has had an extraordinarily large marketing staff, huge marketing budgets by industry standards, an apparently single-minded obsession with a formed "meatball" type product, and an extraordinarily high turnover in top management.

Somewhere, somehow, there must be someone in the upper echelons of GF corporate management who looks down and thinks maybe, just maybe, canned dog food should be lumped into the same category with Viviane Woodward, Kohner Bros., Burger Chef Systems, and W. Atlee Burpee Company—other ill-fated GF expansion efforts of the late 1960s.

Postscript (August 1985)

In May 1984, just 23 months after this article appeared in *Advertising Age*, General Foods announced its intent to sell its entire Pet Foods Division, including Cycle, to Anderson, Clayton & Co. (AC) in Houston, Tex., whose president, W. Fenton Guinee, Jr., a former Quaker Oats marketing executive, figured he would do something with Gaines' product line. The sale, in June 1984, was for $156.8 million in cash, and AC assumed about $30 million in debts. James L. Ferguson, chairman of General Foods, was quoted as saying at the time, "...we see difficulty in supporting Gaines to the full extent it needs and deserves."

An executive of another pet food manufacturer, who saw the Gaines books when it was put up for sale, later told me, "I never saw such a mismanaged operation."

7 Marketing a Marketing Information Service

Most of what has been written about new-product development in the marketing literature has been based on high-velocity package goods, mostly because that's where the action has been. But things have been changing rapidly in recent years, and service firms—more and more—are getting into methodical development of new services. In the marketing information industry, a new product is a new information service—and next to nothing has been written about the process leading to the development of such services.

The following story about the TestSight service developed by the A. C. Nielsen Company will, I hope, throw some light on the unique considerations, capital requirements, and technological implications of setting up a sophisticated information system.

The interview with Arthur C. Nielsen, Jr., which follows, is a candid revelation of how such projects look to the man on top.

The Launch

"Any comments?"

No answer.

"Then let's go."

With this terse statement, tantamount to an order because the speaker was Arthur C. Nielsen, Jr., at the time CEO of the A. C. Nielsen Co. (ACN), an extraordinary meeting of ACN's management committee on April 1, 1983, ended at 6:30 p.m. Nielsen had just blessed a venture, long in planning, that within two years would involve an investment of $16 million, create a new, stand-alone profit center employing 130 people, and send ACN into head-on conflict with a brash new competitor, Information Resources, Inc.

The day-long meeting, held in conference room 2A in the huge ACN headquarters building in Northbrook, Ill., included almost all the top brass of the world's largest marketing/advertising research organization—Henry Burk, Gene Harden, Don McCurry, Frank Herold, and about a dozen others. Since it was Good Friday and many had personal plans, the normal expectation would have been for an early adjournment. Instead, the last item on the agenda, the presentation of a new business plan by Tom Busyn, went on for three hours.

Busyn, a 25-year veteran of the company, had six months before been promoted from manager of ACN's Boston sales/service office to manager, test marketing services, a newly created post. One of his tasks was to find a way for ACN to regain prominence in the heavy-spending new-product test marketing field. "I didn't expect to come out of that meeting with a decision," Busyn told me 20 months later. But now, in retrospect, it appears that April 1 was pivotal; ACN, a sleeping giant not renowned for adventurous moves in recent years, was awakening. Nielsen has put a decisive foot down.

Many of ACN's management committee knew well that the company's founder, the late Arthur C. Nielsen, Sr., had pioneered test marketing when, in 1933, he made a panel of audited grocery stores available to package goods clients for "experimentation." But they also knew that ACN had through the years, lost prominence in that large, lucrative segment of the U.S. marketing research business because, simply, competitors had developed innovative local-market, fixed systems that had more appeal to big-spending clients like General Mills, Procter & Gamble, Quaker, and General Foods.

There follows the inside story of how ACN studied its competitive problem, developed a plan to solve it, and brought in the people needed to make that plan come to life—plus how one of Art Nielsen's golfing buddies turned out to play a major, perhaps decisive, role. The story is out of the ordinary because, while marketing research firms like ACN often counsel clients on new product development and marketing tactics, no one heretofore has permitted documentation of how they go about developing a new product (i.e. service). As you'll see, in the case of ACN and what would later surface as the TestSight Service of ERIM (Electronic Research for Insights into Marketing) Information Services, the new ACN profit center, the cobbler's children have shoes. You'll also see that ACN, despite its stodgy image, is quite willing to take some big risks.

The story begins, appropriately, with a market survey.

Market Study

The executive most directly involved with ACN's test marketing business in the U.S. is Donald R. McCurry, executive vp and divisional manager of the Marketing Research Group USA. He and MRG's director of marketing, Frank L. Herold, had in late 1982 hired a consulting firm to do a study entitled "A Strategic Assessment of Opportunities in the Market for Test Marketing Services." It was based on interviews with marketing/research executives in large packaged goods firms, some advertising agencies, and other research firms specializing in test marketing services.

The final report, delivered in January 1983, analyzed the market (size, trends, etc.) for test marketing services and how it was segmented by various types of commonly used services. One key finding: "Nielsen is not usually seen as a test marketing company, although most users are generally aware of the range and type of services it offers." One reason was that there was no stand-alone unit at ACN to handle test marketing clients, a unit that could nurture its own reputation for expertise and a specialized client service staff. Because of this, ACN's test marketing services—although sizable in dollar volume—tended to be viewed by clients as an extension of the national syndicated services, a la NFI. (In fact, when Busyn came in, ACN's Major Market Service, Data Market Service, custom store audits, and local Scantrack services were consolidated under his management.)

The study also pointed out that the fastest-growing segment of test marketing services involved panels where product movement data were collected via scanning of UPC codes on package goods at checkout. This, and other developments in electronic data collection, were tending to give test marketing a high-tech image, and ACN was not perceived as being particularly advanced in that area, although—generally—the company had an above average image for data collection/sampling ability, quality of data, etc.

IRI Leads the Way

One phenomenon studied closely by Busyn was the rapid growth of Information Resources, Inc. (IRI). This Chicago-based firm, founded in late 1978, started its BehaviorScan measuring system in two small markets: Marion, Ind., and Pittsfield, Mass. in 1980.

An immediate hit with some major packaged goods companies, these systems—almost entirely electronic—established the concept of a "single data source" field laboratory for the test marketing of new products and the testing of advertising and promotion variables on established products.

IRI funded the installation of UPC scanner systems in BehaviorScan market supermarkets and then recruited, in each market, panels of about 2,500 households, each of which had a plastic identification card. When a panel household shopped for groceries, the checkout clerk could insert its ID card, and then information (brand, package size, price paid, etc.) about each item purchased was entered into the family's file—a continuous, computerized record of its purchasing activity. Since IRI had developed a classification file on each household, purchases could then be linked to family composition factors, such as age of children, income, etc. Also, through cable tv systems and some sophisticated electronic hardware, test tv commercials could be beamed to specific panel households. So, for instance, one group of panel households known to be breakfast cereal users could be exposed to one commercial over time while another group was seeing a different commercial. In time, any changes in purchasing behavior could be observed.

In addition, tv viewing in some BehaviorScan panel households was monitored by meters affixed to tv sets. The time the set was on and the channels being watched were recorded continuously.

Finally, through a local staff, IRI could monitor other factors influencing purchasing behavior, such as special price promotions, on-shelf display of goods, etc.—hence the term "single source." All relevant data were collected by one integrated system and then analyzed on IRI computers via proprietary systems and software.

IRI quicky became the *wunderkind* of the research industry, especially with those involved in test marketing. Its revenues grew from $389,000 in 1979, to $2.7 million in 1980, to $5.9 million in 1981, to $12.3 million in 1982. ACN knew IRI's revenues in 1983 probably would exceed $21 million, and that a good hunk of that was lost Nielsen business. IRI had added two more BehaviorScan markets (Eau Claire, Wis., and Midland, Tex.), and two more were in the planning stage.

Just a month before Busyn's presentation to ACN's management committee, IRI announced plans for a public stock issue. There was every reason to believe that this would be successful, and says Busyn, "This fortified the fact that IRI was for real." He knew, as did many others, that in earlier days IRI was often hard-pressed for the capital needed to set up BehaviorScan markets, and, in fact, IRI had approached ACN trying to work out some sort of deal, which ACN rejected, mostly because they felt IRI's plans at the time were too sketchy.

In late March, IRI's public offering went out through Hambrecht & Quist, a West Coast underwriter renowned for handling high-tech company issues, especially around Silicon Valley. IRI netted $21.35 a share, or $18.5 million, and ACN was now faced with a not-so-small competitor with plenty of capital to fund its ambitious growth plans. (IRI stock, shortly after the offering, briefly shot up to $64 a share, or 131 times 1982 earnings. The company had become very conspicuous, and there were numerous flattering articles in the trade and business press.)

It was within this context that Busyn made his presentation of April 1. After reviewing the outside consultant's findings and describing the impact of IRI and its probable growth, funded by the stock money, he concluded: "If ACN wants to stay in the test marketing field, we have to get into electronic test markets." A request for start-up money was made and granted—but the long-term implications were far greater. ACN was playing catch-up, and to be really successful, it had to beat IRI at its own game.

Staffing Up

Over the next two months, Donald McCurry, as he traveled around the country visiting ACN clients, raised questions about ACN's position in the test marketing business. He learned that his company's reputation had been dented by a project in Rochester, N.Y., in 1980 when ACN recruited panels of households—a la BehaviorScan—around some Wegman grocery stores. Clients got the impression that ACN didn't have the software or experience to process the sequential purchase files that result from such panels. So, it seemed prudent to hire an executive with extensive panel experience.

The solution to that one turned out to be Laurence N. Gold, vp-client services, at Market Research Corporation of America, a large diary-panel company which, as luck would have it, had Gold stationed at its Chicago office about a mile from ACN's offices. Gold had over 18 years experience in selling and servicing the kind of clients ACN would need to make its new test market system go, and he would assume the title of vp-marketing.

Another important addition to Busyn's staff was Aleta Bluhm, a statistician by training, who had recently rejoined ACN after leaving several years earlier to work for Burke Marketing Research and Needham, Harper & Steers. Officially, Bluhm was associate manager, test service planning. Unofficially, she recalls with a chuckle, "My new job description was 'Do whatever is necessary.'"

Over the summer of 1983, Gold and Bluhm traveled over the U.S., having in-depth interviews with marketing and research executives in prospective client companies, the purpose of which was to learn what they would like—ideally—in a new test marketing service and, incidentally, to probe for IRI's weaknesses, as perceived by perspective clients.

They did take time out, however, to take a course on project management from Jim Cumberpatch, a consultant hired by ACN. "He was critical to our success," says Gold; "I doubt we would have made it without him." What they learned was put into immediate practice. The three—Busyn, Gold, and Bluhm—locked themselves in a conference room for one week and started to develop a plan, listing every need-to-do and contingency they could think of.

"We filled up blackboards with lists," recalls Gold, "and it seemed endless."

Adds Bluhm, "We identified 134 tasks and subtasks and set up the critical paths necessary to get them done on schedule." It was for Bluhm to expedite these plans, define the people needed to staff them, and to coordinate with other units of ACN, like the Media Research Group and computer services, which at the time weren't as accessible as desired because ACN was switching over from Honeywell to IBM computer systems, and "resources were strained."

Gold, in turn, was starting to shape up a client service staff, a particular concern because he was convinced that ACN could probably outdo IRI in that area. The decision was made to go outside ACN and hire people with relevant experience. ACN client service people would be recruited to the extent that they had the inclination and aptitude.

In early October, now very conscious of their resource needs, Busyn and his group made a progress report to McCurry and his staff. The main message: the market, as exemplified by BehaviorScan, was growing fast; IRI was vulnerable; ACN should speed up its efforts to build a comparable, or better, system. On November 4, 1983, Busyn wrote a 23-page memo—privileged and confidential, for internal use only—to outline the plan for a new service to be called ERIM (for Electronic Research for Insights into Marketing—a pick-up from ERIM-France, a leading test marketing company in France and an ACN subsidiary since the mid-1970s). The first service of ERIM, ACN's version of BehaviorScan, would be called TestSight.

Busyn's plan called for two TestSight market systems to be on-line by September 1984—just 10 months away. The crunch was on.

New Offices

In December 1983, the ERIM staff moved into its own offices in Deerfield, Ill., a short distance from ACN's headquarters. Space was much needed; staff was piling in. Irving J. Kuperman had come from MRCA to head systems/production. In a short time, he would recruit over 15 systems people, and it had been decided that an IBM 3083 in ACN's Green Bay, Wis., Computer Center would be the mainframe for ERIM operations. Jack E. Ryan, an ACN employee, moved over to head market operations, the actual fieldwork required to set up TestSight panel and retail store systems. Jim Wyza, media director of HBM/Creamer, Chicago, came on to handle that aspect of the TestSight service.

In January 1984 with its project charter in hand and a new ACN fiscal year starting, ERIM became a profit center within the Marketing Research Group USA, reporting to McCurry. An ERIM advisory task force, including representatives from Media Research Group (technical and statistical), MRG (statistical research and UPC scanning), and Systems/Production, was set up to facilitate internal cooperation.

The Missing Link

ERIM's goal from the start was to develop a system that was technically superior to IRI's BehaviorScan, if possible. But so far the only tangible step in that direction was to specify that TestSight markets to be in the

40,000–150,000 population class. This was in response to some client criticism of IRI's smaller markets. The other plus ACN hoped for was to have superior client servicing, but such things are, at best, subjective.

There was another development hanging fire which, potentially, could scuttle the whole ERIM plan. Just to equal BehaviorScan, ACN had to acquire or develop an electronic mechanism that would make possible specific household targeting of tv commercials, as applied to cable tv systems. Equipment in use at the time had patent strings attached.

The previous October, ERIM had gone to the Dunedin, Florida, R&D lab which backed up ACN's Media Research Group, developing the meters that are attached to tv sets in audience measuring systems. "We told them what we wanted, what we needed," says Gold, "and they thought about it for a while and said something like, 'We might be able to develop such a box—given two or three years.' When I told this to Art [Nielsen], he said, 'That's unacceptable. I've got an engineer you ought to talk with.'"

That engineer turned out to be the late Homer Marrs who was retired from Motorola, Inc., but still on the board—along with Nielsen.

"We gave him our wish list," recalls Gold, "and he said, 'Gimme a couple of days.' When he came back, he said, 'The fellow you should be talking with is Earl Gomersall.'" Gomersall, an ex-Motorola corporate vp, signed on with ERIM as a consultant.

About this same time, the FCC loosened its regulations regarding micro-band broadcasting, effectively opening numerous new channels on offbeat frequencies. This opened a big door for Gomersall; assuming it could obtain licenses in the markets desired, ERIM could theoretically, broadcast test tv commercials live over its own station—and completely bypass cable tv systems. What was required was a device that, when attached to a panel household's tv set, could cut in on hearing a broadcast signal, show the test commercial instead of what was on air naturally, and then cut back out—all so smoothly that people watching the tv set wouldn't be conscious of what had happened.

This, potentially, was the big break. If Gomersall could design the needed equipment, TestSight could bypass patent concerns related to the cable cut-in equipment as was being used in BehaviorScan, select test markets quite independent of their development as cable markets, and if patents would apply, have a lock on new technology. Especially important: this would enable ERIM to end-run some client concerns about cable system households, who are believed by some to be atypical in their demographic and tv-viewing characteristics. Hopes were high; this solution was far beyond what was hoped for—and it gave ERIM some high-tech of its own to crow about.

Two weeks later, Gomersall returned and said, "We can build such a box," and better yet, many of the component parts of the new device, called Telemeter, could be purchased "off the shelf." The Telemeter—in fact, a microcomputer with 64K RAM and 16K ROM—had to monitor tv viewing (just like the regular ACN meters used in audience measurement systems), had to perform the function of a sophisticated tv commercial traffic cop (cutting in test commercials as desired), had to be field-programmable, and had to provide videotex capability (permit two-way communications with the household), should that ever be required.

By August 1984, a prototype had been designed and bench-tested, but mass production and the sophisticated software needed to drive Telemeter were still formidable obstacles. The D-Day for TestSight to be up and operating in the first two markets, according to a revised time table, was just 11 months away.

ERIM contracted with Pensar, an electronics company in Appleton, Wis., to produce 20,000 Telemeters. A software company called TMQ, Inc. in Wheeling, Ill., and ERIM jointly formed a new company ICOM, in Buffalo Grove, Ill., to custom develop the software—without which the Telemeters were useless. If everything went smoothly, everything would be ready by the end of 1984 in time to install the first two TestSight markets in Sioux Falls, S.D., and Springfield, Mo. The Telemeter system development cost to date: about $2 million.

Going Public

On Thursday, September 6, 1984, just 30 days after the successful Telemeter bench test, ERIM splashed a public introduction of the TestSight System. Mailgrams were sent to 750 prospective clients. Fancy four-color brochures were ready for distribution. There were breakfast show-and-tell conferences for advertising and marketing executives in New York and Chicago, with Art Nielsen hosting one, Don McCurry, the other.

Talk was bold. Busyn said plans called for opening six to ten TestSight markets, given client demand; planning for the next two was underway, he added. Gold said that clients would have on-line access to TestSight databases. Much was made of the larger size (vis-à-vis BehaviorScan) markets and the ability to be independent of cable tv systems, although a description of exactly how that was to be accomplished was general in nature. "Sure, we took a risk," says Gold now, "but that's what this business is all about, taking risks."

ERIM's publicity campaign was timed to start with the conferences in New York and Chicago. Color advertisements appeared in *Advertising Age*, *Adweek*, *Marketing News* and *Marketing Communications*, and they ran through November. (A second, lighter schedule ran in January–May 1985.) News releases prepared by ACN's public relations department went out to trade and business publications. Articles on ERIM appeared in *The Researcher*, a quarterly publication ACN's Marketing Research Group sends to about 10,000 marketing and research executives, and *Newscast*, the comparable publication put out by ACN's Media Research Group.

ERIM executives were already programmed in as speakers at ARF conferences in New York and Chicago, and a special ARF Workshop on heavy-up advertising. One of Mr. Gold's speeches was printed as a pamphlet and mailed to a list of about 2,500 prime prospects for the ERIM service. ERIM started printing its own quarterly publication, *Testing Techniques*, for the same prime prospect list. Looking back, Mr. Gold says, "We got awareness fast."

Now the serious—make that imperative—business of selling clients on using the TestSight system started, with assurances that test data would be available in early 1985, and for-pay projects could start in June. This was uphill, inasmuch as clients were being asked to book on faith at this point, and an average advertising test in systems like BehaviorScan or TestSight can run from $150,000 to $200,000, and a full-fledged new product test market can cost from $250,000 up.

This selling was facilitated, however, by some subtle preselling Gold had done in the previous eight months. He had organized a series of meetings with prospective clients, some including up to 12 people, to advise about TestSight development plans and to solicit suggestions/advice. "We wanted their experience and involvement," says Gold, "and, of course, we wanted them to know about the quality we were building into the system." Wasn't he afraid that those people would tip off IRI about ERIM plans? "No," says Gold, "and we don't know of any case where that happened." What goes unsaid is that major research buyers like to see competition; it tends to drive prices down and provide bargaining leverage. Hence, they would provide verbal encouragement, if not financial support, for a new system like TestSight.

Scott Johnson had come from ACN client service the previous May to work for Gold as business development manager, and between them they lined up about $1 million worth of future projects before the end of 1984. The first clients to put money on the table: General Mills and Gillette, one of the accounts Busyn had handled when he ran ACN's Boston office.

Concurrently, Jack Ryan, ERIM's project manager for market operations, and his staff were rushing to set up Sioux Falls, S.D., and Springfield, Mo. (Another choice, Enid, Okla., had to be dropped because of lack of grocery trade cooperation.)

In each market, it was necessary to work with local grocery trade factors to agree on cooperation fees (an inducement to those stores not already equipped with UPC scanning equipment to install same); recruit a panel of about 2,500 households and build a household classification file; build a tv transmission station and tower; install Telemeters in panel households along with special antennae on their rooftops to pick up ACN commercial test signals; and recruit and train the local staff needed to operate and maintain such an installation. Things were ready by March to start running test data and get to the debugging.

Back in Deerfield, Gold was setting up his client service staff—a group of 16 headed by two group account managers. Bluhm had designed an extensive client service training course, and new employees were being trained on the job—down to giving them some of the rich history of ACN, which was founded in 1923.

D-Day

On June 30, 1985, just 26 months after Busyn's presentation to ACN's management committee and Nielsen's mandate to "go," the first, live for-money client project started in TestSight. There were 10 projects from seven client companies on the books, and several more were expected once prospective clients were convinced that TestSight was "for real." ERIM was planning two additional markets, and a New York sales/service office was scheduled to open in January 1986.

One last promotional shot in the arm by ERIM marketing: a mailing to its 2,500 prime prospect list, which included a coupon good for $25,000 off an ERIM test, which hit just as ERIM service started.

All told, about $16 million had been invested—salaries, equipment, marketing, general administration, and overhead. As for what it took to get from here to there, Busyn says, "We've burned people up."

Interview with Arthur Nielsen, Jr.

I interviewed Arthur C. Niesen, Jr. on July 3, 1985, just three days after the first for-pay project started in the TestSight system.

Much had happened since the meeting on April 1, 1983. The Nielsen family interests, on May 18, 1984, announced plans to sell the A. C. Nielsen Co. to Dun & Bradstreet Co. for $1.1 billion in D&B stock. Nielsen, now one of the largest individual stockholders in D&B, took a place on its board of directors and started to phase out his involvement in the Nielsen Co., where he relinquished his titles of chairman and CEO.

Although out of touch with day-to-day developments of the ERIM project, Nielsen still has lively reminiscenes of how it all came to be, and after some general discussion of how the Nielsen Co. pioneered in electronic data collection techniques back in the 1930s, we focused down on ERIM. Here's how it went....

Marketing a Marketing Information Service   111

HONOMICHL: Were you suprised by the success of IRI [Information Resources, Inc.]?

NIELSEN: I think so, Jack; I didn't think it would be as big as it turned out to be.

HONOMICHL: When did people here at ACN really begin to take it seriously?

NIELSEN: I guess probably about two years ago.

HONOMICHL: About the time they went public?

NIELSEN: Maybe even a little later than that. We thought it was a good method of testing, but we didn't realize how much more advertising testing, apparently, would be done if there was a better technique.

HONOMICHL: You think IRI expanded the market?

NIELSEN: I think they did. Also they have another feature—I think they call it a Fact Book—a compendium of the markets they measure which shows the sales of product classes and composition of buyers. I've always thought that that composition of the buyers or the demographics was a very important part of diary-panel research. It's useful in advertising; you find out who buys a product, you know where to direct your advertising.

I've always been less sure of the claim that the panel makes that it can shorten the time interval of finding out whether a new product is successful. Theoretically, if you can find out that a family bought the product and it continues to buy the product, then you are on the right track; you've got something that has merit. However, the samples are awfully small. Some people buy it and some people don't buy it, and I've always felt you had to allow a decent interval to go by for people to decide whether they really liked it; they might go back to their old product. So I've favored the slower method, which would be readily apparent in a store audit project; if the share began to rise, you knew that people were taking to it.

But I think there is a natural desire among businesspeople to find out as quickly as possible whether they have a good idea, a new product to invest in. They want to know that, and they want to get it out in the marketplace before a competitor picks up the idea and takes some of the opportunity away from them by matching it.

HONOMICHL: When ACN set up ERIM, a separate group, and allowed it to go outside, hire whomever they wanted, and so on, to get the job done—there's never been anything like that at ACN previously has there?

NIELSEN: That was an unusual departure for us. Traditionally, we would put it under an established organization and hire additional people who would be managed by the established organization.

HONOMICHL: Do you think that when a company gets to be as big and prosperous and as compartmentalized as ACN, it's almost necessary to set up one of these side groups to get something new going and get it going fast? A lot of companies believe this, you know.

NIELSEN: I don't know whether that's the best way or not. In the literature which you've read and I've read, a lot of companies do that with good results, so it must be an effective method. My own style of management, I try not to get involved. If the group president thinks that's the best method, and if it's a reasonable assumption, I would not oppose it. I think if I were the group president in this case, I would not have done it that way.

HONOMICHL: You would have done it strictly in-house?

NIELSEN: I think the reason I favor that method—and it's just a personal matter of organization—you can rely on people whom you've worked with for years; you know who will do the work, and on whom you can rely. If you have to go out and hire new people and give them authority and responsibility, and so on, inevitably you find people who are not trained in your methods, and you always have the possibility that they're not the kind of people you'd hoped they would be, and you make a few mistakes there. So, that's the other side of it—and, also, I don't think you have the muscle to turn on a project.

If you have a good production vice president under your regular organization, and you succeed in gaining his enthusiasm for a new project, he has a lot of resources he can put to work on it. If you do it the other way, you have to go slower; you have to hire people, train them, and so on.

HONOMICHL: Let's assume ERIM is a success. Do you think then you would change your mind and, as ACN got into other relatively new areas, you'd follow the same pattern—set up a separate thing off to the side and let the man do what he wants to do to make it go?

NIELSEN: Well, I think this, Jack: if you get too many of those, it gets too darned hard to manage; I don't think a manager can look after too many different pieces. Somebody has to be responsible for each one of these.

Having said that, I think that if the project that you're going into is something that you know a fair amount about, you're better off to stick with your own organization, because those people understand it and they can learn it and go to work. If you get too far from home, and you start something that's radically different and you can't really put anybody on it from your organization who knows much about it, you're better off if you go outside and get some people. Maybe then it would be better to hire a manager who understood that industry and let him make some of the decisions, and not try to tell him what to do when you don't know yourself.

HONOMICHL: When ERIM was launched back on April 1, 1983, did you have any idea it was going to get to be as big as it is today with 130 people...?

NIELSEN: If I had been the active manager, I wouldn't have done it that way. My theory on starting something is to go around and talk to the potential users and get their ideas, listen carefully to what they have to tell you, then see if you can fashion something that, if successfully implemented, would meet their requirements. And you would hope that they would support that work, not only by encouraging you, but that they would also execute some contracts so that it would be a binding relationship. I think that is what I would have done, and I've done it in most cases in the past. Here, there was a great deal of enthusiasm. BehaviorScan had a notable success, and I think the fellows here were of the opinion that all they had to do was fashion something that was somewhat similar and that the market would be there. Maybe it is, but that's taking a long chance. My way is perhaps more conservative; at least, you don't get your neck out quite as far.

HONOMICHL: It's past tense now; you've incurred all the developmental money on the Telemeter, the systems, and all that. Doesn't that speak for trying to take the ERIM system into other countries—Germany, France, etc.—and trying to amortize that development work over a lot of your different markets?

NIELSEN: I think that makes good sense, Jack.

HONOMICHL: Are there plans to do that?

NIELSEN: I think you'd be better off talking to Dick Vipond [Richard W. Vipond, president of the Marketing Research Group]. He would be able to tell you. It's a matter, I guess, of timing. Frankly, I'm not up to date as to how many European stores have scanners and whether you could find the right markets.

My contribution, if anything, to this ERIM project was to point out the limitations of cable. The number of households that have cable—if you had to use that as the method of directing the advertising—would not produce a representative sample.

I've done a lot of surveys, as you have, and you know that the fear is that the people who aren't in the samples are behaving differently than the ones who are.

What I was trying to figure out was, is there any way that you can accomplish the objective and get the signal into all homes—a really true cross section? This is where I think I may have made a contribution. I hope so.

I've been a director of Motorola for many years; they were the people who developed the Walkie Talkie, and they have tremendous expertise in sending radio signals. If you go in a taxi cab or police car, or fire station, they all use Motorola equipment. The fellow who ran that communications part of Motorola was a very ingenious fellow named Homer Marrs, and some years ago Homer had told me that he had figured out how to save householders costs of heating their water, and also help the power company avoid peak loads. Most people keep water hot all day when the family is out working, so Homer figured out how to send a radio signal to turn off the water heater. When the power company wanted to turn it back on, they could send a signal back. I asked Homer, "Is there any way you could send a signal that would carry a tv commercial? Could you figure out how to do that?"

He was always the kind of man who was challenged by a new idea, and he said, "I don't know, but let me think about it." A couple of weeks later he called and said he thought he'd figured out how to do it. He had just retired from Motorola, so I said, "How about helping on this thing? Maybe we could make something out of it; you could be our consultant." So he came over, and he talked to me, and we went into it a little more. Then he went back, and he called again and said, "I really think you ought to hire a man who is younger, has more technical competence. I know the theory of this, but you've got to have a practical fellow to design the equipment and so on, and I'll bring him over." This was Earl Gomersall.

Since my relationship with Motorola was such I didn't want to be in a position of inducing one of their valued employees to quit and come to work for us, I talked to the fellows at Motorola. They were very kind to me and said, "Sure, if this is what you need, Art, go ahead and hire Earl." So Earl came over, worked on this thing night and day, and manfully brought the equipment up and got it going. It reminded me quite a bit of my dad's early efforts to develop the Audimeter.

HONOMICHL: ACN was a pioneer in electronic data collection back in the '30s. Somewhere along the way ACN lost that— call it what you will—high-tech, innovation thrust.

NIELSEN: We were like the tortoise; we kept coming along. I could show you probably 15 variations of the Audimeter, for instance. Not too many people were interested in measuring tv or radio by meter —maybe Arbitron, ourselves, and maybe a couple of others. So we had to develop our own; we had to set up our own laboratory.

There are not enough units made to justify some other outside supplier doing it, so we had to manufacture them ourselves, and we have perfected the thing; at least, I'll say we've improved it year after year.

But in any engineering thing like that [ERIM], you run into problems, and you have to solve them. Earl is a very clever fellow, and he hit the problem and solved it.

I think a problem with the ERIM project has been that the fellows are too optimistic about the time that it takes in an R&D project to overcome the obstacles—because you just don't know what they are going to be. Tomorrow there's another one, and you have to work on that, and then the next day there's something else. It was the same with the Audimeter in the early days—certain things that keep bothering you.

HONOMICHL: It's getting so that the engineering people are becoming the most important people to a research company, it seems, with all this emphasis on electronic data collection, and innovations in that.

NIELSEN: It was a great day for marketing research back in January of 1946 when I made my first recommendation of any importance to my dad—that we buy a machine which I had seen in the Army and had built the building to house it. It was the Univac 1, the first commercial electronic computer. Interestingly enough it took five years to build that. And IBM, hard to believe now, didn't think it would work and turned it down when we went to them and asked them to help build it. So we got in on the ground floor of the computer. I know that helped our company because it did two important things: it reduced the cost of doing our work and that enabled us to sell more people who couldn't afford—at least they claimed they couldn't afford—our work, and also speeded up delivery of the reports.

HONOMICHL: Collateral to that, of course, is patent lawyers, being able to protect an innovation or get around the competitors. Companies like ACN must have patent lawyers on retainer all the time. It's all getting so darned legalistic.

NIELSEN: We have had a hard time on this. One of the problems we have in the Television Index, for instance, is that the U.S. law is such that you have to get your hot hands—if you'll pardon that expression—on the other fellow's equipment and then demonstrate to the judge that he had infringed your patent. We have had a total lack of cooperation from Arbitron for years. At one point we proved that they were infringing our patents and got a license from them. They paid us for it, but then we got into a position where they claimed that we were monopolizing the business, and they got the Federal Trade Commission to say that they didn't have to pay us anything. We have felt for years that they are infringing our patents, but we can't prove it because they won't give us the machine. And there's no way in the legal process in the U.S. that we can get our hands on it without stealing one, and we're not going to do that.

HONOMICHL: The court won't mandate that they give you the equipment?

NIELSEN: No, and they refuse to do it.

HONOMICHL: On the grounds that it's proprietary?

NIELSEN: I don't know on what grounds, but they take the position that they won't show it to us, and they just say, "We're not infringing." Well, how do we know? We spent a lot of money inventing these things and other people copy them. The same thing was true in Japan. We know that Dentsu violated our patents, but we didn't have any protection there. So, what I'm trying to say, Jack, is you can have patent lawyers but...I'm not sure it does you a heck of a lot of good.

8 The Marketing of Arm & Hammer

The "I've got a secret..." advertising campaign that ran for Arm & Hammer baking soda, starting in February 1971, has come to be recognized as a classic. But the full, behind-the-scenes story of how imaginative and aggressive marketing propelled sleepy old Church & Dwight Company into extraordinary growth and rejuvenation had never been told before the following story appeared in Advertising Age, *on September 20, 1982. Indeed, it would not have been told thoroughly without the full cooperation of Robert A. Davies III, president of Church & Dwight at the time.*

The interview with Davies, at the end of this chapter, is extraordinarily candid—and revealing. Unfortunately, space limitations in Advertising Age *kept the full interview from being published. The full story follows on these pages.*

Editor's Note: *Mr. Honomichl's Arm & Hammer article won top prize for 1982 in the annual Journalism Awards Competition sponsored by Compton Advertising, Inc., which is meant to "honor the writers of those articles [about advertising] which are particularly creative and thought provoking."*

The Marketing Story—The Product as Hero

The hero of this story is the product, which is a marketing manager's dream come true.

The raw material is plentiful and relatively cheap to mine and process. The product itself is a colorless, odorless powder with a slightly salty taste. It has a multitude of uses ranging from an ingredient in cookie recipes to the deodorization of septic tanks, to use on movie sets to simulate snow. Many of its uses have not yet been exploited commercially, and each year thousands of consumers write to tell about new uses they think they've discovered. The product's brand name has unaided recognition among 97% of female heads of households in the United States, and the goodwill it enjoys is awesome. The package is a simple cardboard box, and for all practical purposes, there is no limit on shelf life. Almost all grocery stores stock it. Surveys show that, at any point in time, about 95% of all U.S. households have one or more packages in use. There are no branded competitive products of consequence.

Product usage in some, if not all, instances is very responsive to advertising. The marketing strategy since 1980 has been to lower price to give the product an even better cost/value relationship. The biggest problem marketing management has is the broadening of usage through consumer education programs and the development of flanker products—and, more recently, cost competition from no-name generic brands.

This paragon of marketing virtues is Arm & Hammer Baking Soda, a brand marketed by the Arm & Hammer Division of Church & Dwight Company, Inc., Piscataway, New Jersey. Its affectionate nickname in-house is "mother baking soda," and its history dates back to 1846 when cofounder John Dwight opened a "plant" in his kitchen to process and package the fine powder that it is, technically, sodium bicarbonate, or $NaHCO_3$.

Church & Dwight's net sales in 1982 were expected to be about $150 million, almost a tenfold increase over the level ($15.6 million) in 1969 when the company started its much-publicized product proliferation program under the spur of Robert A. Davies III, who came from a group product manager post at Boyle–Midway (division of American Home Products) to become vp, marketing at Church & Dwight. In 1976 Davies moved up to vp/general manager, Arm & Hammer Division, and in March 1981 he was named president and chief operating officer of Church & Dwight.

Up until 1969, Arm & Hammer Baking Soda was a sleepy, one-dimensional brand—albeit a staple on the grocer's shelf—with an advertising budget of less than $500,000 a year, mostly in print. What has happened since then, however, is a fascinating story—the saga of a high-pressure campaign to exploit the venerable Arm & Hammer name and logo by (1) an advertising blitz to promote new uses for the product and accelerate the use-up rate, (2) the development of new flanker items keyed to specific usage/applications, and (3) the creation of entirely new products.

What follows is an insider's story of this campaign, which includes consumer research data and internal C&D figures never before made public. And if you're one of those many people who has always been a mite hazy about what this thing called "marketing" is all about, hang on: you're about to get a cram course that should make it perfectly clear.

Cool Sales Spur

The single most dramatic move Arm & Hammer made—and the one, of course, that has received most attention in the press—was the stimulation, via advertising, of an extended use for baking soda, namely putting an open box inside a refrigerator as an air freshener/deodorant.

Advertising was prepared by Arm & Hammer's agency (Kelly, Nason at the time; it's now defunct), and a test was run in 1972 on a network television West Coast feed. (In the balance of the country, the company was then airing a commercial boosting baking soda for light-duty cleaning chores.) Table 8.1 shows the dramatic results of that test, as measured by tracking surveys done via telephone. Eventually, the penetration numbers leveled off at about 80%.

Table 8.1 Result of 1972 Television Test Advertising for Regrigerator-use on the West Coast

Households Saying They Have Used Baking Soda in Refrigerator as a Deodorant (West Coast)	
May 1973	63%
March 1973	57
October 1972	43
June 1972	38
May 1972	27
February 1972	19

Well, you gotta believe the early results of that test got the marketing adrenalin flowing back at the home office. "Our brokers started calling in," recalls Burton B. Staniar, who had come from Colgate–Palmolive to C&D in 1970 as a group business manager, "and they said the shelves were empty; there were out-of-stock problems all over the West Coast. We knew we had discovered gold."

Quite naturally, Arm & Hammer moved quickly to get that refrigerator copy onto the total network, and results (shown in table 8.2) were equally dramatic. Eventually, these numbers leveled off at about 90%.

The bottom line is that in 1971 C&D sold 2,300,000 equivalent 24-pound cases of Arm & Hammer Baking Soda into grocery channels. In 1974, it sold 3,965,000 cases. That's a 72% increase, and almost all of it was due to the refrigerator deodorant campaign.

Table 8.2 Results of 1972 National Television Campaign for Refrigerator-use

Households Saying They Have Used Baking Soda in Refrigerator as an Air Freshener/Deodorant (Total U.S.)	
March 1973	57%
October 1972	45
June 1972	38
February 1972	1

A logical extension of this very successful move was to go a step further—run advertising to suggest that another box of Arm & Hammer Baking Soda be put inside the refrigerator's freezer compartment for the same purpose. Table 8.3 shows how that expanded usage campaign produced.

Table 8.3 Results of National Television Campaign for Freezer Use

% Households Saying They Have Used Baking Soda in Refrigerator Freezer as a Deodorant (Total U.S.)

Year	%
1981	28%
1980	24
1979	18
1978	12

Successful as these campaigns were, they also pointed up a weakness in the refrigerator/deodorizer usage pattern, namely: someone might go for the concept, buy a box of baking soda, put it into the refrigerator (or freezer), and then forget it. It could sit there for months, and that didn't induce repeat purchasing. So, how to speed up that process? The answer was advertising designed to get the box out of the refrigerator. The idea was that after the box of Arm & Hammer had worked in the refrigerator for a while, remove it and pour the contents down the kitchen drain to deodorize it, too. Table 8.4 shows the results of that limited campaign.

Table 8.4 Results of Limited Television Campaign for Re-use

Households Saying They Have Used Baking Soda in the Drain of their Sink as a Deodorizer (Total U.S.)

Date	%
June 1977	67%
January 1977	62
July 1976	53
April 1976	46
November 1975	43

Behind the Campaign

"There are at least 10 guys running around New York claiming some credit for the refrigerator campaign idea," says Gerald Schoenfeld, president of Gerald Schoenfeld, Inc., a consulting firm specializing in new product concepts. He should know; Schoenfeld is the most conspicuous of the 10. You may have noted the advertisements his firm runs in *Advertising Age*; the headline is "Who Put Baking Soda in the Refrigerator?"

Back in 1969–76, however, Schoenfeld was president of Kelly, Nason, and creator of the now-famous refrigerator commercial, "I've got a secret ...[in the refrigerator]." In addition to Schoenfeld, I've also talked with Reynald M. Swift, who in 1971 came from American Cyanamid to C&D as product manager on baking soda. Between the two, I have tried to piece together the true story of how the West Coast test came to be. This should help dispel the many "personalized" versions that now circulate.

Circa 1969–70, many focus groups were exploring new product use concepts, and most of the attention was on the cleaning applications of baking soda. Among other things, recalls Schoenfeld, who moderated many of the groups himself, respondents were exposed to some of the very earliest print ads for Arm & Hammer, one of which promoted the use of baking soda for cleaning the inside walls of iceboxes.

"The idea was in existence when I came aboard," adds Swift; "it already had project status. But it was nothing new; 'put some in the refrigerator' was a usage suggestion on Arm & Hammer boxes back in the mid-1930s." He also notes that, historically, baking soda had been widely accepted as a mild cleanser for the cleaning of refrigerator surfaces, so it was a short and logical bridge for the consumer to accept use of it to clean the air too.

"The theme of sweetening, freshening kept coming up [in focus groups]," recalls Schoenfeld, "but at first I didn't pay much attention; we were concentrating on cleaning ideas. It kept coming up though, and I started to get excited that we might be on to something."

"When we put the proposition to respondents directly—'Your refrigerator smells, and baking soda will cure that'—it didn't go over at all," says Swift. "But when we came through the back door and worded the proposition in such a way that it didn't imply the woman was a lousy housekeeper, they showed a lot of interest in the idea." That realization led to Schoenfeld's oblique "I've got a secret..." copy.

One hunch expressed by Schoenfeld is that some women feel guilty that they do not clean their refrigerator as often as they think they should. Putting a box of baking soda inside at least cleans the air, and that alleviates some of the guilt—and no work is required.

Not everyone at C&D was enthusiastic about the idea—especially the old guard—and, Staniar recalls, "It was just one of dozens of ideas we were considering. The important thing is the strategic decision, featuring just one use in advertising instead of several and going onto network tv."

In any case, momentum for testing the refrigerator copy on-air kept building amongst the C&D marketing group, and the result was a cause célèbre in American marketing history. As for Schoenfeld, he told me, "It's been a meal ticket for me."

Previous Expansion Efforts

Famous as the refrigerator caper is, it was not the first attempt by Davies and the company to expand the usage of Arm & Hammer Baking Soda. A network television campaign in 1971 promoted its use in bath water to smooth dry, flaky skin, and, as noted, a commercial promoting household cleaning chores was on-air nationwide in 1972. Together, these experiments in single-use advertising and tv had produced a sales increase of about 10%.

But both of these efforts were overshadowed by an even more ambitious—and audacious—move to broaden the Church & Dwight business base. In 1970, Davies decided to exploit a growing public concern with ecology by introducing a non poluting laundry detergent under the Arm & Hammer name, a move not so surprising when you know that, prior to Boyle–Midway, Davies had been a product manager in the Household Products Division of Colgate–Palmolive. (Before that, he was a salesman with Procter & Gamble.) But when a company with annual revenues of about $16 million takes on P&G and Colgate in their most important product category...that's gutsy (or, if you should fail, stupid).

You may recall that at the time there was considerable public concern about phosphates in detergents feeding algae growth in public streams, and products that were not biodegradable were being banned in grocery stores in some communities.

Arm & Hammer Heavy Duty Detergent—which, incidentally, has never had a baking soda ingredient—found immediate acceptance. "We had a $25 million business almost overnight," says Staniar. In some markets, share of market topped 10%, and nationally the brand today still holds about 3% share although it is not in full distribution. (In 1981, this product was restaged; price was lowered, and a "value price too" strategy was adopted.)

Church & Dwight's sales had gone from $15.6 million in 1969 to $57.9 million five years later. Given that this had been achieved by a brash bunch of new marketing employees (recruited from General Foods, Block Drug, P&G, Colgate-Palmolive, and American Cyanamid) who had faced up to P&G and held their own and who had launched one of the most successful advertising campaigns in history, it is not surprising that a giddy attitude of "we can do anything with the Arm & Hammer name" had come to prevail at Church & Dwight. Obviously, it had become difficult for the "old guard" to oppose new ideas, no matter how off-the-wall they might have seemed, and growth was largely self-financing.

In this atmostphere then came an avalanche of new business-building moves, which can be grouped as follows:

- *Promoting increases in established uses for the basic baking soda, mostly via suggested uses on package and advertising.*
  Cleaning kitchen surfaces, additive to bath water, baking ingredient, laundry additive, and general household cleaning chores.

- *Creating new uses for basic baking soda, again mostly by advertising and suggestions on package.*
  Refrigerator/freezer air deodorant, cat litter deodorant, dog deodorant, water treatment in swimming pools, septic tank deodorant, kitchen drain deodorant, and as a dentifrice (plaque removal claim).
- *Development of flanker products—basic baking soda in special packaging aimed at specific use segments.*
  Rug/carpet deodorizer, cat litter deodorizer, and a kitchen cleaner that failed.
- *Development of entirely new products, capitalizing on the Arm & Hammer name/logo.*
  Heavy-duty laundry detergent, oven cleaner, liquid detergent, and two conspicuous failures—a spray underarm deodorant and a spray disinfectant.

Some packaging innovations also stemmed from this effort—for instance, the introduction of a four-pound box of Arm & Hammer Baking Soda to tie in with heavy-use applications, such as swimming pools and septic tanks, and the creation of entirely new packaging, which, in the case of cat litter deodorizer, got baking soda into the supermarket's pet food section, near cat box litter.

Research Guidance

Sifting and evaluating so many new ideas—plus many more that died aborning—suggests a considerable amount of consumer and marketing research, and Church & Dwight has had a very active program, about spending about $500,000 a year, on average. But to this day, C&D does not have a marketing research staffer.

In lieu of the traditional research setup, C&D has since 1971 funnelled almost all its research—well over 150 studies at this point—through one research firm, Behavioral Analysis, Inc., in Irvington, N.Y., and its president, Richard Reiser.

"We've done just about every kind of study there is," says Reiser, citing segmentation studies, tracking of usage and awareness, on-air and off-air copy testing, product placement tests, price elasticity studies, promotion testing, image studies, and—obviously—concept testing, some of which has been focused on special ownership segments like septic tank or swimming pool owners.

"This continuity is important," notes Reiser, "because we've been able to build up a comprehensive body of knowledge that probably wouldn't result from a bunch of unrelated, ad hoc studies. Also, we've wasted little time and money in studying the same phenomenon twice."

The Bottom Line

Behavioral Analysis, Inc. (BAI), on the basis of studies they've conducted, estimates how much of the basic Arm & Hammer Baking Soda volume is consumed by end-use applications in the home. (These estimates *do not* include plus-volume gained via flankers or new products; they just relate to the basic Yellow Box volume, which in turn accounted for about one-third of total Church & Dwight dollar volume in 1981.)

Back in 1970, the year of departure, Yellow Box volume was 2.3 million cases. BAI estimates for that year say that the single most important end use was cleaning refrigerator surfaces, which accounted for about one-third of the tonnage. The second most important uses were bath water treatment and general household cleaning. Other important end uses were as a skin rash treatment, deodorizer, and the cleaning of teeth. Use in baking, it is estimated, accounted for only 6% of end-use volume, which might be surprising since the product is called "baking soda." It was too late to change the product's name, however.

By 1981, case volume on Yellow Box had grown to 5 million cases. But now the main end use, by far, was to deodorize refrigerator air, which accounted for about 25%. The second most important use was general household cleaning, and secondary uses were bath water treatment, cleaning refrigerator surfaces, skin rash treatment, rug deodorizer, cat box litter deodorizer, kitchen drain deodorizer, septic tank deodorizer, swimming pool treatment, etc.

In 1981, baking still accounted for 6% of the estimated end-use consumption, but, since the base had doubled, it meant that over twice as many cases were being used for that purpose. And that's an interesting result of all the promotion—the introduction of new uses did not take from the established uses of 1970; if anything, it expanded the tonnage they represented, if not the relative importance.

"If we had done anything less," says Staniar, "it would have been a failure. The Arm & Hammer name has such phenomenal strength, such good equity, it was hard to do anything wrong. Even if we screwed up—as we did with the underarm deodorant, that was a bad product—the consumer forgave us."

"The Arm & Hammer name, in fact, presents a very serious research problem," says Reiser. "Whenever we associate it with a new product or concept, consumer acceptance and 'will buy' intentions are always unrealistically high; consumers are reluctant to reject Arm & Hammer. Factoring down to the reality of the situation is always difficult."

(In 1975, Helene Curtis Industries, Inc. edged too close to the magic Arm & Hammer name by marketing an underarm deodorant called "Arm and Arm Deodorant." Church & Dwight brought a trademark infringement suit and won. The settlement of $2 million in 1979 was one of the largest in U.S. legal history.)

The Current Situation

A concern at Arm & Hammer currently is the importance of no-name, generic baking sodas; these products now have about 10% of the category volume. This has led Church & Dwight to emphasize the word "pure" on boxes (reminiscent of the Bayer aspirin effort some years back to further differentiate their product from low-price competition by stressing quality control), the lowering of price (twice within the past two years), and an ever-growing use of trade and consumer deals, including coupons.

This situation, of course, spurs even further efforts to develop "enhanced" baking soda-based products that cannot so easily be duplicated by manufacturers of the basic soda ash.

On the brighter side, Davies is presently very enthusiastic about a new use for baking soda: when it is added to cow feed, the cows reportedly produce more and better milk. Now, when you stop to think about how many milk cows are being fed every day...maybe, just maybe, the refrigerator deodorant campaign might turn out to be the second most important case history at Church & Dwight.

Baking Soda: What Is It? How Does It Work?

Baking soda is a derivative of trona ore. One of the richest deposits in the United States is located from 600 to 2,400 feet below ground in southwestern Wyoming, where Church & Dwight has its largest production facility. These deposits were an accidental find, the by-product of gas and oil exploration drilling in the 1930s.

Technically, trona ore is a mineral composed of about 85% sodium sesquicarbonate—a hard crystal-like material. It is mined much like coal and brought to the surface through deep shafts. The ore is crushed and heated to about 500° F. to burn off foreign materials and convert it to sodium carbonate, or soda ash as it is most commonly known. The yield is about 60%. Church & Dwight purchases soda ash and then in its own plants reacts it with water and carbon dioxide to produce sodium bicarbonate, or baking soda—a granular substance that is colorless and odorless with a characteristic salty taste.

The job baking soda does in eliminating odors inside a refrigerator, for instance, is best understood if you think of odors as chemicals, whose presence in the air can be measured. ("But the instruments we use aren't as sensitive as a human nose," says Dr. Richard Lehne, director of corporate regulatory affairs at Church & Dwight. "The average nose is still the best instrument made to detect odors.")

Some such odors are acidic and have a negative electrical charge while some are basic with a positive electrical charge; both are neutralized by baking soda. Other odors, the nonionic or neutral ones, are absorbed in a

The Arm & Hammer Baking Soda box, once simplistic, is now a montage of marketing elements, partly because of an increasingly competitive environment. A one pound box like this can contain (1) a proof-of-purchase seal, (2) a cookie recipe, (3) a money-back guarantee statement, (4) usage (deodorizer and cleanser) suggestions and instructions, (5) a cook book ("All Time Baking Soda Favorites") offer, and (6) usage directions as an antacid. The familiar Arm & Hammer logo is one link to the past; it has been in use on baking soda since 1867.

sponge-like process. At any time, a refrigerator could have all three types of odors or chemicals in the air, and the deodorization process going on is quite complex.

"In fact," says Lehne, "we're not completely familiar with the entire mechanism, despite considerable testing. In any case, the process is so effective that even if a box of baking soda weren't opened, odors would be filtered right through the cardboard and absorbed/neutralized. Also baking soda has a finite chemical life, but it does not start to work its absorbent magic and lose this life until an odor is in the air to react with it."

In a "normal" refrigerator, with "normal" odors, tests show a one-pound box of baking soda can absorb/neutralize about two months' worth of odor chemicals.

Human bodies also manufacture sodium bicarbonate, which helps to maintain the proper acid-base balance in the blood stream. When you take an antacid with sodium bicarbonate, what you are doing, in effect, is supplying a concentrated dose of sodium bicarbonate directly into the excess stomach acid that the body has been unable to neutralize in a "normal" fashion. Incidentally, notice and description of sodium bicarbonate as a pharmaceutical product first appeared in U.S. medical literature in 1840.

In baking, baking soda serves as a leavening agent since, when heated or put in contact with an acidic material, it produces gaseous carbon dioxide and a sodium salt. Baking soda also works as a cleaner, since it is a mild alkali which, when mixed with fatty acids normally found in dirt and grease, makes a form of soap. This "soap," in turn, cleans, aided by a gentle abrasive texture.

And what happens when milady adds baking soda to her bath water? The human skin is always growing, and the top layer consists of protein scales (called keratin), which feel flaky. Baking soda reacts with keratin in a softening process, and the result is a smooth-feeling skin. How does it work? "We're not exactly sure," says Dr. Lehne, "but it does a good job."

According to Dr. Lehne, no single man-made substance could do all the jobs baking soda does as effectively; it would take several such products.

Bob Davies Looks Back: "If I had to do over again"

Robert A. Davies III came to Church & Dwight in 1969 as vp-marketing in the Arm & Hammer Division. In 1976, he became general manager of the Arm & Hammer Division, and in 1981, president of Church & Dwight Company.

In August 1982, I interviewed Davies at Church & Dwight headquarters in Piscataway, N.J., during which he reflected on the past 13 years, the good and bad decisions, and the advice he'd give to other companies interested in a broad new-product expansion program.

HONOMICHL: Looking back, if you had it to do over again, what would you do differently?

DAVIES: First of all, I'm kind of pleased with what we've done. But if I had to do it over again? Well, I think of a series of things. The first thing I would have done is recognize the value of baking soda itself as a brand much earlier because we spent fully the first two or three years working on anything but baking soda. There was a fair amount of wasted money in there, certainly a lot of wasted time, a lack of focus.

There was a going-in assumption that the strength here was the brand name, Arm & Hammer, and there was an equal assumption that baking soda was an unexciting product in and of itself that was profitable and could generate some money, but had little value in terms of building the brand. I think the number one thing is to have recognized that earlier.

A second thing is that I would have moved slower. We were in a great rush to be successful and to proceed, and to grow, and to develop. When I joined the company, it was only very modestly profitable in relation to its operations; the profitability it enjoyed was mainly the result of its portfolio, its investments. There was a great rush to get the operating business larger and more profitable, and this caused mistakes to be made, caused some products to be marketed that should not have been marketed, caused a lot of marketing development dollars—both in R&D technology and marketing research—to be spent that need not have been spent. It caused products to go to market before they were ready to go to market, and it caused some decisions to expand broadly when the proper thing to do was to continue test marketing. So, the second thing would be to not have rushed nearly as much.

A third thing I would have done, which is consistent with the second, is that I wouldn't have staffed nearly as rapidly. I built a lot of staff quite early, and the staff began to take on a life of its own to justify its existence. We were able to attract extraordinarily bright and talented people to the company—quite frankly, more people than we could possible keep busy and consume and find resourceful jobs for—and too many people working on a problem is, I guess, every bit as bad, if not worse than—in fact, I'll say it was worse—than too few people working on a problem.

At one point in time—gee, I don't remember for sure—not too long after I was here, maybe after three years, we must have had 10 or 12 people in the marketing department. That was a lot of people given the status of the business. We were always staffing to meet next year's, or the following year's, or three year's from now perceived needs. And that didn't further the perceived development of the business; in fact, I think it tended to hinder us, to tie us up.

A fourth thing I would have done—I went through a period when I relinquished too much authority to the marketing organization. I had this relatively large group of talented, energetic, hardworking, resourceful, inventive people, and I was a young guy—I was in my mid-30s at that point in time—and I went through a period where I thought it was a good, sound management practice to get best results by giving lots and lots of authority to very capable people. That's a very positive practice to energize people, to turn them on, making them alive and resourceful and whatnot, but if you don't at the same time use your own experience base and judgment and keep very careful control on what is going on, a lot of dollars and time can be wasted. There was a period—three or four years—when I went too far down that road; I think that was an error.

I would be very, very careful in the new products area (I don't think this comment is equally applicable to established products)—to acting on a situation in the interest of competitive pressures—I'd be very, very careful of that. At one time, we saw some of our good ideas being snapped up by competitors or would-be competitors, and, of course, when you see your idea about to be implemented by somebody else, this gets the hackles up; not only are you afraid you're going to lose the opportunity, but there is a whole emotional thing that overrides, that says, "By heavens, we've been working on this idea, and no one else should do anything with baking soda except this company." This precipitated some decisionmaking that turned out not to be sound for the company. I would be very, very cautious making decisions in the new product area because of competitive pressure. With established products, I think that would be a poor rule; if you don't react to competition in your established products, you'll be dead.

HONOMICHL: What do you regard, in retrospect, to be the largest single mistake you made?

DAVIES: The most costly error we made was to go national with personal deodorant at a time that wasn't appropriate, with a product that wasn't ready to go to market, with a selling proposition that wasn't finely honed, with what I think turned out to be the wrong form of product; that was the most costly error we made, in terms of costs you can see.

However, the larger error—one that I've already touched on—was maybe in simply not moving more slowly, more deliberately, in terms of organization, structure, strategy, product development—following the principle that a more deliberate, measured, careful approach will get you ahead further. It's the tortoise and hare story.

HONOMICHL: Wouldn't that have lost you some of your momentum, the enthusiasm that was building up?

DAVIES: I'm sure we would have lost something, but if you stop and think that if with that you had staffed for a more deliberate and slow approach—and I don't mean to communicate that the place would have become a sleepy little corner; that's not part of my thinking—but a more measured, deliberate, studied approach—crawling before walking, walking before running—I think it could have been on a basis that would still have been exciting. Could be wrong.

HONOMICHL: Weren't the people around here, including yourself, terrified at the prospect of a $15 million company facing up to Procter and Colgate in their home turf, in their biggest and most important product category?

DAVIES: To answer that perfectly honestly, I think we weren't all smart enough; we should have been more concerned about that than we were. At the time, we were not.

HONOMICHL: A lot of people out there probably have thought about doing something similar but backed off because they were afraid of the consequences. What would you advise them? You're one of the few people who have gotten away with it.

DAVIES: Give it a shot—if—if you have some kind of basic strength that can carry the day through. If you're up against Procter, you're probably not going to enjoy any cost advantage, or any marketing or advertising or sales clout. You have to have an edge. We had an edge: the Arm & Hammer name.

HONOMICHL: And you could move more quickly; they can be muscle-bound in many respects.

DAVIES: That's true; they were particularly tied up in their policies regarding phosphate at that time.

HONOMICHL: And it's particularly interesting in that you were working through brokers.

DAVIES: Oh, yeah. I think very highly of brokers. Procter & Gamble enjoys a lesser cost sales organization; their cost of sales compared to ours—as a percentage of sales dollars—would be approximately half of ours. That's a nice advantage. However, in terms of effectiveness, I think very highly of food brokers. Church & Dwight has been able to attract a very, very fine group of brokers; seldom has our sales force let us down.

HONOMICHL: You have the traditional regional salespeople setup?

DAVIES: We have about eight regional salespeople of our own and a national sales manager. And we have a national field sales manager to handle nonfood, and then about 80 food brokers.

HONOMICHL: Do you think the Arm & Hammer act would travel? Could you take it into international markets? Or is it so native American that it wouldn't travel?

DAVIES: Well, are you talking about baking soda under the Arm & Hammer name?

HONOMICHL: Yes, and for pretty much the same uses.

DAVIES: We've spent a fair amount of time assessing that, and certainly there is no clear-cut answer; it's never been tried. And it's no lead-pipe cinch, or we would have tried. I think there's a decent chance; it's a 50–50 kind of chance. There are some definite problems. Baking soda is indigenous to this country; it's part of the root structure of Americana. But it is sold in some other countries in some channels of distribution, food and drug stores in Germany and France. But its volume base is miniscule as compared to this country.

HONOMICHL: I've gotten the impression that this cow feed additive thing could be bigger than everything else some day. You could be on the verge of another historic leap ahead in volume.

DAVIES: That is possible. But that's a technical question; that's sheerly based on the technology, the functionality of the product.

HONOMICHL: As based on productivity—increased production related to cost?

DAVIES: Yes. We are doing a lot of work in this area, and we enjoy a nice dairy business. But to take on the dimensions of what you indicated, we would be required to go a good deal further—which is possible.

HONOMICHL: What's coming next? What are you working on now—that you can talk about?

DAVIES: Well, we're testing a liquid laundry detergent under the value strategy in New York state right now, and that brand is doing fairly well. That's under evaluation as to where that will lead us. Could be that over time there will be other things of that nature.

The name itself—Arm & Hammer—we regard to be an underutilized asset. In terms of baking soda, we still see the future as infinite—baking soda or baking soda new products. Baking soda is used for about 15 different basic use areas, and then it breaks down to literally hundreds of uses from those areas. And we've only tapped into a few of the basic ones so far. I regard that as a mine where we've only tapped the first vein. There are a lot more veins; I don't know how many more, but a lot more.

HONOMICHL: Have the big guys in the grocery business tried to buy you? I assume you would have been a hot acquisition prospect—a tightly held company with a great growth record.

DAVIES: Dwight [Dwight C. Minton, chairman of the board and chief executive officer] handles that, but I think it's safe to say there is a level of interest that is fairly constant. But we're very much oriented to running our own business, and I think we're doing a reasonably creditable job of doing it so we don't encourage that sort of thing at all.

HONOMICHL: You have a company that is, as I understand it, controlled about 70% in-house. What difference has that made? Could you, Bob Davies, have done what you did here in a larger, more broadly held company?

DAVIES: I think it might have been difficult. I think you're onto a key point. I think the strength of the company is its shareholder group; it's very, very loyal.

A lot of the shareholders are third, fourth—I suppose even fifth—generation Churches and Dwights who regard their stock with a certain family pride, so they take a slightly different, more long-term attitude towards the property. This has been a definite, clear strength to the company.

HONOMICHL: What was the role of marketing research in all this? Was it a driving force or a supportive force?

DAVIES: It was a guiding force; it wasn't a leadership force.

HONOMICHL: You have done something rare; you've never built up an internal market research staff, and you've placed all your research work with one firm.

DAVIES: It enabled us to, on a constant basis, relate to an extraordinarily capable individual, Dick Reiser, who has been very, very helpful to us. However, I'll say that the help has been in counseling, guidance advice, observation as opposed to a prime moving force. On the whole, it's been good, sound advice and research as opposed to a leadership position in terms of what we should do—but it has had some elements of leadership.

HONOMICHL: Would you recommend that approach to other companies the same size of Church & Dwight?

DAVIES: I would be very cautious in a company of our size of an internal marketing research capability. This company could not attract or hold on to the talent of a fellow like Dick Reiser; even if the expense would be warranted, which it probably would be, the individual wouldn't be interested. He would become disenchanted; it wouldn't be enough for him. He would become bored. So, I definitely would advise it— assuming one has a fellow the quality of Dick Reiser available to him.

HONOMICHL: Has Church & Dwight—with its growth—become an R&D-oriented company?

DAVIES: We regard the company in many respects to be a technology company and make a major commitment. That commitment has grown a fair amount in the past year or two; it's been much higher in recent years. We had no technological capabilities 13, 14 years ago.

The issue is the degree to which you inherently believe you have potential in your business. We believe there is a fair amount in sodium bicarbonate and we can pursue it—and we realize that here we are working an area that has not been very heavily worked in American industry.

HONOMICHL: What would you tell all those other marketing guys who watch Church & Dwight and say, "That's what we should be doing"?

DAVIES: My first thought goes to all those people who have done better than we have done. There are some very successful operations that have taken place in the last 10 years.

Remember, we started with a small base. When I came here in 1969, sales were about $16 million. Earnings were modest. But the company had a dynamite product, baking soda, and a dynamite name, Arm & Hammer. So, we started with sound assets.

The real question is "What did we do right?" First of all, we tried. I've been critical about some of the things we did wrong, but you can only do that if you've been trying. You've got to have the basic enthusiasm. You've got to have the drive, you've got to have the will, you have to get out there and be willing to make errors. We had a lot of that; we had it in spades.

HONOMICHL: Do you think that could be accomplished in a very large company?

DAVIES: Yes, I expect it could. You can get a business unit charged up—I think it has to do with excitement and leadership and vision. I think one of the things I've done well here is to constantly stir up things, constantly have people excited. We've had some bad times, tough times, but it's fun to come to work—and we've had an atmosphere where new thinking, including unconventional thinking, is welcome. You can do that in a large organization, but it's easier in a small organization.

Another thing we've done right would be not to assume that there is not opportunity right in what you're doing right now. Too often, I think, you take a look at your business and you orient yourself to the problems; you can spend all your time focusing on the problems. You never go to a joy meeting, okay? You can get pretty down on things. To allow yourself as a result to fail to see the inherent opportunities in what you already have, and what you already are, and what you already possess, is a mistake. The fine group of people we had working on baking soda before we got going on it thought they reasonably had done everything that could be done. In fact, I myself spent the first two or three years assuming that was the case. So, don't overlook the possibility that there is opportunity in what you're doing right now.

Postscript (August 1985)

For 1984, Church & Dwight Company had annual sales of $184.6 million, and earnings of $11 million were an all-time record. Consumer products alone, basically the Arm & Hammer Division, had sales of $144.4 million, up from $110.4 million in '83.

By the summer of 1985, the company had moved its corporate headquarters from Piscataway, N.J., to Princeton, N.J., and Robert A. Davies

III, who had left the company—abruptly—in September of 1984, surfaced as president and stockholder in California Home Brands, Terminal Island, Calif., a company best known as packers of Skippy dog food.

Dwight C. Minton, 50, chairman and CEO of Church & Dwight, emerged as the company's spokesperson, and in a *Forbes* article (July 15, 1985), he suggested that C&D's new products program had perhaps been too much too fast, and that they should scale back—and stay closer to the mother product, baking soda.

As for the mother product, A&H baking soda, 1984 case sales equaled the best levels achieved in the past. The new pricing and promotional strategies had helped arrest private label sales to about 10% share of market. A&H laundry detergent, now fully established nationally, has nearly a 7% share of market; it is priced 25% below competing powder detergents and is unadvertised. The liquid laundry detergent is now national in distribution, and further growth is envisioned. New products in test include A&H fabric softener dryer sheets; dry bleach; and Dental Care, powder dentifrice with baking soda, fluoride and mint flavor. As for the use of baking soda as an antiacid additive in cow feed, growth in this area has been inhibited by cutbacks in government support for dairy farmers.

9 How Detroit Reacted to the Imported Car Threat

In the spring of 1980, when it was cruelly evident that the U.S. automobile industry had been devastated and that one of the main reasons was its slack, apparently ill-informed response to the growing flood of well-made and relatively cheap imported cars, Rance Crain, editor of Advertising Age, *asked me to do a piece on the subject. I was to try to determine just where, when, and why Detroit's marketing efforts lost touch with the American consumer, or—as Mr. Crain summarized it—"How did they ever get into such a mess?"*

I spent four months on the article, which finally appeared in Advertising Age *on August 4, 1980. The story traced back to 1953, when American Motors introduced the Rambler, a car positioned as a gas saver. Detroit laughed.*

Most of my information came from executives—marketing and marketing research—who held key, bird's-eye positions in the U.S. auto industry from 1950 to 1970. The idea was to learn what they knew about how the U.S. auto market was changing at the time, and how top management reacted. It's a grim story, especially when you realize that once upon a time, the auto industry was estimated to account for about 18% of our Gross National Product.

In retrospect, I pulled my punches in all this article; it should have been more critical of Detroit's apparent lack of regard for product quality and quality control; in that respect, they held the door open for the Germans and Japanese.

Early Background—The Compacts

Here's the U.S. auto industry bent double. Over 28% of the Big Three's workers are idle, dividends are being cut, and by year's end [end of 1980], it is estimated, 11 major plants will have been closed and one-fourth of the industry's dealer franchises will have filed for bankruptcy. Our third largest auto maker is now being managed by the federal government; the second largest is in deep financial trouble.

How in the world did an industry that accounts for about 18% of our country's GNP get into such a bind—a bind that probably will get worse before it gets better?

In dire circumstances like these, there's a natural tendency to pile the main blame onto the top management of Detroit's Big Three—Ford, General Motors, and Chrysler. They were out of touch with the consumer; slow to react to the growing demand for small, fuel-efficient cars; and prone to underestimate the marketing prowess of foreign exporters like Nissan, Toyota, Volkswagen, Peugeot, et al.

In retrospect, there's some truth in all that. The full story, however, is far, far more complex and traces all the way back to the early 1950s when American Motors introduced the Rambler to compete with the "gas-guzzling dinosaurs" favored by Detroit's Big Three.

In an attempt to put today's predicament into perpsective, to get the full story on how the small, economy-car phenomenon evolved in the U.S. auto market, and to identify turning-point decisions along the way, I have recently interviewed numerous auto executives, most of whom held key executive positions in Big Three companies or their advertising agencies back in the 1950s, 1960s, and 1970s, and some, currently. Many of these informants worked in marketing research and, hence, were privy to marketing information that was available—and how top management reacted to it.

Out of this, a fascinating story has unfolded, and if there are lessons to be learned, it seems to me they are these:

1. Today's situation didn't just happen; it evolved over time.
2. The U.S. auto industry is living with some very cruel economic facts of life.
3. Some courses of action, easily espoused by outsiders—including the federal government—are, in fact, very difficult, expensive, and time-consuming for the auto industry to implement.
4. The same thing could happen to your business; learn from it.

The Dinosaur

A gallon of regular gasoline was selling for 26.8 cents a gallon, on average, in 1953 when George Romney, the feisty, outspoken, and—in retrospect—prophetic president of American Motors introduced the Rambler. The selling proposition: many Americans wanted a relatively spartan, gas-conservative car. To Detroit's surprise, Rambler sales took off—despite a relatively weak dealer network. One GM agency executive on the scene at the time recently told me, "GM's top management couldn't believe it; they thought it was a fluke."

To put things into perspective in 1952, 30,000 foreign-made cars—mostly British—were being imported into the United States, and they accounted for less than 1% of new car registrations. This dropped to 28,000 in 1953, and to 23,000 in 1954, the year, incidentally, when VW's famous Beetle first moved to the top of the import list with 5,000 units.

It was in 1955 that the Paley Commission, now nearly forgotten, made its report on strategic minerals to Congress. A major finding was that, in due course, the United States faced a shortage of oil. Some Big Three executives believed this, too.

Eventually, the Rambler was withdrawn from the market, but a point had been made, and this was not lost on the Big Three. "It was in the mid-50s," recalls George H. Brown, who was marketing research manager for the Ford division of Ford Motor Company at the time, "that the concept of market segmentation started to be recognized in Detroit."

Charlie Brown's Falcon

By 1958, when a gallon of regular gasoline sold for nearly 30 cents, the annual imports of foreign-made cars had increased by 16 times their 1953 level to 380,000 units—and Detroit was ready to launch its first major counterattack: Ford's little economy car, the Falcon, and its kissin' cousin, the Mercury Comet.

The decision to tool and go into full-scale production of a "compact" was made in 1957, and the Falcon was introduced to Ford dealers on September 2, 1959, via a closed-circuit telecast in 21 cities, and to the general public via a 20-page section in the *New York Times* on October 4.

J. Walter Thompson Company was the agency, and they made Charlie Brown, the "Peanuts" cartoon character, the spokesman for Falcon. The marketing plan called for a whimsical Charlie Brown newsletter, which was mailed to hundreds of thousands of foreign car owners. The production goal for Falcon was 97,000 units by year's end.

George Brown, who headed Ford's research on the Falcon, in a speech before the Detroit chapter of the American Marketing Association in December 1959, reported on 14 research studies that led to the Falcon production decision. He said:

> In the early part of 1958 it was quite apparent sales of domestic cars were dropping while sales of foreign cars had picked up and were rising.
>
> This was about the time we were reading charges in newspapers and magazine articles that the auto manufacturers were failing to anticipate consumer preferences. This is not true. Research had already been long under way—but was under wraps. Ford began to act at a very early date, first analyzing the foreign car competition as far back as 1953.

We knew...that foreign cars were selling in considerable volume in some market areas, or pockets, and had attained 1.5% of the total market. This was projected to envision a future 6%.

What do people want? Broadly, it figured out like this. They wanted such a car to be just like the standard car, but it should cost only $1,500 and travel 30 miles on a gallon of gas.

As we went along, we became convinced the market for the economy car was a cross section of the total car market.

Remember, this was 15 years before the first oil embargo, and most Americans had never heard of Saudi Arabia, let alone Iran. Still, the demand was there.

Brown recently told me the Falcon was a tough sell to Ford's top management, who cited the bad sales experience with their own small cars that had been imported into the U.S.

It's important to recognize that during the 1950s, Detroit's Big Three were well established in the European small car market. GM subsidiaries in Germany were making the Cadet and the Opel and, in England, the Vauxhall. Ford had the English Ford. Chrysler, in 1956, bought an interest in Simca, Inc., the French auto manufacturer. Hence, for several years Detroit had been well aware of the production economics—and profit possibilities—of small, high-mileage cars, designed as they were for countries where gasoline cost much more than in the United States.

And that gets us to *Economic Fact of Life No. 1:* It was natural, at first, for the big three automakers to try to import their own small cars into the United States; the production nut was already covered by sales in Europe and other parts of the world, and an import represented variable costs only. There would be no need to expend the millions of dollars necessary to tool up for manufacture of similar cars inside the United States.

These same economies, of course, work for the German and Japanese auto manufacturers too, and that made it relatively easy [read: inexpensive] for them to penetrate the United States market later on.

But early efforts to import and sell such cars as the Opel and Vauxhall through GM's Buick and Pontiac dealers fell flat; only about 25% would handle the little imports. And that brings us to *Economic Fact of Life No. 2:* Standard American cars offered dealers a "profit potential," as they say in Detroit, of 23–25%; small economy cars offered only 15–17%. So, for each small car sold at the expense of a larger one, the dealer lost revenue both in absolute and relative terms.

And that gets us to *Economic Fact of Life No. 3:* The auto manufacturers' true customers are the dealers; if they're not excited about a new car offering, they can resist, drag their sales feet. And auto dealers tend to be short-term thinkers, intent on weekly—make that daily—sales and cash flow. The top management of Detroit's Big Three through the 1950s and '60s were extraordinarily sensitive to the opinions of the people who owned their dealerships and relatively blasé about the ultimate consumer's wants and needs.

U.S. News Story
An item of note took place in 1958, just about a year before the Falcon introduction. *U.S. News & World Report* magazine published a study, done by Benson & Benson, Inc., in Princeton, regarding the auto preferences of Americans. This quote from *Advertising Age* tells the story:

> The Detroit auto wizards who have been hopefully assuming the small foreign car market in the U.S. is an offbeat market of atypical buyers, hence no serious threat to domestic car makers, will derive no joy from a small car report just published....
>
> The market for small foreign cars is virtually the same market for new domestic cars—mostly the upper income managerial and professional families—the report concludes.

This study went on to say that, among those who planned to buy a new car within the near future, the favored brand among both foreign and domestic makes was Volkswagen, which was named first by 28% of the respondents. Following, in order, were Chevy, Ford, and Romney's Rambler.

The general reaction in Detroit, I have been told, was: "That's what consumers say, but once they get into the showroom, they trade up." And, indeed, there was a great deal of truth in that.

It is important to pause here and recognize that, compared to most consumer products, market research involving car buyers has a unique, built-in advantage—the exact names and addresses of buyers are known—and it is relatively easy to follow up on people who have bought a particular type of car or to study a group of owners of older cars who are due to come back on the market for a new model.

And GM was well on to this. Starting in 1934, they instigated what is known as the Continuing Automotive Market Information Program (CAMIP), which is a mail survey each year of from 80,000 to 90,000 recent new car buyers. The purpose: to continuously monitor who is buying what, why, and subsequent satisfaction. The CAMIP study continues today.

Getting back to the Falcon—naturally, GM responded; they introduced the sporty Corvair and the Chevy II, or Nova (which, incidentally, was the first body size with an "X" car designation at GM).

But Ford was preparing to go a step further. In 1962, they announced plans for a 156," front-wheel-drive vehicle with a German-made engine priced at about $1,700. Code name: the Cardinal. Later in 1962, Lee Iacocca, then general manager, announced that plans for the Cardinal were being deferred because of "the tremendous transition and changes away from economy cars." Had Ford gone ahead then, the situation could have been much different.

The Middle Years—The Monza and Others

Back to the concern to create attractive profits on the "compact" cars—one possible solution for the Big Three was to jazz up their compacts with sporty options, all of which were very profitable to dealers.

GM's success with the Corvair Monza—with two doors, buckets, and stripes—was a key development here. It was followed by a souped-up Falcon called the Futura and an upscale Comet called the S-22.

So, at the time, the trend in Detroit was to take the compacts and turn them into what passed for a poor person's sports car—with a larger profit potential.

The sales of Falcons, Corvairs, and other such "compacts" were a well-established fact in Detroit going into the 1960s, and judging from this statement by Marley F. Copp, assistant chief engineer at the Ford Division of Ford Motor Company, the small-car situation was felt to be well in hand. Citing the advent of the Falcon in late 1959, Copp said, "We'll make anything the public wants to buy, so long as a reasonable proportion of the public wants something. That is the basis under which we are doing our long-range thinking at Ford, and I'm sure this is the promise of the future for all U.S. motor car producers."

Copp went on to credit American Motors for their "good job" and "agility" in marketing the Rambler, but warned that foreign car manufacturers will "feel our strength, too."

Be that as it may, the heartfelt convictions of Big Three top management were probably summarized in the 1960 statement of Harlow H. Curtice who had been president of GM through 1958: "I don't think the American buyer really wants a compact car—the trend will be for bigger cars." A researcher, at the time a GM employee, who made a presentation in 1962 to GM's board of directors and concluded with the recommendation that they market a car on the same wheel base as a VW Beetle, told me the reaction was "violent." Why? "Our dealers would never sit still for it."

Unsafe at Any Speed

Through the 1960s, the Big Three continued to crank out "compacts"—Pinto, Vega, Gremlin, Valiant, etc., none of which are renowned for quality engineering—but by the end of that decade, with a gallon of regular gasoline selling for about 35.7 cents, foreign imports accounted for 17–18% of new car registrations in the United States. And a new specter had arisen—consumerism, as personified by one Ralph Nader who attacked small cars, and especially GM's Corvair, as being "unsafe at any speed." This and other developments started to bring the U.S. government into Detroit's act; regulations would be soon to follow.

Detroit's interest in consumer behavior also was shifting. In 1960, GM started what was known as the Product Image and Awareness Study

(PIAS). Instigated by James M. Roche, who became president of GM in 1965, the original purpose was to continuously evaluate the effectiveness of GM advertising, according to Donald B. Batson, currently director/technical services at GM. This consumer research program, which was designed by a committee of research people from all of GM's advertising agencies, was assigned in 1962 to Audits & Surveys, Inc., New York. Based on 18,000 personal, in-home interviews, this PIAS program cost about $1 million a year, and it probably was the most sophisticated measure of attitudes, buying intentions, and subsequent purchasing behavior sponsored by American industry. (In the early 1970s, with the cost of in-home interviews escalating, the program switched over to telephone interviews through Amrigon, Inc., a Detroit-based research company.)

The point is this: it is difficult to say Detroit didn't know what was going on in the marketplace from the ultimate consumer's point of view. But how these data were interpreted and reacted to—well, that's another subject.

Half-Hearted Response

Based on what had happened by the end of the 1960s, no one could say Detroit's Big Three had not responded to the small car market or tried, in their own way, to shut the door on foreign imports. But the imports continued to grow in popularity. Why? In retrospect, the reasons seem to be as follows:

- American-made cars didn't compare well with imports in terms of quality construction and, in some instances, styling.
- Detroit was selling "small" per se while imports were selling economy of operation, low maintenance, and dependability.
- Importers were adventuresome marketers; witness the now famous Doyle Dane Bernbach campaign for Volkswagen, cited in 1980 by a panel of experts as the "outstanding advertising effort of modern times."
- Some Americans, at least, seem to perceive foreign-made products as more exotic, distinctive.
- Detroit's top management still didn't have their hearts in small car production; the return on investment wasn't there. Further, despite sales gains, the small car market was perceived as a fringe market, not the core of the consumer demand.

In sum, Detroit had indeed responded to the small car market—but not to the full extent of its capabilities.

Speaking of small cars, "The first ones we did were ugly as hell," recalls William L. Mitchell, vp-design at GM for 19 years and now retired. From a designer's point of view, he adds, "It was hard to get excited about funny little cars, and the pressure wasn't on from management to get outstanding design. Chevette [first marketed in 1975] was the first [GM] effort to make a really good-looking small car." In Mitchell's opinion, "The designers in Europe were way ahead of us."

Another man in a position to know is Norman Krandall, now executive director, corporate strategy and analysis, at Ford Motor Company. Krandall was in product planning in the 1950s and 1960s and succeeded George Brown as director of market research in 1969. At one time, he was manager of a factory that made Falcons.

"Our research interest levels were not well developed in the 1950s and '60s," Krandall told me recently, "and mostly we were sloshing around in demographics." George Brown's statements notwithstanding, Krandall feels, "Not a hell of a lot of research went into the Falcon." In those days, he recalls, "Nobody showed a model to potential customers before going to steel. We were making the cars as cheaply as we could make them."

An advertising agency executive, who prefers to be anonymous because he is still active on a GM account in Detroit, recently told me, "The quality control on those first little cars left much to be desired and, worse, some just weren't comfortable. The interiors were unattractive with cheap little door handles." In contrast, at least in his opinion, "The European cars had internal furnishings and style."

The Foreign Approach

Krandall makes another telling point, which is **Economic Fact of Life No. 4:** Foreign manufacturers have had a great cost advantage over the United States, and they could build more quality into a car. "Today [1980]," he says, "the average labor cost in Detroit is about $16 an hour, including fringes. In Japan it's $7.50 to $7.75, but when you figure in higher productivity, it's more like $6 in our terms." This same relationship existed back in the 1960s, and maybe more so—and that meant the foreign cars could include more hand labor [read: quality] and still be price competitive after being shipped halfway around the world.

This was a particularly important point because it was in the late 1960s that the Japanese started to make their major moves into the U.S. market, and before long funny names like Toyota, Datsun, Subaru, Mazda, and Honda would start showing up on American tv—and in GM, Ford, and Chrysler dealerships.

The European manufacturers, exemplified by Volkswagen, had taken the tack through the 1950s and 1960s of building their own dealer organizations, an expensive and laborious process, which includes brick and mortar, stockpiling of spare parts, and training of personnel, especially service people.

The Japanese manufacturers took a different tack; they selectively sought out established Big Three dealers and convinced them to add their cars to their product line. It was variable costs all the way; there was little to lose and, as we've seen, much to gain. The Japanese auto industry, I've been told, has the capacity to produce 11 million cars a year; the Japanese home market absorbs 5 million. That leaves 6 million to sell strategically around the world. They were in a position to wheel and deal.

And this gets us to **Economic Fact of Life No. 5:** The Japanese ability to cherry pick and ride on the back of established Big Three dealerships in the United States probably, in the beginning, hurt Detroit more than any other single thing.

The huge dealer organizations—GM alone has 11,400—had traditionally brought a great deal of stability to the U.S. car market. Because so many sales choices can be influenced at the point of sale, and because there's a certain amount of momentum from repeat business, the dealer organization could buoy up a bad model year by pushing relatively unpopular cars. So, in effect, if a division of GM made a bad style decision, the dealer organization could help carry sales through to the next model year when it could be corrected.

The Japanese *modus operandi* was to induce a U.S. dealership to take on their line as a sideline and then, as sales grew, to open a separate showroom nearby, featuring just the Japanese cars. So, what the public might perceive as a Datsun dealership could well be just an annex of a weak Ford dealership down the street.

So, if the Detroit product wasn't selling well and the Japanese product was, it was relatively simple to shift key personnel—and sales enthusiasm—down the street. (Ironically, this situation may today be a great help to Detroit's Big Three; some of their dealerships which might have otherwise gone under will survive because of their import sales—and hence still be alive when Detroit makes its comeback.)

The Japanese were alert in other ways, too. According to Mitchell, "Many of them had offices in Los Angeles long before; they were using the best design talent in California, especially the Arts Center College School of Design in Pasadena. Many of those Japanese cars were designed by Americans for Americans, and they didn't get sucked into the flat box look favored by the Europeans; they came in with crowned, curved looks."

Another bright move by the Japanese is to test a new model for one year in the Japanese market before bringing it into the United States. The result is an elimination of "new model bugs," which annoy customers. According to David Power, president of J.D. Power & Associates, a Los Angeles market research company that works for both the Japanese importers and Detroit, there is a lesson to be learned from that. "Since 1972 we've interviewed (via mail) the first 1,000 buyers of almost all new model introductions in the United States. When you ask buyers, within two or three months after purchase, if they have had any problems with their new car, Omni-Horizon buyers say "yes" about 74% of the time. Buyers of new cars from Mitsubishi—the Dodge Colt, Plymouth Arrow, Challenger—have a much lower rate—about 35 to 40%. All these cars are being sold through Chrysler Corp. dealers, of course, so that's constant, and most of the problems relate to delivery conditions of the car. Generally, the U.S.-made cars are faulted much more on body work, body parts."

The OPEC Impact

A gallon of regular gasoline was selling for about 38.8 cents just before the first oil embargo in October of 1973; the price was up to 59.5 cents by 1976, and at least some Americans were starting to scream bloody murder.

And it was in this period—1973-74—that Detroit's Big Three started to put some muscle into their reaction to foreign imports. There are two outstanding examples of this: GM's subcompact Chevette and Ford's Fiesta.

What is now known as the Chevette was being produced by GM through its European subsidiaries long before. When the decision was made to modify its design and to mass produce the result inside the United States, GM borrowed $600 million to cover the tooling expenses. And, as Mitchell noted, "Chevette was the first effort to make a good-looking car." In any case, the first Chevette was introduced in the United States on September 16, 1975.

Concurrent with this effort, Ford was going through an extensive research program, which reputedly cost $2 million, to develop a wholly new small car entry, the Fiesta, the story of which is documented in a book entitled *Let's Call It Fiesta*.

Now it is important to make the distinction between "market" research in Detroit and "styling" research, which is usually sponsored by product development people away ahead of marketing decisions.

The days in Detroit when a new car design "went to steel" before being appraised for consumer reaction had passed. GM lagged way behind Ford in this respect, but now every effort was being made at the design stage—often four years before production started—to eliminate bugs or build in features that would affect the car's sales. This was done through a laborious and expensive process called Advance Product Style Clinics. Prototypes, or mock-ups, of proposed models were made up and quite often shipped to southern California which is believed by Detroit to be a harbinger of U.S. auto tastes.

One of the most experienced companies in this work—Rogers National Research, Inc., in Toledo, Ohio, who has worked for GM, Ford, and Chrysler—offers a good example of what happens. Say the target audience for a new design is young married couples. A group of respondents would be recruited and brought to a showroom in the wraps of considerable secrecy to be exposed to the test car mock-up and competitive models from the world market. Every detail of the car is explored as the would-be prospects pore over it, and the results are then fed back to designers in Detroit.

Much of the $2 million spent on researching the Fiesta was for such style research, and one momentous style clinic was conducted in December of 1972 in the Palais de Beaulieu exhibit hall in Lucerne, Switzerland. Over two weeks, research companies retained by Ford flew in 700 respondents from London, Paris, Madrid, Milan and Dusseldorf. Each separate group, through questionnaires in their own language, reacted to the proposed Fiesta design (which then had the code designation "blue car") vis-à-vis a Peugeot 104, Fiat 127, Renault 5, Honda Civic, and two minimites. In the United States, Rogers National Research was conducting similar style clinics. In such a way, the Fiesta design, which was styled by Alessandro de Tomaso and included front-wheel drive, was appraised for its world sales potential and style competitiveness. Capital investment in production was estimated at $800 million.

This was the "most serious research" ever put into a new Ford car, says Krandall, "and the result is one of the best small cars in the world." Further, now that the Fiesta is on the road, "It has the best consumer acceptance rating of any Ford car," he adds. (It is interesting to note that today the Fiesta is currently advertised as "The Wundercar from Germany—a masterpiece of European engineering." Ford's market research shows that American car buyers believe that foreign-made cars are of higher quality and better design.)

Chevette and Fiesta get us to ***Economic Fact of Life No. 6:*** It is very time consuming and expensive for Detroit to tool up for the production of an entirely new model car.

We've seen that the capital expenditure consequences of Chevette and Fiesta were from $600 to $800 million—and that was in the early 1970s; today, the figures would be closer to $1 billion. And such innovations as the Fiesta can be up to four years in the planning. After such a commitment is made and the car finally comes on to the market, many things can happen —and if you've planned/guessed wrong, you can end up with one very big turkey on your hands.

Detroit's top management certainly would want to be very sure of their ground before making such a major move. And it must be very frustrating to them to have outsiders ask why they don't build this or that in immediate response to the whims of the marketplace.

In fact, early research showed that the Chevette was not a good "import fighter," according to Dave Power. "Our research on the Chevette showed that it was not appealing to the kinds of people who were making the import car market," says Power. "Instead, it was appealing basically to those who were already Chevrolet customers."

At the same time, I think it is important to recognize that Detroit wasn't hurting in those days; 1972 was a near record year, 9.3 million American-made cars; 1973 was the record year for U.S.-made cars, 9.7 million. Detroit was selling all the big cars it could make.

Also, Detroit got a helping hand from Washington. President Nixon, as part of his wage and price fixing program, which started in August of 1971, put a 10% surcharge on imported autos (the import tax had been running at 3.5%). This was removed, however, in 1973, and today [1980] it runs at 2%.

By the mid-1970s, Americans had learned a great deal about places named Kuwait, Bahrain, Saudi Arabia, and Iran. A gallon of regular gasoline was selling for more than 63 cents. The original OPEC price increase in October 1973 had been 70%; the second one in December 1973 had been 130%. It was this second increase, according to one executive at GM, that led top management to conclude that "this is a basic change," and serious plans started to be made to downsize the standard cars.

It was also in the mid-1970s that Volkswagen abandoned the little Beetle, which had served them so well, and started to bring their sporty, second-generation cars into the United States—the Dasher in 1974, the Rabbit in 1975. On April 23, 1976, they announced the decision to build an assembly plant in the U.S.

Shades of the Cardinal—it was in 1975, it has been reported, when Lee Iacocca again recommended to Ford's top management that they bankroll a small, front-wheel drive car—this time using a Honda power train. Since the commitment to Fiesta had already been made, this suggestion was rejected. According to Iacocca now, "It was the greatest tactical error in automotive history. They get an F for management."

Still, Detroit traditionalists could take heart in the fact that by 1975–76 sales of imports had started to decline; their share of new car registrations went from 18.2 to 14.8% in 1976. And this added fuel to the argument, "See, now Americans are getting back to what they've always wanted in the first place—a comfortable, standard-sized car."

The Government's Role

In 1975 Congress—convinced that oil conservation was necessary and that the Big Three were dragging their feet in the development of fuel-economy cars—passed the Energy Policy and Conservation Act, Public Law #94-163. The main stipulation was that, starting with the 1978 model year, Detroit would have to produce a line of cars that, on average, had higher miles per gallon ratings each year, ending with 27.5 by 1985. At the time, Detroit's fleets were averaging about 13 to 14 mpg.

And this brings us to **Economic Fact of Life No. 7:** The federal government, just one step away from direct regulation, has had a heavy hand in Detroit's production strategies for over five years [as of 1980]. Downsizing (to save weight), inclusion of new safety features, and the emission control regulations combine to tie up the Big Three's design time and financial resources.

Was this drastic step really necessary? Well, judging from this quote from President Jimmy Carter's news conference, as reported in the *New York Times* of April 17, 1980, the administration thought so:

> I remember the first months [1977] I was President...talking to the leaders of the American automobile manufacturers...encouraging them to comply with the impending legislation of the Congress to require the production of small and efficient automobiles for the American market.
>
> Their unanimous reply was that this was an inappropriate thing for them to do—that the market was not there for the small and efficient automobile.

Could it really be that Detroit had yet to get (or should I say, accept) the small-car message? There's no way of knowing, of course, how accurately these brief remarks by Carter reflected all the arguments made by Detroit's leaders—but one thing was certain: making fuel-efficient cars had become the law of the land, and manufacturers who could make plastic look like steel were to have a field day.

The "pending legislation" referred to by President Carter was Public Law #95-618, the so-called gas guzzler tax, which stipulated that, starting with model year 1980, a surtax would be levied on autos which have a miles-per-gallon rating under a specified level. Shades of George Romney!

This leads us to **Economic Fact of Life No. 8:** To meet the new economy-car production demands, Detroit itself had become a major importer of foreign-made auto parts. One reason was to save time and money. To rush the Chevette to market after the Arab oil embargo, for example, it was decided to import automatic transmissions from a GM plant in France already tooled and under-utilized. Another reason was cost and quality. A Ford study, as reported in the *Wall Street Journal* recently, indicated that a particular motor needed in the United States could be made for as little as $704, at a particular point in time, by Ford's Japanese affiliate, Toyo Kogyo. The same engine made in the U.S. would cost $1,062. In addition, to produce in the U.S. would involve tooling costs.

One result of all this, according to the *WSJ* report, is that Chrysler's Omni and Horizon get about 14% of their components from outside the United States, including German engines, manual front-wheel drives, transmissions, and starters.

When Ford's new compact car, the Escort, is introduced this fall [1980], the front-drive systems and steering wheels will come from Japan; other steering parts will be British-made; key front suspension parts will be Spanish; and the fuel pumps will be Italian. When Chrysler's new Ariels and Reliant compacts come on the market, the motors will be Japanese.

So, when Ford, Chrysler, and UAW executives trooped to Washington in May 1980 to plead for some sort of restrictions on foreign-made car imports, this situation undercut their arguments for protectionism.

The need to import foreign-made components brings us to **Economic Fact of Life No. 9:** Compared to foreign auto manufacturers, U.S. production facilities are old and in need of modernization.

Of the 18 assembly plants operated by Ford in the United States, the average age is 29 years, according to a recent report in *Forbes*. Of GM's 26 domestic assembly plants, only 3 have been built since 1965; one, a Buick plant in Flint, Michigan, dates back to 1903. Ford's famous assembly plant at Rouge, where the public is invited to take "The Incredible Factory Tour" featured in tv commercials, was built in 1918. In contrast, many Japanese auto plants have been built within the past 10 years.

Money and technology that could have gone to modernize Detroit's plant have instead gone to support the crash programs dictated by government safety and economy regulations, argue United States auto leaders, and that hurts.

In 1979, there were additional blows from the Middle East—a new round of OPEC price increases and, in May, a cutoff of Iranian oil supplies. The need for fuel economy was more dramatic than ever.

By mid-1979, one of the Big Three—Chrysler—was on the verge of bankruptcy, and as part of a government-backed loan, the company effectively came under government control in May 1980 through the Chrysler Loan Guarantee Board, a group of Treasury Department officials. That board is now in a position to tell Lee A. Iacocca, president of Chrysler, how to market the "K" body car, which was meant to be the turnaround for the beleaguered company.

Ford's finances are in bad shape, too. The company's U.S. operations posted huge losses in the fourth quarter of 1979 and the first quarter of 1980, with more expected; only the overseas operations are profitable. By the end of 1980, the situation could be as bad as at Chrysler.

A gallon of regular gasoline now sells for $1.29, and about 27% of the new cars and trucks sold in the United States are imports. The only bright spot in Detroit is the "X" car sales, limited only by production capacity. And, Jimmy Carter, if anything, is now figuring out how to help our crippled auto industry, and he'll probably come up with something simply because it's an election year.

As this article has attempted to point out, it has taken a long time for Detroit to get into this mess, and it is apt to take a long time to get out; the bleak economic facts of life with which Detroit must cope still exist. And no one is apt to argue with this prediction made by Lee Iacocca in late May 1980: "The next six months to a year are going to be pure hell."

Postscript (August 1985)

Closing that article back in 1980 with a quote from Lee Iacocca, it turns out, was highly prophetic. Who could have foreseen at that time that Iacocca would turn Chrysler around, gleefully pay off the big government-backed loan way ahead of time, become the most successful businessman author in history—and be touted as presidential timber? In many ways, Iacocca symbolizes Detroit fighting back.

Things did get worse before they got better, as Iacocca felt they would, but slowly Detroit got upbeat again. Even American Motors had a brief flash of success, which is documented in the Alliance launch story in the following chapter.

But the changes since 1980 are awesome: robot-driven factories— lowering gasoline prices and the caving in of the OPEC alliance—more American auto production moving offshore, and more parts imported from low-cost suppliers ranging from Korea to Spain—a new Nova, by General Motors, out of Toyota—more foreign manufacturers, a la Honda and Volkswagen, building production facilities in the U.S.—the stunning success of specialty vehicles, such as AMC's downsized Jeep and Chrysler's Vancar—community after community clamoring for a chance at GM's exciting new Saturn production facility—a market demand surge for large cars, loaded (as Detroit traditionalists always felt would happen)—and so much more. All that in just five years?

Most of Detroit is profitable now, and the mood is upbeat; the story as told in this article is history, largely forgotten. But it should not be forgotten.

10 Launching Renault's Alliance

After years of gloom and doom in the U.S. automobile industry, a really upbeat marketing effort took place starting September 22, 1982. Two most unlikely partners—American Motors Corp. and Régie Nationale des Usines Renault, the French auto manufacturer—teamed up to market a little subcompact called the Alliance in the U.S. The success of this launch gave AMC a new lease on life, and, perhaps more important, it showed Detroit that a really well-made car, at a reasonable price, will sell as well as the imports, despite a relatively weak dealer network.

W. Paul Tippett, Jr., chairman of AMC, gave me almost complete access to his organization and its consumer/marketing research files—and much of the article (which appeared in Advertising Age *on June 6, 1983) is based on information that had never been published before.*

Of special interest is the candid interview with Tippett, some of which did not appear in Advertising Age *due to space limitations. As you'll see, he is a very flat-out man.*

The Alliance Story

Is a little 56-horsepower car designed in France powerful enough to haul one of America's largest corporations out of its deep financial ditch?

Given that the car is Renault's Alliance and the corporation is American Motors, the answer at this point of time [1983] is a hopeful "yes." United States and Canadian sales of this much-acclaimed, front-wheel drive subcompact are expected to exceed 140,000 units during its first 12 months on the market (October 1982–September 1983), despite a 1.3% price increase in April 1983.

The significance of this consumer endorsement to AMC, which lost $491 million over the three years 1980–82; to Renault, which has been trying to dent the U.S. auto market since 1904; and to 10,800 auto workers in Kenosha, Wis., where the Alliance is manufactured, is almost beyond measure. As for AMC's dealer network, Nat Ross, the happy sales manager of Tappan Motors, Inc., which has been representing AMC productions in North Tarrytown, N.Y., for 22 years, recently told me, "The Alliance is a franchise all its own."

151

What follows is an insider's story of the $13.5 million marketing program behind the Alliance's successful U.S. launch, which AMC people consider "one of the smoothest in Detroit's history."

This story, written with the blessing of AMC's top management, dates back to 1977. It details the $1 million consumer research program that guided the Alliance's market positioning and copy strategy, the creative contest between AMC's agencies, Grey and Compton, for "the copy" that would introduce the Alliance, the media strategy, and the "Get to know Renault..." program that was felt necessary to convince old-time AMC dealers that the Renault name, considered a liability by many, could be transformed into a marketing plus.

And, maybe above all, it highlights the hands-on insistence of José J. Dedeurwaerder, the Renault manufacturing executive who joined AMC in 1981 and became president in January 1982, that the Alliance—which, after all, is the star of this saga—has construction quality equal to, or better than, comparable Japanese-made cars. (*Motor Trend* magazine, in naming the Alliance "Car of the Year" for 1983, said, "It may well be the best-assembled first-year car we've ever seen.")

Born of Necessity

The Alliance might be viewed as a child born of a mixed marriage, an automotive marriage of convenience. Courtship started in 1977 when AMC's top management, led by Gerald C. Meyers (chairman from 1978 to January 1982, now retired), concluded that to survive in the U.S. market, the company "had to acquire advanced technology quickly and at minimum cost."

AMC's auto products in those days were "off the same platform," as they say in Detroitese when spin-offs of the same basic design are presented to the public, after some cosmetic, or shell, alterations, as different cars. The AMC Concord, for instance, was a variation of the Hornet, and the Spirit was a revamped Gremlin. "We had changed the skirts on the old girl as much as we could; we needed something really new," says Robert Schwartz, vp-North American sales at AMC from 1982 to January 1983.

This situation led to exploratory talks with several auto makers, both in Europe and Japan, but AMC's urgent needs seemed to mesh most naturally with those of Régie Nationale des Usines Renault, the world's sixth largest auto manufacturer, which is owned by the French government.

In the spring of 1978, AMC and Renault started to deal seriously, and about nine months later they signed an agreement that called for AMC to become the exclusive importer and distributor of Renault-made autos in the United States and Canada. (This was overshadowed at the time by Chrysler's way out of a similar bind—the controversial, government-backed survival loan of $1.2 billion.)

The lure to Renault was AMC's dealer organization (Renault calls them "stores"), which numbered about 1,350 at the time. It was by Ford or General Motors standards, a hodgepodge; some AMC dealers had a strong Jeep orientation; some carried only AMC products; others had had some Renault product experience. Many were relatively small "stores" off of auto row, and as Schwartz observed recently, "Their one distinguishing factor was that they were survivors of the hard times at AMC," dealers who had stayed alive by pushing their service department and/or used car sales, or by taking on one or more competitive lines. (Ross's dealership in North Tarrytown, for instance, handles Mazda, Jaguar, and Dodge's Omni in addition to Jeep and other AMC cars.)

Because of the AMC–Renault agreement, two Renault-made cars were pushed into AMC's dealer network: the mini-compact LeCar and a larger subcompact called the "18i," a blah car with little sales appeal.

Need to Sell Dealers

Dealer enthusiasm for the Renault–AMC pact, the Renault name, and Renault-made products was well under control; in fact, the negative feelings threatened to undermine the long-range plans to launch the Alliance in the United States. As many sales/marketing managers have learned the hard way, sometimes the really hard sell is not the consumer—it's one's own organization.

This problem was on the table up front, says Schwartz, who made a presentation to Renault's board regarding what he thought to be the need for special efforts (and expenditures) to win the dealers over to Renault identification with the new (as yet unnamed) car that would become the Alliance, and to convince U.S. consumers that it was a departure from Renault's lackluster past in the U.S. auto market (1959 was the peak— 91,000 units, two-thirds of which were Dauphines, which it takes a real auto buff to remember). "The French understood," adds Schwartz. (One reason may be that, previously, Renault had retained the management consulting firm of Hoagland & MacLachlan in Wellesley, Mass., to survey AMC dealers.)

In 1979, knowing that a new car (as yet undescribed) was coming, the AMC Dealer Advisory Board voted unanimously against giving it Renault's name, says Schwartz, and, "They would have been in absolute revolt if we didn't do something." The "something" turned out to be a "Get to know Renault..." road show that started with dealers in the Boston area in March 1981. Eventually, this upbeat presentation about Renault's prowess in the European auto market was taken to 30 markets. One result was that about a year later, when the advisory board was told of upcoming plans for the Alliance and the use of Renault's name, no member objected.

The X-42

During the "Get to know Renault..." campaign, AMC dealers knew more Renault cars were coming their way, but they didn't know exactly what. Internally, at AMC's headquarters in Southfield, Mich., executives referred to the car that would be the Alliance by the code name X-42, but only a handful knew that it would be an Americanized version of a Renault car called the R-9, a subcompact designed to compete in what is known in Europe as the "Class 3, small" category.

Built in Renault's new plant in Douai, France (which is considered one of the finest production facilities in Europe), the R-9 has since become the second best selling car in Europe and the best seller in France. It was named Europe's Car of the Year in 1982.

The man in charge of production at Douai and credited with the R-9's quality was José J. Dedeurwaerder, who joined AMC as executive vp in September 1981 to oversee production of the Alliance.

Modifications of the R-9 for the U.S. market included a fuel injection system (to make it peppier), a fancier interior, different headlights and antenna, extended bumpers, a softer suspension, and a two-door model. The car was destined for a market segment Detroit refers to as "subcompact, standard"—which accounts for about 23% of U.S. auto sales in units; it's the guts of the current market. There are 24 nameplates in this category, some of the most prominent being Plymouth's Horizon, Honda's Civic, Toyota's Corolla, Chevrolet's Chevette, and the best seller—by far—Ford's Escort. About 80% of these subcompact cars are purchased as the "primary car," according to AMC research; the balance are viewed as second cars.

This is considered to be an especially price-sensitive segment of the market, and right from the start one of AMC's marketing goals was to give the Alliance a very competitive—you might say "low ball"—price; the basic two-door model, stripped, had a sticker price of $5,595, which was featured in advertising. "Research showed we could have started with a higher price," says David J. Van Peursem, general manager/marketing, at AMC, "but it was a marketing decision to keep it low; we wanted everything going for us, considering the importance of this launch." (The model MT, which is the fully loaded configuration tested by *Motor Trend*, had a sticker price of $9,200.)

Naming the Baby

The consumer research program, which had much to do in defining the qualitative positioning of the Alliance and which eventually cost about $1 million, started in the summer of 1979, three full years before Alliance Announcement Day (to the general public) on September 22, 1982. There were two key players: David G. Garfield, manager/marketing services, at AMC, and Joseph G. Smith, president of the New York-based survey research firm of Oxtoby-Smith, Inc., which since 1972 has, under retainer, provided about 85% of AMC's custom research work.

"We were trying to figure out how to sell the car [X-42], and we didn't know what we didn't know," recalls Garfield. There were several key questions, directed to U.S. customers, such as, "What does 'European' mean?" "What does 'Renault' or 'imported' mean?" Exploration of these and related questions was the purpose of six focus-group interviews, and shortly after, in August 1979, the first auto clinic was conducted in Anaheim, Calif.

Such clinics are commonplace in auto marketing. You rent a showroom and recruit a group of people who are typical of the target group "the car" is aimed at (in the case of the X-42, buyers of compacts, young, relatively well-educated, and import-car-oriented). These people are then allowed to inspect closely, at leisure, a mock-up, or prototype, or real-thing model of "the car," which might be displayed along with other cars that are directly competitive, with or without identifying nameplates. ("Over half of the people can't recognize the cars after the name plates are taken off," says Garfield.)

The first clinic used a fiberglass mock-up since there were no R-9s then, and focused on exterior-only properties. A second clinic in San Mateo, Calif., in April, had three sessions; each presented a prototype in a different light—as a Renault product, as an AMC product, or as a "no name." The key findings were these: the car itself got positive scores, but these were less positive when the car had a Renault identification. The same was true with an AMC identification, but less so. (This clinic also included mock-ups of the new Renault car, code name X-37, which might be considered competitive to the X-42.)

Meanwhile, the question of name was on the table. "About 1,000 were suggested by management, our agencies, suppliers—everyone," says Garfield. These were reduced, judgmentally, to 10 finalists, and consumer research was done to establish the imagery inherent to each because, according to Garfield, one of the goals was to match the car's image with a name that reinforced that image.

The research, which was done by Burke Marketing Research, produced "Alliance," and the only concern was prior claim to the name. (The closest one that could be identified was a tire manufacturer in Israel.) "American" was the runner-up name, and some also-rans were "Radiant," "Pioneer," and "Resolute."

A third series of clinics took place in Long Beach, Calif., in July 1981. Now one of the descriptors could be "Renault Alliance"—the first time the name was used. Respondents at the clinics were interviewed, prior to seeing the cars, as to what car they would be most apt to shop for and buy, given that they were in the market. A comparable interview afterwards provided a measure of the Alliance's ability to "switch off" buyers interested in competitive cars. The Alliance's attraction power was established.

Also going on in the fall of 1981 were focus-group sessions designed to develop hypotheses for a full-scale survey to determine how best to position the Alliance in the American marketplace in order to maximize its chances of success.

Based on face-to-face interviews with 605 respondents in eight cities (mall intercepts), this study was fielded in January–February 1982. Respondents were shown pictures of the Alliance and told of its performance characteristics, and these were pitted against the Escort, Civic, Horizon, and Mazda's GLC. Three "genealogies" were presented: the Alliance was a car (1) of Renault origin, (2) of joint AMC/Renault origin, and (3) of AMC origin. Also measured was the relative importance of stressing quality, technology, or durability. One of the study's key findings, and I quote from Oxtoby-Smith's report:

> Purchase interest in the Alliance, regardless of which geneology was revealed, was much more favorable than predisposition to Renault and AMC generally. Indeed, the car overcame relatively unfavorable predispositions to each manufacturer.

Other conclusions from the study were these: "There was a distinct edge for the Renault genealogy in generating strong purchase interest in the Alliance, and 'Made in America' was much more frequently mentioned as a reason for strong purchase interest...among those exposed to the mixed and AMC genealogies." Also, "Respondents clearly found the durability and technology positionings more attractive...," especially among key target groups (young, more upscale import prospects). The decision was made to emphasize "technology," partly because "durability" proof was down the road, too early to substantiate. "The question now was how to talk about 'technology,'" recalls Garfield, "because buyers were more results-oriented than process-oriented."

Beyond the analytical researcher concerns about the best name or positioning of the X-42, you can well imagine that there were strong undercurrents of opinions fueled by the pride of two pioneer auto manufacturers, both hungry for a winner. Beyond pride was the fact that Renault started in 1979 to acquire AMC stock, and by December 1980, its ownership equity had reached 46.4%.

Since 1979 Renault has, in effect, served as AMC's banker, and that facilitated the election of Mr. Dedeurwaerder as president and CEO—and, in essence, Mr. Quality Control—in January 1982. At the same time, W. Paul Tippett, Jr., who had joined AMC as president in 1978, was elected chairman of the board and CEO.

The Advertising Battle—Grey vs. Compton

Because of the extreme importance of getting the best possible creative to launch the Alliance, Van Peursem did something that may be a "first" for Detroit: he asked both of AMC's agencies (Grey Advertising on autos and Compton Advertising on Jeep products) to prepare creative for consideration. But, no matter which agency won, it was understood that the media planning and billing would be through Grey. How did that go over? "Compton was delighted." recalls Van Peursem, "but Grey was a little thunderstruck—until I explained the reasoning behind the decision. And, after all, it's reciprocal; Grey is now helping with advertising on our new Jeep line."

Both agencies maintain offices in AMC's 25-story headquarters building, American Center, in Southfield, but they quickly turned to their home offices in New York for creative help. A batch of focus-group sessions were done for guidance, some paid for by AMC, some by the agencies. The result was 50 storyboards, 4 of which were converted into animatics (photographing a series of drawings with sound track for testing). These were "Chasm" and "Plastic Car" from Grey and "Way to Go, Renault" and "Love It" from Compton.

Evaluation was done through a pretesting methodology—which emphasizes persuasion measures—developed by Oxtoby-Smith. Respondents recruited in mall intercepts were shown double exposures of the copy within a pilot film context.

Three of the commercials had virtually the same scores, according to Joseph E. Cappy, a former Ford executive who joined AMC as vp-marketing group in 1982. "We leaned towards going with 'Plastic Car,' but production time was estimated to be long and production costs too high, so we went with 'Chasm,'" says Cappy.

"Chasm" pictures two land masses converging; one represents European technology and styling and the other affordability. When they come together, you had the Alliance proposition. (Cappy declined to comment, but agency sources estimate the production cost for "Chasm" to be over $700,000, a number that reportedly sent shock waves through AMC's executive suite when the bills started to come in.)

But when the finished copy on "Chasm" was tested on-air in Burke's DAR system, a not-so-funny thing happened—it got a lower score than norms for other AMC commercials tested through the years. You gotta believe a lot of people wanted to know, "How come?"

So, Oxtoby-Smith was asked to put finished "Chasm" copy through its pretest system; sure enough, it received a lower score than the original animatic test. "But," says Donald E. Payne, senior vp-research at Oxtoby-Smith, "we went a step further; after the normal test, we exposed respondents to the original animatic and then questioned them about differences they perceived." The result was that while both finished version and animatic communicated the same message, respondents didn't like the announcer's voice or music in the finished version as much as they did in the animatic. Also, the color in the finished version seemed pale compared to that in the animatic.

Based on these final results, Grey redid the sound track, putting back in the original announcer and music (Handel's "Water Music"), and the end result is what went on air.

Robots in Kenosha

Kenosha, Wis., population about 126,000, is located on Lake Michigan about halfway between Chicago and Milwaukee. To say that AMC has deep roots there is an understatement; the first Rambler, a one-cylinder auto that sold for $750, was manufactured there in 1902 by a predecessor company, Thomas B. Jeffery Co. (which in 1916 became Nash Motors; in 1937, Nash-Kelvinator; and in 1954, American Motors). That original plant—called Main Plant—is where final assembly work is being done on the Alliance today.

About 1¼ miles away, in a plant called Lakefront, which was a Simmons Mattress plant until AMC bought it in 1958, the Alliance bodies are framed, painted, and trimmed with the help of 24 robot welders, some manufactured by Renault, some by the Japanese. Of the $200 million that has been spent to make the Alliance's production in the U.S. as good as the R-9's in Douai, France, most has gone into Lakefront —including a $11 million paint system that features an electrodeposition priming process that adheres a protective coating to the body. The system also provides for clear-coating of metallic colors. (This shiny outer coat of colorless acrylic enamel really dresses up the Alliance vis-à-vis other cars in the same price class.) The Alliance is 75% domestic made (U.S. and Canada), with the power train—engine and transmission—coming in from France.

The first pilot Alliance rolled off the line at Main in January 1982, the first of four pilot car runs of about 100 cars each—with a month shutdown in between to make sure quality was satisfactory before starting production line volume. Many of these cars were given to employees for evaluation, a common practice in Detroit. But with the Alliance, there was a twist —it wasn't just top executives who got the cars; they went down into the ranks, and everyone had to fill out a performance questionnaire every week, noting any problems.

The first production model Alliance came off-line on June 18, 1982, and nearly 10,000 were produced and shipped to dealers before Announcement Day on September 22.

With a modern factory up and going and product available for review, the stage was set for another important step in the campaign to sell AMC's dealers on the Renault association. In mid-July 1982 about 1,000 AMC dealers (some with sales managers, some with wives, some with both) were brought to an intensive program at the former Playboy Club resort in Lake Geneva, Wis., about 60 minutes from the Kenosha plant.

"We got them right off the plane at O'Hare," recalls Van Peursem, "onto buses equipped with sets. We started showing films about the Alliance [the first time, officially, that the dealers were told the car's name would be Renault's Alliance] and the marketing plan. They watched this stuff on the ride up to Lake Geneva." There followed a showbiz kickoff dinner, tours of the Kenosha plant, and test drives of the Alliance at AMC's testing grounds at Burlington, Wis.

As for the Alliance's quality, Schwartz says the Lake Geneva meetings proved to the dealers "that this time it's not just hype; it's true that we have a great car." The Renault issue was fading.

Task Force

In February 1982, introduction plans—complete with time sequencing diagrams—started to build up steam. First, there was an X-42 task force created with all functions—public relations, sales training, merchandising, service, dealer advertising, market planning, etc.—represented with a member. It was the sole responsibility of the task force manager, William R. Chapin, to pull it all together and expedite its activities. Chaplin is the son of Roy D. Chapin, Jr., a former chairman of AMC, and a grandson of Roy D. Chapin, Sr., one of the founders of Hudson Motor Car Co.) This task force reported—weekly, toward the end—to a top management review committee that okayed major moves.

As for communications, the budget was divided generally as follows: 70% to advertising in measured media, 10% for merchandising materials (dealer kits, point of sale, etc.), 10% for public relations, and 10% for miscellaneous matters such as shows and meetings.

The national advertising plan, according to Howard I. Mosher, director of Renault marketing at AMC, called for 70% of the budget going into broad-reach network, with participation in special events as much as possible. (The first Alliance commerial on-air was on September 13, a week prior to Announcement Day; that was due to an opening on the U.S. Open tennis tournament telecast.) The plan called for 200 to 300 gross rating points per week during the first four-week flight and a 150-point average each week in the balance of the introductory period.

Grey had developed a pool of four commercials, two :60s and two :30s, for the introduction. "We felt the :60s were important," asserts Cappy, "because the Alliance is not a car with just one outstanding feature; instead it rates very high on a lot of features. When you can tell that whole story, testing showed that people said, 'I'd better have a look at that car.'"

The 200 AMC dealer associations were offered 25-second versions with room for an identification tag. "We urged the associations to use our copy to tie in with the total campaign," says Van Peursem, "and most of them cooperated." The factory picked up 45% of the air time costs.

On the public relations front, AMC tried an innovation that may also have been a first for Detroit, according to John G. McCandless, manager/sales and marketing communications. "The idea was to tie in with local public relations firms, just like co-op advertising, with the hope that they—with their knowledge of the market—could create more effective media events than we could dream up from Detroit." This concept was tested in four markets, in conjunction with the local dealer associations, and then expanded to 20 markets. This worked so well, says McCandless, that the network will be used again in new auto launches next fall.

Announcement Day

Everything came together on August 29, 1982, with a National Press Review in three cities and, finally, Announcement Day to the general public on September 22. AMC's pr department had arranged for about 100 Alliances to be spotted around the country for test driving by local automobile newswriters, and dealer showrooms were stocked with about a 20-day supply of Alliances (compared to an industry norm of a 50- to 60-day supply), with special emphasis on the top 200 AMC dealers, who account for about 80% of sales.

Nervous, "How's it going?" questions were being answered by a number of feedback devices. One is the weekly UPS (for "dealer write-ups") report at AMC, in which dealers record store traffic (limited to prospective buyers who register; i.e., give their name and address). Another is a weekly sales report from a panel of 250 key, especially large dealers.

Research fielded by Garfield in Detroit included such things as the Monitor Survey (mail survey of Alliance buyers asking, among other things, how they came to know of the car), and in the case of the Alliance, a showroom shoppers' study, done by Marketing Strategy, Inc., a research firm located in Southfield, to determine what kind of people were being drawn in to see the new Alliance.

And, finally, there is the so-called Rejecter's Study, where known visitors to AMC showrooms are interviewed about four or five weeks later to determine what they ultimately did, and if they decided not by buy an Alliance, "Why not?" "What we found," says Garfield, "was that sometimes the car did better than the dealers; the young, educated buyers we were appealing to now often know more about cars than the floor salesman."

All systems were indicating a good response, and generally dealers were happy although some experienced a shortage of the lower priced two-door models. "I never expected it would take off like it did," says Ross, the AMC dealer in North Tarrytown; "the test drive does it." Another dealer, Vincent A. Soccodato, general manager of Biltmore AMC-Jeep-Renault in Rye, N.Y., was especially pleased, he told me, that the Alliance brought a different kind of buyer into his showroom. (AMC's internal research shows that 90% of all Alliance buyers are new to AMC.)

Marketplace feedback indicated two things: (1) in the beginning, Alliance sales took off most quickly with dealers in the north central part of the United States (and especially in southern Wisconsin, spurred by AMC employee families anxious to support the company), and (2) the "made in America" appeal of the Alliance was especially strong. Consequently, Alliance advertising was modified (revising commercial sound track) to reflect that, and in addition, "Made in America" bumper stickers and window decals were made up and rushed to dealers to put on the cars.

At a press conference in Los Angeles, Calif., on January 10, 1983— just about four months after its introduction—promotional lighting struck the Alliance; *Motor Trend* magazine named it Car of the Year for 1983.

AMC's public relations department knew this was coming two months before and had set up a press campaign to exploit the most welcome endorsement, which—as Mr. Mosher puts it, "gave the Alliance credibility." The day after the announcement, four teams of AMC executives, headed by chairman Paul Tippett, fanned out for press conferences in 23 cities in four days. New bumper stickers and window stickers with "Car of the Year" were on hand in dealer showrooms to affix on cars.

Getting a clear-cut fix on just exactly what the *Motor Trend* award does for the sale of a car is difficult, and that is especially so with the Alliance; as luck would have it, AMC had just announced a new 11.9 percent financing plan at the same time, and how can you separate the impact of two?

In any case, here's an indication of what happened based on weekly sales reports from a panel of 250 AMC dealers. During the best week in September, these 250 dealers sold 791 Alliances. In October, the comparable number was 1,126, and in November, 1,115. The best week in December was 870. Then, in January, in the two weeks immediately prior to the *Motor Trend* announcement, the numbers were 573 and 829. In the third week of January, immediately after the *Motor Trend* announcement, the number was 1,022, and in the week after, 1,233. The best week in February was 1,554 units.

"Half of the people who come in here," says AMC's Rye dealer, Vincent Soccodato, "don't know about *Motor Trend*," but he estimates store traffic quadrupled. "But, I don't think we'll see the full effect until after April 15 when the spring buying season starts," he adds. "Our traffic doubled," estimates Al Kilduff, co-owner of Kilduff Motors, Inc., a long-time AMC dealer in Edgewood, Md. "But you have to remember, a lot of magazines were saying good things about the Alliance at the same time." Most important of all, perhaps, was the huge amount of publicity the Alliance got from newspaper auto writers because of the award, and AMC's pr department has books full of clippings to show.

One of the key questions has been, "To what degree has the Alliance's prominence and success enhanced the image of both AMC and Renault to potential car buyers?" The results of an image study fielded in February 1983, suggests that progress is being made, according to Stu Lahn, senior vp of Oxtoby-Smith, who conducted the study. "The percentage of people who would give positive purchase consideration to Renault has increased 23% over the levels in the last study in December 1981," he said, "and we've also seen significant increases in the positive opinions of both Renault cars and dealers."

Aftermath

The success of the Alliance's launch, with a marketing budget of $13.5 million and a dealer organization of 1,350, unfortunately cannot be compared exactly with those of Ford's Escort and Lynx, which reportedly cost $40 million, or the $20 million spent on the Horizon. In terms of dealer strength, Chevrolet's Chevette had about 6,000—over four times the number of AMC dealers. But what is known does seem to confirm that, pound for pound, AMC's launch was, indeed, one of the most effective Detroit has seen for a long, long time.

Perhaps equally important in the long run, the Alliance's success has enabled AMC to beef up its dealer organization, which was the main lure to Renault in the first place. "For several years," says Jacque O. Polan, manager of AMC's New York Zone office in Elmsford, N.Y., "we were just trying to hold the organization together. About 18 months ago, we started to change all our franchising habits. For instance, now we can be more demanding about adequate training and financing. There was a time when we let a dual dealer take on our cars just to get the exposure, but now when they come around trying to get the Alliance, we can insist on a separate showroom."

That may be—aside from profits—the most important bottom line on what the Alliance means to American Motors.

W. Paul Tippett, Jr., Talks about the Alliance

W. Paul Tippett, Jr., 50, joined AMC as president, chief operating officer, and a director in 1978; in January 1982, he was elected chairman of the board and chief executive officer.

In addition to about 20 years experience in the auto industry (Ford and Lincoln-Mercury divisions of Ford, director of sales and marketing for Ford of Europe, Inc.), Tippett may well be the only top auto executive with experience in high-velocity package goods marketing. He started with Procter & Gamble as a brand manager and advertising supervisor, and at one time was executive vp of STP Corporation.

I talked with Tippett in his office in Southfield, Mich., on April 14, 1983. Tippett was in a good mood; AMC's first public stock offering since 1972 had been snapped up by investors the day before.

HONOMICHL: How does it feel to have the press come to badger you to talk about the Alliance?

TIPPETT: It feels good. I've been rich and I've been poor, and believe me, rich is better. Not an original line, admittedly. Nevertheless, it's been a long, dry spell. We've been sitting here being beaten about the head and shoulders to death by "X" cars, "J" cars, "K" cars, Japanese cars, and without anything to fight back with. Now we've got something, and we've got a lot more coming—that's the important thing.

I think the marketing guys have done a great job with the product. But, as you know—you've done a lot of these stories—marketing can only accelerate the success of a product; it can't substitute for the product. If you market it well, you'll get successful faster.

My first employer was P&G, and everybody talks about what a great marketing-oriented company it is. I say, "You've got it all wrong; it really is a product-oriented company." They work so hard to bring out a better-than-average product; then they do market it well. But the few times they have tried to market a parity, or me-too product, they have fallen on their asses just like everybody else.

HONOMICHL: You are probably the only top executive in the auto industry who knows what high-velocity package goods are all about, with your P&G and STP backgrounds. How much of what you learned in the package goods business have you been able to infuse into the marketing of a car like the Alliance?

TIPPETT: A lot, of course. The principles are certainly the same. You'd better have a product that is at least as good as the competition in most areas, and better than the competition in some key areas. That's to me a principle of good package goods marketing. When you try to come out with a parity product—especially when you are the last guy in, as we were with the Alliance—you've got a lot of trouble; I don't care how good you are, how much you spend.

I've worked in Detroit for a long time—20 years. When I first got here, a car was developed and, like six months before it was scheduled to be launched, the marketing boys were brought in and told, "Here it is; go sell it." In those days you could do that. When we started with the Alliance three, four years ago—it was not just me, it was everybody in the company—we took the attitude, which I strongly believe in, we had better design into the product things that will make it easy to market and give us some advantages, demonstrable advantages, or else we're going to have trouble.

HONOMICHL: What would have happened if the Alliance had bombed?

TIPPETT: It would not be nearly as much fun to be at the office today, Jack.

HONOMICHL: Would it have been the end of American Motors?

TIPPETT: I don't think it would have been the end of American Motors; I don't think it was that desperate. We just had a stock issue....

HONOMICHL: I read about it; it went out very well.

TIPPETT: Yes. We just sold $134 million worth of stock. We just got our banks to increase their lines with us $80 million in spite of the fact we said we were going to sell the single biggest asset we have, AM General. So, not only did we ask them for more money, we said, "By the way, the collateral is going to disappear." That's not an easy sell. So, that's $134 and $80—$214 million. If the Alliance had not been a success, I suspect that neither one of those events would have occurred.

People said, "Can you guys do it? Can you build a new car that is of high quality and technologically superior, and if you can build it...?" They didn't say it that charitably. Most people said first, "You can't build a decent car, and even if you did, you couldn't sell it with all those redneck dealers you've got."

HONOMICHL: How many big banks want to come and have lunch with you at the Detroit Club now when they wouldn't even talk with you two years ago?

TIPPETT: Of the $80 million we just got, $50 million was from our present banks and $30 million was from guys saying, "We'd like to loan you some money." [An aside, with hand cupped to mouth: "Where were you when I needed you?"]

We would not have gone under. I think we could have taken a longer-range view. But I think everybody—there's no question about the fact—was watching this car to see if we could make a good car and sell it in volume.

We have now proved we could do so. We are going to do it again this summer with another car. We are going to do it this fall with a new Jeep. We've done the same thing with these products. The Jeep has six or seven very important product advantages over its competition built in, which we worried about four years ago—not six months. That, to me, is what marketing is all about. I don't care how good a marketer you are; if the product isn't better—and again, if you're the last guy in like we were with the Alliance—you don't have enough money.

Obviously, there's luck involved in anything. We took a marketing viewpoint on this vehicle to begin with. Now pricing is another thing. We knew we'd have to have an advantage going in; nobody is waiting for another new car....

HONOMICHL: You low-balled the Alliance, didn't you?

TIPPETT: No, we did not low-ball it. Well, that depends on how you define it. To me, there are two ways to get a product or marketing advantage. One is "same product, lower price." The other is "better product, same price." So, we chose the "better product, same price" route. If you adjust for equipment, we are pricing right at, or now over, the Escort, which is the biggest selling car in this class. But we've got the better product. Now, if that is low-balling—maybe it is, but I don't think it is;

we don't think our costs are any higher than the Escort—we think we have designed a better product and we've priced it right on them. So people say, "Gee, that's a helluva buy."

To me, that's obviously not only the better but the cheaper way to get an advantage. If you take $100 off the price of the product, that costs you $100. But if you've got $100 of value in the product, that costs us, say, $50.

So, we're not low-ball. We just raised the price by $100 last week. We started with a very competitive price on Escort, and now we're going to start moving it up a bit.

HONOMICHL: How many units do you have to sell a year to get into the black on the Alliance?

TIPPETT: Gee, that's almost an impossible question to answer; it depends on how you allocate the costs. Ford says they are losing money on the Escort. I don't know how they calculate that. The ultimate test—whenever they say they are losing money, then the corollary of that is, "You'd make more money if you stop selling it." Is that right? Most people are not willing to go that far with you, and that's the ultimate test. Would Ford be making more money now if they stopped selling the Escort? I think the answer is "no." It would really be in the soup; the Escort absorbs a huge amount of overhead. From what we know, our costs are generally competitive with what it costs other people to make this size and kind of vehicle, and we're selling it for the same as, or more than, what they are selling for, so it's reasonably profitable for us. I tell you, I would not want to be sitting here today without the Alliance.

HONOMICHL: In digging into your marketing affairs, I found several innovative things. But one, because of my research background, was especially interesting: that is your making a deal with an outside research company to do most, if not all, of your consumer research. How does that work?

TIPPETT: Well, it seems to work out all right. Joe Smith has been with us long enough so that he has some perspective, and yet he's far enough away from us so that he can say, "Hey, you guys, that may sell well in Detroit, but it's not going to sell anywhere else."

This is a somewhat incestuous community, and we have to guard against becoming typical Detroiters. As the fourth guy in town, we can't do what the others do. We've got to be different, not peculiar different, but aggressive different, and—hopefully—imaginatively different. We've got to be right. General Motors can survive—maybe even prosper—after the "J" car debacle, which that really was. They overpriced it and underpowered it. As you correctly pointed out, we would have had a lot more trouble surviving an Alliance debacle. We couldn't afford it; we have to be right every time. We have to be right with the X-37 [named Renault Encore] this summer, and I think we will be. We have to be right in the new Jeep line. We've got to build ourselves up to the point where we can afford a mistake.

HONOMICHL: Does that mean that you have to pay more attention to consumer research than they might?

TIPPETT: I think so. Every time—every single time—we've ignored it, for reasons that seemed convenient at the time, we've lived to regret it. The Alliance cliniced fantastically well; it's been successful. The Eagle cliniced well. We've done some other things that didn't clinic as well, but we said, "Well, what the hell, we like it." And we went ahead and tried it, and guess what...the research was right and we weren't. We ignore it at our peril. We just don't have enough clout to jam it down their throats—and I don't think anyone does any more. There's just too much choice.

HONOMICHL: If you could do it all over again—in retrospect—what would you do differently in marketing the Alliance? Was there something you'd do more of, or less of, or whatever?

TIPPETT: All I can tell you is that we're using the same checklist with the X-37 as with the Alliance. I think most things we did were right.

Oh, yeah—I'll tell you one thing—pr guys never did get the preferred view of the car in their press kits. That's one thing we'd do right next time around.

HONOMICHL: Are cars like actors who want to be photographed from one angle?

TIPPETT: Seriously, I am a nut about this. Twelve to 14 months before we launched that thing, we got professional photographers in and photographed that car from maybe 125 angles—up, down, high, low—and we looked at the transparencies, and everybody gets into it, and we finally conclude the car looks best from this precise angle. Maybe the rear end is a little weaker than the front, or the side view is stronger than...And then there might be two secondary views. But then I don't want to see any pictures of the car—television, print, whatever—that don't use those views; because they're like an actor, or anything else, cars are very funny things. They can look fat, they can look skinny, and they can look big or small, and if you don't get the right view....There is one view that optimizes things. Same with colors.

For reasons that aren't entirely clear, we never did get the pr guys totally in sync with the marketing guys.

We probably spent a little too much money advertising, but on the other hand, no one seems to know exactly what's the precise amount.

It's great now, sitting here feeling euphoric. But knowing what was riding on this car, we started production at 300 cars a day, but we wanted to get to 600 a day because there is considerable lead time. I remember this very clearly: José Dedeurwaerder, the president, and I sat in that room there and said, "We haven't sold car one to a customer, but we've had our dealer announcement shows and the dealers loved it, had the press in and they liked it," and José said to me, "If you really want to not run out of cars, we've got to make a decision by August 14 to go to a second shift." That meant hiring 2,000 people in Kenosha so we could start to build 600 cars a day in the middle of September; it takes about a month, five weeks lead time. We had to order parts, the engine and transmission, from France.

Renault said, "Do you guys know what you're doing?" I said, "No, we're not sure, obviously, but we think we ought to go; the worst thing would be to run out of cars." So, before we'd sold one car, we decided to double production—and it turned out to be the right decision. We went to 600, then to 660, and then today to 860. We didn't go up any faster because we wanted to keep the quality; one of the things that is selling this car is quality.

I really sweated that. One thing we didn't want to do—that is get into the launch and then have to put in rebates or something like that, like our competitors do. Another was to cut production; we knew that would be the worst possible thing we could do for the momentum, success feeling, image, and all that. Remember, that market was lousy then; we launched this thing in a downturn market.

On the other hand, we didn't want to run out of cars. We were spending one hundred zillion, trillion dollars on advertising. So, the famous SWAG (Scientific Wild Ass Guess); we said, "Let's put on the second shift."

Postscript (August 1985)

Shortly after this article appeared, AMC turned a profit for the first time in a long time, but this was mostly due to the new, lighter Jeep, which sold very well—and was relatively profitable. The new Alliance hatchback spin-off, the Encore, sold well—but some of that was steal from Alliance.

But, as time went on, demand for small cars started to slacken, and the market's strongest segment was full-size cars, loaded—where AMC had no viable entry. Alliance advertisements no longer made any references to AMC.

AMC earned $15 million in 1984, but the first quarter of 1985 saw an unexpectedly high loss, $29 million, and the company announced plans for a cutback of 25% in operating costs. The most dramatic step was to threaten the close-down of its Kenosha, Wis., plant where both the Alliance and Encore are manufactured. In desperate need of cash, AMC wanted concessions from the UAW, and after much bitter give and take, in July of 1985, the union agreed to a three-year pact that made sweeping wage and benefit concessions. Right afterward, Régie Nationale des Usines Renault, in deep financial trouble itself, announced a $175 million loan to keep alive AMC plans for a new intermediate-size car to be built at the Brampton, Ontario, Canada, plant.

In the fall of 1984, Paul Tippett yielded the title of CEO to José J. Dedeurwaerder. In the spring of 1985, Tippett said he would discontinue full-time employment with the company. In July, it was announced that Tippett had become president of Springs Industries, the fifth largest U.S. textile firm, with headquarters in Fort Mills, S.C. Dedeurwaerder assumed the post of AMC chairman.

As for the quality AMC had built into the Alliance at first, which contributed so much to its earlier success and Car of the Year Award, that now seems a thing of the past. When the J. D. Power & Associates 1985 Customer Satisfaction Index survey was published (based on interviews with new-car buyers about 12 to 14 months after purchase), AMC/Renault products ranked next to last amongst all major automotive lines. (The winner for 1984 was Mercedes-Benz. The only line ranking below Renault was, ironically, Peugeot, which is imported from France.)

Part 2
The U.S. Marketing Research Industry

Preface to Part 2

The marketing case histories in Part 1 of this book are, of course, peppered with references to specific research studies that were providing important inputs to the marketing decisions as they were being made (or, in some cases, being ignored). Moreover, just as much notice was given to the behind-the-scenes research organizations that were involved as was given to the much more prominent, and public, advertising agencies.

This is as it should be. Marketing, advertising, and public opinion research has been inexorably intertwined with the growth of the advertising and, later, marketing industries. To know how the marketing research industry grew and evolved in the U.S. is to know, largely, how the professionalism of marketing grew and evolved; they are really part and parcel of one another. In fact, some of the more dramatic pioneers of the U.S. research industry were, in retrospect, pioneers of the marketing profession too. That you'll see as you become acquainted with people like Nielsen, Gallup, and Politz in the pages that follow—and come to realize the analytical, professional, and innovative contributions they made to the selling of goods and services.

Yet, it is just within the past 10 years or so that the size, nomenclature, and diversity of the research industry, as it has come to be in the United States, have come to be commonly known. The reasons are many. For one, until recent years, many of the important research service firms were privately held, and they did not make their size public. Almost all of the work they did and the innovations they made were for clients on a proprietary basis and often related to extremely confidential marketing plans or new product development.

Another reason was that—and this is still true today—the industry did not have a trade journal of its own that could throw public light on that information about industry happenings that was publishable. The final reason, and a common one, was that theretofore no one had asked. As is often the case, a lot of the confidentiality was more imagined than real. Put another way, many key people in the industry were, in fact, anxious to have a press that tried to make their good work known and appreciated— within the limits of client restraints and related ethical concerns.

The "press" that did develop, largely, was in the pages of *Advertising Age*, and that was almost entirely due to the editor-in-chief, Rance Crain, who—starting in the early 1970s—made ample space available for research industry news and longer feature articles, such as some of the case histories in Part 1 of this book. Such material, over time, became more commonplace as disclosure barriers melted away.

Today, I estimate about $1.6 billion is spent in the U.S. each year for advertising/marketing/public opinion research; the industry now permeates society to an extent far beyond what most people realize. To be explicit: starting in 1974, Walker Research, Inc. in Indianapolis, Ind., has periodically done a study of the amount of consumer interviewing traffic, and their 1984 study revealed 23% of American adults said they had been interviewed within the past year. The same statistic for 1982 was 23%, and for 1980, 25%. In terms of methodology, telephone interviewing was most common, with door-to-door, mall intercept, and mail following in that order.

More revealing: over one-half (54%) of American adults had been interviewed sometime in the past, and of those who reported being interviewed in the prior year, 56% said they had been interviewed two or three times. Now, when you realize that there will always be a segment of society that will not participate in such activity and there are other segments that—realistically—are not apt to be contacted because of the remoteness of their abode, or language barriers, or because they are institutionalized, or whatever, it is easy to conclude that, indeed, research blankets American society.

Given that, more should be known about the firms and people who make up this vast industry, some of their concerns, and how they go about their work. That's what I've tried to do in this part of the book—lift the curtain, make some introductions.

11 The U.S. Research Industry

Gallup, Starch, Nielsen, Roper, Hooper—these names are well known within the marketing community, and even to the general public, to some degree. Unfortunately, little has been written to document how the marketing/advertising research industry got started—way back in the early 1900s—in the United States, and the roles these now-famous pioneers played.

I tried to briefly summarize the early days in a Research Beat column that appeared in Advertising Age *on April 19, 1976. The story began prior to 1900, and here it is.*

The Early History

Would anybody guess that marketing research goes back nearly to this country's beginnings?

Take political polling. In July 1824, the *Harrisburg Pennsylvanian* printed a report of a straw vote taken at Wilmington, Del., "without discrimination of parties." In that election year poll, Andrew Jackson received 335 votes; John Quincy Adams, 169; Henry Clay, 19; and William H. Crawford, 9. Later the same year, another newspaper, the *Raleigh Star*, undertook a canvass of political meetings held in North Carolina, "at which the sense of the people was taken."

Use of original marketing research by an advertising agency to gain a new account popped up as early as 1879. N. W. Ayer & Son was soliciting the Nichols-Shepard Co., manufacturer of agricultural machinery. Ayer prepared a media schedule that was challenged by the would-be client, according to L. C. Lockley writing in the *Journal of Marketing* for April 1950. Substantiation came from an Ayer survey of state officials and publishers throughout the country asking for information on grain production and media circulation by counties. The client was impressed and Ayer got the account.

In 1895, Harlow Gale of the University of Minnesota was using mailed questionnaires to obtain public opinions on advertising, and George B. Waldron was doing qualitative research for Mahin's Advertising Agency around 1900, according to Lockley. In 1901, Walter Dill Scott, later president of Northwestern University, undertook a program of experimental research on advertising for the Agate Club of Chicago.

It wasn't until about 1910, according to Lockley, "that evidences of market research became frequent enough to indicate that a new field of business activity had made a serious start." In 1911, for instance, J. George Frederick left the editorship of *Printer's Ink* to start what may have been the first business research company, the Business Bourse. Among his early clients were General Electric and the Texas Co. By Frederick's estimates, no more than $50,000 was spent in gathering marketing information, even informally, in 1910.

It was also in 1911 that R. O. Eastman, then advertising manager for the Kellogg Co. in Battle Creek, Mich., interested some members of the Association of National Advertising Managers (as the Association of National Advertisers was then known) to cooperate on a joint postcard questionnaire survey to determine magazine readership. That introduced the important concept of duplication of circulation. Eastman became so involved in this sort of survey that in 1916 he started his own company, the Eastman Research Bureau. His first clients were *Cosmopolitan* and the *Christian Herald*, followed later by General Electric, which wanted a consumer survey to determine recognition of the "Mazda" trademark.

The year 1911 also saw the establishment of a Bureau of Business Research at the Harvard Graduate School of Business, as well as the now famous Commercial Research Division of the Curtis Publishing Co., headed by Charles C. Parlin. This operation was spun off in 1943 to become the company now known as National Analysts. In 1915, U.S. Rubber Co. started a research department headed by Dr. Paul H. Nystrom, and two years later Swift & Co. followed with a department headed by Dr. Louis D. H. Weld.

In the newspaper field, the *Chicago Tribune* pioneered in 1916 with a door-to-door survey of consumer purchasing habits in Chicago. This same paper in the 1950s, under the leadership of Pierre Martineau, sponsored what was probably the largest and most diverse marketing and advertising research staff ever for an advertising medium.

About 1918, the now famous husband and wife team of Percival White and Pauline Arnold started the Market Research Company, which later, under the ownership of Samuel Barton, became known as the Market Research Corporation of America (MRCA).

Some of the more familiar pioneer names in research started to flourish in the 1920s. Dr. Daniel Starch, for instance, first used the recognition method for measuring the readership of advertisements and editorial content in magazines and newspapers in 1922.

Dr. George Gallup also got into advertising readership measurements in 1923, but he is probably best known today for the Gallup Poll, which was first published in 35 newspapers in 1935 and promptly got him denounced as a "charlatan," a fate that also befell such other pioneer pollsters as Elmo Roper and Archibald Crossley.

These men had a common problem: convincing skeptical editors and commercial clients that, indeed, a small sample of the population, if properly drawn, could be used to measure accurately the predilections of society. Led by Gallup in 1936, they turned to public elections; here was a chance to measure just before a public event where real, tabulated results could be compared with survey predictions. Even with the progress since, sampling methodology today still remains the most baffling mystique associated with marketing research.

A young man by the name of Arthur C. Nielsen entered the marketing research field in 1923. He, in effect, invented the concept of share of market, which has held business executives spellbound ever since; they've spent more to get at that than for anything else in the marketing information field. Result: the A. C. Nielsen Co. is today by far the largest marketing research operation in the world.

The 1930s saw an explosion of new companies dedicated to this new thing called "research." Daniel Starch & Staff (now Starch INRA Hooper Inc.) opened its doors in 1932. Also in that period came Lloyd Hall & Associates; C. E. Hooper, Inc.; Crossley, Inc.; Stewart, Dougall & Associates; Phychological Corp.; Opinion Research Corp.; Willmark Research Corp.; and the American Institute of Public Opinion.

Research was starting to become an American export. George Gallup set up affiliate relationships with survey companies in England and France in 1936, and A. C. Nielsen started a subsidiary in England in 1939, when World War II started.

War needs spurred the further development of the fledgling research field. Paul Lazarsfeld, the social research scholar, has stressed this: "During WW II, social research was in heavy demand by all branches of the government—and especially the Army, the Office of Price Administration, and the Office of War Information [OWI]." Much of the OWI work, Lazarsfeld noted, was done by contract through the Department of Agriculture, where a young psychologist named Rensis Lickert headed the Division of Program Studies. Social scientists were, more and more, drawn into public opinion and attitude research.

After the war, Lickert took his team to the University of Michigan to create the now famous Survey Research Center. His counterpart at OWI, research director Elmo Wilson, started his own company, International Research Associates, after the war.

There was a postwar boom in research. Of the top ten research companies in the United States in 1976, all but one (Nielsen) were founded after World War II. This period also saw the advent of the electronic computer, which broke open the way to large-scale data manipulation.

This brief history, unfortunately, leaves unmentioned many of the prominent shapers of the research community in the United States today, and many of the landmark texts, events, and contributions that have enriched the field. Nevertheless, it seems evident that marketing and advertising research are more inextricably involved in our country's history than most would guess, except for a backward look prompted by a bicentennial.

12 A. C. Nielsen, Sr.: Obituary Traces History

In my opinion, no other single man contributed as much to the development of professionalism in marketing as Arthur C. Nielsen, Sr., who died on June 1, 1980, at the age of 82.

In 1923, Nielsen founded the A. C. Nielsen Co., which today operates through subsidiaries in 24 foreign countries; it's the largest marketing research organization in the world by far. In fact, ACN, in terms of annual revenues, is also much larger than the largest U.S.-owned advertising agency, worldwide.

When I learned that Nielsen's health was failing back in the spring of 1980, I suggested to Rance Crain, editor of Advertising Age, *that I prepare a suitable obituary for the man so that, when and if the day came, we'd have a substantial tribute ready to publish. Crain agreed, and I prepared the article that follows—with considerable cooperation from the A. C. Nielsen Co. and members of Nielsen's family.*

Nielsen's obituary ran in Advertising Age *on June 9, 1980, and despite considerable trimming, it was still the longest such personal tribute ever to run in that publication. Here's the full story of the man who invented the concept of "share of market"—and as you'll see, Nielsen's professional career is, in large part, a chronicle of the growth of marketing and advertising research around the world.*

A. C. Nielsen, Sr.

WINNETKA, ILLINOIS–Arthur C. Nielsen, Sr., founder of A. C. Nielsen Company, the world's largest and most renowned marketing/advertising research company, died June 1, 1980. He was 82.

Nielsen, who founded the company in 1923, moved from president to chairman in 1957, when he was succeeded by his

177

son, Arthur, Jr. The senior Nielsen, whose most recent title was chairman of the executive board, had been in ill health for the past few years.

Despite the prominence of the Nielsen name—with the general public through the company's broadcast audience ratings service, and with marketing specialists through its store audit services and coupon clearing house—Nielsen's extraordinary business and personal achievements have been relatively unheralded, especially over the past 20 years. He was a private man.

In 1923, four years after graduating from the University of Wisconsin with the highest scholastic average (95.8) ever recorded in the college of engineering, and after two years of duty as a naval officer in World War I, Nielsen started in business with six employees and $45,000 capital raised from a group of friends.

Thus, Nielsen—at age 26—became a pioneer in a fledgling industry. Prior to 1923, there were just three U.S. companies specializing in marketing/advertising research: Business Bourse, founded by J. George Frederick in 1911; Eastman Research Bureau, founded by Roy O. Eastman in 1916; and Market Research Company, founded by Percival White in 1918. (Two other research pioneers, Daniel Starch and George Gallup, also started their companies in 1923.)

Today the A. C. Nielsen Co., now public and traded over-the-counter, operates out of its headquarters in Northbrook, Ill., through subsidiaries in 21 foreign countries, and has over 17,000 employees and annual revenues of nearly $400 million. In contrast, the world's largest advertising agency, J. Walter Thompson Co., had worldwide revenues of $254 million in 1979. Or, put another way, the Nielsen Co.'s revenues from marketing/advertising services alone ($286 million in fiscal year 1979) are larger than those of the next seven largest U.S. research companies combined.

More important, Nielsen's unique blend of foresight, business acumen, inventiveness, and personal bearing has probably done more to shape the professionalism of the worldwide marketing/advertising research industry than that of any other man. He was truly a statesman.

The Dark Days

During its first 10 years, the Nielsen Co. specialized in surveys— mostly for industrial clients—and the going was rough. "We were broke, and it was a terribly risky thing," Arthur Nielsen reminisced in an interview in the *New York Times* in 1967. "I had a mortgage on everything, and there wasn't another dime in the world that we could beg or borrow." Even so, in 1933—at the nadir of the Depression—he started a new service, the Nielsen Drug Index (NDI), which would become the mainspring for his company's growth in the future.

Developed for package goods manufacturers, NDI was based on what was then a novel idea: draw a sample of drugstores and then visit them periodically to develop, through audits of purchase invoices and shelf stock, a measure of unit sales. This was logical for Nielsen since both his parents were accountants. (His father was manager of the general accounting division of Quaker Oats Co., Chicago.)

These store movements data, when projected, provided a measure of category size sales velocity which then could be related to marketing efforts. In the process, he produced an exciting new concept: share of market. This turned marketing into a horse race, and only Nielsen had the scorecard. More marketing decisions, expenditures, and careers have been influenced by that single statistic—share of market—than any other.

A companion service, the Nielsen Food Index, was started seven months after NDI, and since then, the adaptation of the index methodology to other store categories and the expansion of index services in foreign countries have been the main thrust of the Nielsen company. Today, ACN Index services have over 1,500 corporate clients in 23 countries.

Nielsen was a pioneer in oversees expansion; he launched his first foreign subsidiary in Great Britain in 1939, a bold move for a man who had the personal reputation of being ultraconservative in business and politics. In the years since, many U.S. research companies have followed his lead in exporting research expertise.

In developing the index services, Nielsen did several other things that, in their day, were innovative. He paid retailers for their "cooperation." He sold his service on a syndicated basis, with all clients getting basically the same data—and sharing the cost. He asked clients to sign continuous contracts with stiff terms, which gave his business stability. (In later years, he added an escalation clause to these contracts with automatic rate increases geared to the Consumer Price Index; a good part of the company's revenue growth record has been a result of that clause.)

Nielsen made store panels available for experimentation back in 1933, thus foreseeing the need for "test marketing." And he decided early on to use full-time, salaried employees—mostly college graduates—as field auditors. This cadre produced the managers needed for his company's rapid growth, and hundreds of men so trained have sifted into marketing positions in the package goods industry.

Into Broadcast

Nielsen also was one of the pioneers in broadcast audience measurements, starting in 1936 when radio set ownership grew to the level where there was commercial interest. His Nielsen Radio Index service brought the "share-of-market" concept to the communications industry.

Nielsen's innovative approach to audience measures was something you would have expected from a man trained as an electrical engineer; his famous Audimeter was a mechanical device that could be wired to sets to continuously record time on and station tuned.

This was one of several mechanical devices that intrigued Nielsen. He also developed the Gas-Oil Recordimeter to attach to automobiles which automatically recorded purchases of gasoline and oil, and the House Recordimeter, an in-home device through which consumers could record their purchases (Nielsen's answer to mail diary panels).

The years 1946 to 1955 were tough on audience research services, and the Nielsen Co. reportedly lost $13 million. But, as Nielsen said to me over lunch in 1969, "Think of the free advertising." The radio service was discontinued in 1964, but by then the Nielsen name had become a household word because of his ratings service—and a cussword among entertainers who were canceled because of low ratings.

It was in these years that Nielsen started to receive a professional accolades: in 1951, the Paul D. Converse Award from the American Marketing Association for contributions to the science of marketing; in 1963, the Parlin Memorial Award for "demonstrated meritorious achievement in marketing and advertising research"; and in 1966, citation as Advertising Man of the Year and by the International Advertising Association.

Nielsen's business skill is best exemplified by his company's long-term policy of investment in tangible assets, rare for a service company. Today the company owns outright 11 buildings totaling 557,500 square feet; these, plus land values, are carried on the books—at cost less depreciation—at $37.7 million, which is just a fraction of their probable market value today. Most are located in what are now prime industrial park developments where Nielsen was often among the first to buy in.

Concurrent with his professional growth, Nielsen achieved an enviable record in the world of tennis, a sport he took up while attending Morton High School in Cicero, Ill. At the University of Wisconsin, he was captain of the varsity tennis team for three years and continued to play in tournaments through his advanced years. He twice won the national father–son doubles championship in the Veterans Division (over 45), and once, the national father–daughter hardcourt championship. In 1971, Nielsen was elected to the National Lawn Tennis Hall of Fame.

In his prime, Nielsen worked 60 to 70 hours a week, and his employees were used to being bombarded with his memos, which were long and detailed. Many were drafted in the back seat of his eight-passenger blue Fleetwood Cadillac, which—complete with blue shag rug—was equipped as a moving office. Nielsen traveled by ship as he thought flying was dangerous, and the trunk of his car was equipped to carry the voluminous files he took on his long auto trips through countries he toured in the process of building his overseas empire. He was proud of his car burglar alarm which, said Nielsen, "makes a noise that would scare the gizzard out of you."

Nielsen had the reputation of being a super salesman, which dated back to his personal selling of index services in the 1930s.

I can personally attest to his skills in this area. In 1969, I called on Nielsen to solicit advertising for a new research magazine, *The Analyst*. He invited me to lunch in the private dining room off his office, and I found that—in addition to being most attentive to my plans—Nielsen had prepared for my visit; he had some thoughts that he wanted to sell me, which he did most effectively. On the way out, he said that the Nielsen Co. would buy an ad in every issue of *The Analyst* as long as it was published simply because "it's a good thing for the industry."

The remarkable impression that man made during that brief encounter continues today. One unfortunate aspect of his career is that so few research people outside his company had the experience of knowing him personally.

Nielsen is survived by his wife, Gertrude; two sons, Arthur C. Nielsen, Jr., chairman of the board, and Philip R., vp of the company, and three daughters.

13 Alfred Politz: A German-American Original

In sharp contrast to the highly structured, relatively staid Art Nielsen, Sr., another breed of colorful entrepreneurs characterized the early developmental years of the U.S. research industry. Alfred Politz epitomized this breed, and as you'll see, in addition to introducing research into the highest levels of corporate management, he also—as we come to see in retrospect—ran a training facility for a large number of bright young people who had somehow stumbled into research as a potential career path. Politz, then, was a big pebble in what was then a small pond, but the rings emanating from his personal splash still circle the much larger industry today.

Despite their differences in style—and personal life—Art Nielsen and Alfred Politz had much in common. Both had their academic training in the physical sciences. Both were strict disciplinarians. Both had an uncanny ability to "sell in" at the highest levels of American industry. Both profited lavishly from their labors. Both are recognized today as more than just pioneers; they, by force of personality and personal ability, helped shape an industry.

I approached the Politz biography, an edited-down version of which was published in Advertising Age *on October 31, 1983, with great interest. Pulling the materials together took many months and involved the cooperation of dozens of people. Alfred Politz deserved no less.*

Overview of Politz's Life

In 1937, Alfred Politz, a dapper 35-year-old native of Berlin, repulsed by the rise of Nazism in Germany, came to New York City to start a new life. About all he brought with him was a Ph.D. in physics, a scanty knowledge of the English language, an athlete's body (firm and trim), boundless energy, and—most important—an enormous ego, a supreme self-confidence.

What to do? "I arrived in New York and studied the problem," Politz wrote in his personal papers long after retiring as a millionaire in 1967 and about a year before his death on November 8, 1982: "Which profession

Alfred Politz

makes the most money with the least intelligence? The answer was 'advertising.' But my English was not good enough for this field." He should have added, "At least, not right away...."

That career choice, seen in retrospect, was momentous. Politz was to become a legend in his own time, a dynamic and controversial personage in the relatively—circa 1950s—unsophisticated field of advertising, research and marketing. Extremely critical of prevailing practices in all three, he especially deplored the lack of "professionalism" and "logic." Although a middle-aged outsider with a heavy accent, he was an iconoclast who would prevail. In fact, there are admirers today who would argue that Alfred Politz had more impact and lasting influence in the fields of marketing/advertising/research than William Bernbach, relatively, had in the field of advertising.

Politz's personal life was as flamboyant as his professional life, and that's part of his legend and charisma too. He flew gliders and hot air balloons; he wrote poetry and short stories; he ran a hardware store to learn about business close up; he made a fetish of physical well-being and enjoyed arm wrestling with employees or strangers; he conducted experiments in the physical sciences and put up technical papers for publication; he played the electric organ with vigor, if not skill, and enjoyed singing risque German beer-drinking songs; and, according to numerous close coworkers, he enjoyed most of all the companionship of beautiful—make that "stunning"—young ladies; you could say Politz was an unabashed philanderer.

Many who knew him apply the word "genius," and all remark about his energy and forceful personality. "You never forgot him once you met him," observed Robert Weller (executive vp of Politz's research firm, 1950–64) in a speech at a memorial service, which was attended by a standing room only crowd of about 200 at the Time-Life Building in Manhattan on December 2, 1982.

Alfred Politz Research, Inc.

In 1943, just six years after arriving in New York and still dependent on his wife for help in English, Politz started his own business after being fired by Compton Advertising, Inc., where he had been research director.

By the mid-1940s, now president and 100% owner of Alfred Politz Research, Inc., (APRI), which was incorporated in 1947, Politz was becoming increasingly conspicuous for his acerbic criticism of the quota sampling techniques used by public opinion pollsters, including George Gallup and Elmo Roper, a former employer. (In *Advertising Age*, November 8, 1948, Politz was quoted as saying gleefully in reference to the faulty preelection forecasts made by some public opinion pollsters, "This is good for the research business. This is an excellent influence. It will help get rid of the charlatans. The profession will become more ethical and scientific.") Politz, a champion of random probability sampling in marketing research, came to see his point of view prevail, one of his notable contributions to a fledgling industry.

In 1949, Politz's firm was selected by *Life* magazine to do one of the landmark studies of magazine audience readership; more than any other thing, perhaps, this made him famous. For the next 15 years, he was Mr. Magazine Research in the U.S., conducting what were often pioneering, sometimes famous, and always expensive, studies for the likes of *Look*, *McCall's*, *Saturday Evening Post*, *Redbook*, and *Reader's Digest* as they embraced audience research, and a total reach concept, to gin up boxcar numbers to fight tv, which was then coming on strong.

Concurrently, Politz was building up the marketing research side of his business. He came to count among his personal clients some of the biggest names in American marketing—John R. Kimberly at Kimberly-Clark Corp.; Samuel (and later, Edgar) Bronfman at Joseph E. Seagram & Sons; Rosser Reeves at Ted Bates Advertising; Henry Bristol at Bristol-Meyers Co.; Andrew Heiskell at Time, Inc.; J. Paul Austin at Coca-Cola Co.; and Vernon Bellman at the Mobil division of Socony-Vacuum Oil Co. (as Mobil Corp. was called in those days).

It was characteristic of Politz—whom some considered arrogant and aloof—to deal (or try to deal) with the top man only. He would not recognize the client's research department (if the client had one in those days), and that haughty stance cost him business in later years when the fascination of consumer research wore off in the boardroom and research managers started to gain more power.

Politz U.

One of Politz's most important legacies was that his firm—which was the glamorous "hot shop" of research in the 1950s and early 1960s and renowned for its professional standards—also served as the training ground for a small army of would-be survey research and marketing practitioners. For many it was their first—and most exciting—job, the apprenticeship, the stimulus that was to shape a career.

The best way to explain the ripple effect of Politz and his firm, and to show how his influence continues to permeate the marketing community, is to list some of the alumni of Alfred Politz Research, Inc. (circa 1950s and early 1960s) and to show where they ended up (see accompanying listing). You'll probably note many familiar names, and it is interesting to see that the majority of Politz U. alumni turned out to be entrepreneurs; today they either own or are principals in their own firms. Others are now prominent advertising or media executives.

Alumni of Alfred Politz Research, Inc. and Where They Are Today (A partial listing as of August 1983)

One of the most important legacies of Alfred Politz was that his firm became one of the leading training grounds for a generation of survey research and marketing executives, many of whom still adhere to the practices and standards they learned as proteges of Politz in the period 1950–67.

There follows a partial listing of those people and where they are as of August 1983. Special thanks to Robert Weller, Martin Zeidner, Charles Jacobson, and Jack Ross for helping to compile this listing. Apologies to those we were unable to locate.

AGINS, Sherman L.—Senior Vice President, Group Research Director, Doyle Dane Bernbach, New York City
ALMASH, John—Director of Marketing Research and Information Analysis, Pepsi-Cola Co., Purchase, New York
AMOROSO, Michael—Managing Director, Michael Amoroso, Inc., New York City

BALDI, Joseph F.—President, Directions for Decisions, Inc., New York City
BARNES, Hilda (now deceased)—was Founder, President of Research Information Center, Inc. (RICI), now part of Winona Research, Inc., Phoenix, Arizona
BAYTON, James A.—Professor of Psychology, Howard University, Washington, D.C.
BERLAND, Raymond—Vice President, Marketing Information Systems, Inc., Englewood Cliffs, New Jersey
BLAS, Marshall—Vice President, AHF Marketing Research, New York City
BONFELD, Max—Vice President-Director, Consumer Research Services, Young & Rubicam, New York City
BOWDREN, Donald F.—President, Don Bowdren Associates, Huntington, Connecticut

BROUT, David B.—Market Research Manager, Corporate Services, J. C. Penney Co., Inc., New York City

BRUMBACH, Richard (now retired)—was a Partner in W. R. Simmons & Associates, New York City

CHOOK, Paul H.—Executive Vice President, Marketing and Circulation, Ziff-Davis Publishing Co., New York City

CHARING, Herbert W. (now deceased)—was Area Marketing Research Manager, General Foods, White Plains, New York

CIMBAL, Alan—Vice President, Group Head, Data Development Corp., New York

DE KADT, Pieter P.—President, de Kadt Marketing and Research, Inc., Greenwich, Connecticut

DODGE, Sherwood (now deceased)—was President of the Advertising Research Foundation

EBERHARDT, Richard C.—Group Research Director, Ziff-Davis Publishing Co., New York City

EICHLER, Edward (now deceased)—was Partner, National Marketing Studies, New York City

EPSTEIN, Edward—President, Edward Epstein & Associates, Inc., Syosset, NY

ETTUS, Frank—Director, Research, SE Surveys, Inc., New York City

FABIAN, George S.—Executive Vice President, Director of Research, SSC&B, New York City

FRANK, Robert M.—Executive Vice President, Polaris Research Associates, Inc., New York City

FRANKEL, Lester R.—Executive Vice President, Audits & Surveys, Inc., New York City

FRATTO, Kenneth P.—President, Cambridge Opinion Studies, Inc., Holmdel, NJ

GAY, William K.—Market Research Manager, Home Furnishings and Leisure, J. C. Penney Co., Inc., New York City

GERSHFIELD, Bruce—Research Director, *Seventeen* Magazine, New York City

GOLDEN, Robert J.—Vice President, Director of Client Service, R. H. Bruskin Associates, Inc., New Brunswick, New Jersey

GOLDSTEIN, Joseph—President, Data Development Corp., New York City

GORI, George—Group Product Manager, Schmid Products, Inc., Little Falls, NJ

GREENE, Jerome D.—President, Marketmath, Inc., New York City

HALPERN, Richard S.—Manager, Marketing Communications Research, The Coca-Cola Co., Atlanta, Georgia

HARDY, Hugh S.—Senior Vice President, Public Affairs, Royal Bank of Canada, Montreal, Quebec

HERGUTH, Robert (now retired)—was Area Marketing Manager, Marketing Dept., Reuben H. Donnelley Corp., New York City

HULME, Donald—Market Research Manager, Boehringer Ingelheim, Ridgefield, Connecticut

JACOBSON, Charles D.—Director, Marketing Research, Life Savers, Inc., New York

KING, Larry C.—Eastern Region Sales Manager, Breakfast and Pet Foods Division, General Foods, White Plains, New York
KLEIN, Eva—Partner, National Marketing Studies, Inc., New York City
KNOBLER, William—President, William Knobler Company, Inc., Manhasset, Long Island, New York
KOSSOFF, Jerome—President, Beta Research Corp., Syosset, New York
KURTZ, Richard—President, On-Site Testing, Inc., New York City

LAUER, Robert C.—Manager, Market Services, American Can, Canada, Inc., Toronto, Canada
LEMONICK, Chick—Executive Vice President, R. H. Bruskin Associates, New Brunswick, New Jersey
LINDSEY, Robert R.—Consumer Research Manager, Boyle-Midway Division, American Home Products, New York City
LUSTIG, Phillip—President, Leggett & Lustig Research, Inc., New York City

MACHI, Vincent S.—Vice President, Director, Marketing and Sales Services, Somerset Importers, Inc., New York City
MANN, W. Jack—Director, New Products Research, Edward Epstein & Associates, Inc., Syosset, New York
MC GUINNESS, Peter J.—CEO, Valley Forge Information Service, King of Prussia, Pennsylvania
MILHALY, George—President, Crossley Youth-Student Surveys, Inc., New York
MILLER, A. Edward—Chairman, Miller & Kops, Inc., New York City
MILLER, Karen—Group Supervisor, Data Development Corp., New York City
MIRABEL, Jackie—Assistant Research Director, Clairol, Inc., New York City
MOSKOWITZ, Milton—Business Columnist, *San Francisco Chronicle*

NARDO, Ursula—Vice President, Director, Field Operations, Decision Center, Inc., New York City
NEWELL, Thomas—(formerly research director, D'Arcy Advertising, St. Louis), now Director, Alumni Association, Stanford University, Palo Alto, California
NEWMAN, Lawrence—President, Newman-Stein, Inc., New York City
NOVICK, Morton B.—Senior Marketing Executive, Nabisco Brands, New York

O'CONNOR, Peggy (Steuer)—Field Director, Ross-Cooper Associates, Inc., NYC

RAPHAEL, Peter L.—Associate Research Director, Marschalk, Inc., New York
REINER, Gerald—Vice President, Group Assistant Research Director, Doyle Dane Bernbach, New York City
REIS, Frank—Staff Manager, Market Research, AT&T, Central Services Organization, Basking Ridge, New Jersey
ROSS, Jack—President, J. Ross Associates, Inc., Cranbury, New Jersey
RORTHSTEIN, Melvin—Partner, Rothstein-Tauber, Inc., Stamford, Connecticut

SABATER, Gilbert—President, BECKET, New York City
SALB, Jack B.—Director of Marketing Research, Chase Manhattan Bank, NYC
SANTORA, James F.—Assistant Director, Marketing Research, Chesebrough-Pond's, Greenwich, Connecticut

SCHILLER, Miriam—Corporate Research Consultant, Yankelovich, Skelly and White, Inc., New York City
SCHILLER, Nathan—President, Nathan Schiller, Marketing Research and Consulting, Stamford, Connecticut
SCHUMSKY, Stanley—Senior Vice President, Group Research Director, Doyle Dane Bernbach, New York City
SHAPIRO, Sid—President, SA Shapiro Research Corp., New York City
SHILLER, Clark—Director of Research, Corporate Circulation, Time Inc., New York City
SIEGEL, Alan H.—Senior Vice President, Evaluative Criteria, Inc., Stamford, Connecticut
SIMMONS, W. R. "Bill" (now retired)—Founder, President of W. R. Simmons & Associates (predecessor of Simmons Market Research Bureau, Inc.) and Three Sigma Research Center, Inc., New York City
SIMPSON, Richard T.—Executive Vice President, Telcom Research, Inc., Teaneck, New Jersey
SLURZBERG, Lee—President, Lee Slurzberg Research, Inc., Fort Lee, New Jersey
SMITH, Harry—President, Harry Smith Research Associates, New York City
SOBEL, Charles A.—Senior Vice President, Market Probe International, Inc., New York City
SOLOV, Bernard M.—Executive Vice President, de Kadt Marketing and Research, Inc., Greenwich, Connecticut
SPAR, Edward J.—President, Market Statistics, New York City
SPIZER, Stuart—Director of International Advertising, *The New Yorker*, NYC
SPRUNG, Albert F.—Director, Marketing Analysis, Seagram Distillers Company, New York City
SPUNGIN, Raymond S.—Supervisor, Regional Research Section, Port Authority of New York and New Jersey, New York City
STAHLHEBER, Robert F.—Executive Field Director, Yankelovich, Skelly and White, Inc., Stamford, Connecticut
STOCK, J. Stevens (now deceased)—Founder and Chairman, Marketmath, Inc., New York City
STURMAN, Steven—Senior Vice President, Market Research Director, Wells, Rich, Greene, Los Angeles

TAUBER, Richard M.—Partner, Rothstein-Tauber, Inc., Stamford, Connecticut
TREDENNICK, Donald—Vice President, Director, Research/Marketing Services, Dailey & Associates, Los Angeles
TREWHELLA, Claire—Principal, QUIP—Arbuckle, Cohen & Trewhella, Inc., NYC

UBERSTINE, Elliott—President, Workshop West, Beverly Hills, California

VOLASKI, Albert—President, Coding Enterprise, Forest Hills, New York

WELLER, Robert—Partner, National Marketing Studies, New York City
WEIDER, Sally—Senior Marketing Research Project Director, Colgate-Palmolive, New York City

WILLIAMS, Robert J.—Senior Marketing Researcher, The Dow Chemical Company, Midland, Michigan

YAZMIR, Martin D.—President, Polaris Research Associates, Inc., New York City

YOUNG, Shirley—President, Grey Strategic Marketing (a unit of Grey Advertising), New York City

YULMAN, William—Managing Director, Teleservice Research, Wynnewood, Pennsylvania

YUNG, David—President, Wine & Spirits, Inc., New York City

ZANES, George W.—President, Zanes & Associates, Inc. and the Marketing Research Workshop, Fort Lee, New Jersey

ZEIDNER, Martin—President, Topline Research Corp., New York City

ZIMENT, Larry—President, Ziment Associates, Inc., New York City

---

The Legend

When writing about a legend, it is often difficult to separate fact from fiction. That's certainly been true with Alfred Politz, where the fact is sometimes more bizarre than the fiction. To complicate matters, Politz seldom spoke of his early years, either in Germany or the U.S., and there are inaccuracies in his *Who's Who* write-up. Another complication is that Politz's powerful personality evoked different reactions from people who saw him in different contexts.

In talking with literally dozens of his acquaintances—employees, clients, personal friends—I've heard spontaneous reactions to the Politz name that run the gamut:

"A terrific guy...."

"Intellectually a giant; personally a bastard."

"A baron. The way he wanted it, that's the way it was."

"Absolutely the most brilliant man I've ever met."

"He was a nut."

"The analytical power of the brain of Alfred Politz was a wonder; it cut through like a laser beam."

"I loved the man; he was my model—the reason I went into research."

"He had a big, fat ego."

"He ate up problems like some people eat peanuts."

"He made you feel stupid."

"A very impressive man."

"He really enjoyed argumentation with people he felt worthwhile; the list of people he felt worthwhile was very short."

"A remarkable man, Alfred Politz—intelligent, dynamic, creative, playful, whimsical, and very charismatic."

Equally contradictory are the many versions one hears about Politz's career. There follow what I believe to be the facts of the matter, which I hope will help settle the dust.

Alfred Politz was born in Berlin on July 6, 1902. He attended the Institute of Physics, which was part of Humboldt University in Berlin, and received his doctorate in 1924 at the age of 22. Afterwards, according to his personal papers, he taught evening courses for engineers who wanted to brush up on their math. In his spare time he wrote short stories and participated in amateur boxing matches as a welterweight.

Circa 1928–29, he somehow got to be what amounted to advertising director for the *Berlinger TageBlatt*, an important newspaper in Berlin, and—the rumor goes—made himself unpopular with German advertising agencies by suggesting that advertising copy should be tested for effectiveness. This rankled the creative people who saw it as an insult to their professional competence.

Sometime in the early 1930s, Politz started his own firm, Alfred Politz Webeberatung, a consultancy which worked on the marketing of industrial products. For sport, he belonged to a gliding club. In Germany in those days such "clubs" were often clandestine training units for what was to become the *Luftwaffe*, but it seems clear that Politz wanted no part of the German military (which he felt sure he'd get sucked into because of his training in physics).

In the mid-1930s, Politz had gotten involved with a German firm that mass marketed an analgesic (trade name: Split Tablet; it's still marketed in Germany), and this got him involved in consumer advertising and some marketing research. It also necessitated frequent business trips to Stockholm, Sweden, where he was trying to market Split Tablet. When Politz finally decided to forsake Germany, the escape route was through Sweden.

Early Years in New York

After Politz settled in New York, he continued to travel back to Sweden to promote the Split Tablet business and keep his only source of income alive. Also, he tried to capitalize on business contacts he had made in Germany, one of whom was William Wrigley, the chewing gum tycoon, for whom Politz had done some work. According to A. Edward Miller, Wrigley had told Politz that if he came to the U.S., Wrigley would have a position for him. So, the story goes, as soon as Politz could swing it financially, he took a train to Chicago to see Wrigley who kissed him off with a handshake and two tickets to see the Cubs play baseball. We don't know if Politz ever made it to the game.

In 1939, Politz brought his wife-to-be, Martha Bruszat, from Germany and tried to get his widowed mother out, too. This involved clandestine trips into Nazi Germany, which weren't too safe for Politz at the time. He tried to get FDA approval for the Split Tablet formula so that it could be marketed in the U.S., but that didn't pan out, and the start of World War II cut off his income. Politz had to get a job.

In about 1940, Politz became acquainted with one Richard Wood, an editor at *Fortune* magazine who had previously worked for Elmo Roper, a well-known public opinion pollster at the time. That opened the door to the research field, a job with Roper Research Associates, which lasted for three (what Politz was later to describe as "potboiler") years. He worked his way up to the position of study director, and thanks to tutoring from his wife Martha, who also was working for Roper, his English was improving quickly.

In 1943, Politz was hired away from Roper by Edward Battey, research director at Compton Advertising, Inc., to be his replacement—a job Politz held for about eight months. But his personality didn't set too well with Roger Humphries, research director at Procter & Gamble, the largest account at Compton. Humphries considered Politz's attitude condescending; it seems (according to Battey, with whom I spoke recently) that Politz took it upon himself to teach Humphries research. On Politz's discharge, Richard Compton offered Politz free space in the Compton offices, and he promptly started a company that included his wife Martha and Jane K. Elligett, another ex-Roper employee. (Eva Klein, a longtime associate and friend, joined the firm a couple of years later.) Socony-Vacuum Co. (now Mobil Corp.) was one of Politz's first clients.

More important, growing acceptance of Politz's position on random sampling led to a series of study assignments from the Advertising Research Foundation (the first was in 1944, one of 14 in the continuing study of transportation advertising), and his "revolutionary" sampling techniques were starting to attract attention, fueled by lectures he gave and articles he wrote. In 1946, the New York Chapter of the American Marketing Association (AMA) started an Annual Award for Leadership in Marketing. Politz won. He won again in 1947. In 1948 the New York Chapter discontinued the award.

By 1947, Alfred Politz Research, Inc. had relocated to larger quarters in the old Marguery Hotel at 48th and Madison Avenue in Manhattan, and, in 1949, this small—but increasingly prominent—survey research firm was awarded the plum study of the decade by *Life* magazine. The *Life* study both cemented his credentials and revolutionized the industry. Politz, now age 47, was on his way to fame and fortune in his new homeland.

Cumulative Audience

To appreciate fully the impact that *Life* study had on the publishing, advertising, and research community in 1949, some background is required.

In the 1940s the flagships of consumer advertising in the U.S. were the mass circulation magazines—*Life, Saturday Evening Post, McCall's*—and prior to tv they sold primarily off of paid circulation numbers. Of course, advertisers knew that their total readership (or reach) far exceeded the circulation base because of pass-along, but there wasn't much incentive to document that as long as they were the kings of the advertising hill.

But, to combat tv, *Life* wanted a definitive audience study, one they could sell with. There were two key players: Andrew Heiskell, who was publisher of *Life* magazine at the time, and A. Edward Miller, who was research director for many years and later assistant to the publisher. Miller moved on to be publisher of *McCall's* and, from 1964 to 1968, president of Alfred Politz Research, Inc. As Miller recounted at the Politz memorial service, "My own association with Alfred goes way back...as research head of *Life* magazine, I had the opportunity to go to Elmo's [Roper] office from time to time. I noticed that there was a bright and energetic young man who was seated near the entrance door in a crowded office. After I was involved in a few meetings with Alfred, I became aware that here was one of the brightest, freshest, most creative, most analytical minds I had ever encountered." Both men were impressed with Politz's arguments for probability sampling, and this was bolstered by the success of his Advertising Research Foundation (ARF) studies.

The common sampling procedure in survey research theretofore had been what is known as quota sampling. It's an oversimplification, but basically this procedure called for selecting an interviewing site (PSU), which might be the intersection of two main streets, and then having the interviewer intercept passersby against a predetermined quota—so many adult men, so many adult women, etc.

The conceptual flaws in this procedure, as compared to sampling procedures used in the physical sciences which Politz embraced, were threefold: (1) only people who were out walking around at a specific geographical site at a particular time had a chance of being included in the sample; (2) the interviewer selected who would be stopped for an interview, and there could be lots of bias in that the interviewer might shy away from certain types of people; and (3) the setting of quotas assumed that was really the way it was in the society of the particular PSU under study. (Basically, this is still true in all the mall-intercept interviewing that goes on today.)

Politz advocated a procedure much closer to the impersonal, unbiased selection used in sampling in the physical sciences. His procedure was to randomly select a starting point, which might be an intersection, and then have the interviewer, for instance, walk down to the sixth house on a particular street and interview the adults living there—even if it meant making several callbacks to catch them at home. Then the interviewer would go to the next sixth house down, and so on. This procedure, sometimes called "random walk," did not produce a random sample in the strictest sense of the word, but it was a whale of a lot closer than the quota system, and much more desirable if the data were to be projected. It was also much more expensive because of the lower yields and need for callbacks. Hence, the survey research establishment resisted it because they were having trouble enough getting clients to pay for the fieldwork involved with the simpler quota sampling work. Besides, they would argue, who is to say the results would be all so much different or better if they followed the advice of a German émigré?

(It should be made clear that Mr. Politz didn't claim to invent probability sampling as applied to social research. As he was quoted as saying in an interview in the *Journal of Advertising Research* of June 1977, "It wasn't completely invented by me. The Census Bureau had quite a good sample. The bureau didn't call it 'probability sample,' but 'area sample.' But it was available. Except for some accidental reason, however, the commercial field didn't make use of it—it didn't learn from it. Maybe it was a complete absence of anybody with mathematical training.")

In that context, *Life*, the Big Daddy of publishing, embraced Politz and his methodology. Also, Mr. Politz had another concept that intrigued them: why settle for measuring the reach of a single issue of *Life*? Why not measure the cumulative reach of 13 consecutive issues? Why not, indeed? That would really run up the numbers and provide the ammunition for selling multiunit continuity campaigns!

Heiskell and Miller gave Politz a budget of about $250,000 and turned him loose. In return, they got two surprises. According to Darrell B. Lucas, who was involved as a consultant to *Life*, "In the first place, the Politz survey demonstrated that *Life* had some 7 million fewer readers than their own competition conceded to *Life*. In the second place, Alfred had overestimated his field costs and confronted Andrew (Bob) with some change." (The exact refund, according to Jerome D. Greene who was the study project director at APRI, was $25,000.) Now, if that isn't the stuff of which legends are made, especially in New York, what is?

Politz and Heiskell remained friends. Politz, who had bought a weekend home in Mill Neck on Long Island's north shore, would take Heiskell there and try to teach him how to water ski, another one of Politz's sports interests.

Another landmark came in 1964 when Politz Research was retained to do a $530,000 omnibus readership study that included 11 leading consumer magazines. Politz was powerful enough now that he could demand approval rights on any magazine promotional claims based on the study; there had come to be a "Politz Seal of Approval" in audience research.

This study was a turning point in that it further convinced Politz that magazine audiences should not technically be studied collectively; each one should have its own unique study. So, he did not try to get established in the coming thing, annual syndicated studies that would have industry support. An ex-APRI employee, W. R. "Bill" Simmons, had left to form W. R. Simmons & Associates Research, Inc., and this lucrative business started to gravitate away from the Politz firm.

The Heyday '50 s

The golden age for Alfred Politz Research, Inc. was during the 1950s. Revenues of his firm grew from about $2 million in 1955 to $3.0 million in 1956 to about $3.5 million in 1957. (In later years, they would top out at about $6 million, including Universal Marketing Research, a subsidiary). The company had moved into larger space at 527 Madison Avenue (at 54th Street) in what was the old Wiley Hotel, and the staff was now up to about 220, including about 85 professionals. Politz had built up (a rarity in the business) his own captive field force of 660 interviewers and 61 regional supervisors and trainers. He also was using another 600 nonexclusive interviewers. It took a lot of fieldwork to hold such an organization together, so Politz in 1955 started a subsidiary, Universal Marketing Research, to get around the parent firm's exclusive client policy. By 1958, UMR, now headed by Hugh S. Hardy, had branched into international research (in which Politz personally had little interest) and was doing studies around the world for Mobil and British American Tobacco Co., among others. It later became independent with its own offices at 400 Park Avenue.

The APRI client list continued to grow and came to include, at one time or another, Rhinegold Beer, Lever Bros., Colgate-Palmolive, U.S. Steel, Anheuser-Busch, United Fruit Co., E. I. duPont de Nemours, the Chrysler Corp., Sears-Roebuck, and the Florida Citrus Commission—over and beyond his numerous magazine clients and the large retainer clients: Kimberly-Clark, Coca-Cola, Seagram, Mobil, and Brown & Williamson, the U.S. subsidiary of British American Tobacco Co. With these regulars, he had a one-year agreement, and work on specific projects was billed on an hourly rate, as in law firms.

Servicing the Florida Citrus Commission acquainted Politz with the pleasures of living in Florida, and he vowed to buy a vacation home there "as soon as I could afford it." In 1955, he did buy a home in Odessa, outside Tampa, and he opened what *Tampa Commerce* hailed as a branch office of the "famed market researcher." Also, he acquired a retail-wholesale hardware supply business and liked to press customers to see how a salesperson could switch them off of nationally advertised brands. (The hardware business lost money and eventually was dissolved.)

As for Politz personally, this description from a profile article in *Printer's Ink* (January 24, 1958) is apropos: "Even in his native Berlin, Alfred Politz would be considered a *waschecter Berliner*—a man who could be washed out several times and would still remain an urbane Berliner, witty, scintillating, clever."

Working for Politz in those days was both demanding and stimulating, a story best told by former employees. "Alfred was brilliant, stimulating," Nathan Schiller told me recently, "but he expected complete dedication. Personal life and comfort were secondary; he had no concern for family responsibilities of employees. But he brought out whatever professionalism was within people—he got them to think creatively."

"We used to work 5½-day weeks in those days," recalls George S. Fabian, who was with Politz in 1954–56, "but it was still common for people to come in on Sundays too. If Alfred was there, he'd buy lunch for us all: usually steak tartare—he lived on that stuff—and Bloody Marys." Also, Fabian recalls, "Alfred never looked at a questionnaire before he saw a dummy of the presentation we planned to make a client, with all the stated hypotheses. That forced you to think everything out before designing the questionnaire."

Paul H. Chook, at the memorial service, recalled this incident: "It was a very warm Sunday morning in mid-summer when Alfred was away on one of his trips to his home in Tampa. It was about 10 a.m. Deep in thought, I was startled when the telephone rang. I assumed it must be a wrong number. Anyway, I picked up the receiver and before I could say a word, the voice at the other end thundered, 'Hello, Paul; this is Alfred. What are you doing in the office at this hour?' The words caught in my throat. The point is, of course, that he knew I would be there and he wanted me to know that he knew, that he cared, and that he appreciated it."

"As our employer, Alfred was a leader, a teacher, an inspirer," Chook continued. "He was also in every sense a working colleague, giving each of us on the staff a full measure of professional freedom."

Darrell B. Lucas, an early acquaintance, added this in his tribute at the memorial service: "I learned quickly that Alfred was determined to see that credit for a new idea must go to the one who sparks the idea, whether it be the office boy or girl or some Einstein in his field."

"Dr. Politz was a tireless worker and set a very fast pace for his associates, but he was by no means a 'workaholic,'" Robert J. Williams wrote to me recently, adding: "He would suddenly break into the ongoing work with the suggestion, 'Let's get a cocktail.' Then three or four of us would troop down to the bar in our building (running the stairway two steps at a time) and pause to refresh ourselves and exchange stories. We worked a feverish pace for many hours every week—but I have never since felt more enthusiastic about what I was doing, more stimulated by my work—or more alive!"

Joseph Goldstein recalls most the camaraderie, the in-group feeling among the APRI staff. "Almost every night after work a group would go to the Vegas bar across the street from the office and drink a few beers. If someone said he couldn't come because he had to get home, he just wasn't one of the group that would stay on at Politz."

Sometimes the evening would start in the office. Sam Bronfman, when a client, sent Mr. Politz cases of 200 proof natural grain spirits. "He liked to drink that stuff, would you believe?" says one ex-employee.

"I never saw him bawl out an employee or speak rudely to an employee; clients, yes—employees, no," observed Robert Weller at the memorial service. And Politz's relationship with clients is, indeed, another story.

Quite often he gave them Dutch uncle lectures, approaching the level of rudeness. "Yet, they loved to come to his presentations," says Lester R. Frankel, who was vp-technical director at the Politz firm from 1951 to 1957, "not to hear the study results but to hear Alfred's interpretation of the findings."

Albert F. Sprung, another Politz alum, told me recently, "The application of data to marketing, that was the key; that separated the men from the boys, and Alfred wasn't afraid to make recommendations."

Politz, obviously, played on this. In his *JAR* interview, he said, "I was more a consultant to my clients than just somebody who gathered opinions of the consumers. I had to make my recommendations." One reason Politz got along so well with top executive clients, and employees too, was that he had the knack of taking what could be an extremely complicated technical subject and reducing it to a simple and convincing explanation. Numerous stories on this are available, but I'll stick to the one about the Flying Red Horse, as told by Politz:

> One example was whether or not Mobil Oil should use three-quarters of the space on its station signs for a flying red horse, thinking a flying red horse is more interesting than the name "Mobil."
>
> My theory was that these so-called attention getters in reality might be distraction getters and we would waste space on something completely irrelevant. Since the board of directors didn't quite believe this, I set up an experiment. We equipped automobiles with movie cameras and let them drive along preselected routes where we could find Mobil, Esso and Shell signs. Of course, the numbers were unequal, but we later cut the films in such a way that an equal number of stations was left.
>
> Then we played the movie for selective audiences and asked them which station signs they saw. Mobil got only one-half the mentions that Esso got. Esso did not use an attention getter on its sign; it just called itself "Esso" and one could read the name because there was enough room left on the sign. But Mobil had condensed its name on the sign and the rest of the sign contained a completely irrelevant attention getter. That's perhaps typical of the kind of contributions I tried to make.

Another dimension of Politz, which helped him establish rapport with clients and their advertising agencies, was his sensitivity to the creative process. "He was the only research man I ever met who understood copy," Rosser Reeves told me recently, and added, "partly because he fancied himself a writer."

Politz's fame spread further when Martin Mayer's best-selling book, *Madison Avenue, USA*, came out in 1958. Mayer quoted Politz at length and explained his viewpoint on advertising and research. They became friends, and Mayer was one of the speakers at the Politz memorial service.

Perpetual Motion

Everyone remarks about how hyperactive Politz was. Andrew Heiskell, for instance, recently told me, "He conveyed a sense of enormous energy—as if he were barely able to keep inside his skin." Politz ran to work everyday. (His small penthouse apartment in a chic building on 54th St., just a few blocks from the office, featured a wall mirror, 12 feet high, 15 feet long. "You can watch yourself and others," said Politz; "it's fascinating." In the middle of the small living room was a huge, white electric organ. Sometimes he'd take coworkers to the apartment for lunch—steak tartare and beer—and improvise on the organ while they ate; he gobbled his food and always finished first.)

Arriving at the office, he wouldn't wait for the elevator; he'd run up the eight flights, two steps at a time. (Remember, we're talking about a man well into his mid-50s at this point.) Politz would get restless in meetings after a short time and often would start to do handstands on his desk—after carefully removing loose change from his pockets—to break the monotony. Sometimes before a speech or presentation, to ease the tension, he'd do the same thing, up and down the corridor, according to Lester Frankel. He kept small barbells in his office and seemed, to some, to be doing chin-ups, push-ups, or some other form of bodybuilding exercise continuously. "At his home in Florida," recounts Robert Weller, "Alfred had a high trampoline on which he would jump, do somersaults, twists, and what have you."

"Until the very last years of his life he pursued a vigorous program of daily exercise—running, doing push-ups, chin-ups, and the like," according to Robert J. Williams. "I don't believe he had any real fitness objective in all of this (fitness was certainly not a problem for him) nor any other extrinsic utility. It was simply an expression of his boundless and restless energy, a pleasure in which he indulged himself. He even played chess vigorously."

Beyond his fit body build with broad shoulders and continual physical exercise, Politz was a handsome man—who was usually tanned—and a dapper dresser, often wearing a bow tie. But his stature (he was about 5'6" tall) bothered him. Recalls Rosser Reeves, who was a frequent drinking buddy (their favorite watering hole was the bar at the 21 Club), "Alfred greeted me with something like, 'God, I hate you big bastards; if I was as tall as you, I wouldn't have to use my brains [to make a living].'"

Politz, like many creative people, would work intensively for spurts—usually about 18 days, through weekends—and then take a train to his home in Odessa (he wouldn't fly in an airplane). He'd often take along a secretary or two and work on the way down to Florida. (One coworker recalls, "If he had a new secretary, she'd either come back with a new mink coat, or we'd never see her again.") While in Florida, he'd do water sports and work in his famous aluminum-sided tool shed, a 200-foot by 80-foot structure that he called his "laboratory." It was here that he worked on physical experiments and inventions, the most renowned being a sailboat that had a Venetian blind-like apparatus in lieu of cloth sails, and an almost perpetual motion machine," a huge, ugly, and cumbersome-looking, Rube Goldberg-like device, according to Robert Williams, which after a gentle shove, ran for almost 24 hours on at least one occasion. In the corner of the lab, there was always a watercooler filled with Michelob draft beer.

"He liked astronomy and on top of his home in Florida," says Robert Weller, "he had his own miniature planetarium where he spent many evening hours looking at the stars and universe. This interest in the unknown also spurred him to write short stories which were a cross between science fiction and the occult."

Some of Alfred Politz's Thoughts on Advertising (and Research)

The most efficient advertisement makes the prospective consumer see and appreciate the merchandise. Through emotional and logical channels, it arouses his interest in the merchandise and does not arouse his interest in the workmanship of the advertisement. For the maker of the advertisement, this situation can be disappointing, since he gets no credit for the best workmanship.
—From a letter to the editor, *Advertising Age*, April 30, 1956

Much of the effort devoted to measuring advertising efficiency is mistakenly based on the notion that attention-getting and generation of pleasure are synonymous with successful advertising.
—Speech to the Association of National Advertisers, May 10, 1956

Research is useless unless it is creative. Creative research is the formulation of the hypothesis—the guess, the hunch—that you start with. Research must be willing to take on the burden of creating a hypothesis and testing it.
—Speech to Advertising Writers Association of New York, December 1964

If a salesman making a personal visit with a potential customer were to be guided by the same philosophy on which a great portion of advertising copy is based, he would be considered strange, to say the least. The potential client listening to his irrelevant attention getting might consider the performance not only a waste of time but also an insult to his intelligence.

The reason that most salesmen avoid attention-getting tricks is not the superior intelligence of the salesman. It is the directly observable responses he obtains which make him stop his theoretical error. The advertising experts who are responsible for the production of inferior logic, for irrelevance, for time wasting, for attempted wittiness, are not stupid. They are operating along a plan, along a theory which is hard to be corrected through observations of its effect. Thus, it is most understandable that an effect-reducing theory can easily survive in advertising.
—*Journal of Advertising Research*, 1975

Bristol-Meyers has a deodorant, Ban, and wanted to put on the market one for men. They called it Trig. Henry Bristol wanted me to see all the advertising copy before it went out. The first copy I saw for the new deodorant said, "Deodorants are for women, Trig is for men." That means logically that Trig is not a deodorant. We then had a long argument, and I was accused of thinking that we can introduce logic into something and that a violation of logical rules is something to be afraid of. The idea is that the consumer doesn't think logically himself. This is exactly the same as saying that if I have to teach a class of retarded children, I must have retarded teachers to teach them. Consequently, if the consumer is really as unintelligent as some people seem to think, it would still not be a license for the advertiser to approach him as if he had no logic.
—*Journal of Advertising Research*, June 1977

Fighting the Establishment

After his respites in Florida, Politz would bound back into Manhattan, often to resume his personal battles with elements of the research establishment.

His most audacious move, in the fall of 1961, was to rent a ballroom in a hotel and invite hundreds of people in the advertising/research community to hear a speech, in which he delivered a scathing denunciation of the Advertising Research Foundation (ARF), capping it with a suggestion that the ARF be dissolved. He argued that the ARF had violated its nonprofit function by competing with private research organizations, and in many respects lowered research standards and "contributed to mediocrity" by catering to the lowest common denominator, which was the fate of any committee-run organization. According to Jerome D. Greene, an employee who drafted the speech, "The audience was aghast. Many agreed with Alfred's impeccable logic, but they wouldn't say so in public."

In December 1961, Politz went a big step further. He mailed a 19-page monograph entitled "Is Progress in Advertising Research Endangered by the Advertising Research Foundation?" to 1,500 advertisers, agencies, and media representatives. This caused an uproar, and numerous long stories —plus an editorial—are to be found in the December 1961 issues of *Advertising Age*. One story quoted Daniel Yankelovich, who said (December 18,

1961): "I think the Politz statement will probably do more harm than good. The question whether the ARF is, or is not, competing with commercial research firms is not really very important and is not going to arouse the advertising community just because the Politz pocketbook nerve is being hurt."

Politz also received a lot of press because of his public squabbles with another foreign-born researcher of note, namely Dr. Ernest Dichter, the Vienna-born champion of motivation research, which Politz tended to ridicule. ("If I say, 'It's warm in here'—that is a qualitative statement. If I say, 'It's 78 degrees in here—that is a quantitative statement. Qualitative statements are just quantitative statements made at a sloppy level of approximation.")

This general bias carried over to Politz's attitude towards public opinion research, which he also tended to ridicule, and his firm did not seek such work—with one exception. According to A. Edward Miller at the memorial service, "Responding to a call from C. D. Jackson [an aide to President Eisenhower]...Alfred produced a national public opinion study for President Eisenhower in anticipation of a meeting with Winston Churchill in a matter of two weeks. C. D. later told me this contribution by Alfred had a significant effect on the course of history. A letter from President Eisenhower about his research was one of Alfred's prized possessions." Politz's application for U.S. citizenship was held up until 1944, after World War II when anti-German sentiment was dying down.)

Retirement in 1967

Aside from the barn-burner $530,000 study for 11 consumer magazines in 1964, the Politz star was starting to descend in the early 1960s, partly due to Alfred's "poor health" and deteriorating client relations. (Reportedly, he pushed Edgar Bronfman, clothed, into a swimming pool, for instance.)

A. Edward Miller came to Alfred Politz Research, Inc. in 1964 to take over the presidency; Politz moved up to chairman. In 1966, the Politz firm —which had not had a good profit picture for some time—was sold to Computer Science Corporation (CSC) for about $2.2 million in CSC stock. Miller, who had been given one-third interest in APSI to join the firm, held his stock; (Politz sold his right away, netting about $1.5 million.) After this, Politz started to spend more and more time in Odessa, and in 1967, he officially retired and moved there permanently.

However, Politz did not slow down. Among other things, he started to write long "think-piece" articles for publications such as *Advertising Age*, some of which were published as late as 1974. He was 75 years old when he got a license to fly hot air balloons, and he continued work on his experiments and inventions in the "lab." He also had more time for reading; reportedly, his favorite author was Mark Twain (whom he read in German).

By 1972, the volume of APRI had dried up to next to nothing, and the name—plus the lease on the firm's office, then at 400 Park Ave.—was purchased by Henry D. Ostberg's Admar Research Co. There is still today a listing in the *Green Book* for Alfred Politz Research, Inc., and, according to Ostberg, it still does some studies under that name for agencies of the federal government, a carryover from the old days. "Also," Ostberg told me recently, "when we meet with older top management people, many still know of Politz and think it is still a large company."

November 8, 1982

In February 1981, Politz had his larynx removed. From the day of his operation until he died (November 8, 1982, at the age of 80), he could not speak. He could not eat; he had to be fed some other way every two hours. In August 1982, he suffered a massive stroke and was completely paralyzed—but he could communicate via eye movements.

When he died, within a few days of William Bernbach, the contrast in commemoration was stark. Long, up-front features were written about Bernbach. But Politz's obit in *Advertising Age*, for instance, was a 5-column-inch-long item on page 75 (November 15, 1982).

Be that as it may, Politz was, as they say, "an original." He started in mid-life in a strange land and went on to impact his field as few others have, or probably ever will. He was, indeed, an amazing man. Many would agree with this observation made by Paul H. Chook at the memorial service: "Without question, Alfred, perhaps more than anyone else, helped convert the field of marketing and advertising research from a practical to a real profession." And, I might add, he apparently had a lot of fun while he was at it.

14 Princeton: U.S. Research Capital

If Hollywood ever made a movie about the survey research industry, they'd probably shoot it in Princeton, N.J. Here they could meld into the popular conception (which, in fact, more and more is a misconception) of what the industry is like, one foot in academe, the other reluctantly in commerce.

Be that as it may, the research community in Princeton is something special, a rather insular community which has a personality of its own. That is what I tried to capture in this article, which appeared in Advertising Age *on October 26, 1981. What I said then pretty well stands today; things don't change very fast in Princeton. (It should be noted, however, that George H. Gallup, Sr. died in July 1984.)*

What Princeton Is Like

If the U.S. survey research industry were to have a capital, it most certainly would be the pastoral little community of Princeton, N.J., a historic stagecoach stop about halfway between New York City and Philadelphia. It is the world renowned home of Princeton University, founded in 1756.

Today, Princeton and adjacent Princeton Junction (combined population of about 14,000) are home to 17 survey research organizations or their branches; the administrative office of the American Association for Public Opinion Research (AAPOR), which was founded in 1947 and currently has more than 1,000 members; the residence of Michael R. Kagay, a Princeton University faculty member who consults with the *New York Times*/CBS Poll, and one electronic data processing service bureau that specializes in marketing research work (Multivariance Data Analysts).

In total, just the survey research operations located in Princeton have nearly 600 full-time salaried employees locally and do an annual volume estimated at about $28.7 million. Put another way, there are probably more survey research professionals per square mile, or per 1,000 population, in the Princeton area than there are in any other community in the world.

203

To appreciate the research atmosphere that permeates the Princeton area beyond survey research, here is a list of other organizations that are centered there:
- The technical research laboratories of corporations such as RCA, Mobil, Squibb, FMC, Remington Rand, Exxon Office Systems, and Firmenich.
- The world-famous Institute for Advanced Study, founded in 1930, which today has 26 permanent faculty members and an international colony of about 160 guest members during the academic year.
- Educational Testing Service, the educational and professional testing organization, which gives students fits with Scholastic Achievement Tests. There are about 2,000 ETS employees in the Princeton headquarters.
- The James Forrestal Research Campus of Princeton University, with its Plasma Physics laboratories, home of the famous Takamak Fusion Test Reactor, which has been built at a cost of $413 million. (In 1983, Tokamak is scheduled to perform its first experiment: to achieve scientific breakeven by generating as much fusion energy as is required to heat the fuel. This process will generate temperatures of 100 million degrees centigrade, which is five times as hot as the center of the sun. The long-range goal of Tokamak is to be the ultimate energy source, completely self-sustaining.)
- A seemingly endless number of companies specializing in mathematical services, and computer software development.

Add to this heady mix the 790 faculty members and 5,800 students of Princeton University, and you'll see why I suspect that there are more Ph.D.s per square mile in the Princeton area than, perhaps, any place else in the world (except, perhaps, Los Alamos, N.M.).

All this emphasis on scientific inquiry, of course, contributes to the ambience—and affluence—of the Princeton community, where people do, in fact, wear tweed jackets with leather elbow patches, ride bicycles, and often work in aged buildings covered with ivy.

The center of Princeton, a small park called Palmer Square, is surrounded by chic little shops, and I suspect it looks almost exactly like Hollywood's image of a preppy, East Coast college town—complete with Topsiders, Icelandic wool sweaters from Landau's, and urbane people enjoying a drink around the stone fireplace in the Yankee Doodle Tap Room in the Nassau Inn, with its original Norman Rockwell mural.

And I also suspect it is very much like the layman's conception of what the survey research capital of the U.S. should look like—assuming there was such a thing.

No doubt, the insular, ivory-tower atmosphere of the Princeton community is infused in the survey research practitioners who work and live there. It is psychic income, and most probably wouldn't consider living anywhere else. In addition, they tend to be a mite provincial; most just aren't concerned about what goes on in the rest of New Jersey—except, perhaps, for some Jersey Shore communities like Bay Head or Mantoloking—or in other segments of the research industry.

In fact, you'd be hard pressed to find anyone who could talk knowledgeably about, say, A.C. Nielsen Company or IMS or Arbitron. If you did, it would be difficult for them to believe that such activities could possibly be as relevant or primary as the survey research activities centered in Princeton.

As the president of one Princeton survey company said recently, "I'm sure some of my clients from New York like to work with us because they enjoy coming down to spend a day in Princeton, walking around Palmer Square—maybe going over to the Foolish Fox or the Annex or the Rocky Hill Inn for lunch."

These three local watering holes, plus Charlie's, apparently house congregations of Princeton survey practitioners at lunchtime, and especially on Fridays, when the wine sometimes flows on into late afternoon over shop talk. There's no proof, of course, but salary levels for researchers are probably lower in Princeton than in nearby New York or Philadelphia, but the Princeton area lifestyle is very captivating.

It was 1935 when George H. Gallup, Sr., already a well-known pioneer in advertising research (through a company called Audience Research) decided to found a company in Princeton that would be devoted to public opinion research, today known as The Gallup Organization. It also was in 1935 that the first Gallup Poll was published—in 35 newspapers.

Survey research pioneers in those days, including Gallup, had a common problem: convincing skeptical editors and commercial clients that, indeed, a small sample of the population, if properly drawn, could be used to measure accurately the predilections of society.

Most of these pioneers were popularly denounced as charlatans, and the best way they could legitimize their methodology was to premeasure public election results. The proof of the pudding, then, would be out in the open for all to see. Hence, the poll.

In 1936, Gallup made another innovative move: he established affiliate relationships with research companies in England and France. The Gallup name and methodology then became an export product.

In 1938, Claude Robinson, then associate director for Gallup, left to found Opinion, Inc. (now known as Opinion Research Corp.) in Princeton, and in 1948 the two—Gallup and Robinson—teamed up to found another Princeton company, Gallup & Robinson, to specialize in advertising effectiveness research. As we'll see, most of those who now head research organizations in Princeton are alumni of one or more of the three companies founded by these two men. This adds to the cohesiveness of the Princeton research community.

When asked why he chose Princeton, Gallup, who at age 80 still is active in his company's affairs, said, "Critics have said I did it to get a good dateline for the poll news releases, but actually it was an accident."

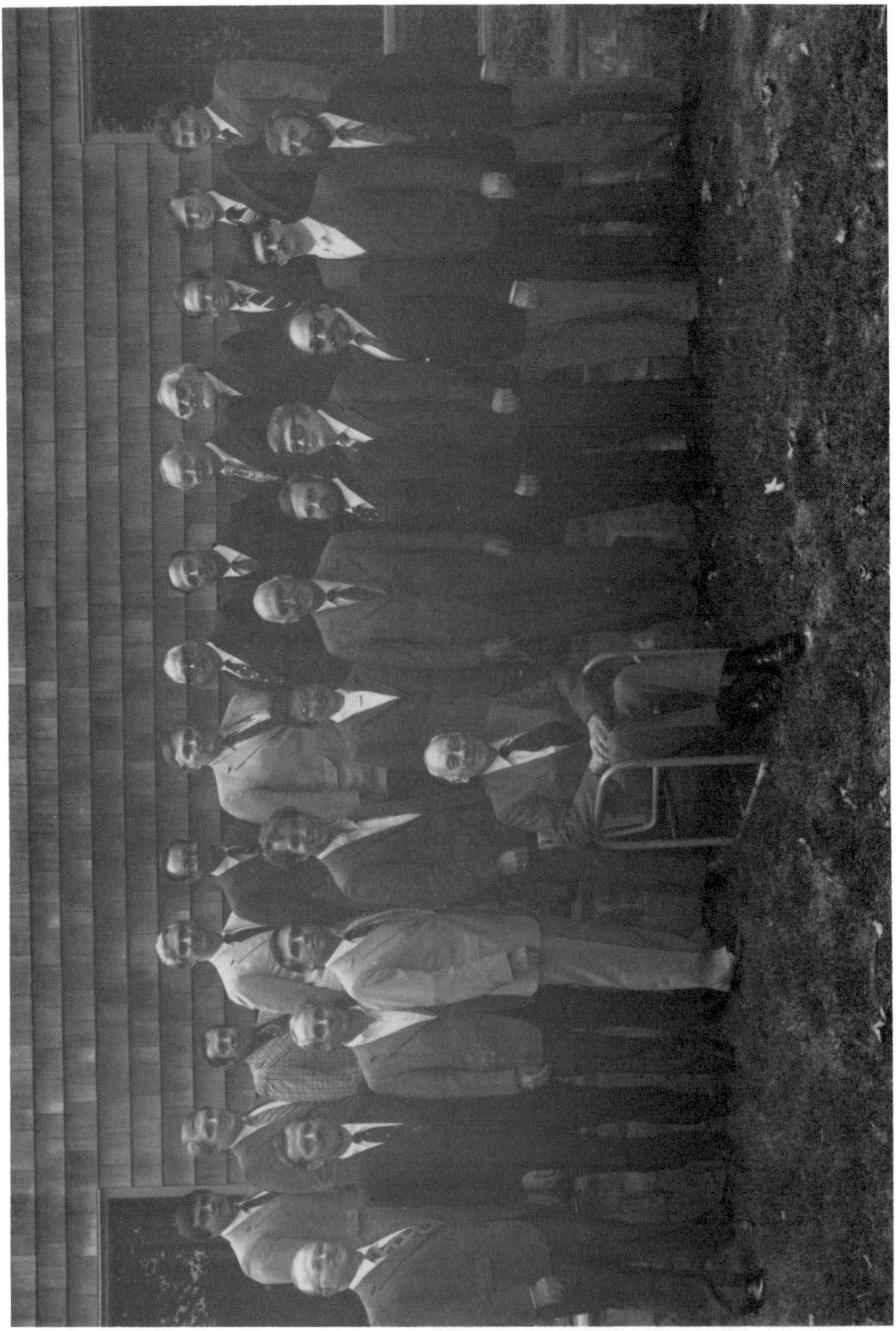

Princeton: U.S. Research Capital **207**

Key to research tree — The Princeton family photo

Members of the Princeton research family: Front row, from left to right, are: (1) Franklin F. Reeder, Frank Reeder, marketing/research; (2) Robert Bezilla, Benson & Benson; (3) Alfred Vogel, Response Analysis Corp.; (4) A. Spencer Bruno, Spencer Bruno Research Associates; (5) Paul F. Hase, Hase/Schannen Research Associates; (seated) (6) George H. "Ted" Gallup Sr., 80, paterfamilias of the Princeton research community; (7) Patricia J. Labaw, R L Associates; (8) L. E. "Brick" Purvis, Gallup & Robinson; (9) Leon B. Kaplan, Princeton Research & Consulting Center; (10) Lorin Zissman, Total Research Corp.; (11) Michael M. Sandler, Research 100; (12) Seth Rubinstein, Multivariance Data Analysts; and (13) Andrew Kohut, The Gallup Organization; Back row, left to right: (14) Alfred B. Ochsner, Schrader Research & Rating Service; (15) Joseph Ridgway, Spender Bruno Research Associates; (16) Jack Ross, J. Ross Associates; (17) Harold "Red" Ross Jr., Mapes & Ross; (18) Charles F. Mapes Jr., Mapes & Ross; (19) Henry A. Schannen, Hase/Schannen Research Associates; (20) Harry W. O'Neill, Opinion Research Corp.; (21) Irwin Miller, Opinion Research Corp.; (22) Ernest A. Rockey, Gallup & Robinson; (23) Reuben Cohen, Response Analysis Corp.; (24) Herbert I. Abelson, Response Analysis Corp; (25) Paul Scipione, Kenneth Hollander Associates; and (26) Ronald E. Vangi, Multivariance Data Analysts.

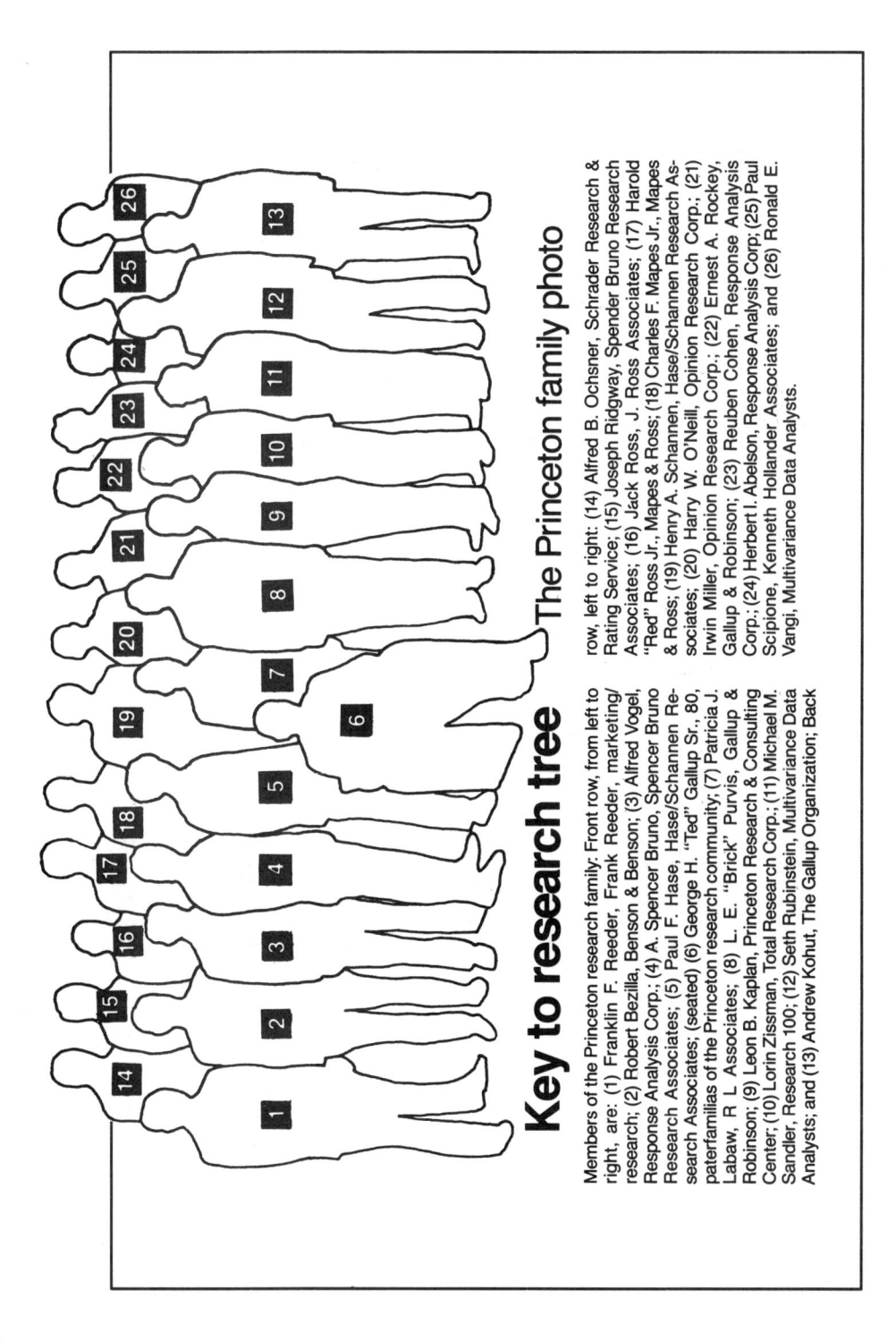

At the time, Gallup was director of research at Young & Rubicam and lived near Scarsdale, N.Y. "We went down to Princeton one weekend in 1934 to visit some friends, and they had arranged for the real estate people to show us around," he said. "We saw a farm we liked and made the decision to move on the spot. We've lived there ever since. Later, I decided that I didn't like to commute into New York, and I started the Gallup Poll."

So but for a chance visit to Princeton, the research capital of the U.S. might be located in some small, out-of-the-way place—like Manhattan.

The growth and evolution of the Princeton survey research community is probably best told in a chronological rundown on the companies themselves, their roots and their current activities. In the process, the family tree relationships become more or less obvious.

Gallup Organization (privately held corporation)

Founded by George H. Gallup, Sr. in 1935, primarily to develop and publish the Gallup Poll, this organization has been a wellspring of the research talent that, in time, started most of the other research organizations now based in Princeton.

The corporate predecessor of The Gallup Organization was a company called Audience Research, Inc., which specialized in audience reaction to motion pictures. The Gallup Poll, which was first published in 1935, shifted the emphasis to public opinion research, and especially the prediction of election results.

In 1936, Gallup in a sense franchised the Gallup name and polling methodology by establishing affiliate relationships in France and England; today there are Gallup Poll affilates in 38 foreign countries, and the coordinating organization is called Gallup International Research Institute.

The Gallup Organization currently has about 100 full-time salaried employees and an annual volume in the neighborhood of $4 million. Its activities fall into five broad areas:

- Public opinion journalism: the Gallup Poll; the Gallup Youth Survey; the *Newsweek* Poll; Gallup *Wall Street Journal*, and the Gallup Opinion Index.
- Multiclient (shared-cost) surveys of general interest.
- Omnibus surveys: syndicated surveys of special populations where clients buy in on a question-by-question basis.
- The Gallup Social Science Research Group: founded to conduct social research for government, business, universities, and other not-for-profit organizations.
- International surveys: fielded through the 38 member companies of Gallup International Research Institute.

Today, Gallup is chairman of The Gallup Poll, chairman of the board of The Gallup Organization and president of Gallup International Research

Institute. Author of numerous articles and six books, he is the recipient of honorary degrees from 13 colleges and universities. Two sons, George H. Gallup, Jr. and Alec M. Gallup, are active in the company as vice-chairmen. Andrew Kohut is president.

Opinion Research Corporation (ORC)
(subsidiary of Arthur D. Little, Inc.)
Princeton's largest survey research company has 143 full-time salaried employees, four branch offices (New York, Chicago, Washington, and San Francisco) and annual revenues of $7.7 million in 1980.

Originally called Opinion, Inc., ORC was founded in 1938 by Claude Robinson, former associate director of the Gallup Poll. It grew to be one of the most venerable names in the U.S. research industry, but its history has been troubled.

A privately held corporation until 1969, when its owners sold out to McGraw-Hill, ORC later suffered a mass exodus by disgruntled employees who were displeased with the sale; these employees started three other Princeton companies: Research 100, Response Analysis and, ultimately, Total Research Corp.—plus other research organizations in other cities.

In 1975, McGraw-Hill sold ORC to its current owner, Arthur D. Little, Inc. of Cambridge, Mass., and Irwin Miller, an ADL employee, joined the company as chairman and chief executive officer. President of ORC is Harry W. O'Neill, a long-time employee.

ORC is a full-service survey research company offering custom studies in the areas of consumer and industrial marketing, market modeling, corporate relations and communications, media, advertising, public affairs and public policy, political (ORC was the research company that handled much of President Nixon's early public opinion polling), financial, and program evaluation.

Syndicated services include the ORC Public Opinion Index, the ORC Marketing Index, and Travel Pulse, the rights to which were recently purchased from Ziff-Davis Publishing Co., as well as shared-cost surveys in the areas of media relations, corporate reputations, etc.

Benson & Benson (subsidiary of Admar Research Company, New York)
Benson & Benson was founded in 1938 by two ex-Gallup Organization employees, Edward Benson (deceased) and Lawrence E. Benson (retired). The story goes that, back in those days, Gallup was sensitive about having the Gallup Poll organization work for commercial clients because that might smack of conflict of interest.

So when commercial clients approached him, he often bucked their projects off to employees who would like to moonlight to make extra money. As that activity increased, the natural outgrowth was new companies, and B&B is an example of that.

Today Benson & Benson, headed by president Robert Bezilla, has 20 full-time salaried employees, and since 1978 has been an independent subsidiary of Admar. About one-half of B&B survey projects are based on personal interviews (individual and group) and about one-half are based on mail questionnaires. The company also does telephone interviewing. Almost all studies are custom designed.

Gallup & Robinson (privately held corporation)

Founded in 1948 by George H. Gallup and Claude Robinson. Gallup & Robinson's specific purpose was to provide advertisers with measurements of the effectiveness of their advertising expenditures and, again, to keep that activity separate from the Gallup Poll.

The company began by introducing Gallup's pioneering print research technique, "Impact." This was based on natural reading with the interviewer to determine the extent of learning and persuasion in the period before the next issue of the same publication was available.

In 1950, services were expanded to include tv, newspaper, outdoor board and product testing. Testing of all prime-time commercials, by industry classification, started in 1962. Pretesting of commercials in a theater setting shifted to on-air reception in 1970.

The most famous alumnus of G&R is David Ogilvy, a young Scottish copywriter who worked there when he first came to the U.S. Recently the now-famous founder of Ogilvy & Mather was asked, "What advice have you for young copywriters?" Ogilvy's answer was, "First, get yourself an education—in any subject except advertising. Furnish your mind. Then learn to write—letters, articles, books, anything. Then get a job with a research outfit like Gallup—and learn what makes your fellow creatures tick."

A data bank based on tests of more than 100,000 print ads and tv commercials is a key element of the current G&R business, which includes consulting on advertising and sales problems, as well as syndicated and customized studies of advertising effectiveness in tv, print and radio.

In the early 1960s, ownership of G&R passed to L. E. "Brick" Purvis who continues today as chairman of the board. President of G&R is Ernest A. Rockey. There are 70 full-time salaried employees and a branch office in Philadelphia.

Schrader Research & Rating Service (SRRS)
(privately held corporation)

Founded in 1952 by Donald P. Schrader, an ex-Gallup employee, SRRS originally was named National Quality Interviewing. This organization, which was funded in part by George H. Gallup, was to serve as a field service for The Gallup Organization. Both Gallup and Schrader (now retired) divested their interests. Today, SRRS is a full-service survey research company with 10 full-time, salaried employees. The president is Alfred B. Ochsner.

SRRS specializes in print advertising, radio commercial, package, taste, and tv commercial testing, mostly through a fleet of 20 mobile trailer units located around the country. These units can be positioned at intercept points that are in accordance with study sample requirements.

Response Analysis Corporation (RAC) (privately held corporation)

Founded in 1969 by five ex-employees of Opinion Research Corporation, Response Analysis Corporation is headed by Reuben Cohen, its president, and Herbert I. Abelson. Today, there are 92 full-time salaried employees and a branch office in Washington; RAC has an annual volume near $5 million.

Since its inception in 1969, RAC has conducted over 1 million interviews for over 175 different clients, many of which are federal agencies or not-for-profit organizations, on a broad range of social and public issues, as well as studies for commercial clients.

An RAC division, Advanced Research Resources Organization (ARRO), handles research, development and evaluation of problems that are related to the organizational, behavioral and social sciences.

Total Research Corporation (TRC) (privately held corporation)

Founded in 1970 by Lorin Zissman, a former employee of Opinion Research Corp. and, briefly, of Response Analysis Corp., TRC today is primarily a survey research company, but—rare indeed in Princeton—it also does custom store audit work.

There are 80 employees, 30 of whom are full-time and salaried. A separate division, TRC data surveys, has a centralized telephone interviewing service for nationwide data collection as well as capabilities for personal interview data collection within the state of New Jersey.

In addition to traditional quantitative and qualitative research techniques involving all types of data collection, TRC offers the following special services:

- High Technology Market Research—including simulation modeling, conjoint scaling, ad impact optimization, brand maximization, price elasticity measurement, and multivariate analyses.
- Stratplan—a comprehensive strategic marketing research and consulting service that focuses on key strategic market factors.
- Accuaudit—a retail brand share and distribution service for consumer durable goods.

- Integrated New Product Development—a multiphase iterative research program to yield new products.

Research 100 (privately held corporation)

Research 100 was founded in 1970 by five ex-employees of Opinion Research Corp., headed by Michael H. Sandler (who continues as president) and Walter H. Meyer, who now is with Contemporary Research Center, Toronto.

Research 100 today does both national and local studies, employing personal and telephone interviewing, product and concept tests, test market studies, repeat purchase surveys, and attitude and opinion surveys. There are 14 full-time salaried employees with the company.

Spencer Bruno Research Associates (SBRA) (partnership)

Founded in 1970 by A. Spencer Bruno, an alumnus of both Gallup & Robinson and Compton Advertising, where he was senior vp, creative research director, SBRA today has 26 full-time salaried employees and offers a variety of services: product testing, WATS interviewing, mall intercept interviewing, new product and new strategy concept studies, packaging and mail studies, print and radio day-after-recall testing, and copy concept evaluations.

In 1981, SBRA purchased the New York-based survey company of J.A. Ward, Inc., and relocated its operation to Princeton.

Mapes & Ross (privately held corporation)

Specializing in on-air pretesting and posttesting of tv commercials, providing both recall and persuasion measures, Mapes & Ross was founded in 1972 by two former Gallup & Robinson employees, Harold L. Ross, Jr. (chairman) and Charles F. Mapes, Jr. (president).

M&R commercial evaluation takes place through syndicated testing in three markets or on a custom basis in some 33 cities among general samples or target respondents.

There are 40 full-time salaried employees, and the Mapes & Ross Television Commercial Evaluation Service, which incorporates both day-after-recall and persuasion measures in a single on-air test, has been used to evaluate more than 8,000 commercials.

Frank Reeder Marketing Research (privately held corporation)

Frank Reeder, who, among other things worked for both The Gallup Organization and Research 100, started his operation in 1973, doing concept, product and packaging studies. There are on-premise group session facilities.

R L Associates (RLA) (privately held corporation)
Founded in 1975 by two former ORC employees, Michael A. Rappeport (president) and Patricia Labaw, RLA now has seven full-time salaried employees.

RLA specializes in stragetic research in four main areas: financial institutions; factors in the travel and tourism industry; nonprofit organizations in the area of policy and public affairs; and various agencies of the federal government in the area of health, education, and human services.

About 50% of RLA volume comes from for-profit corporations, about 40% from not-for-profit agencies and trade associations and about 10% from federal agencies.

Mathematica Policy Research (MPR)
(subsidiary of Mathematica, Inc.)
MPR was founded in 1968 to operate the nation's first large-scale social policy experiment, the New Jersey Negative Income Tax Experiment, which provided policymakers with the first hard data and practical experience with an income maintenance program that provided cash benefits to intact families and that incorporated features designed to minimize disincentives to work. At the heart of the program was a continuous longitudinal panel survey program to monitor the progress of individual test families.

This pioneering research effort soon expanded into the Urban Opinion Surveys Division of Mathematica Inc., and in 1976 it became Mathematica Policy Research, a separate subsidiary of Mathematica. MPR president is William A. Morrill, and there are 271 full-time salaried employees. (Mathematica, the parent company, was originally a subsidiary of Market Research Corp. of America.)

The survey division of MPR, headed by Kenneth C. Kehrer, has 30 professionals on its staff and provides full survey capabilities in support of all MPR projects, as well as direct contract work for agencies of the government. The survey division headquarters is in Princeton, with a branch office in Washington, D.C. In addition, there are currently 10 field offices operating around the country and a roster of over 2,000 on-call field interviewers.

The survey division has developed a computer-assisted telephone interviewing system (CATI) that combines interviewing, data entry, and editing into one operation. In addition, the division has entered into a partnership with the Survey Research Center at the University of California at Berkeley to further develop their UNIX-based CATI system to engage in a broad spectrum on CATI, and to apply the Berkeley system in large-scale surveys.

An MPR film, *Interviewing,* is used for training by over 150 academic and commercial survey organizations and by government agencies, incuding the Census Bureau for the current population survey.

J. Ross Associates (RA) (privately held corporation)

This company was founded in 1976 by Jack Ross who previously had been director of market research for the health care division of Johnson & Johnson, New Brunswick, N.J. Today there are nine full-time salaried employees.

A custom marketing research company functioning in both quantitative and qualitative areas, RA conducts surveys, stores audits and qualitative research, such as focused group sessions, for both new and established products and services.

Hase-Schannen Research Associates (HSR)
(privately held corporation)

HSR was founded in 1976 by Paul F. Hase and Henry A. Schannen (current president), both of whom came from Research 100, another Princeton company and prior to that, Opinion Research Corp., Princeton. Projected volume is $1.9 million for 1981, and there are 19 full-time salaried employees.

HSR is a full-time service company offering all types of interviewing —including qualitative and WATS telephone, statistical analysis of data, bio-behavioral/psychological research and test market forecasting.

A division of HSR, Data + Medics, which specializes in medical and health care research, is located in Greenwich, Conn., and another division, which speciaizes in financial research problems, is in Chicago.

Kenneth Hollander Associates (privately held corporation)

This Atlanta-based survey company, which is headed by Kenneth A. Hollander, established a branch operation in Princeton in 1978. The Princeton operation is headed by Paul Scipione, a vp of the parent company, and there are three salaried employees who are located in the Princeton office.

The parent company specializes in Quantitative Communications Test (QCT) to assess the impact of tv/radio/print messages, financial services research, market segmentation and market modeling, corporate image studies, and Hispanic consumer research.

Princeton Research & Consulting Center (PRCC)
(privately held corporation)

Founded in 1979 by Leon B. Kaplan, previously an employee of Opinion Research Corporation (ORC), this company has six full-time salaried employees and a branch office in Weatogue, Conn.

PRCC is a full-service survey research and consulting company involved in both consumer and industrial areas. The company offers product development and product testing, usage and attitude studies, and tracking services.

Audits & Surveys (Government Research Division)

A new venture launched by Audits & Surveys, New York, was founded in 1981 and is headed by Stanley M. Zdep, who came from Opinion Research Corp.

This division specializes in survey projects for federal, state, and local governments, as well as other clients in the academic and research communities who, in turn, conduct research for federal agencies. There are now three full-time salaried employees, but this is expected to go to six in the near future.

The documentation of Princeton and The Gallup Organization as a breeding ground for two generations of prominent survey research practitioners could go on and on. To wit: Mervin D. Field, now president of Field Research Corporation in San Francisco, Joe Belden, Roy Morgan, Joe Batchelder and Irving Crespi—just to name a few.

But the point has been made: Princeton has, since the beginning, been a leader in survey research and a training ground for professionals in that rapidly expanding industry. And many of them have opted to stay right there—in the center of what rightly lays claim to being the survey research capital of the U.S.

15 Top Forty U.S. Research Firms

Back in 1971, when I first started to write for Advertising Age, *the editor, Rance Crain, asked why there was no annual summary of how the top research firms did, comparable to* AA's *U.S. Agency Income Profiles. I answered that it would be difficult since so many of the large firms were privately held and secretive about their finances. Moveover, there was a definitional problem: exactly what type of firm should be included in such an industry overview?*

However, there was a real need for such a compilation. Hardly anyone outside the industry (or inside, for that matter) had the vaguest idea about the size of other obviously important firms, and some—notably Gallup and Harris—had a reputation far larger than their revenue size because of the prominence of their syndicated newspaper columns. Other, much larger firms were virtually unknown away from their immediate client base and ex-employees. Further, if we had an accurate year-to-year record of how the major firms, in toto, were growing in revenue, that would provide an important piece of marketing news: a barometer of the industry's growth in the U.S. (and, indeed, it was growing very rapidly in those days).

Rance kept on the subject, as is his wont, and finally in the Advertising Age *of July 18, 1974, I published the first such listing, which was limited to just those 10 firms that were believed to be the largest. However, to do that, I first had to define what type of organization qualified: hence, this definition:*

A for-profit corporate identity which has as its main enterprise the development of proprietary measures in the field of marketing, public attitudes, media consumption, or advertising stimuli, that are basically related to the sale of goods or services. This definition includes, at one extreme, the measure of market size and share of market, and at the other, the perceptions that can be gained from one, small focused group interview.

As we look back now, that was simplistic and crude. But it was something to use as a base, a frame of reference.

The first listing drew a lot of very critical mail. People argued with my definition and, more specifically, with the implied notion that annual dollar volume equates with quality of service. Underlying much of that criticism was a very human response: "Hey, you left my firm out!"

Rance Crain urged me to do it again in 1975, and that listing too was based on just 10 firms. However, other events were starting to shape this annual review. One was that some large research firms went public, and others were acquired by larger, public companies, which had a different policy towards financial disclosure. In any case the listings in 1976, 1977, and 1979 were based on 20 firms. It went to 23 in 1980, 25 in 1981, 28 in 1982, and 30 in 1983. In 1984, we took it up to 35, and the 1985 listing, which appeared in Advertising Age on May 23, listed 40 organizations—and introduced a new listing, Marketing Information Service firms, kissing cousins to the research firms.

Each year, in addition to the number of firms listed, the compilation increased in accuracy and detail. Today, it is recognized as a workably accurate barometer of the industry's growth, and, in fact, these trend data overshadow individual company descriptions.

Another by-product of this annual listing is that now the research industry's growth and size can be compared with that of closely allied industries, such as advertising agencies. Further, the size of leading research firms can be compared to leading advertising agencies—often producing surprises for the Madison Avenue fraternity whose firms are so much more prominent. Often a relatively obscure research firm was larger than its agency!

There follows what had come to be, after years of evolvement and increased industry cooperation, the definitive Who's Who of the American research industry, circa 1984.

U.S. Research Industry Grows 13.7% in 1984

The U.S. marketing/advertising/public opinion research industry ended 1984—a year characterized by changes in ownership—with a 13.7% increase in revenues over 1983, according to this, the 11th Annual Review of Industry Performance compiled exclusively for *Advertising Age*.

This year's listing, expanded to the 40 leading U.S.-based research organizations, some of which are conglomerates, differs significantly from the 1983 listing in that one firm, Audits & Surveys, Inc. is not included due to lack of input, and six new firms have been added: Decision/Making/Information, Ad Factors Marketing Research, Kapuler Marketing Research, Oxtoby-Smith, Response Analysis, and Decision Research Corporation.

Also new this year is a valuable "all other" input thanks to the Council of American Survey Research Organizations (CASRO). Some CASRO member firms make their annual revenues known on a confidential basis, and the total revenues of 54 such survey research firms, over and beyond those already included in the Top 40 listing, have been made available to add to the Top 40 list revenues. This, then, is the most comprehensive index of industry growth yet developed because the "all other" group reflects firms smaller than the Top 40 organizations.

We then end up with six ways to look at industry growth:

	Revenue Growth, 1984 over 1983	
	U.S. Only	Worldwide
Top 40 firms alone	+17.4%	+13.7%
CASRO "all other" group	+12.5%	+12.5%
Total, Top 40 plus CASRO	+16.9%	+13.6%

As it pertains to worldwide volume, the Top 40 list, and the total, is heavily weighted by the two huge internationals, A. C. Nielsen Co. and IMS International. Both, in recent years, have been negatively impacted by the strong U.S. dollar vis-à-vis foreign currencies, and in 1984 their combined offshore revenues of $339.2 million were up only 3.4% over 1983.

As it pertains to U.S. only, the inflation rate in 1984 was 4.3%, according to the U.S. Department of Labor Consumer Price Index-U, monthly average. So, if the Top 40 plus CASRO, U.S.-only growth rate of 16.9% is adjusted downward accordingly, the industry's so-called real growth in 1984 was 12.6%. If we do the same for worldwide revenues, the real growth was 9.4%, the figure used on figure 15.1, to make it comparable to the calculation used in previous years. (Figure 15.1 appears on page 221.)

Table 15.1 1984 Revenue Record* of the 40 Leading U.S. Research Organizations

Rank 1984	Rank 1983	Organization	Research Revenues* (Millions)	Change vs. 1983**(%)	Research Revenues from Outside U.S. (Millions)
1	1	A.C. Nielsen	$491.0	$5.9%	$255.3 Est.
2	2	IMS International	151.4	10.1	83.9
3	3	SAMI	118.4	19.0	—
4	4	Arbitron Ratings Company	105.8	12.3	—
5	5	Burke Marketing Services	66.0	9.8	1.7
6	8	M/A/R/C	37.6	39.8	—
7	7	Market Facts	35.9	26.7	—
8	12	Information Resources	35.8	69.7	—
9	9	NFO Research	29.5	10.1	—
10	10	NPD Group	29.2	17.7	—
11	13	Maritz Market Research	24.7	24.3	—
12	11	Westat	24.5	3.8	—

Rank 1984	Rank 1983	Organization	Research Revenues* (Millions)	Change vs. 1983**(%)	Research Revenues from Outside U.S. (Millions)
13	14	Elrick and Lavidge	23.3	21.4	—
14	16	Walker Research	19.4	21.7	—
15	19	YSW Group	17.0	13.3	.85
16	18	Chilton Research	16.5	23.1	—
17	15	ASI Market Research	16.4	20.0	—
18	17	Louis Harris and Associates	15.3	13.3	4.0
19	23	Opinion Research Co.	14.5	34.3	—
20	20	Ehrhart-Babic Group	13.2	5.6	—
21	22	Winona Research	12.9	9.0	—
22	25	Simmons Market Research Bureau	12.5	21.4	—
23	21	Data Development Co.	10.5	16.7	—
24	26	Decisions Center	10.2	15.9	—
25	24	Harte-Hanks Marketing Services Group	9.7	25.0	—
26	27	McCollum/Spielman Research	9.4	10.6	—
27	28	Admar Research	9.3	8.0	—
28	32	Custom Research	8.6	34.3	—
29	29	National Analysts	7.9	8.2	—
30	—	Decision/Making/Information	7.8	100.0	—
31	30	Management Decision Systems	7.7	8.1	—
32	31	Gallup Organization	7.7	14.9	—
33	33	Starch INRA Hopper	7.5	19.6	—
34	35	Mediamark Research	7.2	23.0	—
35	34	Market Opinion Research	6.8	13.6	—
36	—	Kapuler Marketing Research	6.0	34.0	—
37	—	Ad Factors Marketing Research	5.9	66.1	—
38	—	Response Analysis	5.6	44.6	—
39	—	Decision Research Corp.	5.5	36.0	—
40	—	Oxtoby-Smith	5.0	18.0	—
		Subtotal, Top 40	$1,449.1	+13.7%	$345.8
		All Other (54 CASRO companies not listed in Top 40)***	117.2	+12.5	—
		Total	$1,566.3	+13.6%	$345.8

*Total revenues that include nonresearch activities, for some companies, are significantly higher. This information is given in the individual company profiles.

**Rate growth from year to year has been adjusted so as to not include revenue gains from acquisition.

***Total revenues of 54 survey research firms—over and beyond those listed in Top 40 list—who provide financial information, on a confidential basis, to CASRO.

Figure 15.1 U.S. research industry (Year-to-year revenue growth rate)

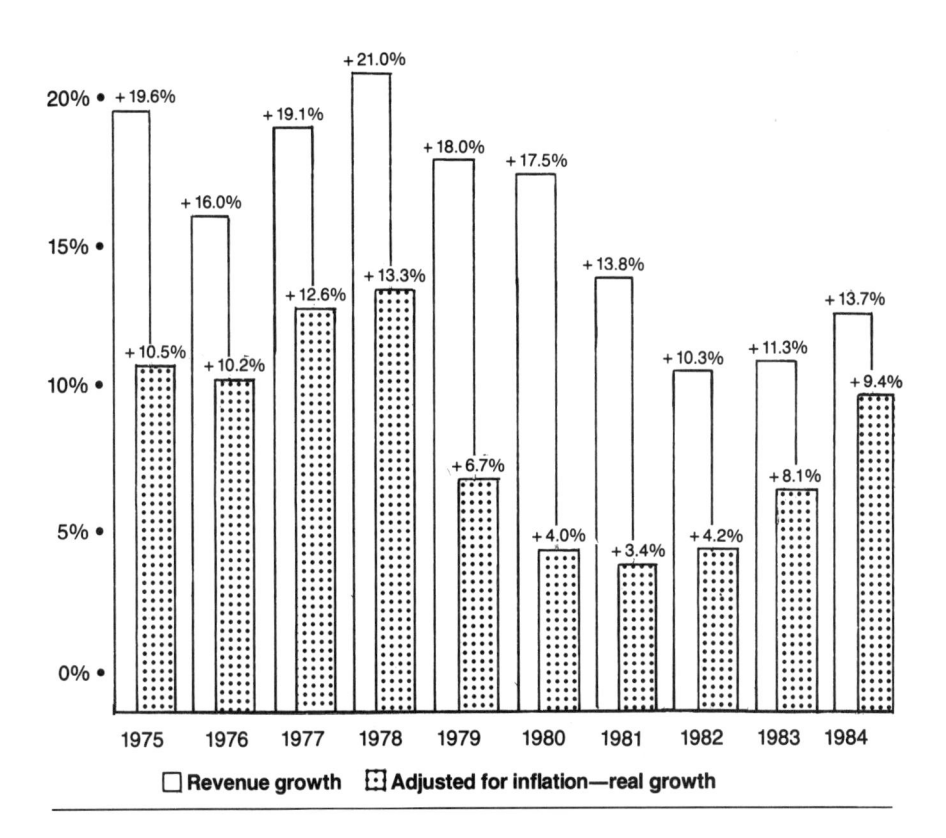

Year	Revenue growth	Adjusted for inflation—real growth
1975	+19.6%	+10.5%
1976	+16.0%	+10.2%
1977	+19.1%	+12.6%
1978	+21.0%	+13.3%
1979	+18.0%	+6.7%
1980	+17.5%	+4.0%
1981	+13.8%	+3.4%
1982	+10.3%	+4.2%
1983	+11.3%	+8.1%
1984	+13.7%	+9.4%

It is interesting to note that the Top 40 group U.S.-alone growth rate of 17.4% compares to 17.3% for the Top U.S. advertising agencies (see special issue of *Advertising Age*, March 28, 1985.) However, these numbers are not perfectly comparable because in the case of Top 40 research companies, any growth attributable to acquisitions has been calculated out. For instance, if one research company purchased another during 1984, revenues of the two firms for all of 1983 and 1984 were used to calculate growth. If that weren't done, the industry's growth rate would appear higher than is the fact. It was impossible to do that for the advertising agencies, so their growth rate, to some degree, probably is inflated by acquired revenues.

Table 15.2 How the Top 40 U.S. Research Companies Compare With the Top 40 U.S. Advertising Agencies

	Top 40 U.S. Advertising Agencies*	Top 40 U.S. Research Companies**
Revenues—1894 (in millions)		
Worldwide	$5,779.2	$1,449.1
U.S. only	3,876.1	1,104.3
Revenue growth rate (1984 over 1983)		
Worldwide	+16.3%***	+13.9%
U.S. only	+17.3%***	+17.4%

*Source: *Advertising Age* U.S. Agency Profiles, March 28, 1985.
**These figures account for marketing/advertising research operations only. In fact, many of the companies listed have larger total revenues, as is explained in individual company profiles.
***These percentages are not perfectly comparable to the Top 40 research growth rates in that some of the agencies may reflect revenue growth in 1984 attributable to acquisitions. In the Top 40 research list, this has been corrected for by using the two (company plus acquisition) total revenues for both 1983 and 1984 to calculate growth rate. It was not possible to do this for the advertising agencies.

The Urge to Merge

The factoring out of growth by acquisition was particularly important because, since this analysis was published last year, there has been an unprecedented number of changes of ownership. Just among the Top 40 group, it looks like this:

- Dun & Bradstreet acquired A.C. Nielsen Co. (#1 on the list) for approximately $1.1 billion.
- Harte-Hanks Marketing Services Group (#25 on list) divested two research properties. TRIM, Inc. was sold to MAJERS Corp. (see Marketing Information Service Firms at the end of this chapter), and the MARKETRAX service in Los Angeles and St. Louis was sold to The NPD Group (#10 on Top 40 list).
- ASI Market Research (#17 on list) acquired Teaman/Lehman Associates, Norwalk, Conn.
- The Arbitron Ratings Co. (#4 on list) bought approximately 45% interest in Burke Marketing Services, Inc. (#5 on list), with an option to purchase the balance by 1990.

- Admar Research Company (#27 on list) was acquired in January 1985, by Sprigg Lane Investment Co.
- Information Resources, Inc. (#8 on list) acquired Management Decision Systems, Inc., Waltham, Mass. (See #31 on list and the section on Marketing Information Service Firms at the end of this chapter.)
- YSW Group (#15 on list) was acquired by Saatchi & Saatchi, the British advertising agency.
- Data Development Corp. (#23 on list) divested its interest in Central Location Testing, a subsidiary.
- IMS America (#2 on list) acquired Pipeline Research in the fourth quarter of 1984.

Size of U.S. Market

The 94 research organizations included in the Top 40 listing plus the CASRO all other groups had gross worldwide revenues of $1,566,400,000 in 1984, and of that, $1,220,600,000—or 78%—was from operations within the U.S.; that number, it is estimated, accounts for over 85% of the commercial market for marketing, advertising, and public opinion research (excluding nonprofit research organizations, survey work down in-house by agencies of the federal government, and the value of research done in-house by some marketers of goods and services and their advertising agencies). So, the size of the total market is still left to estimation, as is the total industry growth rate.

However, the 1984 figures dramatize once again the degree to which the U.S. research industry is big business with ownership in the hands of large nonresearch corporations, such as Control Data Corp., Dunn & Bradstreet, Time Inc., Maritz, Inc., Equifax, Inc., Saatchi & Saatchi, American Broadcasting Co., IDC Services, Gannett Co., Arthur D. Little, JWT Group, Harte-Hanks Communications, Booz Allen & Hamilton, Temple, Barker & Sloane, and Mills & Allen International, to name some. In fact, of the $1,449,200,000 in Top 40 firms' revenues for 1984, only 13% is still controlled by privately held corporations. That percentage, the way things are going, should be significantly lower in the next year's Annual Review of Industry Performance.

Individual Company Profiles

There follow profiles of each of the Top 40 research organizations, with a summary of changes they made in 1984—and intend to make yet in 1985.

1. A. C. Nielsen Company
Northbrook, Illinois
Founded in 1923; since late 1984 a wholly owned subsidiary of Dun & Bradstreet Corporation. Research revenues in 1984 were $491 million, up 5.9% over 1984.

For the 12 months ending November 30, 1984, the world's largest marketing/advertising research organization had research revenues of $491 million, about 52% of which is estimated to have come from ACN operations in 24 countries outside the U.S. (Total revenues for all ACN operations are no longer public because of D&B acquisition—*Advertising Age*, May 21, 1984—but in 1983, research operations accounted for 67% of the total.)

Of the $491 million, 79%—or $338 million—was accounted for by ACN's Marketing Research Group, an increase of 5.3% over 1983, and $103 million was accounted for by the Media Research Group, an increase of 8.2% over 1983.

ACN's Marketing Research Group provides, basically, custom and syndicated measures of product movement on both a national and local market level. This group does about 65% of its business outside the U.S. and continues to be hurt by foreign currency exchange problems.

In 1984, the Test Marketing Services unit of Marketing Research Group USA set up a profit center called ERIM to develop a new, single-source product/advertising exposure measuring service called TestSight, at first in two markets—Sioux Falls, South Dakota and Springfield, Missouri—with several more planned to come on-line through 1985 and 1986. A unique feature of the TestSight system is the ability to make tv commercial cut-ins to specific households (in TestSight consumer panels of 2,500 households per market) on-air, thereby bypassing cable transmission on which other such systems are dependent. (See chapter 7 for details on the development of ERIM.)

ACN's Media Research Group in the U.S. during 1984 continued its expansion of local tv meter-measured markets, opening up Washington, Dallas, and Boston, bringing the total so-equipped to 10; Miami and Denver will come on-line in the fall of 1985. The Media Group has also expanded its national people meter test to 300 households, and further expansion is planned for later in 1985.

Chairman–CEO of ACN is Henry Burk, 58, who is also a member of D&B's board. Burk studied at the Universities of Zurich, St. Gallen, and Freiburg in Switzerland and has a degree in economics. N. Eugene Harden, 50, is president, COO; he is a graduate of Lawrence University. Richard W. Vipond, 57, is president of the Media Research Group. Arthur C. Nielsen, Jr. is now a member of the D&B board.

2. IMS International
New York, New York
Public corporation traded otc; founded in 1954.
Research revenues in 1984 were $151.4 million, up 10.1% over 1983.

Revenues do not include Pipeline Research, which IMS America acquired in the fourth quarter of 1984.

Of this worldwide conglomerate's total revenues of $223 million, about 68% came from its marketing research operations in 60 countries. Of the research revenues alone, 44.6%—or $67.5 million—was from the IMS subsidiary in the U.S., IMS America, which is headquartered in Ambler, Pennsylvania. So, IMS U.S. revenues in 1984 were up 30.6% and international research revenues were down 2%, in part due to the same currency exchange problems besetting the other big international on this list, A. C. Nielsen.

IMS market research activities are divided into pharmaceutical audits, reports on the sale of ethical (and in some cases, proprietary) pharmaceuticals collected from panels of drugstores (which account for 21% of total research volume); medical reports based on information collected from panels of practicing physicians who report on the diagnosis and treatment of patients (12%); other syndicated audits of purchases made by hospitals, and cosmetics and toiletries (13%); sales territory reports (customized geography) started in U.S., now being expanded to other countries (34%); custom ad hoc surveys and studies in such industries as cosmetics, veterinary pharmaceuticals, medical supplies and equipment, office equipment, and agriculture. Some IMS data are available in numerous countries via an on-line Data Base Systems network.

The IMS marketing research operation has 2,300 full-time salaried employees.

In 1984, Robert Louis Dreyfus, 38, became president, CEO of IMS International, succeeding Lars H. Erickson, who became chairman. Dreyfus has an M.B.A. from Harvard University, and his office is in London. Serge Y. Okun, 38, is president of the U.S. subsidiary and also a vp of the parent company. He is a graduate of the National School of Statistics and Economic Administration in Paris.

3. Selling Areas-Marketing, Inc. (SAMI)
New York, New York
Wholly owned subsidiary of Time Inc.; founded in 1966.
Revenues in 1984 are estimated at $118.4 million, up 19% over 1983.

SAMI's main service amalgamates warehouse withdrawal data on thousands of individual package goods items sold through food stores and produces 13 reports a year separately for each of 51 marketing areas representing about 86% of the total U.S. ACV. Spin-offs of this main service produce customized reports on stores servicing minority segments (black or Hispanic) of the population and product availability (SARDI service). Starting in March 1985, SAMI will add three new market areas—Portland, Maine/Concord, New Hampshire; Shreveport, Louisiana/Jackson, Mississippi; and Green Bay, Wisconsin—to its system, bringing the total to 54 marketing areas representing 88.4% of total ACV.

In addition, SAMI operates three minimarkets, each with 2,500-household panels, where purchases can be recorded via UPC scanner at checkout and then related to individual households. Sales and service of this system, which is called SAMSCAN, are handled by the BMSI Test Marketing Group (see #5 on list).

Starting in 1985, SAMI will operate a drugstore reporting system comparable to its basic grocery store service, starting in Chicago, New York, Los Angeles, and San Francisco. Ten market areas will be on-line by the end of 1985, and 18 by mid-1986, says SAMI.

SAMI has 344 full-time, salaried employees in three offices.

Carlyle C. Daniel, 54, is president of SAMI; he is a graduate of Lynchburg College. Daniel is a vp of Time Inc.

4. Arbitron Ratings Company
New York, New York
Founded in 1949; since 1967 a wholly owned subsidiary of Control Data Corporation.
Revenues in 1984 were $105.8 million, up 12.3% over 1983.

During 1984, Arbitron purchased approximately 45% of Burke Marketing Services, Inc. and an option to purchase the balance by 1990. BMSI revenues are shown separately (see #5 on list).

Arbitron produces radio, tv, and cable tv audience studies at the local-market level using either mail diaries or panels of meter-equipped households. Surveys in 210 tv markets account for 52.7% of Arbitron revenues; 47.2% comes from measurement of 261 radio markets. Customers for Arbitron data include radio and tv stations, advertisers and their agencies. There are 1,020 full-time employees in eight U.S. offices. A phone interviewing center with 55 stations is located in Laurel, Maryland.

During 1984, Arbitron completed a long-range meter-market expansion program, and meter service is now on-line in 11 major markets. Also in 1984, Arbitron introduced a number of microcomputer systems to help stations manage and analyze radio and tv ratings. Product Target Aid, a new service, uses lifestyle cluster information to help tv stations plan a commercial schedule to target customers of a particular product or service.

In 1984, Arbitron and BMSI, in a joint venture, started to develop an advanced market measurement service—linking tv viewing with purchases of specific packaged goods—called ScanAmerica. A pilot panel of households in Denver is now equipped with special equipment which enables the consumer to scan, via wand, the UPC code on products purchased, which then can be accessed via telephone lines along with viewing data. First data from Denver are expected in late 1985.

Chairman and CEO of Arbitron is Theodore F. Shaker, 63, a vp of Control Data; he attended Colgate, Northwestern and New York Universities. A. J. "Rick" Aurichio, 48, is president and COO. He is a graduate of Fairleigh Dickinson University.

5. Burke Marketing Services, Inc. (BMSI)
Cincinnati, Ohio
Privately held corporation; founded in 1947.
Revenues in 1984 were $66 million, up 9.8% over 1983.

In the fall of 1984, about 45% of BMSI was purchased by Arbitron Ratings Company (see #4 on list) which, in turn, is a wholly owned subsidiary of Control Data Corporation. Arbitron holds an option to buy the balance of BMSI. Infratest, a German research company, owns 5% of BMSI, and, in turn, BMSI owns 5% in Infratest.

The BMSI conglomerate consists of the following: (1) Burke Marketing Research which specializes in custom survey research and pre- and post-tv copy testing; (2) Test Marketing Group, a unit consisting of what was AdTel and Market Audits, which operates six controlled test markets and which markets and services, through a joint venture, SAMI's (see #3 on list) three test market SAMSCAN service; (3) BASES which specializes in market modeling; (4) Burke Institute which conducts seminars and courses for students of marketing/advertising research; (5) Burke Canada, a wholly owned subsidiary which accounts for about $1.7 million in revenue; (6) Burke International, a joint venture with Infratest; and (7) COMTEC, a joint venture with the Gartner Group, Inc., to operate a panel of 8,000 business establishments which report on their intention to buy a variety of computer and telecommunications products.

Starting in 1984, BMSI entered a joint venture with Arbitron Ratings Company to develop a new electronic market/advertising measurement system, ScanAmerica. Now in pilot phase in Denver, ScanAmerica equips panel households with people meters to monitor tv viewership and a device through which participants can record the purchase of specific packaged goods via scanning of the UPC code with a small wand that is an inherent part of the meter.

Burke has 475 full-time employees in 42 offices in the U.S. A central WATS phone center has 200 stations, 140 of which are CRT-equipped.

In May 1985, about 1,000 BMSI employees now located in five office sites in Cincinnati will come together in one headquarters building, a 21-story structure in the downtown area which was once the *Post and Times Star* building.

Also, in early 1986, Burke plans to add a seventh market to its AdTel system.

Jack E. Brown, 41, is chairman of BMSI. He attended the University of Cincinnati.

6. M/A/R/C, Inc.
Dallas, Texas
Publicly held corporation traded otc; founded in 1965.
Research revenues in 1984 were $37.6 million,
up 39.8% over 1983.

Total M/A/R/C revenues for the fiscal year ending March 31, 1985, were $41.4 million. (Excluded from the revenue trends above are certain nonresearch activities.)

This has been an eventful year for M/A/R/C. The company's name was changed (from Allcom, Inc.), and in December of 1984, it filed with the SEC for a public offering which has since taken place. M/A/R/C also broke ground for a new six-story corporate headquarters near Dallas–Ft. Worth airport and, early in 1984, constructed a new 144-station, CRT-equipped central interviewing facility in Denton, Texas.

M/A/R/C, with 314 full-time, salaried employees plus 162 hourly staff workers in 10 U.S. offices, is divisionalized as follows: (1) the Corporate Group, which supplies support services such as personnel, marketing, and accounting to the operating groups; (2) the Marketing Research Group, which provides syndicated buyer studies, computer software systems, interviewing and marketing research consumer panels; (3) the Marketing Services Group, which develops and maintains data bases of prime users of products; develops, executes, and fulfills promotion efforts; and operates the Promotion Test Lab. (About 67% of this group's revenues are from research activities.)

Plans for 1985 include expansion of the LMN network to 30 markets, consolidation of the New York and Boston client service groups into a Westport, Connecticut, facility, and bringing on-line an IBM 4381 to handle large data bases.

Chairman, president and CEO of M/A/R/C is Cecil "Bud" Phillips, 60, a graduate of Southern Methodist University. President of M/A/R/C's Corporate Group is E. L. "Jack" Taylor, 58; he has an M.B.A. from the University of Texas.

7. Market Facts, Inc.
Chicago, Illinois
Public corporation, traded otc; founded in 1946.
Revenues for 1984 were $35.9 million, up 26.7% over 1983.

MF revenues do not include those of Market Facts-Canada ($5.7 million in 1984), which is 50% owned by MF.

MF's U.S. operations include: (1) the Consumer Mail Panel, a fixed mail panel of over 220,000 households; (2) Consumer Opinion Forums—six completely uniform shopping mall interviewing facilities; (3) Marketest, a store auditing and controlled score testing service in seven permanent markets; (4) focus group facilities; and (5) two WATS telephone interviewing centers with a total of 104 stations, about 65 of which are CRT-equipped. The survey research activities at MF are separated into operating groups, as so: consumer, public, sector, and financial services.

During 1984, MF introduced a new system for evaluating tv commercials. Called TRACE, the system utilizes microprocessors to obtain moment-to-moment reaction to commercial messages and other advertising stimuli.

There are six client service offices at 16 other field organization offices in the U.S. (four others are located in Canada). There are 520 full-time, salaried employees.

President and CEO of Market Facts is Verne B. Churchill, 52, who received his M.B.A. from Indiana University. David K. Hardin, 57, is chairman; he received his M.B.A. from the University of Chicago and is past president of the American Marketing Association.

8. Information Resources, Inc.
Chicago, Illinois
Public corporation traded otc; founded in 1977.
Revenues in 1984 were $35.8 million, up 69.7% over 1983.

The main business of this much-publicized company is the BehaviorScan system, a network of eight minimarkets that are equipped for advertising and control store testing. In each BehaviorScan market, the service captures consumer purchase behavior of a wide variety of packaged goods via UPC scanner equipment in major grocery stores, collects purchase data from a panel of about 2,500 households via the use of plastic identification cards that tie in panel households with point-of-sale scanner data, alternates tv advertising over cable tv to groups of preselected households which are meter-equipped, and collects other measures of in-store merchandising/promotions. During 1984, BehaviorScan added drug stores to its system in two more markets, making a total of six so equipped.

Another service, Marketing Fact Book, provides access to a data base of consumer purchasing activity on a large number of packaged goods. During 1984, IRI added data from selected neighborhoods in Chicago, Los Angeles, and New York to the Marketing Fact Book system.

Also in 1984, IRI introduced a new service called TV Buying Guide, which provides media planning information based on integrated scanner-collected purchase data and metered by tv viewing data for a sample of 7,000 households. Also in 1984, IRI introduced FASTRAC, a system for evaluating the volume potential of new products prior to test marketing.

IRI has 496 full-time employees, and most of them were consolidated into a 150,000-square-foot corporate headquarters building during 1984.

In a letter of intent signed in February 1985, IRI announced its plans to purchase for stock worth approximately $30 million the research/marketing information firm of Management Decision Systems, Waltham, Massachusetts. (See Marketing Information Service Firm section at the end of this chapter and #31 on this list.)

During 1985, IRI plans to add drugstores to its BehaviorScan system in two more markets and selected neighborhood data from 10 additional major cities to its Marketing Fact Book data base.

Chairman–CEO of IRI is one of the founders, John Malec, 40, a graduate of the University of Wisconsin. President–CEO is Gian Fulgoni, 37, who has a Master's degree from Manchester University in England.

9. NFO Research, Inc.
Toledo, Ohio
Founded in 1946; since 1982 wholly owned subsidiary of AGB Research.
Revenues in 1984 were $29.5 million, up 10.1% over 1983.

NFO, with 675 employees (340 of whom are full-time, salaried), is located in offices in Toledo; New York; Chicago; St. Louis; San Francisco; Newark, New Jersey; Greensboro, North Carolina; and an executive headquarters recently relocated to Greenwich, Connecticut.

The main business of NFO is a fixed mail panel, which was expanded to 320,000 households in 1984. Multiclient Services Division of NFO offers TRAC syndicated research based on diary-type purchase panels to report on consumption of beverages, men's tailored apparel, and the personal home computer and video game market.

NFO operates two telephone interviewing facilities with more than 200 interviewing stations with interactive interviewing capabilities in both locations.

In 1984, NFO formed a new company, NFO International Research, in New York to specialize in European research for American multinational companies. Also in 1984, NFO entered into a joint venture with MMSL (another AGB Research subsidiary located in London) to form Patient Searchlight, a New Jersey-based unit specializing in research for the pharmaceutical industry.

William E. Lipner, 38, is president–CEO of NFO; he is a graduate of the University of Toledo.

10. The NPD Group
Port Washington, New York
Privately held corporation; founded in 1953.
Revenues in 1984 were $29.2 million, up 17.7% over 1983.

The NPD Group, which has 560 employees, 320 of whom are full-time salaried, is divisionalized as follows: NPD Research, Inc., a 14,500-household national diary purchase panel specializing in package goods and more than 25 local-market panels with about 40,000 households; NPD Special Industry Services, purchase diary and mail panels specializing in such product classes as toys/games, textile/apparel, petroleum products, sports equipment, and records/tapes; GDR/CREST Enterprises, a panel reporting on meals eaten away from home and also providing custom research and consulting to the food service industry; and Home Testing Institute, a fixed mail panel of 175,000 households. A new unit, Marketing Models Division, which specializes in proprietary models such as ESP (for pretest marketing, new product forecasting) and PSA (for preference structure analysis), was created in 1984.

New in 1984: the Special Industry Services Division started a Jewelry Tracking Service and an Apparel Point-of-scale Tracking Service was added to the Toy POS data base. The Packaged Goods Division introduced a behaviorally derived Nutritional Segmentation System, a joint venture in the apparel diary panel area was established with Kurt Salmon Associates, and the HTI Division established a 150,000-household syndicated survey regarding insurance and related financial products. NPD's Chicago office was relocated into a new 24,000-square-foot facility, and a new office was opened in Los Angeles.

In early 1985, NPD purchased the Marketrax scanner-based consumer panels in St. Louis and Los Angeles from TRIM, a subsidiary of Harte-Hanks. This service, which is used to analyze consumer response to promotional activities, will be expanded to other major markets in 1985.

President–CEO of The NPD Group is Tod Johnson, 40, who holds an M.S.I.A. degree from Carnegie-Mellon University. Founder, chairman, and joint owner is Henry Brenner, 70.

11. Maritz Market Research, Inc.
Fenton, Montana
Founded in 1973; wholly owned subsidiary of Maritz, Inc.
Revenues in 1984 were $24.7 million, up 24.3% over 1983.

The Maritz organization includes the following: full-service divisional offices in six cities (one of which, Parsippany, New Jersey, was new in 1984); CRT-aided WATS survey centers in three cities (which in total have 115 stations); single-client, dedicated interviewing and data processing centers in three cities; and a network of field interviewing facilities (phone, focus group, central location, and mall studies) in 16 major cities. The company's Econo-Net Interviewing system grew, in 1984, to a network of 12 cities utilizing a total of 200 microcomputers for telephone and mall interviewing. Each city's system communicates with any one of three HP mainframes. Maritz's Agricultural Research Division, with annual revenues of nearly $2 million, is one of the largest specializing in that market.

In total, there are 150 full-time, salaried, exempt employees at Maritz, and approximately 2,500 part-time interviewers and supervisors.

In 1985, Maritz will open new client service offices in Dallas and Atlanta and plans two new services: MAPPS for product planning and positioning and MIVIS for interactive videodisc interviewing.

President of Maritz Market Research is William H. Lewellen, 54, who has an M.S. degree from St. Louis University.

12. Westat, Inc.
Rockville, Maryland
An employee owned corporation founded in 1961.
Revenues in 1984 were $24.7 million, up 3.8% over 1983.

Revenues include Crossley Surveys, a wholly owned subsidiary. Westat specializes in survey research, and about 85% of the work is done for agencies of the U.S. government. The staff includes 240 salaried, exempt professionals and an average of 60 salaried, nonexempt, plus about 350 involved in telephone interviewing, support and survey processing, and national field studies. There is an office in New York City in addition to the headquarters staff in Rockville, and phone facilities include 75 dialing stations, half of which are equipped for CRT interviewing.

President–CEO of Westat is Joseph A. Hunt, 49, who has an M.S. degree from Massachusetts Institute of Technology. Edward C. Bryant, 69, the founder, is chairman; he has a Ph.D. from Iowa State University.

13. Elrick and Lavidge, Inc.
Chicago, Illinois
Founded in 1951; a wholly owned subsidiary of Equifax, Inc. since 1980.
Revenues in 1984 were $23.3 million, up 21.4% over 1983.

Revenues include those of Quick Test Opinion Centers, a separate operating unit within E&L, with a network of 18 shopping mall interviewing sites, plus a new one in Manhattan devoted to focus groups.

E&L, which specializes in survey research for consumer and business-to-business clients, operates six telephone interviewing centers, two of which are dedicated to the TELSAM/PULSE system for Bell operating companies. The other four have, in total, 144 interviewing stations, 112 of which are CRT-equipped.

There are 163 salaried, exempt employees at E&L, plus 55 salaried, nonexempt, and 761 hourly paid in-office, located in 29 domestic offices.

During 1985, E&L plans to relocate and expand its San Francisco facility, which will include 24 CATI interviewing positions. New Quick Test Opinion Centers are being added in the San Francisco area and Denver, and the one in Tampa Bay is being doubled in size. Plans also call for two new full-service offices, one on the West Coast and one on the East Coast.

President–CEO of E&L is Robert J. Lavidge, 63, who received his M.B.A. from the University of Chicago. He was national president of the American Marketing Association, 1966–67.

14. Walker Research, Inc.
Indianapolis, Indiana
Privately held corporation; founded in 1964.
Revenues in 1984 were $19.4 million, up 21.7% over 1983.

Walker, a survey research firm, is divisionalized as follows: Custom Research Division, which provides traditional ad hoc marketing research services through client service offices in six U.S. cities; Operations Division, which offers data collection and data processing services through a network of six offices and interviewing via telephone, mall intercept, pre-recruited central location, and direct mail. There are, in total, over 240 telephone interviewing stations, the majority of which are outfitted for CATI.

During 1984, Walker started two new marketing divisions: Performance Measurement Systems, which specializes in ongoing service industry measurement research, and MarketPULSE Measurement Systems, which offers syndicated research programs to the healthcare industry. Also in 1984, Walker established a Marketing Science Group, which provides advanced conceptual and analytical consulting services.

In 1984, Walker started construction of a new 90,000-square-foot corporate headquarters building, which will be ready for occupancy in October 1985. Employees at Walker include 128 full-time salaried, 152 full-time hourly, and 476 part-time.

Chairman and CEO of Walker is Frank D. Walker, 50, a graduate of DePauw University. President and COO is James E. Sammer, 46, who received his M.B.A. from Michigan State University.

15. YSW Group
New York, New York
Founded in 1958; since 1984, a wholly owned subsidiary of Saatchi & Saatchi.
Research revenues in 1984 were $17 million, up 13.3% over 1983.

YSW Group includes what was Yankelovich, Skelly and White and McBer & Company, a research-based consulting company (McBer's research revenues only are reflected here). YSW was acquired by Saatchi & Saatchi in late 1984.

This multifaceted survey research organization is organized as follows: Consumer Marketing Group (which includes, among others, TRAC Forecasting models, the LTM simulated test marketing system, the Monitor tracking study, and custom surveys); Corporate Communications Group (corporate image studies, corporate advertising assessments); Policy Planning Group (public policy, corporate priorities, multiclient studies); Industrial Marketing Group; Human Resources Group (work force attitudes); and McBer & Company (selection, training, rewards, key employees). In total, there are 195 full-time, salaried employees in three offices.

About 5% of YSW revenues come from operations outside the U.S.

In 1984, YSW inaugurated three new multiclient studies under the "Viewpoint" name (Architect Viewpoint, European Viewpoint, and Hispanic Viewpoint), and during 1985 it plans to add a Small Business Viewpoint.

Founder and chairman of YSW is Daniel Yankelovich, 60, a graduate of Harvard University. President and CEO is Florence R. Skelly, a graduate of Hunter College.

16. Chilton Research Services
Radnor, Pennsylvania
Founded in 1957; since 1979 a wholly owned subsidiary of American Broadcasting Company.
Revenues in 1984 were $16.5 million, up 23.1% over 1983.

This survey research organization does custom, ad hoc marketing, and social science studies for industry and agencies of the federal government. While a significant number of CRS surveys utilize mail or face-to-face interviewing, the majority are conducted via telephone via one of the industry's largest and most sophisticated CATI systems, which has on-line sample control and interactive cross tabulations. This system has 185 interviewing stations and is linked to Chilton's twin IBM 4341 computers.

CRS has 142 full-time salaried employees.

Director of CRS is Gilbert Barrish, 45, a graduate of Temple University.

17. ASI Market Research
New York, New York
Founded in 1962; a wholly owned subsidiary of IDC Services since 1983.
Research revenues in 1984 were $16.4 million, up 20% over 1983.

Revenues include those of Teaman/Lehman Associates, a full-service survey research firm, Norwalk, Connecticut, which ASI acquired in January 1984. Also during 1984, ASI divested some of its properties. The gross revenues for both years have been adjusted accordingly to a common base to calculate growth rate.

ASI, which represents about 90% of the total, is organized into two divisions: (1) Advertising Research, which specializes in controlled audience pretesting and on-air testing of tv commercials, testing of print ads, and evaluation of entertainment projects, including pilots for tv and movie films; and (2) Marketing Research Division (over $5 million of total), which conducts custom, ad hoc surveys, focus groups, and—in 1984—set up a qualitative division in New York. MRD operates central telephone interviewing facilities with 120 stations, 20 of which are CRT-equipped.

During 1984, the Advertising Research Division launched Apex, a new tv copy testing system which provides on-air recall, on-air persuasion, and diagnostics, with all exposure occurring naturally within the home.

President and CEO of ASI is Gerald Lukeman, 53, who is a graduate of Dartmouth College. He is also executive vp of IDC Services.

18. Louis Harris and Associates, Inc.
New York, New York
Founded in 1956; a wholly owned subsidiary of Gannett Company since 1975.
Revenues in 1984 were $15.3 million, up 13.3% over 1983.

Twenty-six percent of Harris revenues come from subsidiaries outside the U.S.—Louis Harris International, headquartered in London; Louis Harris France, headquartered in Paris; and Louis Harris International Medical Surveys, also located in London.

The U.S. operation is composed of seven divisions, five of which are located in New York, one in Washington, D.C., and one in San Francisco. They specialize in public opinion and attitude research in the following markets: telecommunications, computers, health care, banking and financial services, automobiles, public policy and corporate public affairs. Multiclient surveys track corporate, financial, public and leadership opinion. A CATI-based telephone interviewing facility with 52 stations (34 CATI-equipped) is located in New York. There are 137 full-time, salaried employees in the total Harris organization.

Chairman and CEO is the company's founder, Louis Harris, 64, whose syndicated column appears in 170 newspapers. He is a graduate of the University of North Carolina at Chapel Hill. President and COO is Humphrey Taylor, 50, a graduate of Cambridge University in England.

19. Opinion Research Corporation
Princeton, New Jersey
Founded in 1938; since 1975, a wholly owned sudsidiary of Arthur D. Little, Inc.
Revenues in 1984 were $14.5 million, up 34.3% over 1983.

ORC provides survey research, analytical and consulting services, with emphasis on the following: market research, modeling and simulation, cable and video, financial services, telecommunications, health care, government research, employee relations, and public opinion research.

In addition, ORC periodically conducts several share-cost surveys—the Financial Relations Image Assessment Program, the Corporate Reputation Survey, the Executive Corporate Image Survey, the Business and the Media Survey, the Public Opinion Index, and Caravan Omnibus Surveys. In total there are over 200 full-time, salaried employees in Princeton and four branch offices.

In early 1985, ORC opened a new 100-station (30 equipped with CRTs) telephone center in Somerset, New Jersey, in addition to its 25-station facility in Princeton.

Chairman–CEO of ORC is Irwin Miller, 56, who has a Ph.D. from Virginia Polytechnic Institute. Vice chairman is Harry O'Neill, 56, who has a Master's degree from Pennsylvania State University. President is Andrew Brown, 40, who has an M.B.A. from Temple University.

20. The Ehrhart-Babic Group, Inc.
Englewood Cliffs, New Jersey
Privately held corporation; founded in 1959.
Revenues in 1984 were $13.2 million, up 5.6% over 1983.

The Ehrhart-Babic Group, with 110 full-time, salaried employees, specializes in "in-store" research through the following four groups: (1) E-B Custom Research which executes sales measurement studies including minimarkets, controlled store tests, projectable and trendable sales audits, weekend audits, and product purchases; (2) National Retail Tracking Index (NRTI) which conducts regularly scheduled syndicated retail observation studies in 110 major markets, including all SAMI areas (see #3 on list)—a total of 8,000 retail outlets, including food, drug, mass merchandisers, convenience and hardware/home centers; (3) National Liquor, Wine & Beer Index which provides comprehensive distribution information quarterly in over 2,600 off-premise outlets and semiannually in over 3,100 on-premise outlets; and (4)—new in 1984—Measurement of Trade Cooperation (MTC), a syndicated survey of weekly in-store promotional support by chain supermakets for all or selected brands within a category. About 1% of E-B revenues comes from outside the U.S.

Cofounders of E-B are chairman Thomas A. Ehrhart, 60, a graduate of Pace University, and president Louis J. Babic, Jr., 52, a graduate of Boston University.

21. Winona Research, Inc.
Minneapolis, Minnesota
Privately held corporation; founded in 1953.
Revenues in 1984 were $12.9 million, up 9% over 1983.

This full-service survey research company has 125 full-time, salaried employees in four offices—Minneapolis, Dallas, New York, and Phoenix. The Phoenix site houses a WATS phone interviewing facility with 160 stations, 120 of which are CRT-equipped.

In addition to large-scale telephone interviewing, Winona also does product testing and custom retail store audits of product movement.

President and CEO of Winona is Richard McCullough, 41, a graduate of the University of Minnesota. He is the immediate past chairman of the Council of American Survey Research Organizations (CASRO).

22. Simmons Market Research Bureau (SMRB)
New York, New York
Subsidiary of JWT Group; founded in 1978.
Revenues in 1984 were $12.5 million, up 21.4% over 1983.

This survey research/database organization was created in 1978 through the merger of W. R. Simmons & Associates (founded in 1952) and Axiom Market Research Bureau.

Each year SMRB creates a data base based on a survey of 19,000 adults. Through several interviews with each respondent, data are obtained on the following: purchase and use of products and services in 800 categories, including some 3,900 brands; media exposure; demographics; and life style orientation in terms of VALS classifications. The data are merged with a Donnelley Marketing Information Service data base to create a service called ClusterPlus, and with the Claritas Corporation's PRIZM system, to pinpoint geo-demographic market segments. Clients are offered on-line access to this data base, which is also utilized by SMRB in conjunction with proprietary marketing research conducted for individual clients.

During 1984, SMRB started a joint venture with Scarborough Research Corporation to provide syndicated newspaper audience measurement in major markets; data from the first survey will be released in June 1985. Also in 1984, SMRB launched Trade Magazine Total Audience Studies and announced a tie-in with A. C. Nielsen's Media Research Group through which ClusterPlus data were related to local broadcast audience ratings. Also in 1984, Teen Study, a study of product and service usage, media exposure, etc., among 2,000 teenagers, was published.

There are 125 full-time, salaried employees at SMRB.

President, CEO of SMRB is Frank Stanton, 55, who has an M.A. degree from the University of Pennsylvania.

23. Data Development Corporation
New York, New York
Privately held corporation; founded in 1960.
Revenues for 1984 were $10.5 million, up 16.7% over 1983.

DDC revenues for both 1984 and 1983 have been adjusted to reflect the sale of DDC's equity position in Central Location Testing, a subsidiary.

This full-service, custom survey organization, which has 100 full-time salaried employees in three offices, includes DDC, New York Conference Center, and Telephone Center, which has 70 interviewing stations, 45 of which are CRT-equipped because of installation of a larger computer (HP-3000-48) during 1984.

DDC emphasizes strategic research and its proprietary services include COMBO (product testing), COPY II (copy strategic development), and ADOPTER (pretest market measurement system), which is a joint venture with Edward Tauber, University of Southern California.

During 1984, DDC opened an office in San Francisco and three offices located in Connecticut, New Jersey, and Rye, New York, were consolidated into one facility in New Rochelle, New York.

Jerry Rosenkranz is chairman of DDC, and Joseph Goldstein is president–CEO. Both are 49 and graduates of the City College of New York.

24. Decisions Center, Inc. (DCI)
New York, New York
Privately held corporation; founded in 1965.
Revenues in 1984 were $10.2 million, up 15.9% over 1983.

DCI, which has 115 full-time, salaried employees, includes Decisions Center, Qualitative Decisions Center, Analytic Insights, DCI International,

Murray Hill Center (three focus group conference rooms), and Facts Center, a 94-station telephone interviewing facility.

DCI specializes in custom survey research—large-scale market and strategy studies, tracking and trade studies, copy research, concept testing, and product testing.

In 1985, DCI will launch Express Data Center, which features computerized transmission of survey data from a network of locations about the U.S. to the company's mainframe in New York. Tabulation is instantaneous, and clients will be able to access the data from their own PCs.

DCI is managed by three partners: Bernard Ruderman, 53, who has an M.S. from Pennsylvania State University, Bernard Levine, 59, and Steven Roth, 39, both of whom received their M.B.A. degrees from New York State University.

25. Harte-Hanks Marketing Services Group
River Edge, New Jersey
Wholly owned division of Harte-Hanks Communications; founded in 1975.
Revenues in 1984 were $9.7 million, up 25% over 1983.

During 1984, Harte-Hanks sold two research units: Tele-Research, a tv copy testing operation, and TRIM, which specialized in controlled store tests. Revenues for both '83 and '84 have been adjusted accordingly to calculate growth.

This conglomerate, put together by a large Texas-based publishing company—which went from being a public, NYSE-listed company to a privately held one in 1984—consists of (1) RMH Research, Inc., a full-service survey company specializing in communications/media research; (2) National WATS Service, a telephone interviewing facility with 60 stations, 12 of which are CRT-equipped; and (3) Urban Data Processing, a Burlington, Massachusetts-based EDP service firm specializing in custom processing of census data for marketing uses.

There are approximately 100 full-time, salaried employees in three offices.

President of the Harte-Hanks Marketing Services Group is Richard Hochhauser, 40; he holds an M.B.A. from Columbia University.

26. McCollum/Spielman & Company, Inc.
Great Neck, New York
Privately held corporation; founded in 1968.
Revenues in 1984 were $9.4 million, up 10.6% over 1983.

M/S activities are divided into two groups: (1) Communications Division which does quantitative/qualitative–effectiveness/diagnostic testing of tv and radio commercials and print advertising utilizing closed-circuit, theatre-like interviewing facilities in 12 cities, as well as custom studies in the communications area, and (2) Associates Division, including Child Research Services, which tests children's (and frequently parents') reactions to commercials, programs, packaging, products and concepts, as well as custom studies in the area of ad tracking, corporate image, and syndicated services.

In 1984, the Communications Division introduced two new services: (1) STEP ONE, an early, primarily diagnostic service for advertising development, and (2) AC-T/SP (a joint service with NPD Research; see #10 on list), which predicts sales volume for new products and is based on NPD's ESP model combined with AC-T advertising information. Some M/S services are available in Japan, the United Kingdom, Canada, and West Germany through affiliates.

M/S has sales/servicing representation in four U.S. cities, and there are 90 full-time, salaried employees.

CEO of M/S is Harold M. Spielman, 58, who received his B.S.S. degree from City University of New York. President is Donald H. McCollum, 62, who received an M.A. from the University of Denver.

27. Admar Research Company, Inc.
New York, New York
Founded in 1960; since January 1985, a wholly owned subsidiary of Sprigg Lane Investment Corp.
Revenues in 1984 were $9.3 million, up 8% over 1983.

Revenues include three subsidiaries: Market Trends, Inc., Amherst Research Group, Inc. and Consumer Interviews, Inc. (a central WATS phone facility with 28 stations in Floral Park, N.Y.). There are 60 full-time, salaried employees.

Admar specializes in tracking surveys, product testing and advertising studies, employing research programs copyrighted by the company. A central phone facility has 22 stations.

Founder, chairman, and CEO of Admar is Henry D. Ostberg, who received his Ph.D. from Ohio State University. President is William J. Battison, 38, who joined the company in early 1985. He received an M.B.A. from the University of Virginia.

28. Custom Research, Inc.
Minneapolis, Minnesota
Privately held corporation; founded in 1974.
Revenues in 1984 were $8.6 million, up 34% over 1983.

This custom survey firm is divisionalized as follows: (1) Consumer Research; (2) Medical Research Bureau; (3) Custom Business Research; (4)

Custom Research Telephone (central telephone WATS interviewing facility, CRT-equipped, with 50 stations); and (5) Corporate Services. There are 70 full-time, salaried employees and branch offices in Union, New Jersey, and Chicago.

During 1984, CRI introduced the System, a new-product development system, which takes all the research steps a company normally goes through and puts them into one cohesive system.

CRI is managed by two partners: Jeffrey L. Pope, 44, who received his M.B.A. from the Kellogg School of Management, Northwestern University, and Judith S. Corson, 42, a graduate of the University of Minnesota.

29. National Analysts
Philadelphia, Pennsylvania
Founded in 1943; a division of Booz Allen & Hamilton, Inc. since 1970.
Revenues in 1984 were $7.9 million, up 8.2% over 1983.

NA, with 81 full-time, salaried employees in Philadelphia and New York, conducts custom qualitative and quantitative studies in support of its strategic research and consulting services, and commercial clients account for about 80% of its business. The balance is accounted for by agencies of the federal government, universities, and other not-for-profit institutions.

NA's professional staff specializes in such fields as telecommunications, financial services, pharmaceuticals and medical equipment, automotive, package goods, and litigation support. During 1984, NA converted to a new integrated EDP system to support its specialized work in market segmentation, trade-off analysis, and other multivariate modeling.

President of NA is Marshall G. Greenberg, 49, who received his Ph.D. from the University of Michigan.

30. Decision/Making/Information
McLean, Virginia
Privately held corporation; founded in 1969.
Revenues in 1984 were $7.8 million, up 100% over 1983.

This survey firm, which has 65 full-time employees (34 of whom are salaried, exempt) is divided into two divisions: Marketing Research and Political/Public Affairs. One big reason for the extraordinary revenue gain in 1984 was D/M/I political work for the Reagan-Bush '84 Committee and numerous other Republican candidates for office. Concurrently, D/M/I's nonpolitical business grew considerably too.

There are D/M/I offices in Santa Ana, California, and Provo, Utah, where the company's phone interviewing facility (100 stations, 40 of which are part of a PC-driven computerized interviewing system) is being centralized.

Founder and chairman of D/M/I is Richard B. Wirthlin, 52, who holds a Ph.D. from the University of California, Berkeley. He is best known as President Reagan's personal pollster. Vincent J. Breglio, 44, rejoined D/M/I in early 1985 as president and head of the Political/Public Affairs Division. He holds a Ph.D. from Brigham Young University.

31. Consumer Research Division, Management Decision Systems, Inc.
Waltham, Massachusetts
Privately held corporation; founded in 1967.
Research revenues were $7.7 million in 1984, up 8.1% over 1983.

Of the total MDS revenues of $25 million (see company profile under Marketing Information Service Firm listing at the end of this chapter) about 31% are attributable to the Consumer Research Division.

CRD's primary research service is the ASSESSOR simulated test market system, which predicts the probable market performance of a new product prior to market introduction. ASSESSOR's predictions are based on consumer response to advertising, shopping in a simulated store, and repurchase after in-house use. Although originally developed for consumer package goods, modifications of the ASSESSOR system have been used for automobiles, other consumer durables, and services.

CRD also provides a wide range of research and consulting services to support early opportunity identification and positioning stages. DEFENDER, CRD's newest service, is a model and market measurement system for determining the best response to a competitor's new product.

In February 1985, Information Resources, Inc. (see #8 on list) signed a letter of intent to purchase Management Decision Systems.

There are 34 full-time, salaried employees in CRD offices in Waltham, Chicago, and Los Angeles.

Manager of the CRD is James J. Findley, 40, who has an M.S. degree from the Sloan School of Management, Massachusetts Institute of Technology. He is a vp of MDS.

32. The Gallup Organization
Princeton, New Jersey
Privately held corporation; founded in 1935.
Revenues in 1984 were $7.7 million, up 14.9% over 1983.

This survey research organization, founded by the late George H. (Ted) Gallup, Sr., who died in 1984, whose syndicated newspaper column, Gallup Poll, appears in 100 newspapers, specializes in quantitative attitude and public opinion research. About one-half this work is custom, ad hoc, and the balance comes from syndicated surveys in the area of financial services, packaged goods, and video products.

Data collection is through face-to-face interviewing (national sample, 360 primary sampling units, and about 50,000 interviews a year) and a WATS telephone facility with 72 stations located in a separate facility outside Princeton. There are 115 full-time, salaried employees.

During 1985, Gallup announced a joint venture with SRI Research Center, Inc., to conduct hospital market research.

Acting chairman of Gallup is George H. Gallup, Jr., 56, son of the founder. He is a graduate of Princeton University. Joint CEOs are Andrew Kohut, 42, a graduate of Seton Hall University, and Leonard A. Wood, 45, who has an M.B.A. from Rider College.

33. Starch INRA Hooper, Inc.
Mamaroneck, New York
Public corporation traded otc; founded in 1923.
Revenues in 1984 were $7.5 million, up 19.6% over 1984.

Revenues for this survey research organization, best known for print ad and print media audience studies, include those of a wholly owned subsidiary, the Roper Organization, New York, the newly resurrected Hooper Telephone Interviewing Service (over 30 stations), and revenues derived from being part of the INRA network of affiliate companies in 31 countries. There are 165 full-time employees, 51 of whom are salaried exempt.

SIH's oldest service, Starch Ad Readership, hit an all-time high in revenues and profits in 1984, and the company launched two new services: (1) Starch Travel Agent Readership Study (STARS), which is offered on a biannual basis with first reports due in June 1985, and (2) a large-scale pilot study with male elites in four South American countries, which the company hopes will lead to a full-scale audience research project in Latin America later in 1985.

President–CEO of SIH is William J. (Jay) Wilson, 48, a graduate of Yale University.

34. Mediamark Research, Inc.
New York, New York
Company, which was founded in 1979, is 80% owned by Mills & Allen International PLC and 20% owned by its principal officers.
Revenues in 1984 were $7.2 million, up 23% over 1983.

Mediamark operates a syndicated media/product research service based on personal interviews with 20,000 adults each year regarding their exposure to advertising media and, via a leave-behind questionnaire, purchased data on a broad line of products and services. There is on-line access to this data bank, and advertising agencies, advertisers, broadcasters and cable networks subscribe to MRI's 25 reports.

MRI also produces three special reports each year based on a two-year data base: a business-to-business report and the Upper Deck (affluent market), as well as reports related to the top 10 local markets, including data on newspapers and broadcast stations. Also, in 1984, MRI produced a report on Consumer Innovators, describing the purchasing behavior, demographics, and media exposure of those people identified as innovators and their propensity to try new products.

In January 1985, MRI set up a Custom Studies Division.

There are 24 full-time, salaried employees at MRI.

Timothy Joyce, 51, is chairman-CEO of MRI; he has a Ph.D. from Cambridge University in England. Alain J. Tessier, 51, is president-CEO; he has an M.A. degree from the University of Notre Dame.

35. Market Opinion Research
Detroit, Michigan
Privately held corporation; founded in 1941.
Research revenues in 1984 were $6.8 million, up 13.6% over 1983.

Of this firm's total revenues, about 81% are derived from research-related activities. This survey research organization is divisionalized as follows: (1) consumer and industrial marketing research; (2) media studies; (3) social and public policy research; (4) information systems; and (5) political. Since Robert M. Teeter, MOR's president, is prominent as a political pollster/consultant and MOR has as clients numerous Republican senatorial, congressional and gubernatorial candidates, 1984 was a boom year.

MOR has 80 full-time employees (48 of whom are salaried, exempt) located in five offices, one of which is in Toronto. One of the five, Washington, D.C. was new in January 1985. A central phone survey facility includes 86 stations, 20 of which will be CATI-equipped by mid-1985.

Chairman–CEO of MOR is Frederick P. Currier, 61, who received his M.A. degree from the University of Illinois. President is Robert M. Teeter, 46, who received his M.A. from Michigan State University.

36. Kapuler Marketing Research, Inc.
Arlington Heights, Illinois
Privately held corporation; founded in 1974.
Revenues in 1984 were $6.0 million, up 34% over 1983.

Kapuler, through branch offices in Los Angeles and Dallas and a full-time, salaried staff of 51, offers a complete array of marketing research services and consultation.

Quantitative services are based on telephone surveys through the Kapuler Survey Center, a 120-station facility with 28 CRT-equipped. Qualitative research is centered in UniFocus, a system that completes over 3,000 one-on-one in-depth interviews per year to obtain data on lifestyle, social trends, benefit-value structures, new-product development, and diagnostics for advertising creative.

President of the firm is Stanley J. Kapuler, 44, who has an M.B.A. from the University of Chicago.

37. Ad Factors Marketing Research
Glen Ellyn, Illinois
Privately held corporation; founded in 1975.
Revenues in 1984 were $5.9 million, up 66.1% over 1983.

Primary business is custom, ad hoc surveys, both consumer and industrial, a la continuous market measures, tracking studies, test market evaluations, product in-home use tests, and general opinion/attitude/viewership studies. Services include computer-generated national-local samples, questionnaire development, interviewing, data processing and analysis. In-house WATS telephone facilities include 240 monitored dialing stations, 100 of which are CRT-equipped.

Ad Factors employs approximately 300 people, 44 of whom are full-time, salaried, exempt. There are branch offices in Montrose, Connecticut, and Cinnaminson, New Jersey. During 1984, the company installed a fully interactive CRT/DP computer system with data transmittal capabilities linking all offices.

President of Ad Factors is Donald B. Chapman, 43, a graduate of Portland State University.

38. Response Analysis
Princeton, New Jersey
Privately held corporation; founded in 1969.
Research revenues in 1984 were $5.6 million, up 44.6% over 1983.

Revenues do not include RA's ARRO Division in Bethesda, Maryland, which specializes in human factors and performance evaluation/skill testing procedures.

This survey research organization which specializes in large-scale projects for agencies of the federal government, nonprofit organizations as well as private sector commercial clients, has 99 full-time, salaried staff members.

RA maintains a central telephone interviewing facility with 40 stations, 15 of which are CRT-equipped.

CEO of Response Analysis is Herbert I. Abelson, 59, who received his Ph.D. from the University of Maryland. He is past president of the Association for Public Opinion Research (AAPOR) and past chairman of the Council of American Survey Research Organizations (CASRO).

39. Decision Research Corporation
Lexington, Massachusetts
Wholly owned subsidiary of Temple, Barker & Sloane, Inc.; founded in 1971.
Revenues in 1984 were $5.5 million, up 36% over 1983.

This full-service marketing research firm specializes in custom, ad hoc survey work for consumer goods and business-to-business marketers. In addition, DRC does jury simulation work for legal clients, running mock trials during which various arguments and appeals are rated. There are 40 full-time, salaried, exempt employees, and a phone center has 30 interviewing stations.

During 1984, DRC opened an office in Palo Alto, California.

General manager of DRC is Robert S. Duboff, 36, who received his J.D. degree from Harvard Law School.

40. Oxtoby-Smith, Inc.
New York, New York
Privately held corporation; founded in 1956.
Revenues in 1984 were $5 million, up 18% over 1983.

This survey research firm, which has 70 full-time, salaried employees, is distinctive in that about one-half its revenues come from clients for whom Oxtoby-Smith assumes responsibility for all, or largely all, of the consumer research functions, filling the role of both internal department and outside research supplier. Among such clients are American Motors, Block Drug, and Coca-Cola Foods.

The balance of Oxtoby-Smith volume comes from custom, ad hoc survey products and, of growing importance, consultation, research, and testimony relating to legal regulatory matters, among them trademark litigation and advertising claim substantiation.

On-site facilities include a central telephone interviewing facility with 20 stations, all of which are being CRT-equipped in 1985, and a focus group facility.

President and CEO is one of the firm's founders, Joseph Smith, 58, who received his Ph.D. from the University of Iowa.

Marketing Information Service Firms Grow Rapidly During 1984

They don't look like research firms, they don't talk like research firms, and they don't walk like research firms—but a large, fast-growing genre of marketing information service firms is, increasingly, competitive with the traditional marketing/advertising research firms for a larger share of monies marketing management spends for decision-making data.

It is most appropriate, then, that starting this year *Advertising Age* is publishing profiles of such marketing information service firms in conjunction with its annual list of Top 40 U.S.-based marketing/advertising research firms.

The six organizations profiled—Claritas L.P., EPSILON, Interactive Market Systems, MAJERS, Management Decision Systems, and SPAR—had combined revenues of $114.6 million in 1984, up 29.5% over 1983, and —as you'll see—their activities are becoming more intertwined with the traditional marketing research firms and their business sprawls around the world.

Since most of the firms that fit naturally into this marketing information service firm category are privately owned or subsidiaries of large, public corporations, they are not accustomed to making their revenue data public. Indeed, Donnelley Marketing Information Services, a Dun & Bradstreet corporate unit; American Demographics, Inc., a subsidiary of Dow Jones & Company; and the Market Analysis Division of C.A.C.I., Inc., marketers of the Acron Market Segmentation and Targeting System, are not allowed by their parent companies to reveal revenue data.

Other privately held firms, like National Decision Systems and Marketing Intelligence Service, Ltd., when invited by *Advertising Age* to participate in this first listing, replied in essence, "Not this year, but probably next." Others, like Telmar, just declined. And others—notably, Urban Decision Systems, Calle and Company, Data Resources, Inc., and National Demographics & Lifestyles—didn't bother to acknowledge *Advertising Age's* request at all.

Be that as it may, these organizations and their ilk probably represent, in total, $300 to $400 million in annual revenues, and judging just from the six organizations listed below, they are growing much faster than most marketing research firms. As more such firms participate in *Advertising Age's* annual listing, their collective performance will create an index of industry growth.

Marketing Information Service Firm Profiles

There follow profiles of some leading members of the Marketing Information Service Firm category—in no particular order.

Claritas, L.P.
Alexandria, Virginia
Founded in 1971; since 1984 a partnership which included Claritas senior management and a noncontrolling interest held by VNU Amvest, the U.S. subsidiary of VNU (United Dutch Publishing Company), Holland's largest publishing/communications firm.
Revenues in 1984 were $6.2 million, up 41% over 1983.

A specialist in market segmentation and target marketing, Claritas is best known as the developer of PRIZM, a neighborhood classification model that assigns each census block group and tract, as well as each postal carrier route and ZIP, to one of 40 unique lifestyle groups. The PRIZM Interlock concept permits marketers to cross-correlate PRIZM profiles drawn from nearly two dozen different PRIZM-coded survey research data bases and services, including Arbitron, Birch, Home Testing Institute and NPD, Market Facts, Accountline, Scarborough/LNR, Simmons Market Research Bureau, SRI/VALS and SRI/Financial, and TRW.

Claritas' software and data bases are heavily utilized in support of its analytical project services, and they are also distributed under license to end users for operation on their own computers.

A key resource is the Claritas GeoBase, an integrated data base of Census demographics, geographic code systems and mapping boundaries, which is utilized for retail trading area analysis, sales potential studies, and computer mapping applications.

During 1984, Claritas launched a new service for targeting the Affluent Market.

The 75 members of Claritas' professional staff are located in its central R&D production facility in Alexandria, Virginia, and four regional client service offices. Two more regional offices will be opened in 1985.

President and CEO of Claritas is Samuel G. Barton III, 42, who has an M.B.A. from Stanford University.

EPSILON
Burlington, Massachusetts
Public company, traded NASDAQ; founded in 1969.
Revenues in 1984 were $44.7 million, up 34% over 1983.

EPSILON, which refers to itself as "the Database Marketing Company," was originally founded by four graduates of Harvard University's Business School. In 1979, the company went public, and today over half its revenues come from commercial clients.

EPSILON provides a full range of data management and direct marketing services, including marketing data base management; market research and analysis; direct response/direct mail creative and production; inquiry fulfillment; inbound and outbound telemarketing; sales lead management; and strategic consulting.

The company specializes in (1) developing and maintaining accessible marketing information systems—marketing data bases—designed to store detailed historical and profile data for support of direct marketing programs, and (2) creating and executing targeted direct marketing programs that use the data base to increase accuracy.

In 1984, EPSILON moved into new office facilities, and on through 1985, expansion plans include expansion of client on-line access systems and increased development of services for the financial service, pharmaceutical, publications, and fund raising markets.

President and CEO of EPSILON is Thomas O. Jones, 40, who received his M.B.A. from The Sloan School, Massachusetts Institute of Technology.

Interactive Market Systems (IMS)
New York, New York
Founded in 1969; since 1983, a partnership which includes IMS senior management and a noncontrolling interest held by VNU Amvest, the U.S. subsidiary of VNU (United Dutch Publishing Company), Holland's largest publishing/communications firm.
Revenues in 1984 were $15.8 million, up 10.1% over 1983.

IMS includes the following units: (1) IMS itself, which provides on-line access to over 300 marketing and advertising data bases for clients in the U.S., Canada, Europe, Asia and Australia; and (2) Leading National Advertisers (LNA), which offers the Publishers Information Bureau Advertising Expenditure Services, publishes the LNA/BAR multimedia expenditure report, publishes Rome Reports (both domestic and international) and offers the PERQ medical industries service to media agencies and pharmaceutical companies for media analysis and administrative functions.

IMS employs more than 260 people in offices in New York, Chicago, Los Angeles, San Francisco, Honolulu, Oslo, Brussels, Paris, Hong Kong, Melbourne and Sydney. Its services are offered through utilization of four DEC 2060 computers in New York and additional computers in London and Melbourne.

Richard F. Makely, 44, is president and COO of IMS; he attended New York University. Chairman and CEO is Leon H. Liebman, 44, who received an M.S. degree from The Sloan School, Massachusetts Institute of Technology.

MAJERS Corporation
Omaha, Nebraska
Privately held corporation; founded in 1963.
Revenues in 1984 were $24.7 million, up 36.5% over 1983.

The main service of MAJERS, called Mastertrack, tracks and evaluates feature ad support, display support, manufacturer's coupons, and shelf positioning for package goods, daily and weekly, in retail grocery chains in all major markets. Mastertrack data, in addition to hard copy, are available to clients via an on-line delivery system called Instant Replay.

MAJERS provides consumer research through its FeaturLab service, which offers a pretesting environment for the testing of response to various featuring options. This syndicated service is offered to manufacturers on an exclusive category basis.

MAJERS' education division, MAJERS Marketing Institute, located in Omaha, provides open and in-house seminars to manufacturers, advertising agencies, brokers, and retailers on the effective planning implementation of promotion strategies and tactics.

During 1984, MAJERS purchased TRIM, Inc. from Harte-Hanks Communications (see #25 on Top 40 Research Firm list). TRIM provides continuous UPC scanner audits and controlled store test services in 30 markets. Also in 1984, MAJERS established the Summa Consulting Group, whose mission is to identify new promotion strategy planning concepts.

MAJERS has 519 full-time employees and regional offices in Stamford, Connecticut, Chicago, Atlanta, and San Francisco.

Founder, president and CEO of MAJERS is Adrian J. "Ed" Scribante, 55; he is a graduate of Kansas State University. Executive vp and COO is Frank Schanne, 44, a graduate of Holy Cross University.

Management Decision Systems, Inc.
Waltham, Massachusetts
Privately held corporation; founded in 1967.
Marketing information service revenues in 1984 were $17 million, up 25% over 1983.

Of total MDS revenues of $25 million in 1984, 68% were attributable to the marketing information segment of the business, which includes marketing decision support (DDS) services. (The balance is attributable to the MDS Consumer Research Division, which is #31 on the Top 40 research organization list.)

Management Decision Systems provides integrated, strategic marketing applications, including EXPRESS EASYTRAC, a marketing decision support system that makes it possible for marketing managers to address daily reporting and analysis needs, such as forecasting, sales analysis, survey analysis, project planning and control, simulation/risk analysis, pro forma analysis, etc. (EASYTRAC, in 1984, won an ICP million-dollar award.)

In addition, EXPRESS EASYCAST, another MDS service, offers marketing managers and production planners a unique, interactive means of combining their judgment with computerized statistical forecasts. PROMOTER, a new service announced in February 1985, helps marketing managers evaluate and improve the effectiveness and profitability of consumer goods promotions. Also, MDS offers customized consulting services.

MDS has 168 full-time, salaried employees located in Waltham and five sales/service offices in the U.S., plus London and Paris.

In early 1985, MDS announced its intent to merge with Information Resources, Inc. (see #8 on Top 40 research organization list).

President of MDS is John S. Wurts, 37, who is a graduate of Massachusetts Institute of Technology.

SPAR, Inc.
Tarrytown, New York
Privately held corporation; founded in 1967.
Revenues in 1984 are $6.2 million, up 30.4% from 1983.

In early 1984, SPAR, Inc. acquired the Gelco Marketing Services Division of Gelco Corporation, Eden Prairie, Minnesota. Revenues reflect both organizations for both years (fiscal year ended March 31), as does the growth.

SPAR (formerly Pan Eval) is a pioneer in the field of systematic evaluation of economic impact of trade promotions, primarily high-velocity package goods in the grocery field. Services include the following: SPARLINE, a measure of what manufacturers or retailers sell in the absence of promotions; SPARBASE, an on-line promotional and brand data base system that integrates all the key syndicated data with manufacturer factory shipments; and SPARTRAC, the next-day promotional reporting system to improve promotional execution.

Gelco Marketing, now to be called SPAR Marketing Services, offers in-store measures of product availability, stocking conditions, and promotional activity in 106 market areas.

There are full-time regional field managers in 12 cities and district managers in 52. SPAR, Inc. has about 100 full-time, salaried employees in offices in Tarrytown, Minneapolis, Chicago, London, and Melbourne.

President–CEO Robert G. Brown, 42, received his M.B.A. from Columbia University. Senior vp William Bartels, 43, has an M.S. from Occidental College.

16 Top Fifteen World Research Organizations

Each year, after Advertising Age *publishes my annual review of the largest U.S. research firms, a bigger, global question comes up: "How do the U.S.-owned firms compare with other research firms owned and headquartered in foreign countries?"*

I first developed a Top World list in 1983, which was published in the Advertising Age *of July 18. To do so, I had to document nearly 100 non-U.S. research organizations, but I had a lot of expert help from Eileen Cole, at the time chief executive, Research International; Wolfgang Ernst, CEO, Infratest Forschung GMBH & Co.; Morten M. Lenrow, director, international marketing research, PepsiCo; Jack Brown, chairman, Burke Marketing Services, Inc.; and Ms. Gunilla Broadbent, vp-director of INRA, at Starch INRA Hooper. It was quite an education.*

Updating this material, circa 1984, produces more than a listing; it helps document just how international in nature the research industry has become, with the trend accelerating over the past three years. Those developments are inherent in the individual company profiles that follow.

The World of Research

There follows a listing of the 15 largest marketing/advertising/public opinion research organizations in the world, circa 1984, all of whom have annual revenues of about $25 million and up.

Before reading the profiles of each, please note the following:

1. I am citing research revenues only. Some of these organizations—notably Nielsen, IMS, and AGB—have significant additional revenues from nonresearch activities.
2. All revenues are for calendar 1984 or the latest obtainable.

3. There are currency conversion values (vis-à-vis the U.S. dollar) to consider, and these vary almost from day to day. For 1984, I have had to use average rates, such as 31¢ for the West German DM and $1.25 for the British pound, and so the European company figures may be slightly off, depending on just exactly what was the precise average rate that prevailed over 1984.
4. Further, in recent years, some of these organizations have made acquisitions that didn't necessarily result in 100% ownership. Exactly how much of that acquired volume is reflected gets a bit hazy at times.

So, all things considered, I suggest that you consider these revenue figures—all stated in U.S. dollars—to be magnitude estimates but certainly close enough to establish an order of ranking.

Table 16.1 World's 15 Largest Marketing/Advertising Research Organizations as of 1984

Organization	Home Country	Approx. Research Revenues 1984 (U.S. Dollars Add 000,000)	Number of Countries With Office
1. A.C. Nielsen Co.	U.S.A.	$491.0	25
2. IMS International	U.S.A.	151.4	60
3. SAMI	U.S.A.	118.4	1
4. Arbitron Ratings Co.	U.S.A.	105.8	1
5. AGB Research	U.K.	77.5	21
6. Burke Marketing Services	U.S.A.	66.0	2
7. Information Resources	U.S.A.	60.8	1
8. Research International	U.K.	52.0	29
9. M/A/R/C	U.S.A.	37.6	1
10. Market Facts	U.S.A.	35.9	2
11. Infratest	W. Germany	32.2	5
12. GFK	W. Germany	30.9	6
13. NPD Group	U.S.A.	29.2	1
14. Maritz Market Research	U.S.A.	24.7	1
15. Westat	U.S.A.	24.5	1

It was especially frustrating to try to get a fix on large Japanese research organizations. One thing, however, seems certain: those well-known Japanese organizations that specialize in marketing/advertising research—such as Dentsu, Chuohchosasha (Central Research Service), the Japan Marketing Research Association, or Video-Audience Research—are not nearly large enough to make a world Top 15 listing (nor is the largest French firm, SOFRES).

One enigma is this: the huge Nomura Research Institute in Tokyo, which has revenues in the range of $50 million. Nomura does economic forecasting and social research, much of which is based on secondary data. But it also does a considerable amount of custom survey research. What percentage that is of the total Nomura volume is unknown, but I have no reason to believe it is large enough to make the following list.

Company Profiles

1. A.C. Nielsen Company
The world's largest marketing/advertising research firm is the A.C. Nielsen Company, with international headquarters in Northbrook, Ill. Research revenues in 1984 were $491 million, about 52% of which came from ACN subsidiary (most are wholly owned) companies in 24 countries outside the U.S. (To put that revenue level into perspective, consider that Young & Rubicam, the largest U.S. advertising agency, had gross revenues worldwide of $480.1 million in 1984—and that was from all its operations, including nonadvertising. That, of course, is $10.9 million less than ACN's research revenues alone.)

Founded in 1923 by the late Arthur C. Nielsen, Sr., truly one of the giants of the world research industry, ACN operations basically consist of large syndicated systems that track product movement at the retail store level (Mr. Nielsen, in effect, invented the concept of share of market) and tv audience size and composition.

Nielsen was a pioneer in exporting U.S. research know-how overseas; he set up ACN's first subsidiary in the U.K. in 1939, on the eve of WW II.

A public company traded over-the-counter until late 1984, when it was purchased by Dun & Bradstreet Corp. for $1.1 billion, ACN continues now as an integrated part of D&B, and it took special permission from D&B to get the ACN research revenue figures for 1984.

2. IMS International
This vast organization, which operates through subsidiaries in 60 countries, is the A.C. Nielsen of the worldwide pharmaceutical industry. Of its total research revenues of $151.4 million in 1984, 44.6%—or $67.5 million—was from the U.S. subsidiary, IMS America, which is headquartered in Ambler, Pennsylvania. (These revenues do not include those of Pipeline Research, which IMS America acquired in the fall of 1984.)

Generally, IMS uses panels of stores or hospitals or physicians to report on purchases, usage, and diagnosis/treatment of patients. Unlike ACN, IMS has been built largely through acquisition. The organization, as it exists today, was founded in 1954.

Although incorporated in the U.S. and a public company traded over-the-counter, IMS has traditionally operated out of headquarters in London.

3. Selling Areas-Marketing, Inc. (SAMI)

Technically the Selling Areas-Marketing, Inc. subsidiary of Time Inc., this large firm was founded in 1966 by the late J. Clarke Mattimore to utilize grocery warehouse withdrawal data, amalgamated at the local-market level, to produce continuous records of product purchasing.

Today, the basic SAMI system produces data on 54 different U.S. market areas on grocery products, and in 1985 it started a comparable system based on drugstores in four major markets.

Another SAMI service called SAMSCAN operates in three local-market systems which are used for test marketing of new products; the sales and servicing of SAMSCAN is handled by Burke, the sixth-largest organization on our international listing. SAMI headquarters are in New York City, and its revenues for 1984 are estimated at $118.4 million.

4. Arbitron Ratings Company

Founded in 1949 by James Seiler as American Research Bureau, this organization was purchased by Control Data Corporation in 1967 and renamed Arbitron. Revenues for 1984 were $105.8 million, and headquarters are in New York City.

Arbitron produces radio, tv, and cable tv audience measurements at the local-market level using mail diaries or panels of meter-equipped households. Surveys in 210 tv markets account for 53% of revenues; the balance comes from 261 radio markets.

In 1984, Arbitron purchased about 40% of Burke Marketing Services, Inc., the sixth company on this list, and there is an option to purchase the balance by 1990. (If Arbitron exercises this option, the combined operations could move ahead of IMS and become the world's second largest research organization.) The two, Arbitron and Burke, started a new operation called ScanAmerica, a local-market system (now being tested in Denver), which links metered measures of tv viewing with household purchasing data gathered via wand that reads UPC codes on packaged goods. Those data, then, can be accessed via telephone along with the tv viewing data.

5. AGB Research PLC

This London-based conglomerate, which was founded by Sir Bernard Audley in 1962, has operations in 21 countries, including three subsidiaries—NFO Research, acquired in 1982, Information & Analysis, acquired in

1983, and AGB Television Research, founded in 1984—in the United States. Total revenues for the fiscal year ending April 1984, were $77.5 million. These did not include the full impact of another AGB acquisition, Survey Research International, a network of seven survey firms in Southeast Asia, due to a delayed purchase plan. In short, the full research revenues of AGB as it exists today are probably significantly higher, but not enough to replace Arbitron as #4 on our listing.

In the U.K., AGB operates consumer panels and tv audience measurement systems. AGB currently operates 14 different tv and audience measurement systems around the world, 10 of which utilize the so-called People Meter. One of these systems is in Boston, Mass.

6. Burke Marketing Services, Inc. (BMSI)

This Cincinnati-based conglomerate was originally founded by Alberta H. Burke as a field service firm in 1931; in 1947 it evolved into what today is known as Burke Marketing Services, Inc. As of 1984, about 40% of BMSI was purchased by Arbitron Ratings Co. (see #4 on list), which has an option to purchase the rest. Also, BSMI owns 5% of Infratest (see #11 on list), and in turn Infratest owns 5% of BMSI.

BMSI in the U.S. is a multidivisional organization, which includes Burke Marketing Research (tv copy testing and custom survey research); BASES (market modeling); AdTel (six controlled test markets used for advertising and new product testing); Burke Institute (educational seminars on research); and ScanAmerica, a joint venture with Arbitron (see #4 on list).

A subsidiary, Burke Canada, specializes in custom ad hoc survey research in that country.

BMSI revenues in 1984 were $66 million.

7. Information Resources, Inc. (IRI)

This Chicago-based organization was founded in 1977 by John L. Malec, Gerald Eskin, William Walter, and Penny Baron. It has leapfrogged ahead in our listing because of its own extraordinary growth rate (up 70% in 1984 over 1983) and its 1985 acquisition of Management Decision Systems. The combined operations had revenues of $60.8 million in 1984.

The first and most dramatic product of IRI was its BehaviorScan system, a network of eight minimarkets equipped for advertising and control store testing. By combining data from these systems, IRI produced a Marketing Fact Book service, which provides clients with purchase dimensions on a variety of high-velocity package goods products.

MDS is basically divided into two divisions: (1) Consumer Research Division, which is best known for its ASSESSOR simulated test market system, and (2) Marketing Information Division, which markets a line of proprietary systems and software for forecasting, project planning, simulation/risk analysis, and other marketing applications.

The two organizations and their top management were undergoing a merger and reorganization in July 1985.

8. Research International (RI)

This London-based conglomerate, a wholly owned subsidiary of Unilever, specializes in survey research through a network of its own offices in 29 countries, including one in New York City. Revenues in 1984 were $52 million, including Marplan in West Germany and the U.K., both of which are subsidiaries of RI.

This organization, which was founded in 1973 by Eileen Cole (now retired) banding together in-house research operations of Unilever, now operates as a separate stand-alone research facility; about 70% of total revenues come from non-Unilever clients.

In a given year, RI estimates that it conducts about 2 million interviews, and in that sense, it is the world's largest ad hoc sample survey firm.

9. M/A/R/C, Inc.

This Dallas-based firm, with revenues of $37.6 million for a fiscal year ending March 31, 1985, was founded by Cecil (Bud) Phillips in 1965 as a outgrowth of Tracy-Locke, an advertising agency.

M/A/R/C, which issued public stock in 1985, is basically a survey research firm specializing in WATS line telephone interviewing. It also operates a network of local-market panels related to central location testing facilities in (by year's end) 54 locations in 30 markets.

10. Market Facts, Inc.

This public company, traded over-the-counter, was founded by William F. Odell (now retired) in 1946. Revenues for 1984 were $35.9 million but this does not include Market Facts of Canada, Ltd., in which MF owns 50%.

MF's U.S. operations include the Consumer Mail Panel, a fixed mail panel of more than 220,000 households; Consumer Opinion Forums—six shopping mall interviewing facilities; Marketest, a store auditing and controlled store testing facility in seven markets; and focus group facilities. The company does considerable sample survey work too, and in 1984, it started a tv commercial pretesting service.

11. Infratest

Infratest Forschung GMBH & Co. KG, with headquarters in Munich, and its subsidiaries had revenues of $32.2 million in 1984, according to information furnished *CONTEXT*, a West German trade journal.

Infratest was founded in 1946 by the husband–wife team of Wolfgang and Lena-Renate Ernst; its first project was audience measurement studies for Bavarian radio. Today Infratest specializes in ad hoc consumer surveys, advertising and media research, and political/public opinion polling. In addition to four subsidiary firms in Germany, Infratest in 1980 expanded in Europe by purchasing five subsidiaries of Burke Marketing Services, Inc. (see #6 on list) in Italy, the U.K., Sweden, France, and Germany. Infratest now owns 5% of Burke, and the two jointly operate Burke International Research, a network of affiliated companies in 12 countries.

12. GFK

GFK Nurnberg Gesellschaft F Konsum und Absatzforschung & V., headquartered in Nuremberg, West Germany, and subsidiaries had revenues of $30.9 million in 1984, according to data furnished to *CONTEXT*.

Founded in 1934 by Wilhelm Vershofen, GFK has always been a nonprofit trade association serving a closed list of member firms.

GFK specializes in a broad range of research activities: ad hoc survey research; advertising research; syndicated surveys; package and product testing; industrial, financial, medical and agricultural marketing research. GFK has operations in six European countries.

13. The NPD Group

The core company in this organization, NPD Research, was founded in 1953 by Henry Brenner, who continues as chairman. (Another NPD unit, Home Testing Institute, was also founded by Brenner and later acquired by NPD.) Headquarters are in Port Washington, Long Island, N.Y., and 1984 revenues were $29.2 million.

The main business of NPD is a 14,500-household national diary-type purchase panel specializing in packaged goods, and more than 25 local-market panels with about 40,000 households. HTI is a fixed mail panel with 175,000 households. NPD operates several special interest panels in the fields of wearing apparel, away-from-home eating, and toys/games.

14. Maritz Market Research

A wholly owned subsidiary of Maritz, Inc., this St. Louis-based conglomerate was founded in 1973. Revenues in 1984 were $24.7 million.

Maritz has been built almost entirely through acquisition; four survey firms have been purchased since 1980. The company operates a network of field interviewing facilities (phone interviewing, focus group facilities, central location and mall facilities) in 16 major U.S. cities.

15. Westat, Inc.

Founded in 1961 by Edward C. Bryant, who continues as chairman, this large survey research organization with headquarters in Rockville, Md., is employee-owned. About 85% of its work comes from studies for agencies of the federal government, with the balance from commercial clients. In 1983, Westat acquired Crossley Surveys, Inc.

Westat revenues in 1984 were $24.5 million.

Postscript (August 1985)

Eileen Cole, writing in *Advertising Age* (November 1, 1984), estimated the world market for marketing/advertising research in 1983 at $2.94 billion. If we project that to 1984, a good estimate would be about $3.4 billion; the 15 organizations listed here had revenues of $1.3 billion, accounting for about 40% of that total. The largest organization, A. C. Nielsen, had about 14.4% share of market.

Only 3 of the Top 15 were founded prior to World War II; the balance were born postwar, and the youngest, IRI, started in late 1977. Only 2 are privately owned; the balance are either public companies, or wholly or partially owned subsidiaries of larger, nonresearch corporations, or employee-owned. The founders of most Top 15 companies are still alive, and several are still active in the business.

17 How Much Is Spent on Research in the U.S.?

"How much is spent for research in the U.S. each year?"

That's the question that comes over my phone most often, especially just after publication of the top U.S. marketing/advertising/public opinion research company listing I prepare for *Advertising Age* each year. Further, if there is one number that has been guesstimated with reckless abandon in articles in the popular press about the research industry, this is it.

I am getting weary of explaining—and I'm sure frustrated callers are tired of listening to—all the reasons no one has an exact answer to that question. "But," some callers insist, "can't you make an estimate?"

The answer, of course, is "yes"—and that's what I'll do now. However, since this magic number is apt to be picked up and bandied about, I urge you to follow closely the explanation of how it was derived, what's included—and what is not. Laborious this may be, but in the process you'll come to understand how complex the research industry is and why I haven't had a snappy one-line answer for callers through the years.

Adding Up the Numbers

The solid base from which I depart is the latest listing of the Top 40 U.S. companies, which in 1985 was published in *Advertising Age* on May 23 (see chapter 15). These 40 organizations had combined revenues of $1,449,100,000 in 1984, but only $1,103,300,000 of that represented work done within the United States. Also, only revenues from research activities are included; several of these organizations have sizable revenues from nonresearch activities, and, fortunately, most of that can be separated out.

As such things go, this base number of $1,103,300,000 is a hard number. Many of the organizations on the Top 40 list are public or owned by public companies or commonly make their revenues public to interested parties. For those that are privately held, I require that their public accounting firm submit a statement of confirmation. Also, with rare exception, the research revenues for these firms have all been adjusted to reflect calendar 1984, no matter what their fiscal year.

Equally important, these Top 40 firms represent all segments of the industry and data collection techniques—survey, syndicated and ad hoc; store audits, syndicated and custom; product movement data gathered via warehouse withdrawal and UPC scanner systems; mall intercepts; tv copy testing, in theatre and on-air; print ad testing; mail panels; media audience measurement systems; continuous diary-type purchase panels; focus groups; etc. In a word, these 40 top companies represent the diverse spectrum of services for which "research money" is spent, in the common understanding of the term.

To this base number of $1,103,300,000 we can make a knowing addition, thanks to the Council of American Survey Research Organizations (CASRO). CASRO is the trade association of those U.S. for-profit firms which specialize in survey research, and currently there are about 125 members. Some, not all, supply—on a confidential basis—a statement of their annual revenues to CASRO, which, in turn, prepares a combined statement. For the year 1984, Diane K. Bowers, executive director of CASRO, subtracted out those revenues reported by CASRO firms already included in my Top 40 listing, and that left $117,200,000 from 54 other CASRO reporting firms, which was almost entirely commercial survey work done within the U.S. (this averages out to $2,170,750 each). This takes our total hard number up to $1,220,500,000.

However, that still leaves numerous conspicuous commercial firms that were either not large enough to make the Top 40 listing, or who belonged to CASRO but did not comply with its annual revenue requests, or who have no relationship with CASRO. Here are some prominent firms included in this category: MRCA Information Services; Birch Research Corp.; Frank N. Magid Associates, Arbor, Inc., J. D. Powers and Associates, Burgoyne, Inc., NABSCAN USA, TRIM, Inc., Westgate Research, Research Systems Corporation, Store Audits/Q.E.D. Research, Inc., Lance Tarrance & Associates, Arthur J. Finkelstein & Associates, McHugh & Hoffman, Audience Research and Development, Reymer & Gersin Associates, and Peter D. Hart Research Associates. I would like to go on being more explicit, but there is one big unknown: what CASRO firms not in the Top 40 did not participate in its annual revenue compilation?

The point is this: based on what is known generally, at least 25 research organizations belong in the class described above, and I would estimate they have—on average—revenues of about $3.5 million a year. So, that adds $87.5 million to our running total, bringing it up to $1.308 billion.

In addition to the 120 firms accounted for so far, there are at least 100 other research suppliers, many of which are one-, two-, or three-person shops, operative in the U.S. As to the revenue this boutique segment of the industry represents, I can only speculate. An average of $300,000 each seems conservative; if you agree, add $30 million to our running total, bringing it up to $1.338 billion.

Let's pause now to emphasize *what is not included* in the running total so far. Most important, I do not include the numerous service firms that are basically field service. Some are quite large, and a few provide full service, ranging from design through analysis. But, for the most part, adding in such operations would result in double-counting of revenues; that is, basically, their revenues come from subcontract work on projects being conducted by the larger firms we've already included. The same is true for the numerous firms that specialize in WATS telephone interviewing data collection, most of which is done on a subcontract basis for advertising agencies, large full-service research firms, or advertisers. Same reason: it would be double-counting.

Also not included are numerous marketing information service firms on the fringe of the research industry, which mainly specialize in the manipulation and/or analysis of either public domain data bases (a la the census) or client data. This is a big, fast-growing segment of the total marketing information service industry, and in the *Advertising Age* of May 23, 1985, I started to describe such firms and, to the extent possible, their revenues (see chapter 15). Some notable examples are these: MAJERS, SPAR, Management Decision Systems, Claritas, National Decision Systems, Telmar, etc. Also not included are firms like Technomic Consultants, Frost & Sullivan, and Business Trends Analysis, who basically specialize in analyses of secondary source data.

Back to our running total. From here on, we have to face up to inputs that are, at best, knowing estimates. For instance, there are numerous in-house research operations of consequence operated by firms such as General Mills, General Foods, Quaker Oats, Procter & Gamble, and advertising agencies, especially Foote, Cone & Belding, Grey, Leo Burnett, Young & Rubicam, J. Walter Thompson, and Ted Bates. In addition, some large public relations firms, like Hill & Knowlton and Ruder & Finn—and some publishers too, notably McGraw-Hill—have sizable in-house research staffs.

Some numbers I've pulled together suggest that Procter & Gamble, Quaker Oats, General Mills, and General Foods, combined, spend in the neighborhood of $25 million a year through their in-house research departments. The problem is that these departments, in turn, may subcontract some phase of the total project—notably fieldwork—to some of the firms we've already accounted for, and that gets us back to the double-counting bugaboo. The same is true with advertising agencies. Grey Advertising, which has one of the largest agency research departments, for instance, does all its field and tab work through Data Development Corporation, one of the 1984 Top 40 firms.

So, how much do we add for unduplicated in-house research work? I submit that $15 million is a reasonable and conservative number (which translates into about $30 million worth of work purchased at "outside" costs and profit). So, there's a running total of $1.353 billion.

The Nonprofits

There are numerous organizations with nonprofit corporate charters that specialize in survey research in the U.S. According to the Survey Research Laboratory at the University of Illinois, there are 49 such organizations that are affiliated with and/or operating units of universities alone. The *Survey Research Newsletter* at the University of Illinois did a survey in 1981 that indicates that university groups—and there wasn't full reporting—did something in excess of $84 million in survey work a year. Now, if you think that's all academics talking to one another, you're mistaken. Prominent university-affiliated research centers like NORC at the University of Chicago, the Survey Research Center at the University of Illinois, the Survey Research Center at the University of Michigan, the Research Triangle near Duke University and the University of North Carolina, et al. do some of their work for commercial clients.

Some are very aggressive in pursuing such business. For instance, a couple of years ago, I received a sales letter to potential industrial clients from an outfit called University Resources, which is affiliated with The Barney School of Business and Public Administration, University of Hartford (Connecticut). It turns out, as a nonprofit organization, University Resources claim to have done 350 studies (surveys) for commercial clients over the previous seven years. It does no work for the faculty at Barney. In a word, this is a bunch of academics in business under a quasi-academic guise.

I believe that the university-related nonprofit organizations should add at least $90 million currently to our running total, taking it up to $1.443 billion.

In addition, there are nonuniversity-affiliated nonprofits that get involved in survey research, such as the Bureau of Social Science Research and the Rand Survey Research Institute. These outfits, like many of the university units, feed off grants from agencies of the federal government and/or foundations who are heavily into societal investigations. There are dozens of such organizations operating in the Washington, D.C. area alone, although their ranks have been thinned in recent years by cutbacks in federal budgets, both under the Carter and Reagan administrations. (They really thrived under the Johnson administration and the so-called Great Society spending programs.)

No one has a firm fix on how much this group accounts for, but from my personal experience, I'd say many such organizations subcontract a good part of their survey work and/or the field portion to commercial survey research firms or university-affiliated nonprofit organizations. So, even if we had a dollar volume estimate, we'd still be back to the problem of double-counting.

Now we arrive at the biggest spender for, and doers of, research of all—agencies of the federal government. No one has an exact fix on this traffic, but Charles Turner and Elizabeth Martin of the National Academy of Sciences have studied the files of the Statistical Policy Division of the Office of Management and Budget (OMB) and come up with some interesting estimates. Regulations require that agencies of the executive branch of the federal government submit questionnaires and a statement of study plan to the OMB for approval before conducting a survey. One of the reasons is to prevent duplication of effort; another is to prevent overburden of potential respondents.

In any case, this results in an overview of survey traffic—not at all complete; for various reasons, some studies can bypass the OMB review. Looking just at studies where individuals would be interviewed, Turner and Martin found, as of November 1980, the OMB had 202 active files on surveys, and if all went as planned, they would result in 5,245,000 interviews —mail, telephone, face-to-face. This, they felt, provided an approximation of the annual federally sponsored survey traffic.

Of the 202 studies, 127 were being conducted through nongovernment suppliers—i.e., commercial firms on my Top 40 list, like Westat, Chilton Research Services, National Analysts, or Response Analysis, especially, or university-affiliated survey centers, or nonprofit survey firms— expenditures I've already tried to account for. The balance, 75 studies, were to be conducted by federal agencies, in-house.

The most conspicuous example of in-house government research is the Demographic Survey Division (DSD) of the Bureau of the Census, one of the world's largest survey research organizations. (The bureau's Field Division has about 400 full-time employees, 3,200 part-time interviewers, and 12 regional offices.)

Most of the surveys done through DSD are funded by agencies of the federal government, but on occasion studies have been done for commercial clients, like trade associations. The DSD had, in fiscal year 1981, "reimbursable revenues" of about $62 million, and in addition did about $4 million worth of work from their own budget. This level tends to remain pretty steady from year to year because so much is locked into ongoing studies funded through time. So, just from this one government source, let's add $66 million to our running total, bringing it up to $1.509 billion.

That still leaves other federal studies done by, as they say in Washington, "the statistical community," for which I have no documentation, especially the National Center for Health Statistics (a unit of HHS—Health and Human Services), which does its own studies and some for outsiders, and the Bureau of Labor Statistics, which surveys in-house for other federal agencies. And, added to that, there are thousands of industrial organizations, news media, etc., which do all sorts of surveys now and then, mostly in-house (many of which, from my experience, are methodological monstrosities). No one will ever be able to tote up all these expenditures, but let's guess that it's at least $75 million, most of which is federal in-house.

When we add that to our running total, we come up with $1.584 billion.

So, the next time someone calls to ask my estimate of how much is spent for research in the U.S. each year, I'm going to say, "Currently, I'd estimate about $1.6 billion—conservatively, without double-counting. But that number could have an error range of plus-minus 5%."

Going back to the Top 40 list for 1984, you can now see that these organizations, in toto, account for about 69% of the total.

18 TV Copy Testing Flap

Well over $51 million a year is spent on tv copy testing in the U.S., excluding the time charges associated with on-air tests. But the consternation caused by this activity is far out of proportion to the monies spent; this is the most anguished-about segment of the research industry because to many—mostly creatives in advertising agencies—the loose numerical measures of a commercial's probable effectiveness stifle imaginative, breakthrough advertising.

This controversy continues today, and I did my best to put things into perspective in the following article, which appeared in Advertising Age *on January 19, 1981. Unfortunately, that presentation dropped out a segment that reflected the viewpoint of some prominent agency creatives. That has been restored, and here's the full story.*

TV Copy Testing Flap: What To Do About It

Then I said, Woe is me! For I am undone...
    Isaiah 6:5

"'Copy' and 'testing' have become two of the dirtiest words in our vocabulary," pined Richard F. Chay, director of marketing research, S.C. Johnson & Son, in a speech to the American Marketing Association Research Conference in New Orleans in September 1980. He went on to lament the "open hostility" within the marketing community on this issue, the "abuse" of copy testing techniques, and the "bad image" this flap is imputing to the whole research industry.

And, indeed, no segment of the research industry has been subject to as much public hand-wringing, introspection, and hyperbole as that which specializes in systematic testing of tv copy.

Attended at the last two American Research Federation conferences and Advertising Age Week have heard numerous articulate and emotional critiques from such heavy hitters as Allen G. Rosenshine, president of BBDO; Shepard Kurnit, chairman of DKG Advertising; Burton Manning, chairman and CEO of J. Walter Thompson, U.S.A.; and Normal L. Muse, at that time executive vp-creative services, Leo Burnett Co. Their common lament: creative people "don't want 'report cards' and 'imperfect rules' measuring their work," as Kurnit puts it.

"All of us, agencies and clients alike, have submitted ourselves to justification by the numbers instead of using those numbers only as an aid to judgment," adds Rosenshine. "We have had more faith in Mr. Burke, Mr. McCollum, Mr. Spielman, Mr. Mapes, and Mr. Ross than we have had in ourselves. None of this is what excellence in advertising is all about."

To hammer their point, agency speakers often cite case histories—most specifically, the now-famous "Mikey" commercial Doyle Dane Bernbach created for Life cereal and the Pepsi "spirit" commercials created by BBDO—which "wouldn't have been produced and run" had copy testing scores prevailed. And that is one of the rubs. Says an executive at a research firm that specializes in copy testing: "These creative people are much more impressive public speakers than we [researchers] are—and one of the reasons is that they don't have to stick to the facts."

The "Mikey" commercial is a case in point; it was "a very rare instance" when Quaker Oats management put a commercial on air without testing. And, while marketing insiders at Quaker say it resulted in "highly effective advertising," they also point out that during the early period when Life sales gains were so impressive, there were "lots of other marketing factors operative"—such as expanded distribution, deals, and new flavor flankers. Life billings are now at BBDO.

As to the Pepsi "spirit" commercials, there is reason to believe that those highly artistic, "mood" spots have been much more effective in markets where Pepsi is the leader over Coke, where Pepsi's total market presence is greater. In markets where Coke is the leader, the nuts-and-bolts blind taste-test copy has been much more effective in moving Pepsi ahead in its share-of-market race with Coke.

Be all that as it may, today advertising agency leaders—creatives and researchers alike—client marketing people, and some copy research company executives are being especially critical of the whole process through which a creative execution passes before finding itself propelled onto the airwaves with a multimillion dollar budget. And, singled out for special denunciation are the single "magic number" results of on-air recall testing, as exemplified by Burke DAR scores.

Concurrently, advertisers—reacting to the ever-increasing cost of tv time—seem to be putting more heat than ever on their agencies and research consultants to find a better way to minimize risk, make copy testing more predictive of sales efficacy.

Improvement Is Possible

There follows a discussion of this controversy, a synthesis of thinking gathered from numerous in-depth discussions with some of the most knowledgeable people in the business. The reader should not expect a panacea to plop out at story's end, but I do believe you'll come to share my conclusion: there is much that can be done now to put matters into perspective and, hence, alleviate much of the friction that exists.

32,500 Commercial Exposures a Year

Let's start with an appreciation of the difficult problem facing an agency creative. Each day the average American spends about four hours watching tv, and, given the proliferation of 10-second spots, this could mean an exposure to 35 commercial messages an hour, depending on whether viewing is concentrated in daytime, prime time, late fringe, etc. That makes for about 140 commercial exposures a day, or a potential of 51,100 a year. But, given time off for trips to the toilet and refrigerator, plus some vacation, the estimate of Dave Vedehra, president of Video Storyboard Tests, seems reasonable: 32,500 tv commercial exposures a year. And with heavy viewers, there could be many more.

Our creative friend is told, simply, to do something that will—without running up production costs—cut through that awesome amount of communications traffic (all done by professionals vying for attention), capture a target audience, make a sales message stand out, and persuade people to buy. That task could be coming from a client with a weak, me-too product in a low-interest category—and be communicated secondhand by an account person who isn't too bright. And, oh yeah—we need roughs in a week.

It's easy to understand the creative's frustration when, some time later, he or she is told that, according to the norms of some standardized copy testing service, the test of rough copy has fallen short. Go try again.

But I think the other side of that coin is that the demand for such creative talent far exceeds the supply, and then even the best of the creatives can have an off day or have next to no enthusiasm for some particular project that's dumped into their lap.

And that brings us to the Golden Rule.

Those Who Have the Gold, Rule

This proposition was stated clearly by Jack R. Andrews, director of marketing research at General Foods, at the 1980 ARF Conference: "Few advertisers can afford to invest millions of media dollars and risk important consumer franchises on copy which has only the author's stamp of approval to attest to its effectiveness."

The answer: some quantification of sales/communication efficacy—a test—with the client paying for it mostly, either directly or indirectly. And it usually is the client who is specifying the methodology (or service) that is used in measuring rough or finished copy.

Simply, clients tend to agree with Lord William T. Kelvin (1824–1907), the British mathematician and physicist, who said:

> When you can measure what you are speaking of and express it in numbers, you know of what you are discoursing. But when you cannot measure it and express it in numbers, your knowledge is of a very meager and unsatisfactory kind.

An M.B.A. temperament and training can pick up this concept easily. But, as Gerald Lukeman, president of ASI Market Research, Inc., notes: "Writers, producers, and art directors—I'll refer to them as 'creatives'—resist and are afraid of numbers on all levels."

And there's another rub: the very act of quantifying, of turning to the language of mathematics for expression, goes against the creative temperament. Witness this comment by Dennis Altman, senior vp-creative director, D'Arcy-MacManus & Masius/de Garmo: "I know this sounds elementary, but you have to remember we're not dealing [referring to clients] with overpowering mentalities here. We're dealing with people who doubt their own ability to rely on anything other than a number."

Adds Lukeman; "'Researchers,' in turn, are afraid of/cut off from intuitive processes, suspicious of them, overly rational."

And so the lines are drawn: tests mean quantification, and quantification creates a communications barrier—at least with some people.

But, equally important is this thought laid down by JWT's Burt Manning in his ARF speech in 1979:

> Can you blame a copywriter or an art director for being preoccupied with getting a good test score? For trying to beat the system? When creative people know that a commercial has got to score on the test or it doesn't get on the air, they try to learn the tricks, the devices, the gimmicks that seem to be associated with high scores.
>
> Even more dangerous, I think, is that creative people begin to reject, to pre-censor ideas that do not look promising in the test situation—even if every instinct tells them these ideas might do far better for the product in the real market place. This inhibition of the creative process may be the most costly side effect of all.

Why Blame Copy Testing?

The pique creatives display toward copy testing seems singular and distorted to some research executives. They point out that, from the time a creative has an idea through the time it eventually goes on the air (or is rejected), that idea could have gone through a series of critiques, each of which changed it, or watered it down, a bit.

For instance—first it must clear the creative group head. Perhaps then the agency research department does some in-house testing. Then there could be a review by the agency's creative board. Then the lawyers nitpick the claims, and exactly how they are stated. Production people come up with a production estimate, which may call for some cutting back. The client's ad director makes a tentative approval and then maybe it goes through a committee of marketing executives at the client's company. Then there's authorization of a budget for rough, or finished production. Maybe then it goes into pretesting with an outside service and, finally, an on-air post test.

"It seems to me," comments one research executive, "that when those creatives get up in public and lambaste that final step—an on-air recall test—they are copping out. It is their employers, the agency and client, who are curtailing their creative freedom—if, in fact, anyone is—and that process has taken place before we ever see the reel."

Multifaceted Inquiry

The term "copy testing" is used in a singular sense most often, and that contributes to misunderstanding. In fact, the field is diverse, as was summarized by Burt Manning in his 1979 ARF Conference speech:

> This is a manual on copy test ... put together by the J. Walter Thompson Research & Planning Department, to serve as a guide to what our research professionals described as "The Leading Methods of TV Copy Testing in Use Today." It describes twenty-four different methods—twenty-four different ways of testing advertising.
>
> I'm told there are a lot more. These are just the twenty-four leading methods. And, interestingly, these twenty-four do not represent subtle or minor variations on a common approach.
>
> There are some radical differences among them—some use one exposure to a test commercial; others use two exposures or more. Some are in-home; others in central locations. Some use recruited audiences and forced exposures; others do not.
>
> Some show commercials in a variable program context, others in a constant context, and still others in no context. Some focus on a recall and playback, others on persuasion, others on brand perceptions or diagnostics. Some use verbal measure only; others trace physiological changes—eye movement, voice pitch, brain waves, and on, and on, and on, and on.

This profusion of techniques has several negative implications. For one, some techniques were developed to focus on just one aspect of the tv commercial communication prowess at one stage of the developmental process—and are, in fact, used by clients eager to save money to serve a broader purpose—misused and abused.

Another implication is that copy testing is a competitive business, and one service may well try to make hay by knocking the competitor's methodological weakness; this negative selling seeps through to creatives who then conclude "a pox on all your houses." And, finally, profusion leads to a communication barrier, as articulated by Lukeman:

> There are very few meaningful, ongoing training programs designed to familiarize writers with copy testing procedures. Meaningful familiarity with these procedures would eliminate 50% of the difficulties. We tend to be less resistant to, and less suspicious of, things we understand.

Another dimension of copy testing activity comes from estimates developed in a recent confidential study: over 9,800 commercial tests (not commercials tested; any one could go through two or more tests) done in the U.S. each year at a cost of about $34 million. On-air recall testing alone, it is estimated, has an annual volume of $12 million.

Fighting the Curve

One of the attractions of large standardized testing procedures—such as ASI, Burke, McCollum/Spielman, Mapes and Ross, ARS, The Sherman Group, Gallup & Robinson, et al.—is that since they have tested so many commercials in basically the same way, they have developed norms— data banks of scores from thousands of commercials, against which a new commercial score can be compared. That helps put the new commercial into perspective: "How does, for instance, a new HBA product commercial compare to those other HBA efforts that have gone before?" These scores come to constitute a statistical field of their own, and, as with any such large base of observations, you would expect to find a normal distribution curve.

This distribution, which is the same process a student at school is subject to in a course where the teacher grades on the curve, is a relative measure and, by its very nature, conducive to friction; by definition, half the commercials tested will be below the norm or average. And that leads to a situation where a specific creative, or advertising agency, scores below average—an ego-bending notion that obviously gets creative hackles up.

Are some clients so arbitrary that they stop production of a commercial that is below average? Yes, indeed—it's a policy in some companies, but not all. According to Donald E. Siebert, vp-DAR activities at Burke Marketing Research, "It does happen, of course—but not as much as people think—the real cutoff is the bottom quartile."

Another function of the curve is that, by definition, most commercials are clustered in a central, average field; very, very few will get extremely high scores.

Ten Ways to Improve the Situation

Earlier in this discourse, I alluded to the fact that much could be done right now to alleviate much of the friction that exists between creatives and the copy testing syndrome—starting with trying to put the whole flap into perspective. Accordingly, I pass on 10 specific suggestions which, collectively, represent the best advice of some of the most knowledgeable people immersed in the problem. Take them to heart, and you, too, might get better creative from your agency.

1. Appreciate the difficult problem a creative faces—cutting through, impacting is much easier said than done.

2. Don't expect the discipline of copy testing to go away. It's wise to heed this observation of the late Dr. Oscar Morgenstern, the famous econometrician: "Wherever mathematics has entered, it has never again been pushed out by other developments. The mathematization of an area of human endeavor is not a passing fad; it is a prime mover of scientific and technological progress." Change, improve—yes; go away, no.

3. Involve the creative in the research process; the more he or she feels part of it and understands what is being measured and why, the more he or she is apt to learn from the process rather than resent it, which is counterproductive. (For people just coming into business, I recommend the AAAA-sponsored booklet, "What Every Young Account Representative Should Know About Creative Research," by Daniel M. Lissance and Leland E. Ott.)

4. Work with the agency as a partner. "I've been giving presentations for 20 years, and my estimate is that 80% of the time the agency and advertiser are in an adversarial relationship," notes Lukeman. "This is really mind-boggling when one thinks about it."

5. Spend the money to do it right. "When you compare the cost of information to broadcasting costs, it is obviously self-defeating to skimp on copy testing," says Michael von Gonten, late of Research Systems Corporation, and now with the BASES division of Burke. The corollary says, "Don't take the results from one test, which was designed to measure just one aspect of the communications process, and expect it to serve as a substitute for another service, which was designed to measure others."

6. A clear-cut statement of copy strategy, up front, saves much anguish later. Often the copywriter is not given explicit direction, and later a piece of copy written to accomplish one objective is tested and evaluated according to how well it did something else.

7. Always remember, when copy testing, the abominations—blithefully labeled creative—that flood into the system and, appropriately, should get screened out by testing. "What I'd love to do," says the

president of one copy testing service, "is follow one of these creative spokesmen at ARF and show a reel of commercials that got low scores. Nothing could make the point better; most of the stuff that gets shot down is awful—in fact, some of the stuff that gets on the air is awful."

8. Beware the middleman. Almost every copy testing executive I talked to underscores the deadening effect of middlemen—functionaries who get between copy testing experts and creatives. "The system keeps us apart," says one, "and the creatives are never invited to our presentations. If they could hear what we say first-hand, I don't think there would be nearly as much antagonism."

9. Copy testing has an adverse effect on an agency's bottom line. The more testing, the more rejections of copy executions, the more meetings, and the more creative staff manhours needed to handle the business—the higher the cost of doing business. Agencies are in business to make money when all's said and done, and it's natural that they would have an aversion to anything that makes that harder.

10. And, finally, always ask: "Am I part of the problem?"—a copy testing executive who knows little about the process of advertising or marketing; the copywriter who indiscriminately scoffs at copy testing over lunch at Crist Cellas but who—for the life of her or him—couldn't explain how the various services work; or the client who gets spooked at the slightest negative along the creative process way.

In a word, the whole copy development procedure is fraught with communications breakdowns/barriers, many of which are manmade. Intelligent individuals can get rid of many of them.

Copy Testing Techniques

Day-After Recall

The history of day-after recall measures of a commercial's ability to cut through and etch memorability in a natural on-air viewing situation—the roots of Burke's DAR—traces back to Princeton, New Jersey in the late 1940s. Dr. George Gallup, Sr., then active in Gallup & Robinson, Inc., became intrigued with the problem of measuring commercial effectiveness, which then was within a context of 60 seconds, no clutter, and sole-sponsor shows. He started by acquiring the rights to R&D done by a Commander Thompson in conjunction with the training of Navy pilots in WW II.

G&R experimentation led to a 24-hour (day-after) recall with aided recall to the product class level. (Later, with proliferation of set ownership and commercials, aid was extended to the brand name level.) Numerous advertisers were interested in his work, recalls Earnest A. Rockey, now president of G&R, but a young assistant to Dr. Gallup in those days. A syndicated service was started by G&R in 1950, and the concept was "Impact."

A bit later, Compton Advertising started work on a similar system called CSMI (for Compton Sales Message Index). "We started with the forgetting curve work of Ebbinghaus [1886]," recalls Howard Kuhn, now retired, but manager of research at Compton in those days. "We tested the recall on commercials 12, 24, 48, and 72 hours after exposure and finally settled on 24 hours—an arbitrary decision—where there was still enough recognition of copy ideas to evaluate impact."

An extensive amount of testing was done, "all at the initiative and expense of Compton," says Kuhn "and we examined all the variables—type of show, differences from city to city, daytime/nighttime, internal spots versus those at the beginning and end of a show, and so on." Out of all this, there were two major conclusions: (1) "artificial exposure of a commercial" in a controlled setting was "no good" because it led to artificially high recall; and (2) of all the variables tested, "the key measure was the 'staying power' of the commercial message over and beyond any advertising history the brand had." The CSMI service was finalized in 1952.

Development of CSMI techniques was followed closely by Procter & Gamble, which was doing some R&D of its own, including double-bind tests. The result was what at P&G were then called "in-the-market studies," and the fieldwork was handled through a then-small research company in Cincinnati called Burke. "We fell heir to business," recalls Donald L. Miller, past president [and owner] of the company that today is known as Burke Marketing Services, Inc., "because we had the only field force capable of doing it [i.e., executing the P&G questionnaire with numerous open-end questions]. The first DAR we did for P&G was in Bloomington, Ind., in 1952 on the 'Loretta Young Show'—and it was all door-to-door interviewing in those days."

When P&G was sold on the technique, all their advertising agencies were urged to use it, and the fieldwork went through Burke. But tabulation and analysis remained within P&G's MRD as it does to this day.

"P&G was very secretive about the technique," says Miller, "and they guarded it like one of their product formulations; they felt they had a considerable advantage over the competition;" Consequently, for several years, all Burke's work was for P&G agencies. Slowly, but surely, P&G alumni at other companies wanted the same, and this led to Burke's making DAR measures available to other companies in the early 1960s.

No doubt, the mystique of a secret project for P&G had much to do with the ultimate acceptance of Burke's DAR service.

As to P&G, one of their few public statements on the subject appeared in the *Journal of Advertising Research* in February 1972; John D. Henry, manager of P&G's MRD then and now, wrote this:

> We do on-air testing, and we talk to consumers following exposure without ever having recruited them to look at the advertising. In

our judgment, this is the way one should look at the advertising. In our judgment, this is the way one should measure communication: as it has to take place in the real world—fighting for attention and memory and reaction against all the advertising that competes for a share of the consumer's mind. That's doing it the hard way, I guess, but that's how it is in the real world as we see it.

"Two agencies—Compton and DFS—promoted the technique," notes Miller, now retired, "but mostly agencies have bad-mouthed it since the beginning."

In addition to Burke, there are five other research companies now providing recall measures, including ASI's Recall Plus, Gallup & Robinson, and Mapes and Ross, Inc.—both Charles F. Mapes, Jr., and Harold L. Ross, Jr., are former employees of G&R. An estimated $12 million is spent each year on such work, and some large package goods manufacturers do their own recall studies in-house.

Here is one final observation from Sanford L. Cooper, past president of Burke Marketing Research: "DAR only tells you about 20% of what you want to know about a commercial—but that's a very important 20%."

Persuasion Testing

The concept of measuring simulated sales response to a commercial exposed to a target audience in a controlled, off-air setting to determine sales efficacy traces back to Horace S. Schwerin who, in 1946, founded Scherwin Research Corporation along with colleagues Henry H. Newell and Leonard Kudisch.

Schwerin, who in the beginning was doing delayed recall studies, too, came to believe "the obvious truth that a claim can be well remembered but completely unimportant to the prospective buyer of the product—the solution the marketer offers is addressed to the wrong need," as he puts it in his book, *Persuasion in Marketing*, published in January 1981. "Pretesting in a central location using a motivated, considered-purchase measure seemed to offer the most likely means of predicting campaign testing." Thus, the emphasis was on shifts in attitude, or predisposition to buy a product, within a well-defined target group.

The impact of Schwerin and his early work in this direction is evidenced by the number of former SRC employees who are now prominent in the tv copy testing industry: Gerald Lukeman, president of ASI Market Research, Inc.; Harold M. Spielman and Donald H. McCollum, copresidents of McCollum/Spielman & Company, Inc.; Martin Weinberger, executive vice president of Oxtoby-Smith, Inc.; and Margaret H. Blair, president of ARS-Research Systems Corp. (Blair and her partner, Reginald B. Collier, purchased SRC from Schwerin in 1968. Schwerin is currently vp-market planning, Canned Foods Division, Campbell Soup Co.)

From the beginning, Schwerin decided to sell to advertisers—not advertising agencies. The reason was this:

> Agencies weren't good long-term prospects; as soon as they got a bad score, they would want to fire you. Besides, in those days, most agencies were doing their own copy testing, and naturally they wanted clients to believe their way was best. One large advertiser who has seven agencies asked them to rate all the copy testing services. Six rated their own first and SRC as second. Only one rated SRC first.

In *Persuasion in Marketing*, Schwerin notes that in those days,

> The majority of major advertisers were retaining either SRC or ASI for the purpose [pretesting of commercials] and that the technique was even more savagely attacked than is Burke recall today was merely symptomatic of the fact. It might indeed be said that, to vary the old fable, agencies have found that one King Stork has been substituted for another.

"You see," Schwerin told me recently, "we were attacking the basic legend—that an ad agency is like a doctor; you take his pills. We said, 'An agency is a creative source.'"

Particularly strong supporters of Schwerin and his attempts to measure persuasion were Charles Beardsley, president of Miles Laboratories; Irving and Neison Harris of Toni; and Leonard Lavin, president of Alberto-Culver. Lavin, especially, was quite outspoken about advertising—and agencies. "Agency review boards cause more damage than any other single group of people in the advertising process, except perhaps for clients," he is quoted as saying. Other early supporters, according to Schwerin were General Mills and AT&T Long Lines.

Physiological Testing

The concept of physiological measures, as applied to tv copy testing, is that consumers have emotional responses—basically subliminal—to stimuli (such as elements which make up a commercial) which cannot be verbalized or, if they were verbalized, might be misleading. But these responses can be measured through controlled studies of bodily functions.

This leads to the development of sophisticated equipment that records, as the respondent is being exposed to an advertising message, such bodily fluctuations as eye pupil dilation, brain wave activity, and changes in voice pitch, to mention the most prominent.

This physiological school of inquiry is currently enjoying a boomlet for three reasons: (1) technical improvement in the recording equipment, making it lighter, more portable, and more accurate—coupled with computer analysis; (2) increasing emphasis on "emotional" commercials where, in lieu of a flat-out, reason-to-buy copy point, the consumer is exposed to a series of nonverbal gratification promises which associate with the product inferentially; and (3) increased heat from advertisers to find some sort of predictive breakthrough in communications research.

Further, it represents the desire to take what is both a nebulous and ephemeral happening (i.e., exposure to a commercial) and subject it to the dictum of August Comte, the French mathematician–philosopher (1798–1857): "There is no inquiry which is not finally reducible to a question of numbers."

Lee S. Weinblatt, president of Telcom Research, Inc., a firm specializing in eye-movement analysis, puts it this way: "We're called upon to distinguish between 'entertainment' and 'communication.'"

Glen A. Brickman, president of Vopan Marketing Research, the leading firm in voice pitch analysis, adds this: "What we're after is the degree of feeling behind a consumer's verbal expression of attitude. Is the consumer committed, or paying lip service?"

Interest in physiological reactions goes way back. According to one expert, jade dealers of yore would shield their eyes when examining stones for purchase; they knew their pupils would react when they viewed a particularly attractive one, a tip-off for the seller to ask a higher price. And poker players wear eye shades for the same reason—and so on.

Clinical psychologists in academe have worked with physiological measures for years, and it was one such—a Dr. R. Hess from the University of Chicago—who worked with Marion Harper, the flamboyant head of McCann-Erickson (and Marplan) in the early 1960s, to measure eyeball movement of respondents as they scanned ads. Behind Harper's auspices, experimentation in physiological measures became fashionable in advertising circles—and used by such heavyweights as Coca-Cola, Buick, and Miles Laboratories.

The Marplan group specializing in this work broke up in the late 1970s, and two alumni now head firms prominent in eye-movement research and analysis: Lee Weinblatt of Telcom Research, Inc., and Elliot Young of Perception Research Services, Inc.

The role of brain wave analysis is best described by these excerpts from literature published by Psychophysiological Research Management Co., which is headed by William Harvey:

> Recent advances in psychobiology—the study of brain and behavior—have allowed researchers to apply techniques developed for medical and psycho-physiological research to the field of advertising....The evoked potential is a brain wave test in which a computer teases out the amplitude with which a person's brain registers a piece of information. The evoked potential is so fine a measure of attention that mere milliseconds in the response a person makes to a word or image makes the difference between high or low

attention value....The right/left hemisphere ratio score tells which half of a person's brain is reacting. If the right dominates, the person's brain is reacting to a picture and/or emotions; if the left dominates, it is reacting to words and/or logical reasoning.

Are advertising agencies receptive to this sort of probing? "It's a given that they'll [creatives] be negative at first; it really depends on how you present yourself," says Brinkman. Weinblatt is more outspoken: "For an industry that is supposed to be informing and changing buying habits, they [the agencies] are the most resistant when it comes to learning new things, changing their own habits." Add this observation of John E. O'Toole, president of Foote, Cone & Belding, re the whole physiological scene: "The entrails of sheep are just as valid."

Most physiological testing is specified—and paid for—by advertisers.

Top Creatives—What They Say

I sought out three prominent, highly successful creatives to make sure their point of view could be included in the context of this chapter. They are David J. Scott, executive vp, Ogilvy & Mather, Inc.; Lois G. Ernst, president, Advertising to Women, Inc.; and John E. O'Toole, president, Foote, Cone & Belding.

All three agree, albeit reluctantly, to three things:

1. The current flood of public denunciation of copy testing stems in large part from frustration; the creatives perceive that now, more than ever, the numbers people are winning the game. "It's getting worse," laments Scott. "The numbers bind is worse today," adds Ernst.
2. Most of the bad-mouthing comes from the less successful copywriters, not from the top-flight people. As Ernst points out, "About 90% of the time it's the weak copywriters who get the bad scores—but then there's the 10% when it's something brilliant—visionary —that scores low; that's the problem."
3. Some copywriters job hunt on the basis of being able to manipulate the system—i.e., produce copy that scores well. "It's a minority," observes O'Toole, "and they don't exactly say it flat out—but as they show their reels and Burke scores, the inference is clear. It would be a disservice to our clients if we hired on that basis."

(Jacking up an awareness score is, obviously, an open part of creative trade talk: "There isn't a copywriter worth a damn," says O'Toole, "who doesn't know how to get a good Burke." Advises Ernst: "Putting something irritating up front always gets a higher score." And, adds

Scott, who is more articulate than the whole copy research industry combined, "I just put a gorilla in a jock strap when I want a good Burke.")

"I don't fight copy testing," says Ernst, "and I think any copywriter who does is not wise; after all, you can't expect an advertiser to spend money without some assurance. It's useful—if used correctly." And that's the rub—it's so often misused, in her opinion. "Take the way focus groups are used to evaluate concepts and commercials—they [the client] say they just want to 'get a feel, an impression,' and then just one person makes a negative remark and an excellent idea can get killed; there's too much emphasis on 'quick and dirty' research that doesn't quantify anything." Ideally, concludes Ernst, "The agency and client should truly be business partners—work together to make a good judgment—with 49% of the decision based on test scores and 51% based on experience and professional judgment."

"It's a savage business," says Scott, "but all creative people want is a 'fair shot.' The commercial is everything; consumers buy the commercial, not the product—and the commercial should create a rehearsal for purchase. But not enough money is spent up front in putting together the selling equation. Then we need to send through more torpedoes (i.e., copy executions), the more the better, to get home runs instead of singles."

"What is frustrating," adds O'Toole, "is that creatives do not reject copy testing for the usual reasons, the ones stated so often, such as resistance to a 'report card.' The main reason is that they can't be convinced logically that the tests predict probable effectiveness on-air; results are just too inconsistent—sometimes it seems as if it's just a matter of luck. And," he adds emphatically, "to turn down a commercial on the basis of low recall score is a repudiation of everything that has gone before. It's an irrational act—madness."

And a final observation, again from O'Toole: "Both sides have dug in to the point where they don't listen to one another any more."

19 The Research Function in Top U.S. Advertising Agencies

Given that research has been inherent in the advertising agency business since almost day one—and as far back as 1929 Young & Rubicam set up what is believed to be the first formal agency research department (headed by a young statistical professor from Indiana, George H. Gallup, Sr.)—you'd expect that today the large agencies would be very much aware of what one another was doing in the research field.

To my suprise, I found this was not so. This revelation came from talking with the people who headed some of the largest agency research departments in the summer of 1982. While most could talk knowingly about one or two competitors, they were at a loss to describe knowingly what was going on generally.

So, when the following round-up article appeared in Advertising Age *on October 18, 1982, it contained what was to many surprising revelations, especially in how the emphasis on research (in terms of staffing and expenditures) differed from one major agency to another.*

I have since learned that now, when young people want to job jump from one agency's research operation to another, they cite material from this article to explain their reasons.

An Overview

In 1879 N.W. Ayer & Son, the famous advertising agency then based in Philadelphia, was soliciting a new account, Nichols-Shepard Co., a manufacturer of agricultural machinery. Ayer prepared a media schedule that was challenged by the would-be client, according to L. C. Lockley, writing in the *Journal of Marketing* (April 1950). Substantiation came from an Ayer survey of state officials and publishers throughout the country asking for information on grain production and media circulation by counties. The client was impressed, and Ayer got the account.

In that respect, at least, things haven't changed much over the past 105 years. When agencies pitch new business, the presentation is often larded with information about the would-be client's marketing problems. But now a large, in-house staff of professional researchers is usually available to gin up the sales ammunition. ("We usually end up setting the tone for the whole presentation," says one agency research director, "because we're the one who have the facts.")

Young & Rubicam claims to have started the first formal agency research department in 1929, the year that a famous statistical professor from Indiana, Dr. George H. Gallup, Sr., came to New York City at the behest of Ray Rubicam to start a department.

Y&R's claim may be disputed, but there is no doubt that research —advertising, media, and market—has been an integral part of U.S. advertising agencies' service capabilities for a long, long time. The roots are deep.

But, currently, there may well be what one research director termed "an identity crisis," with some agency research department heads, at least, casting about for new and more important ways to serve their constituencies and a clear-cut "mission." This has been induced, in part, by the growing sophistication of their clients' research departments; clients aren't so dependent on agency research backup as they once were. Put another way, it's gotten much more difficult to snow a client research-wise.

Also, one of the most sensitive areas of research, testing of tv copy and advertising effectiveness in general, has been under heavy attack—and it is implied that an agency's research staff should somehow alleviate the problem, which continues to fester.

In any case, advertising agencies today fund a sizable segment of the U.S. research industry. For instance, the 25 largest agencies (in terms of gross income derived from U.S. operations alone in 1981) now employ 1,550 people working directly in research of whom 1,162 are considered professionals—according to a unique census recently conducted for this article. And this count does not include about 200 other employees who work in agency libraries or information centers as backup to the research staffs or hordes of part-time employees and consultants. So, looking at just the 25 largest U.S. agencies, they collectively employ 5.4 professional researchers per $10 million of gross income.

But the disparity among the 24 largest U.S. agencies in terms of their apparent emphasis on the research function is surprisingly high, as the analysis in table 19.1 shows. The number of research professionals employed per $10 million in income ranges from a high of 9 (Needham, Harper & Steers) to a low of 2.6 (Ogilvy & Mather). This same variance shows in the percentage of the total agency's payroll going to research staffers. In U.S. agencies with $13.5 million in gross income or more, the mean is close to 4%. But the range is from a high of over 7% in one agency to a low of less than 1% in another. Such a swing can't be explained away by caliber of staffs or salary levels; it simply demonstrates that some agencies place much more emphasis on the research function, and that aspect of service to clients, than others. I might add, that is also true when it comes to expenditures for research R&D, agency support for broad-based original research that might prove useful to all clients, as well as the advertising community in general.

Table 19.1 How 24 Large U.S. Advertising Agencies Rank: The Number of Research Professionals Employed per $10 Million in Gross Income (U.S. Only)*

		Total Number Professionals Employed	Number of Professionals Per $10 Million Income
1.	Needham, Harper & Steers	53	9.0
2.	BBDO	106	8.3
3.	Leo Burnett	100	8.1
4.	Foote, Cone & Belding	79	6.8
5.	Ted Bates—New York	40	6.5
6.	D'Arcy-MacManus & Masius	47	6.4
7.	Young & Rubicam (excl. Marsteller)	106	6.1
8.	Kenyon & Eckhardt	29	6.0
9.	Dancer-Fitzgerald Sample	41	5.4
10.	Cunningham & Walsh	20	5.4
11.	Doyle Dane Bernbach	62	5.4
12.	J. Walter Thompson USA	83	5.4
13.	SSCB—New York	22	5.3
14.	Benton & Bowles	43	5.3
15.	Marschalk Campbell-Ewald	34	5.2
16.	N. W. Ayer	35	5.1
17.	Grey Advertising	47	5.0
18.	Ketchum Communications	17	4.4
19.	McCann-Erickson	30	4.0
20.	Bozell & Jacobs	23	3.7
21.	Martsteller Inc.	16	3.2
22.	Wells, Rich, Greene	20	3.1
23.	Subsidiary companies of Ted Bates & Co., combined—mostly notably Wm. Esty	39	2.9
24.	Ogilvy & Mather	41	2.6

* This analysis was based on gross agency income, U.S. only, for the year 1981, as reported in the *Advertising Age*, 1982 edition, "U.S. Agency Income Profiles." The research staff counts were furnished directly to the author. The analysis is complicated by the number of subsidiaries include in some agency totals, and for the 10 largest agencies, this is explained in the profile. When possible, data on some of the largest subsidiary agencies are shown separately. Compton Advertising, which is one of the 25 largest agencies, would not contribute to the summary.

Beyond various dimensions of size, it turns out that there are other significant differences among major agency research operations. For instance, in some, almost all the top research personnel are female; in others, the opposite is true. In some agencies, there is a titular head of research operations—a prominent front man or woman—who has a grandiose title (but not necessarily much line authority); in other agency setups, the research staffs scattered around in branch offices and subsidiaries are, for all practical purposes, autonomous. Some agencies have through the years built up internal data collection capabilities—focus group facilities, WATS phone centers, or mall locations for central interviewing—while others farm out almost all their work. Some agency research departments stress their role in helping to make good, effective advertising; in others, the emphasis is on planning of marketing strategy. Some agencies have a monolithic, highly structured point of view toward some research methodologies (for instance, one tv copy testing service versus another); in other agencies that does not exist, or so I've been told by research suppliers who work almost entirely with agencies.

These agency research organizations are not nearly as homogeneous as one might expect, and the differences transcend those that might be expected because of their particular client base. This, I think, will become very evident as the reader progresses through the profiles of the 10 largest U.S. agency research operations, which appear later in this chapter.

Agencies, Clients Differ

Not surprisingly, agencies—it seems—tend to see the research services they offer to clients as being well received and valuable, but the client's evaluation is not necessarily as rosy. The best documentation I can find of this comes from an *Advertising Age* Sounding Board survey conducted in January 1979. These data are based on a survey of over 100 marketing and advertising executives on the client side and top agency executives. The results, as they pertain to the importance of research at agencies, are shown in table 19.2.

These data, while certainly not definitive, do suggest that advertising research is the important thing from the client's point of view. The importance of marketing research, relatively, is much less. But, in terms of evaluating how agencies deliver on client expectations, tables 19.3 and 19.4 show the degree to which a gap exists (at least in 1979).

So, from the agency point of view, 23% say clients are extremely satisfied with agency contributions to advertising research, and none say clients are unsatisfied. The client point of view, in sharp contrast, shows that only 4% say they are extremely satisfied, and 23% are unsatisfied.

This is not to say that down deep top executives of major agencies do not recognize this gap and feel it is important enough to take action. It is interesting to note that since 1979, two major agencies—Young & Rubicam and Ted Bates—have brought in new top research management, to a large extent replaced almost all their research professionals, greatly expanded their research staffs, and started to invest in R&D.

Beyond these conspicuous cases, there appears to be a considerable amount of shuffling around at major agencies in response to current criticism and pressure. Here are some examples:

- Leo Burnett, as part of reorganization in mid-1980, moved senior research staff members physically into the creative department to promote day-to-day cooperation and rapport. The results have been very positive, says Calvin W. Gage, Burnett's research director. At Y&R, New York, senior researchers have been assigned to creative group heads, although they haven't physically moved their offices.

- Almost all major agencies now stress ongoing lifestyle research, a continuous monitoring of societal changes and shifts in attitudes and purchasing behavior, to give their agency and clients an early warning system on the future—and, presumably, to give their research depart-

Table 19.2 How Clients Feel About the Importance of Agency Services

	Absolutely Necessary (%)	Very Important (%)	Of Less Importance (%)	Not Very Important (%)	NA (%)
Advertising research	23	50	23	2	2
Marketing research	4	25	54	10	7
Marketing strategy and plans	6	52	35	2	5

Table 19.3 How Satisfied Agencies Believe Their Clients Are with Agency's Performance

	Extremely Satisfied (%)	Satisfied (%)	Unsatisfied (%)	Don't Use/Offer (%)	NA (%)
Advertising research	23	69	—	—	8
Marketing research	11	66	—	9	14
Marketing strategy and plans	46	51	—	—	3

Table 19.4 Client Degree of Satisfaction with Their Agency's Performance

	Extremely Satisfied (%)	Satisfied (%)	Unsatisfied (%)	Don't Use/Offer (%)	NA (%)
Advertising research	4	54	23	8	11
Marketing research	4	35	13	33	15
Marketing strategy and plans	4	60	13	15	8

ments a futuristic image. One researcher, who headed a large agency research department in New York, sees this emphasis on macro research—the big picture—as a way to compensate for the fact that clients are less and less interested in workaday research from their agencies. And it's good publicity for the agency, too.

- Many of the large agencies are starting to play up "strategic planning" in both job titles and operative roles. Presumably this stance—in part semantic manipulation—adds prestige and luster, beyond what can be obtained via research alone. (This has been going on in British agencies for some time. I've been told that it's tough to find a "researcher" in London agencies these days; the operative description now is "strategic planner.")

- A growing response to criticisms about traditional copy testing is evident, too. One conspicuous illustration is the funding by Foote, Cone & Belding of a new, on-air tv commercial testing procedure they felt was most suitable for evaluating the impact of highly emotional copy treatments, with emphasis on nonverbal communications, rather than the traditional day-after-recall techniques, which tend to place most emphasis on a respondent's ability to feed back (i.e., verbalize) key copy points, or a selling proposition. In an unprecedented move, FC&B executives put together a road show and made public presentations of the findings to meetings of advertising executives in several major cities.

- Another illustration is the PACT report, supported by a group of 20 or so major agencies, which attempts to publicize a standard point of view about tv copy testing procedures, which—ideally—would influence all agencies and their clients, settle some dust, etc.

Quite independent of how large agencies shift and mold their research operations in the future to position them in a changing climate, the fact remains that they have been, and continue to be, a large and important part of the U.S. industry. A profile of each of the 10 largest agency research operations follows, and the scope of their operations speaks for itself.

Agency Research Profiles

Young & Rubicam
New York, New York

Y&R, the largest agency in terms of U.S. gross income ($222.8 million in 1981), is—along with a group of branch offices and wholly owned subsidiaries, including Marsteller, Inc.—the largest employer of research personnel: a total of 136, of whom 122 are professionals. (This number does not include a library staff, business managers, and clerical support staff; under the Y&R organization in New York, secretaries are on another budget.)

This works out to an average of 5.5 professionals per $10 million in gross income. However, for Y&R properties excluding Marsteller, it is 6.1; for Marsteller alone, it is 3.2.

It wasn't always this way. Since Joseph T. Plummer came from Leo Burnett Company to be executive vp/director of research, at Y&R USA in 1979, the Y&R research staff has nearly tripled in size. Also, there has been a far greater investment in basic R&D plus a reorganization that emphasizes close working relationships with creatives. (A researcher is assigned personally to each senior creative chief.) The research emphasis, according to an agency statement, has shifted from "How did we do?" to "Are we touching the consumer?"

"This shift from 'counting noses' after the fact to 'sticking our necks out' up-front has had an important impact on creative strategy, creative development, and agency new business efforts," according to a Y&R spokesperson.

The Y&R research department was founded by George H. Gallup, Sr., in 1929, and that—says Y&R—makes it the oldest agency research group in the United States. Today, the organization includes the traditional account research groups (seven) assigned to clients. This staff is headed by John Eighmey.

In addition, there is a Consumer Research Services group, under the direction of Max Bonfeld, which works in the areas of copy testing, survey design, modeling and computer application, and consumer values/lifestyle research.

Also, a group called Creative Research Services, headed by Susan Gianinno, works on creative problems and manages the Discussion Lab, an in-house focus-group facility.

Paul Murphy is director of research for all Y&R specialty companies (excluding Marsteller, Inc., whose research head is John H. Morris), who can turn to Y&R USA staff for "additional horsepower" on research projects, as required.

Joseph Plummer, 41, in addition to being an executive vp of Y&R USA, is a member of the board of directors. He received his Ph.D. in communications from Ohio State University.

BBDO
New York, New York

While ranking fifth among U.S. agencies in gross income ($127.9 million in 1981), BBDO ranks first in emphasis on research in many respects. The parent plus a passel of subsidiaries, including the recently acquired Tracy-Locke, employ 143 people in research, 106 of whom are professionals. (These numbers do not include 7 employees in the Information Resource Center, which is touted as "the most extensive collection of secondary research resources in the business.") Of the professionals, 96 are in marketing/advertising research, and 10 are in media research.

This translates into 8.3 professionals per $10 million in gross income, far above the industry average of 5.4. In terms of the percentage of its gross income expended on research operations, BBDO is believed to have one of the largest percentages of all large U.S. agencies, if not the largest.

At BBDO there is the traditional research group, headed by either a research director or an associate director, assigned to each account. The senior research person also is a member of a Brand Planning Group which includes the responsible individual from creative, account management, media, and senior management; this group, which overlaps the traditional agency account structure, has major coordinating responsibility for a given brand.

In addition, at BBDO–NY, there is a Marketing Sciences Group of 25 people headed by R. Dale Wilson, which is responsible for marketing model development, computer operations, and new product forecasting and analysis.

A third group, Marketing Horizons, is responsible for monitoring changing lifestyle trends and "futures research." A fourth group, Special Projects, is charged with the development and improvement of techniques used by BBDO research, broad-scale consumer attitude and lifestyle research, and BBDO position papers on research questions.

In-house facilities include Hotline, a 10-station WATS phone facility in the New York office, as well as Ad-Lab, a focus group facility.

Regarding hiring research staff, an agency statement says, "We value integrity and the kind of personal strength that makes integrity possible. We value hard-working people, people who love advertising and the challenge it offers. We value intellect and creativity, and find it difficult to distinguish between the two." BBDO does some recruiting direct from graduate schools ("that's where you find the brains"), and transfer from research into other agency functions is discouraged.

Lewis G. Pringle, 41, is executive president/director of research services, at BBDO. He joined the agency in 1968 and was elected to the board of directors in 1978. Pringle is a graduate of Harvard University and received his Ph.D. from the Massachusetts Institute of Technology.

Leo Burnett USA
Chicago, Illinois

Burnett, the largest agency in Chicago and the sixth largest in the U.S. with a gross income of $124 million in 1981, can lay claim to the largest agency research staff under one roof—136, of whom 100 are professionals. (This figure does not include 3 librarians or about 54 part-timers associated with the department.) That works out to 8.1 professionals per $10 million gross income, the third highest among major agencies.

The Burnett operation is distinctive in other respects. For one, since mid-year 1981, researchers assigned to creative actually have offices in the creative department to promote close, day-to-day cooperation and rapport. Also, Burnett pioneered 25 years ago the use of central location interviewing. (Today, the Burnett facility is located near a mall in a Chicago suburb. A focus group facility is located in the agency's main office in Chicago's Loop.)

According to an agency spokesperson, "Virtually all of our research is conducted in-house, except for fieldwork done outside Chicago." A Burnett Lifestyle Program, started in 1967, monitors societal changes and their relevance to advertising problems.

"While we deal with a great range and variety of research," says a spokesperson, "five areas account for the majority of our projects: focus group discussions, copy research, lifestyle analysis, the planning/evaluation of new product introductory programs, and experimental work to improve our understanding of how advertising works—and to find better tools for studying the ways people are affected by advertising."

Organizationally, Burnett assigns each account a research group headed by a vp/group research director (who is physically located in the creative department), who is backed up by associates and analysts. In addition, there are four groups of specialists: (1) Qualitative Research (focus groups, depth interviews); (2) New Product Research (tracking studies, study of new-product introductory copy); (3) Consumer and Marketing Research Programs (lifestyle program and the modeling of relationships between advertising and sales/purchase behavior); and (4) Copy Development Research (R&D on copy testing procedures).

Burnett research recruits staff from universities. Also, the agency's client service department, as part of its training program, puts recruits into research for a year or so.

Head of Burnett research is Calvin W. Gage, 51, senior vp/director of research, who joined the agency in 1955. He has a master's degree in American studies from the University of Minnesota.

Foote, Cone & Belding Communications
Chicago, Illinois

FCB has six research units: FCB–Chicago, DBC–New York, FCB–Honig, San Francisco, FCB/Honig–Los Angeles, Aitkin-Kynett–Philadelphia, and Duetsch, Shea & Evans. In toto, these autonomous units employ 112 people in research, of whom 79 are professionals. Since the total FCB gross income in the United States in 1981 was $116.5 million, this works out to 6.8 professionals per $10 million in income, well above the industry average. (These numbers do not include an additional 18 staffers who work in FCB's information center in Chicago, a depository of secondary research materials.)

FCB research is distinctive in terms of the emphasis put on operating philosophy, the gist of which is embodied in a 17-page policy statement entitled "The Role of Research at FCB." The operative statement is, "FCB researchers work on advertising strategies and advertising. Advertising is their subject, not research. Research is the tool of the trade." Also, there is an emphasis on timing: "Research early in the creative process—delivered fast before decisions have had to be made without the research—can become part of the solution of even the most difficult advertising problems. But late research delivered slowly, can instead compound advertising problems."

FCB claims a battery of 30 different research techniques "which have been invented, developed, extended, or adapted to become FCB tools of research." These are viewed as the minimum capability of each research group. An illustration of such tools is Diagnostic Copy Test, an evaluative procedure (mostly face-to-face interviews in a mall setting) for rough and developmental copy. Along this line, FCB research made news by underwriting an on-air tv commercial testing procedure that they felt was most suitable for evaluating the impact of highly emotional copy treatments, with emphasis on nonverbal communications, rather than the traditional day-after-recall techniques that tend to place most emphasis on a respondent's ability to feed back (i.e., verbalize) key copy points or a selling proposition. Results of this study were presented to the whole advertising agency community via a series of meetings in major cities.

Organizationally, FCB research staff is divided into teams, headed by either an associate research director or research supervisor, which then have account assignments. A media research group is headed by Hugh Zielske.

In addition, FCB maintains in its Chicago office a focus group facility which has its own staff.

Head of FCB research is David Berger, 54, senior vp, corporate director of research, who has been with the agency since 1959, part of the time in account management work. A graduate of Columbia University, Berger also has an M.B.A. degree from Harvard Business School. He is a member of the FCB Strategy Board.

J. Walter Thompson USA
New York, New York

JWT–USA had a gross income from U.S. operations of $153.7 million in 1981, ranking it third in size. (This is not to be confused with the parent company, J. Walter Thompson Group, which includes among other properties Hill & Knowlton, the world's largest public relations agency, which has a sizable research department of its own, and Simmons Market Research Bureau, the staffs of which are not included in this analysis). JWT–USA employs 106 people in research in six offices; 83 of these are professionals, so that works out to 5.4 professionals per $10 million in gross income, average for large agencies.

"The research operation at JWT, as the name Research and Planning signifies, goes well beyond data collection," I've been told. "It is functionally integrated into the agency's Target Planning System. Department professionals work with the account team on a continuing basis in the planning, development, execution, and evaluation stages of marketing and communications strategies for our clients," says a spokesperson. Researchers are organized on an account group basis, with client assignments, and the lead researcher is a member of the agency's Target Planning Team.

JWT says its commitment to research is "most strongly demonstrated through its longstanding investment in a continuing R&D program." As examples of this, JWT cites the following: a study of the public's perception of television violence and its effects on the performance of advertising; a new demographics for defining the changing role of women—and responses to traditional and contemporary portrayals of women in advertising; tracking studies of consumer responsiveness to generic products; and a study of the potential value of long-form commercials available on demand via Cableshop.

In addition to account group assignees, JWT research staffers are organized into groups of functional expertise: media research, statistical analysis, sampling, marketing models, forecasting, information retrieval, etc. Some consultants are used on an as-needed basis.

JWT has semiannual, two-day seminars, which are attended by the senior research professionals from its U.S. offices as well as its affiliated U.S. and Canadian operations. The purpose: share research expertise and ideas.

Sonia Yuspeh, who joined JWT in 1972, is senior vp-research and planning. In 1982 she was appointed chairwoman of the agency's U.S. Research & Development Committee. She also chairs the New York office Strategy Plans Board. Yuspeh earned a master's degree in sociology fom Cornell University.

Ted Bates & Company
New York, New York

Bates was the fourth largest U.S. agency in 1981 with a gross income of $129.1 million (excluding Wm. Esty, a recent acquisition). In addition to the parent company, Bates today includes seven subsidiaries, most notably Campbell-Mithun and, recently, Wm. Esty. In toto, these eight organizations employ 99 people in research, 79 of whom are professionals. (About one-half of this staff is with Bates–NY.) For all Bates properties, this works out to 4 professionals per $10 million in income. However, the calculation for Bates–NY alone is 6.5, and for all the other properties combined, 2.9. (These counts do not include 9 librarians employed by these agencies.)

As for Bates–NY, the research staff is two and one-half times as large today as it was in 1980 when John A. Fiedler came from Leo Brunett to be senior vp/executive research director. Further, the professional staff today, with a couple of exceptions, is new to Bates since 1980.

As for philosophy, the new stance goes like this: "The mission of Bates Research is implicit in the agency's philosophy and discipline, the U.S.P. Explicitly, our goal is to help get better copy, quicker."

Structurally, Bates research in New York is divided into four operating units: (1) four professional groups, each headed by a vp-research director, which have client assignments; (2) the Marketing Sciences and Services Group, overseeing research development activities and liaison with the academic research community; (3) Research Operations Group, which is responsible for the fielding of research studies, coding and tabulating; and (4) the Information Services Group, which has direct computer access to over 50 major data bases.

In addition to the line organization, the Bates department is simultaneously organized into five specialized task forces ("probably a misapplication of matrix management," according to Fiedler), to wit: Motivation Research Group headed by Rudy Schroeer and Jack Bookbinder; the Test Marketing Experimental Design Group headed by Paul Keller; the Copy Research Group headed by Sheri Nadel; and the Market Structure Segmentation Research Group headed by David Gantman.

The Bates department periodically issues a report, New Product Scan, which monitors all new products in test market and national launch. It has worked closely with Stanford Research in the design and execution of their Values and Lifestyles Research Program. In addition, Bates has worked with the music and marketing departments of Columbia University on studies regarding the effect of music in advertising. Also, in conjunction with SUNY–Purchase, the agency has begun experimental research in the area of psychophysics (brainwave activities).

Fiedler, 40, received his M.B.A. degree from the University of Chicago and is a member of the Bates board.

Doyle Dane Berbach, Inc.
New York, New York

DDB, which includes eight different operating groups in the United States, had a gross income of $115 million from U.S. operations in 1981, ranking it eighth among agencies in size. There are 82 people (mostly headquartered in New York) working in research—71 in advertising and marketing research, 11 in media research. Of these, 62 are professionals, and that works out to 5.4 per $10 million in income, right near the industry average.

(This does not include 8 staffers in the agency's research library, which features on-line terminal access to various data banks.)

This staff is organized into two groups, with one reporting to a vp/manager of research (Sy Collins), and another reporting to a vp/manager of marketing services. Under research, there are six group research directors, each a vp, and each of these has a staff of professionals with titles such as associate group director, research supervisor, etc. Each group has a list of client assignments, except for one that specializes in international research and special agency projects. (Some members of the marketing services staff are involved in secondary research, and these are included in the counts above.)

In addition to conducting a wide range of day-to-day studies—from brand image to media mix and weight studies, from legal support to product test, and a variety of copy development tests in conjunction with DDB's creative staff—the DDB research group has developed several techniques that they feel to be innovative. For instance: METER, a tv pretesting technique called Multiple Exposure Television Effectiveness Research; CONTEST, a system to test alternative advertising strategies; GOALS, a five-step systematic, disciplined approach to the Generation of Advertising Leverage Strategies; and two unique systems for measuring the "intrusiveness" of radio commercials and the readership of print ads (which includes a mock newspaper where test ads can be tipped in).

The top research executive at DDB is Ruth Ziff, executive vp and director/research and marketing services. Prior to joining DDB in 1979, she was vp and manager of research at Benton & Bowles. Ziff is a member of the agency's management review board and a director of DDB. She received a Ph.D. in sociology from the City College of New York and, in 1973, was named Advertising Woman of the Year by the American Advertising Federation.

Grey Advertising, Inc.
New York, New York

Grey, with an estimated $94.4 million in U.S. gross income, ranked ninth among agencies in 1981. The agency has 76 people working in marketing, advertising, and media research (of whom 47 are professionals) in four offices: New York, Chicago, Los Angeles, and San Francisco. This works out to 5 research professionals per $10 million in income, slightly below the industry average.

Beyond that, the Grey research setup is distinctively different from that of other major agencies. For one, Grey solicits studies from organizations that are not Grey clients for advertising. Also, Grey research has a long-standing, contractual relationship with Data Development Corporation (New York) to handle the fielding of all Grey studies, including the pretesting of tv commercials through the Pre Search methodology utilized by

Grey. Data processing is done on Grey's in-house computer, and, of course, analysis and presentation are handled by Grey's professional staff. Consequently, Grey positions itself as a full service agency for clients in addition to the normal consultation to clients and internal agency staff.

Organizationally, Grey research has a group of nine associate research directors, each of whom—along with backup analytical staff—has responsibility for all primary research done for his or her account assignments, regardless of the type of study involved. In addition, under a separate manager, Grey offers a continuous consumer social trend analysis service. This group monitors behavioral trends, from secondary sources, and prepares reports for client and internal consumption.

There are three internal department functions that provide backup to this staff: (1) research operations—data collection supervision and control, in-house EDP; (2) technical operations—under the supervision of an outside consultant, Leland E. Ott—provides sampling and multivariate statistical services; and (3) an information center which maintains a file of secondary research data on all aspects of the agency and client businesses (the staff of which is not included in the counts above.)

In the United States, Grey Research executes about $5 million in custom primary consumer research volume a year, including projects done outside the United States but processed through New York.

Head of the Grey research operation is Barbara S. Feigin, senior vp/director of marketing and research, who has been with the agency since 1969. Previously, she held research management posts at Marplan and Benton & Bowles. Born in Berlin, Germany, Feigin has a B.A. degree from Whitman College (where she is on the board of overseers) and has completed a graduate program in business administration at the Harvard Business School.

Needham, Harper & Steers Advertising, Inc. Chicago/New York

Although it ranked 20th among U.S. agencies in 1981 in U.S. gross income ($59.2 million), NH&S ranks eighth in terms of the size of its research staff (74, of whom 53 are professionals) and first in terms of the number of research professionals per $10 million in income—9 as compared to a large agency average of 5.4.

There are five NH&S offices in the United States, but most of the research staff is located in the largest—Chicago and New York. These operations, apparently, are completely autonomous with Chicago headed by William D. Wells, senior vp/director of marketing services, and New York headed by Jacqueline Silver, senior vp/director of research. They are described as "peers," and each has the responsibility for guiding the strategic planning activities in his or her respective office.

"NH&S if often thought of for its campaigns that have the ability to touch human emotion though both 'the heart and the head.' We believe our advertising reaches out because our knowledge of the target is both complete and insightful," says an agency spokesperson.

Structurally, NH&S stresses multivariate statistical and forecasting procedures. "This area is so important at NH&S," the agency says, "that we have implemented a special group [headed by James C. Crimmins], which is concentrating on model development."

In addition to day-to-day consultation with clients and the design and execution of research studies, NH&S also stresses its annual lifestyle study, which focuses on changing attitudes, trends, and product usage patterns. This study is now in its seventh year.

Wells, who joined NH&S in Chicago in 1974, received his Ph.D. from Stanford University. Silver joined NH&S in New York in 1976.

D'Arcy-MacManus & Masius
New York, New York

DM&M has research departments in each of its seven U.S. offices, and, in total, they employ 70 people, 47 of whom are professionals. Since DM&M gross income for the United States in 1981 was $73.9 million, this works out to 6.4 professionals per $10 million in income, well above the industry average of 5.4 for large agencies. (DM&M owns a research company, Mid-America Research, Mount Prospect, Ill., which specializes in central location interviewing through four mall sites. Mid-America staff is not included in this analysis.)

Each of the DM&M research staffs operates autonomously, and there is no one person within the DM&M organization who is, at least, the titular head of research. However, the research directors from these seven locations are members of DM&M's research operating committee, which meets quarterly to exchange ideas and consult on problems of common interest.

DM&M, not surprisingly, finds virtue in the decentralization of research, namely that each office tends to have a different type of client base—packaged goods, durables, industrial, etc.—and hence each office can staff/adjust accordingly.

DM&M operating philosophy stresses "up-front research—used developmentally—on behalf of all clients—as the most effective and efficient deployment of resources," according to an agency spokesperson.

The DM&M units do share a central information services department —including central library (librarians are not included in the staff counts above), and there is information retrieval through CRTs. Also, a "new products prediction model" called RAM, which was developed by DM&M Chicago, is available to all DM&M clients. Two of the DM&M offices have lifestyle researchers on staff, and there are arrangements with several universities as consultants in special areas such as statistics, psychology, and sociology.

DM&M research directors are as follows: Tom Kutsko, Atlanta; Lucien DiSalvo, Bloomfield Hills, Mich.; Marshall Ottenfeld, Chicago; George Scott, Minneapolis; Patricia Greenwald, New York; and Philip Baker, St. Louis. (The San Francisco post is open.)

Part 3
The Future
of Marketing

20 Turmoil in the U.S. Research Industry: What Will the New Order Bring?

For several years now, the U.S. marketing research industry has been in what might be described as a state of turmoil. This is understood very well by some who are rightfully concerned about what will be the consequences, from their personal point of view. Most, however, see only part of what is happening or has happened; they are, generally, oblivious.

I felt the urge to describe these happenings, but, as is often the case, it takes a prod from the outside to get things moving. That prod came in the form of an invitation to be the luncheon speaker at the 25th Anniversary Conference of the Professional Marketing Research Society (of Canada) in Toronto on June 5, 1985. The Canadian research community, as with the total Canadian economy, is usually impacted by events in the U.S. although changes may take a year or two to ripple across the border. So, my speech took on the tone of an alert. Here's the text.

The Speech

I was very pleased to be asked to participate in the PMRS 25th anniversary commemoration. There were three reasons, I felt, why participation would be especially enjoyable.

One was that—try as I have through the years to document the changes impacting the U.S. marketing/advertising/public opinion research industry—I must admit to very dated knowledge of what is going on in Canada. So, the visit would help remedy that shortcoming.

Second, all my previous visits to Canada—Quebec City, Montreal, Toronto, and the Laurentian Lowlands—have been most pleasant. So, I'm always looking for a good excuse to return.

Last, but perhaps most important, I have had building up in me for some time now the compulsion to explain—in a concise and summary fashion and in the past tense—the upheaval that has gone on within the U.S. research industry, and which continues now at a rapidly accelerating pace. The corollary, of course, is, "Will this upheaval I perceive eventually spill over the border into your Canadian industry?" And, if so, will you find that good or bad, or something in between?

Many of you, I'm sure, will be familiar with bits and pieces of what I will describe. But it is when you put them all together, and then back off and examine the result in retrospect, that you see that the old order has crumbled; a new order—whose shape is pretty well defined—is taking shape; and everyone who makes or does traditional marketing research, or who buys it in large quantities, will be impacted.

Let's start by reviewing the merger/acquisition history of the U.S. research industry over the past 25 years.

Exhibit 1

As you can see (from table 20.1), there have been 95 changes of ownership over this time span. And I hasten to add, this list is not necessarily complete; I may have missed a couple along the way. Also, this does not mean that 95 different research firms have changed ownership; in fact, some have changed hands two, even three times. Granted, some of these organizations were mere shells of their illustrious past when they changed hands. Alfred Politz Research is a case in point (see chapter 13).

Be all that as it may, note the flurry of activity in the period 1968–71; 26 turnovers took place. Not many people paid much attention at the time, but this was a harbinger of what was to come. For one, large nonresearch organizations decided it would be kicky to own a research firm—and I might add, precious few had the slightest idea of what they were getting into. Further, a couple of people at least hit up the idea of setting up conglomerates—research supermarkets—via acquisition. The now-defunct INMARCO organization put together by Pierre Marquis with money from Columbia Pictures Industries is a case in point.

Now note the period 1972–80. Not much activity at all, just an average of two sellouts a year.

Then, starting in 1981, all hell broke loose. In the period 1981 through June of 1985, there have been 40 changes of ownership, including some blockbusters like the acquisition of the A. C. Nielsen Company for $1.1 billion by Dun & Bradstreet and the acquisition of Burke Marketing Services by Arbitron, which is owned by Control Data.

There have been four acquisitions so far in 1985 (through May), and I can almost guarantee that there will be at least six more before year's end.

This current flurry of activity is much different than that of the 1968–71 period. Today's buyers know much more about what they are about, and the main idea is to create conglomerates. Two prime cases in point are Maritz, Inc. and Equifax, Inc. Together, these two large nonresearch corporations have purchased six research firms which, in total, now have annual revenues of $48 million. And they are looking for more.

Table 20.1 Research Company Turnover History, 1960-1985 (Through June)

Year	Number of Turnovers	Year	Number of Turnovers
1985	4	1972	3
1984	9	1971	6
1983	6	1970	5
1982	10	1969	11
1981	11	1968	4
1980	4	1967	3
1979	4	1966	2
1978	3	1965	—
1977	1	1964	1
1976	1	1963	—
1975	2	1962	—
1974	2	1961	—
1973	1	1960	2
			95

That brings me to one of the main points I'd like to emphasize here today: the U.S. research industry today is owned in large part by very large nonresearch corporations, most of which are publicly held. Here are a few examples: Dun & Bradstreet, Time Inc., Control Data, Gannett Co., ABC, Harte-Hanks Communications, J. Walter Thompson, Equifax, Saatchi & Saatchi, Mills & Allen International, and IDC Services. This is an impressive—and by no means complete—list of corporate blue chips. If there is a common thread, it is that most have roots in the publishing/communications industry—and advertising agencies are included. (It is interesting to note that, just recently, a Canadian research firm, Dialogue Canada, was acquired by Pegatex, Inc., which is owned by the Reader's Digest Association, Canada.)

Another common thread is that, mostly, the research—or marketing data base management—segment of their business is a small part of the total. SAMI, as big as that is within the context of the traditional marketing research industry, received hardly a mention in the Time Inc. annual report until two years ago. Louis Harris and Associates is just a tiny part of the total Gannett operation, and so on.

Here, maybe, is a better way of looking at who owns what. Last May 23, I published my annual compilation of leading U.S. research organizations in *Advertising Age*. There were 40 organizations listed this year, and they had total revenues—calendar 1984—of $1.5 billion.

Exhibit 2

In table 20.2, as you can see, I've grouped these 40 organizations by the nature of their ownership, that is the situation that existed as of June 1985.

Table 20.2 Status of Ownership (as of June, 1985) 40 Leading U.S. Research Organizations

	1985 Dollar Revenue (Research Only) (Add 000,000)	% Top 40 Volume 1984
Public Companies (Stock traded)		
IMS International	$151.4	
Information Resources (Incl. MDS Consumer Research)	43.5	
M/A/R/C	37.6	
Market Facts	35.9	
Starch INRA Hooper	7.5	
Total	275.9	19.0%
Subsidiary of Large Public, Nonresearch Company		
A. C. Nielsen/D&B	$491.0	
SAMI/Time Inc.	118.4	
Arbitron Ratings Co./Control Data	105.8	
Burke Marketing Services/40% by Control Data	66.0	
Elrick and Lavidge/Equifax	23.3	
YS&W/Saatchi & Saatchi	17.0	
Chilton Research Services/ABC	16.5	
ASI/IDC Service	16.4	
Harris/Gannett Co.	15.3	
ORC/Arthur D. Little	14.5	
Simmons Market Research Bureau/ J. Walter Thompson	12.5	
Harte-Hanks Marketing Services Group/Harte-Hanks	9.7	
Mediamark/Mills & Allen International	7.2	
Total	913.6	63.0%
Subsidiary of Large Nonresearch, Nonpublic Corporation		
Maritz Market Research/Maritz, Inc.	$ 24.7	
Admar/Sprigg Lane	9.3	
National Analysis/Booz Allen & Hamilton	7.9	
Decision Research Corp./Temple, Barker & Sloane	5.5	
Total	47.4	3.3%

	1985 Dollar Revenue (Research Only) (Add 000,000)	% Top 40 Volume 1984
Subsidiary of Large Public Research Company		
NFO/AGB	$ 29.5	2.0%
Employee Owned		
Westat	$ 24.5	1.7%
Private, Closely Held		
NPD Group	$ 29.2	
Walker Research	19.4	
Ehrhart-Babic	13.2	
Winona	12.9	
Data Development Corp.	10.5	
Decisions Center	10.2	
McCollum/Spielman	9.4	
Custom Research Inc.	8.6	
D/M/I	7.8	
Gallup	7.7	
Market Opinion Research	6.8	
Kapuler	6.0	
Ad Factors	5.9	
Response Analysis	5.6	
Oxtoby-Smith	5.0	
Total	$158.2	10.9%
Grand Total	$1,449.1	100.0%

Of the total $1,449,000 in annual revenues, you see that 19%—or $275.9 million—is accounted for by individual research organizations that are publicly held.

The largest group, however, is comprised of organizations which are owned by large nonresearch public companies. These, in toto, represent $913.6 million in revenues, or 63% of the total. Another 3.3% is represented by firms which are owned by nonresearch, but not public corporations. The fact they are not public does not mean they are small. Maritz, Inc., for instance, has annual revenues in excess of $600 million.

The main point here, however, is the list at the bottom—those firms from the Top 40 which are still privately held. In toto, they have revenues of $158.2 million—or just 10.9% of the total. Almost every one of these 15 organizations is approached regularly with offers to sell out. One, or more, probably will by year's end.

Now, more than ever, the image of marketing/advertising research firms being owned by a small group of personal entrepreneurs with a research orientation is a myth. Instead we have all the accouterments of big-time corporate America—staff support—and strictures; employee benefit plans, which add to labor cost; in-house financial support; and emphasis on growth—and profit. The people who run these research organizations are businesspeople first, researchers second. The companies that own them tend to view what we have known as the research industry as marketing information, with a data-base orientation.

Running parallel with this development is the growing awareness of a breed of firms that I refer to, for lack of anything better, as marketing information service firms. Some examples are MAJERS, Interactive Market Systems, Claritas, Management Decision Systems, the Market Analysis Division of C.A.C.I., and National Demographics and Lifestyles—to name a few. These organizations are surprisingly large, and they seem to be growing faster, as a group, than the traditional marketing research firms. While they do not think of themselves as marketing research firms, and while they do not necessarily talk our language, they certainly are competitors for the monies marketing management spends for decision-making data. (See the last section of chapter 15 for more information about these companies.)

The point is this: you are now seeing such marketing information service firms taking on some of the characteristics and activities of marketing research firms (some through acquisition), and some large marketing research firms taking on more of the characteristics and point of view of the marketing information service firms (some through acquisition). For many reasons, I believe this trend, which is well established, will continue—accelerate, if anything. This concept is simply a one-stop marketing information service firm, nationwide in scope, which offers services ranging from lowly field and tab up to consulting (a way to get clients to pay for the client service they now often get for next to free). And the whole shebang will be owned and bankrolled by a large, public, nonresearch corporation. The traditional marketing/advertising research services will be just one department in this new data supermarket.

Here I have tried to show a model of what these new conglomerates will look like. There are seven areas of activity, each a separate profit center. (Also see figure 20.1 on page 306.)

CHARACTERISTICS OF NEW MODEL MARKETING INFORMATION SERVICE FIRMS (AS HYPOTHESIZED)

- Top management that is business (in lieu of research) oriented
- Very capital-intensive (need by buy exclusivity and stay abreast of new technological developments)
- Professional staff management (i.e., personnel, accounting systems, plant maintenance, etc.)

- Strong R&D orientation (to develop new products and, again, to stay abreast of new technological developments in data collection/processing)
- Selling client service for money (i.e., consulting)
- Systematic marketing of services (on a national scale through a network of client service offices)
- Very promotional-minded—advertising/public relations

Back to the U.S. research industry—while the Arbitron-Burke and IRI-MDS organizations are well advanced towards my model of what is to come, numerous other U.S. research organizations are moving, in their own way, toward the model. Some have acquired a consulting company; some, in fact, are owned by consulting companies—namely National Analysts by Booz Allen & Hamilton, Inc., and Opinion Research Corporation by Arthur D. Little, Inc. Some have changed their names. A conspicuous example is Market Research Corporation of America, which a year ago became MRCA Information Services. Market Facts, on the cover of its new annual report, refers to itself as "a growing information company." And so on—the research landscape is littered with other little indications that many other major U.S. research companies are moving toward the model I hypothesize—but perhaps with modifications, or within their own limitations—and ambitions—and financial resources.

So, in addition to size, diversification, and large capital requirements, what would be the nature of the new model marketing information service firm conglomerate, re by model? I have tried to state some of the characteristics, at least, on this exhibit.

Exhibit 3

In the real world, the outfit closest to the model shown in figure 20.1 today is the combined Arbitron-Burke organization, which has—or soon will—six of the seven boxes in place. Combined, the two had revenues of $172 million in 1984. Their owner is Control Data Corporation, which in 1984 had revenues of $5.2 billion.

Another organization moving strongly in this direction is Information Resources, Inc., which recently consummated its acquisition of Management Decision Systems, Inc. Together, these two will have annual revenues in excess of $61 million, and the parent—IRI—has plenty of cash due to its hugely successful public stock offering.

In passing, it is interesting to note how similar this marketing information supermarket concept—and the acquisition trip—is to what is going on in the advertising agency field. Note this section from a recent advertisement run by what was Ogilvy & Mather Worldwide, but which recently changed its name to Ogilvy Group.

Figure 20.1 Marketing Information Service Firm (A Model for the Future)

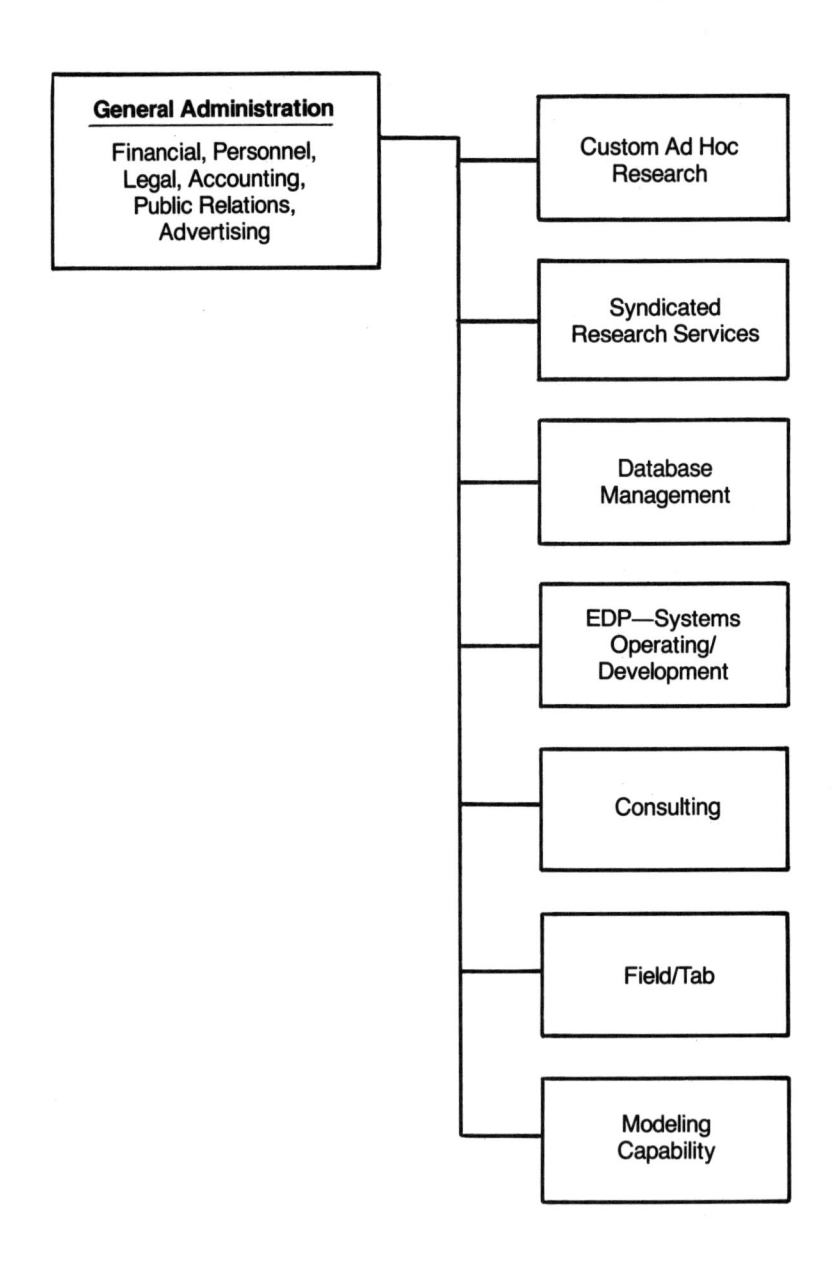

- General Administration: Financial, Personnel, Legal, Accounting, Public Relations, Advertising
  - Custom Ad Hoc Research
  - Syndicated Research Services
  - Database Management
  - EDP—Systems Operating/Development
  - Consulting
  - Field/Tab
  - Modeling Capability

Exhibit 4

You'll note from figure 20.2 that what was once a simple, but elegant, little advertising agency is now a conglomerate. The new tag line, in the copy of the ad, refers to the Ogilvy Group as having "one-stop client service."

Figure 20.2

Ogilvy & Mather Worldwide

U.S. offices: Atlanta, Chicago Hawaii, Houston, Los Angeles, New York, Washington D.C.

O&M Direct

O&M Graphic Services

O&M Hispanic

O&M Partners
(a full-service, medium-size agency)

O&M Presents
(corporate film, video, special events)

O&M Promotions

O&M Public Affairs

O&M Recruitment Advertising

O&M Yellow Pages

A. Eicoff & Company
(specialized broadcast marketing)

Dudley-Anderson-Yutzy

The O&M Public Relations Company

Euramerica
(multilingual communications)

Rolf Werner Rosenthal
(health-care communications)

Exhibit 5

First of all, the people who manage these new marketing information conglomerates will be businesspeople first, researchers second—if at all. Making money, keeping a corporate parent happy—that's the name of the game.

It is just assumed that new data collection techniques and related data processing systems will require—by past research company standards—extensive capital. Presumably, the corporate parent will be the friendly in-house banker.

All the staff frills of a major corporation—trained personnel people, financial people and accountants, etc.—are a given, along with employee benefits package administration.

A strong R&D orientation will be present. Again, the need to develop new products—the same treadmill the package goods industry has been on for some time—exists. The attempt will be made to repackage staff experience and marketing smarts and sell it for a profit. The management consulting companies, through the years, have probably made more money off survey research wrapped up in a problem-solving context than most quality survey firms who develop the input. Why shouldn't research firms do the same?

Marketing will be more systematic—and nationwide. A network of client service offices is a must. And, as you've probably noted, many of the large U.S. research firms are heavy, sophisticated advertisers today, utilizing the services of an advertising agency. Some have retained big-time public relations counsel. Any of you who have attended the annual ARF conference in New York have seen the profusion of exhibit booths, which tend to become more elaborate—and expensive—each year. And the collateral materials—direct mail pieces, brochures, etc.—are, again, getting more professional—and expensive.

But the main shift in selling, I suggest, will be a much more open, less provincial, view of marketing-data sales opportunities. For instance, the traditional research company, mostly, sold in through a company's research department and its staff. For the big, impersonal syndicated services, a la SAMI or Nielsen, the selling point was marketing management.

The new breed, I suggest, will think in terms of selling marketing information to whomever, wherever—corporate planners, brand managers, R&D, corporate officers, marketing research, sales management, etc. In a word, instead of selling "marketing research" to marketing researchers, they will be selling marketing information to the end users of that information. It will call for more knowing, sophisticated selling—a management information specialist, for lack of a better term.

I trust I've made my point by now, so I'll wind down. If I've accomplished what I set out to do, you'll be aware of what's happened in the States and what may spill over into Canada. As to whether it is good or bad—well, that's up to you.

21 A Final Word

When you can measure what you are speaking of and express it in numbers, you know what you are discoursing. But when you cannot measure it and express it in numbers your knowledge is of a very meager and unsatisfactory kind.

Lord William T. Kelvin (1824-1907)
British mathematician and physicist

The material in this book attests to the important, and integral, role of marketing and advertising research in the marketing of goods and services and the economic penalties that come from ignoring feedback from the consumer, as documented by good research. As the past chairman of American Motors, Paul Tippett put it: "Every time—every single time—we've ignored it, for reasons that seemed convenient at the time, we've lived to regret it."

If anything, I sense, the interdependency of marketing and research thickened during the economic recession of 1981–82. In the late 1970s especially, the seemingly endless availability of cheap and easy money encouraged marketers to go ahead with marginal new product/service ventures. The downside penalties for failure—or missing predicted success—were not necessarily deadly. But with the recession and extraordinarily high interest rates, the penalty for failure could, indeed, be deadly. To deny the consumer a place at the new product planning conference—by ignoring marketing research—had become just too dangerous. The need to reduce the risk of failure had, in many companies, become paramount.

Partly because of this shift in attitude, partly to become more competitive, partly to induce a cutting edge, avant-garde state-of-the-art image, and partly to reduce costs, many aggressive marketing research service firms offered up to management an avalanche of new services and techniques during the late 1970s and early 1980s. The names of these new services, if nothing else, demonstrated the industry's creativity in developing acronyms. But beyond that, the main thrust of many of these new methodologies/services was predictability—new, sharper, or just more esoteric methods of making early, up-front estimates of a new product's ultimate sales potential. Also enjoying a boom were marketing models used to simulate a potential marketing environment and permitting quick, relatively inexpensive experimentations in mixes of variables, and closed system marketing laboratories, which come close to providing 360-degree measures of the marketing and advertising environment in which a product can be tested.

These and kindred developments have enjoyed a boomlet as marketing emphasis seems to move away from past-tense measures to estimates, however crude, of things to come. Despite progress, we should heed the words of Niels Bohr (1885–1962), the famous Danish atomic physicist: "Prediction is very difficult, especially about the future."

A trend running parallel to all this is the embrace, by marketing research practitioners, of new (to marketing research) technology that offers to make data collection quicker, more accurate in some respects, and certainly more independent of human labor. Recent breakthroughs in technology in other fields often are adaptable to data collection problems, and, at least theoretically, they promise some enormous breakthroughs in the understanding of consumer response to marketing and advertising inducements. They also promise an absolute deluge of fresh, timely data that—for all practical purposes—could overwhelm the ability of analysts to sift and sort for specific answers to specific problems.

Beyond that, there's the old saw—"The supply of truth far exceeds the demand." To some extent, that is still the situation in marketing, although, as noted earlier, the high cost of failure, especially in the recent recession, has brought many more converts—at least temporarily—to the front of the research preacher's tent asking for a laying on the hands. But total, absolute, wholehearted convergence of marketing into research, and research into marketing, I suggest, will not come to be until two things happen. First, and most important by my reckoning, is urging would-be practitioners of marketing (and advertising) research to start their apprenticeship with hands-on experience in the gritties of marketing—field sales, merchandising, packaging, and the workaday chores associated with media buying and the creation of advertising within an agency. Far, far too many research practitioners today are one-dimensional and, all too often, fail to fully relate their efforts to those of the total marketing scheme, or their personal insights to those of the total marketing team.

The other thing is that would-be marketing people be forced to do an apprenticeship in a research department or agency. There is nothing more sobering or enlightening than having to actually grip a conceptual sampling problem, experience the chuckholes of data collection in the field, or try to divine out of mountains of statistical tabs those few powerful pieces of information that make or break a marketing decision. It's all easier said than done, and most consumers of marketing research input are blithefully ignorant of the process, or discipline, behind good research studies.

Idealistic? Not at all. Astonishing? Yes, especially if you subscribe to this observation attributed to Ralph Waldo Emerson (1803–82), the famous American essayist: "Nothing astonishes man as much as common sense."

Indeed, given the amount of money that is paid for marketing and advertising research, and the latent potential it has to enhance the marketing fortunes of an organization, it seems eminently sensible to properly train those involved in its preration and consumption. Why develop ever more powerful sophisticated, and complex fighter planes—and then skimp or ignore entirely the training of pilots who can optimize their use? Yet, that's pretty much the situation today in marketing research. Some companies, I'm sure, have started to perceive this and, in their own way, have started to address the problem. Others will follow.

When I first envisioned this book and its contents, I wanted it be people-oriented, an introduction to real people, real events; ideally the people involved would tell the story, their story, candidly. That goal, I trust, was realized and, for the most part, you've met some very bright, willful people—people confident enough of their own abilities to say, "Yeh, I made a mistake there . . . ," or "If I had to do it over again, I would have done it differently."

Collectively, their stories would come to realistically describe the state of marketing art, as it is in fact practiced in the United States today, and readers would realize there is still an ample element of by guess and by golly. That is the point of departure because, as in other sectors of human behavior, there is bound to be progress, refinement of technique, and—every now and then—really significant breakthrough. But, no matter how much more sophisticated marketing and marketing research come to be in the future, I tend to agree with the sentiment written by William Maynard, executive vp and managing director of creative services at Ted Bates Worldwide, the large New York-based advertising agency: "Major clients can't survive without research. There's a need to probe, measure, sort, count; to get the facts and turn them into strategy. But you can't print the research. You have to leave room for the magic to happen. Then bring back research to find if the magic works."

In the final analysis, it is people who make magic—in advertising, marketing, and research.

Name Index

A
Abelson, Herbert I., 211, 246
Adams, John Quincy, 173
Altman, Dennis, 270
Anderson, John, 30, 31, 36, 38–39, 41
Andrew, Bob, 194
Andrews, Jack R., 269
Armour, Frank B., 4–5
Armour, Franklin R., 18
Arnold, Pauline, 174
Askew, Reubin, 45
Audley, Sir Bernard, 256
Aurichio, A. J. "Rick," 227
Austin, J. Paul, 185

B
Babie, Louis J., Jr., 237
Bahner, Lesley A., 56
Baker, James A., III, 47, 59
Baker, Philip, 296
Barabba, Vincent, 47
Baron, Penny, 257
Barrish, Gilbert, 235
Bartels, William, 251
Barton, Samuel, 174
Barton, Samuel G., III, 248
Batchelder, Joe, 215
Batson, Donald B., 141
Battey, Edward, 192
Battison, William J., 240
Beal, Richard S., 30, 35–36
Beardsley, Charles, 277
Beaumont, Pamela, 6
Beckham, Raymond E., 57
Belden, Joe, 215
Bellman, Vernon, 185
Benham, Thomas W., 46
Benson, Edward, 209
Benson, Lawrence E., 209
Berger, David, 290
Bernbach, William, 184, 202
Bezilla, Robert, 210
Biden, Joe, 51

Blair, Margaret H., 276
Blott, Richard, 11
Bluhm, Aleta, 105, 109–110
Bohr, Niels, 310
Bonfeld, Max, 287
Bookbinder, Jack, 292
Boschwitz, Rudolph E., 64
Bowers, Diane K., 262
Bowman, Russell D., preface 1
Breen, Marguerita, 80
Breglio, Vincent J., 27, 29, 30, 33–35, 242
Brenner, Henry, 232, 259
Brickman, Glen A., 278, 279
Bristol, Henry, 185, 200
Broadbent, Gunilla, 253
Brokaw, Tom, 44
Bronfman, Edgar, 185, 201
Bronfman, Samuel, 185, 196
Brout, David B., 187
Brown, George H., 137–138, 142
Brown, Jack, 253
Brown, Jack E., 228
Brown, Robert G., 251
Brumbach, Richard, 187
Bruno, A. Spencer, 212
Bruszat, Martha, 192
Bryant, Edward C., 232, 260
Burke, Alberta H., 257, 268
Burk, Henry, 101, 225
Bush, George, 46, 54
Busyn, Tom, 102, 103–104, 106, 108, 110

C
Caddell, Patrick H., 41, 43–46, 49, 50, 51, 65–67, 71
Cappy, Joseph E., 157
Carter, Jimmy, 28, 29, 31, 32, 34, 35, 38–41, 49, 68, 76, 147, 148
Casey, William J., 30, 35
Chapin, Roy D., Jr., 159
Chapin, Roy D., Sr., 159

313

Chapin, William R., 159
Chapman, Donald B., 245
Charing, Herbert W., 187
Chay, Richard F., 267
Chook, Paul H., 187, 196, 202
Churchill, Verne B., 229
Cimbal, Alan, 187
Clark, Agi, 74, 75, 78–82
Clay, Henry, 173
Cobb, Ralph L., 98, 99
Coen, Robert J., preface 1
Cohen, Reuben, 211
Cole, Eileen, 253, 258, 260
Collier, Reginald B., 276
Collins, Sy, 293
Compton, Richard, 192
Comte, August, 278
Connolly, J. Wray, 5
Cooper, Sanford L., 276
Copp, Marley F., 140
Corddry, Paul, 1, 5–7, 9, 11, 16–26
Corson, Judith S., 241
Cox, Lloyd, 14
Crain, Rance, 28, 135, 171, 177, 217–218
Cranston, Alan, 45
Crawford, William H., 173
Crespi, Irving, 215
Crimmins, James C., 295
Crossley, Archibald, 175
Cumberpatch, Jim, 105
Currier, Frederick P., 244
Curtice, Harlow H., 140

D
Dailey, Peter H., 35
Daniel, Carlyle C., 225
Darity, Martin J., 78
Davies, Robert A., III, 117, 118, 122, 125, 127–134
Day, Doris, 93
Deaver, Michael K., 47, 59
Dedeurwaerder, José J., 152, 154, 156, 166–167
De Kadt, Pieter P., 187
Deuschl, Vivian, 78, 85
Dichter, Dr. Ernest, 201
Dinslage, Joe, 79
DiSalvo, Lucien, 296
Dodge, Sherwood, 187
Doggett, Lloyd, 71
Dole, Robert, 47

Domenici, Peter, 47, 64
Dreyfus, Robert Louisa, 225
Duboff, Robert S., 246
Dwight, John, 118

E
Eastman, Roy O., 174, 178
Ebbinghaus, Hermann, 275
Eberhardt, Richard C., 187
Edwards, William H. (Bill), 76, 85
Ehrhart, Thomas A., 237
Eichler, Edward, 187
Eighmey, John, 287
Eisenhower, Dwight D., 76, 201
Elligett, Jane K., 192
Emerson, Ralph Waldo, 310
Encarnacao, Stephen J., 10
Epstein, Edward, 187
Erickson, Lars H., 225
Ernst, Lena-Renate, 259
Ernst, Lois G., 279
Ernst, Wolfgang, 253, 259
Eskin, Gerald, 257
Ettus, Frank, 187

F
Fabian, George S., 187, 196
Fastbinder, George, 80
Feigin, Barbara S., 294
Ferguson, James L., 93, 95, 99, 100
Ferraro, Geraldine, 55, 66
Fiedler, John A., 56, 292
Field, Mervin D., 215
Findley, James J., 242
Francis, Arlene, 93
Frankel, Lester R., 187, 197, 198
Frank, Robert M., 187
Fratto, Kenneth P., 187
Frederick, J. George, 174, 178
Fuhrman, Edward, 99
Fulgoni, Gian, 230

G
Gage, Calvin W., 285, 289
Gale, Harlow, 173
Gallup, Alec M., 209
Gallup, George H., Jr., 209, 243
Gallup, George H., Sr. (Ted), 174–175, 178, 185, 203, 205, 208–211, 242, 274, 275, 281, 282, 287
Gantman, David, 292

Name Index **315**

Garfield, David G., 154–156, 160
Gay, William K., 187
Gershfield, Bruce, 187
Gianinno, Susan, 287
Gilligan, John J., 48
Glenn, John, 45
Gold, Laurence N., 105, 107–109
Golden, Richard, 80, 81
Golden, Robert J., 187
Goldstein, Joseph, 187, 196, 238
Goldwater, Barry, 47
Gomersall, Earl, 107, 114
Gookin, Burt, 5, 6
Gori, George, 187
Greenberg, Marshall G., 241
Greene, Jerome D., 187, 194, 200
Greenwald, Patricia, 296
Grigg, Golden 4, 8
Grigg, Nephi, 4, 8
Guinne, W. Fenton, Jr., 100

H
Hagopian, Louis T., 73
Haldeman, Bob, 46
Halpern, Richard S., 187
Hanan, Delores, 80
Harden, Gene, 101
Harden, N. Eugene, 255
Hardin, David K., 229
Hardy, Hugh S., 195
Harkin, Tom, 71
Harper, Marion, 278
Harris, Louis, 38, 48, 236
Harris, Neison, 277
Hart, Florence, 48
Hart, Gary, 45, 51
Hart, Peter D., 43, 48, 50, 51, 53, 65–72
Harvey, William, 278–279
Hase, Paul F., 214
Heald, Gordon, 82
Heiskell, Andrew, 185, 194, 198
Henry, John D., 275
Herguth, Robert, 187
Herold, Frank L., 101, 102
Herrick, Gerald D., 5-6
Hess, R., 278
Hochhauser, Richard, 239
Hollander, Kenneth A., 214
Howard, Christopher C., 14

Hughes, Tom, 63
Hulme, Donald, 187
Humphries, Roger, 192
Hunt, James B., 71
Hunt, Joseph A., 232
Hurwitt, David, 99
Huxley, Aldous, preface 2

I
Iacocca, Lee, 139, 146, 148, 149
Inouye, Daniel K., 77, 88

J
Jackson, Andrew, 173
Jackson, C. D., 201
Jackson, Henry "Scoop," 48
Jacobson, Charles D., 186, 187
Jepsen, Roger W., 64
Johnson, Jim, 67
Johnson, Scott, 109
Johnson, Tod, 232
Jones, Thomas O., 249
Jordan, Hamilton, 49
Jordan, Jerry N., 78
Joyce, Timothy, 244

K
Kagay, Michael R., 203
Kaplan, Leon B., 214
Kapuler, Stanley J., 245
Kehrer, Kenneth C., 213
Keller, Paul, 292
Kelvin, Lord William T., 270, 309
Kennedy, Edward (Ted), 29, 45, 48, 49
Kennedy, John F., 48, 76
Kilduff, Al, 161
Kimberly, John R., 185
King, Larry C., 188
Klein, Eva, 188, 192
Kluth, Dietmar, 6, 8–11, 14, 15
Knobler, William, 188
Kohut, Andrew, 209, 243
Koors, T. J., 78
Kossoff, Jerome, 188
Krandall, Norman, 142
Kroc, Ray, 12
Kudisch, Leonard, 276
Kuhn, Howard, 275
Kuperman, Irving J., 106
Kurnit, Shepard, 267
Kurtz, Richard, 188
Kutsko, Tom, 296

L
Labaw, Patricia, 213
Lahn, Stu, 161
Lauer, Robert C., 188
Lavidge, Robert J., 233
Lavin, Leonard, 277
Lawson, Sir Christopher, 57
Laxalt, Paul, 47, 77, 88
Lazarsfeld, Paul, 175
Lehne, Richard, 125–127
Lehrman, Lewis E., 44
Lemonick, Chick, 188
Lenrow, Morten M., 253
Lewellen, William H., 232
Lickert, Rensis, 175
Liebman, Leon H., 249
Lindsey, Robert R., 188
Lipner, William E., 231
Lissance, Daniel M., 273
Lockley, L. C., 173, 281
Lucas, Darrell B., 194, 196
Lukeman, Gerald, 235, 270, 272, 276
Lustig, Phillip, 188
Lynch, Dorothy J., 51

M
Machi, Vincent S., 188
Makely, Richard F., 249
Malec, John, 230, 257
Manning, Burton, 267, 270, 271
Mann, W. Jack, 188
Mapes, Charles F., Jr., 212, 268, 276
Marquis, Pierre, 300
Marrs, Homer, 107, 113–114
Martineau, Pierre, 174
Martin, Elizabeth, 264, 265
Mattimore, J. Clarke, 256
Maxey, Thomas F., 74–75, 78–80, 82
Mayer, Martin, 198
Maynard, William, 311
McCandless, John G., 159
McCollum, Donald H., 240, 268, 276
McCullough, Richard, 237
McCurry, Donald, 101, 102, 105, 106, 108
McGovern, George, 49
McGuinness, Peter J., 188

McNiven, Tom, 55
Meese, Edwin III, 30, 35, 47, 59
Meyers, Gerald C., 152
Meyer, Walter H., 212
Mikva, Abner 48
Milhaly, George, 188
Miller, A. Edward, 188, 191–194, 201
Miller, Donald L., 275, 276
Miller, Irwin, 209, 236
Miller, Karen, 188
Minton, Dwight C., 131, 134
Mirabel, Jackie, 188
Mitchell, John, 46
Mitchell, William L., 141–143
Mitofsky, Warren, 42
Mondale, Walter F., 45, 51, 53–57, 60, 61, 65–72, 67
Morgan, Roy, 215
Morgenstern, Dr. Oscar, 273
Morrill, William A., 213
Morris, John H., 287
Moseley, William, 5, 7
Mosher, Howard I., 159, 161
Moskowitz, Milton, 188
Moss, John D., 55-56
Mudd, Roger, 44
Murphy, Paul, 287
Muse, Normal L., 267

N
Nadel, Sheri, 292
Nader, Ralph, 140
Nardo, Ursula, 188
Newell, Henry H., 276
Newell, Thomas, 188
Newman, Lawrence, 188
Nielsen, Arthur C., Jr., 101, 102, 107, 108, 110–115, 181, 225
Nielsen, Arthur C., Sr., 175, 177–181, 255
Nielsen, Gertrude, 181
Nielsen, Philip R., 181
Nixon, Richard, 46, 61, 146, 209
Novick, Morton B., 188
Novitt, Morleen, 80
Nystrom, Dr. Paul H., 174

O
O'Brien, Richard, 94
Ochsner, Alfred B., 211

Name Index 317

O'Connor, Peggy, 188
Ogilvy, David, 210
Okun, Serge Y., 225
O'Neill, Harry, 209, 236
O'Neill, Harry W., 209
O'Reilly, Anthony J. F. "Tony," 10, 18
Orr, Vernon, 35
Ostberg, Henry D., 202, 240
O'Toole, John E., 279
Ottenfeld, Marshall, 296
Ott, Leland E., 273, 294

P
Parlin, Charles C., 174
Payne, Donald E., 157
Pedersen, Robert K., 4–7, 10, 17
Phillips, Cecil "Bud," 229, 258
Plummer, Joseph T., 287
Polan, Jacque O., 162
Politz, Alfred, 183–202
Politz, Martha, 192
Pope, Jeffrey L., 241
Posner, Fred, 80
Powell, Jody, 49
Power, David, 143, 145
Pressler, Larry, 64, 77, 88
Pringle, Lewis G., 288
Purvis, L. E. "Brick," 210

Q
Quayle, Oliver, 48

R
Raines, Howell, 50
Raphael, Peter L., 188
Rappeport, Michael A., 213
Rawlings, William E., 93, 99
Reagan, Nancy, 58
Reagan, Ronald, 27–42, 44, 45, 47–48, 53–56, 74, 77, 82, 86, 87
Reeder, Frank, 212
Reeves, Rosser, 185, 197, 198
Reiner, Gerald, 188
Reiser, Richard, 123–124, 132
Reis, Frank, 188
Richards, Richard, 44, 47
Riegner, Henry G., 74, 76–78
Robinson, Claude, 205, 209
Roche, James M., 141
Rockefeller, Jay, 71
Rockefeller, Nelson, 47

Rockey, Ernest A., 210, 274–275
Rockwell, John, 93, 99
Romney, George, 46, 136, 147
Roper, Elmo, 175, 185, 192, 193
Rorthstein, Melvin, 188
Rosenkranz, Jerry, 238
Rosenshine, Allen G., 267, 268
Ross, Harold L., 212, 268, 276
Ross, Jack, 186, 188, 214
Ross, Nat, 151, 153, 160
Roth, Steven, 239
Ruderman, Bernard, 239
Rund, Charles F., 54
Ryan, Jack E., 106, 109

S
Sabater, Gilbert, 188
Salb, Jack B., 188
Sammer, James E., 234
Sandler, Michael H., 212
Sansone, Robert, 98, 99
Santora, James F., 188
Saslaw, Irving M., 99
Schanne, Frank, 250
Schannen, Henry A., 214
Schiller, Miriam, 189
Schiller, Nathan, 189, 196
Schlinger, Mary Jane, 56
Schoenfeld, Gerald, 120–121
Schrader, Donald P., 210, 211
Schroeer, Rudy, 292
Schumsky, Stanley, 189
Schwartz, Robert, 152–153, 159
Schwerin, Horace S., 276, 277
Scipione, Paul, 214
Scott, David J., 279
Scott, George, 296
Scott, Walter Dill, 174
Scribante, Adrian J. "Ed," 250
Seely, Richard L., 84
Seiler, James, 256
Shaker, Theodore F., 227
Shapiro, Sid, 189
Shiller, Clark, 189
Sidey, Hugh, 45
Siebert, Donald E., 272
Siegel, Alan H., 189
Silbermann, Jon, 83
Silver, Jacqueline, 294
Simmons, W. R. "Bill," 189, 195
Simplot, Jack R., 12, 13
Simpson, Richard T., 189

Skelly, Florence R., 234
Slattery, J. Desmond "Des," 74, 75, 78–79, 85
Slurzberg, Lee, 189
Smilow, Joel, 6, 17
Smith, Brian D., 78
Smith, Harry, 189
Smith, Joseph, 246
Smith, Joseph G., 154
Smith, Philip L., 95, 99
Sobel, Charles A., 189
Soccodato, Vincent, 160, 161
Solov, Bernard M., 189
Spar, Edward J., 189
Spencer, Stuart, 35
Spielman, Harold, 240, 268, 276
Spizer, Stuart, 189
Sprung, Albert F., 189, 197
Spungin, Raymond S., 189
Stahlheber, Robert F., 189
Staniar, Burton B., 119, 121–122, 124
Stanton, Frank, 238
Starch, Dr. Daniel, 174, 178
Stennis, John 48
Stock, J. Stevens, 189
Stockman, David, 82
Sturman, Steven, 189
Swift, Reynald M., 121

T
Tauber, Richard M., 189
Taylor, E. L. "Jack," 229
Taylor, Humphrey, 236
Teeter, Betsy, 46
Teeter, Robert M., 43, 46, 47, 50, 51, 54, 70, 244
Tessier, Alain J., 244
Thatcher, Margaret, 57
Thomas, Martin V., 14, 15
Thompson, Commander, 274
Timmons, William, 34, 35
Tippett, W. Paul, Jr., 151, 156, 161, 162–168, 309
Tower, John, 47
Tredennick, Donald, 189
Trewhella, Claire, 189
Turner, Charles, 264, 265
Tuttle, Donna F., 74, 77–79, 82, 85–89
Tuttle, Holmes, 77, 86
Tuttle, Robert, 77, 86

U
Uberstine, Elliott, 189
Underwood, Terry L., 78

V
Van Peursem, David J., 154, 156–159
Vedehra, Dave, 269
Vershofen, Wilhelm, 259
Vipond, Richard W., 113, 225
Volaski, Albert, 189
Von Gonten, Michael, 273

W
Waldron, George B., 173
Walker, Frank D., 234
Wallace, George, 49
Walter, William, 257
Washington, Harold, 51
Weider, Sally, 189
Weinberger, Martin, 276
Weinblatt, Lee, 278, 279
Weld, Dr. Louis D. H., 174
Weller, Robert, 184, 189, 197, 198
Wells, Lee, 78
Wells, William D., 294, 295
White, Percival, 174, 178
Willer, Robert, 186
Williams, Robert J., 190, 196, 198, 199
Wilson, Elmo, 175
Wilson, R. Dale, 288
Wilson, William J. (Jay), 243
Wirthlin, Jeralie, 48
Wirthlin, Richard B., 27–30, 43, 47–48, 50, 51, 53–65, 70, 242
Wood, Leonard A., 243
Wood, Richard, 192
Woodward, Viviane, 100
Wrigley, William, 191–192
Wurts, John S., 251
Wynegar, Don, 84, 85, 86
Wyza, Jim, 106

Y
Yankelovich, Daniel, 200, 234
Yazmir, Martin D., 190
Young, Elliot, 278
Young, Shirley, 190
Yulman, William, 190
Yung, David, 190

Yuspeh, Sonia, 291

Z
Zanes, George W., 190
Zdep, Stanley M., 215
Zeidner, Martin, 186, 190
Ziff, Ruth, 293
Ziment, Larry, 190
Zissman, Lorin, 211

Company/Product/Service Index

A
ABC. *See* American Broadcasting Co. (ABC)
ABC/Harris Poll, 38
Abenteuer & Reisen, 84
Accountline, 248
Accuaudit (TRC), 211
ACN. *See* Nielsen, A.C., Co.
Acron Market Segmentation and Targeting System, 247
AC-T/SP (McCollum/Spielman and NPD Research), 240
Ad Factors Marketing Research, 218, 220, 245, 303
Ad-Lab (BBDO), 288
Admar Research Co., Inc., 202, 209–210, 220, 223, 240, 302
AdTel (BMSI), 10, 20, 227, 257
Advanced Research Resources Organization (ARRO), 211
Advertising Research Foundation (ARF), 187, 193, 200–201, 274
Advertising to Women, Inc., 279
Agate Club of Chicago, 174
AGB Research, 230, 231, 253
AGB Research PLC, 254, 256–257
AGB Television Research, 257
AHF Marketing Research, 186
Air Jamaica, 75, 80
Aitkin-Kynett, 289
Alberto-Culver, 277
Albertson's Inc., 6, 12
Allcom, Inc., 228
Allen International, 301, 302
Allen Products, 98
Alliance (Renault), 151-168
Alpo (Allen Products), 92, 95, 96, 97, 98
American Association for Public Opinion Research (AAPOR), 203
American Broadcasting Co. (ABC), 223, 234, 301, 302
American Can, 188
American Cyanamid, 121, 122
American Demographics, Inc., 247
American Express, 75
American Home Products, 118, 188
American Institute of Public Opinion, 175
American Kitchen Foods, 8, 9
American Motors, 46, 135, 136, 140, 149, 151–168, 246, 309
American Research Bureau, 256
American Research Foundation, 267
AMFAC, 12
Amherst Research Group, Inc., 240
Amoroso, Michael, Inc., 186
Amrigon, Inc., 141
Analytic Insights, 238
Anderson, Clayton & Co., 100
Anheuser-Busch, 82, 195
Apex (ASI Market Research), 235
Apparel Point-of-scale Tracking Service (NPD Group), 231
APRI, 196, 202
Arbitron-Burke, 305
Arbitron Ratings Co., 205, 219, 220, 222, 226–227, 248, 254, 256, 300, 302
Arbor, Inc., 262
Architect Viewpoint (YSW), 234
ARF. *See* Advertising Research Foundation (ARF)
Ariel (Chrysler), 147
Arm and Arm Deodorant (Curtis), 124
Arm & Hammer, 117–134
ARRO. *See* Advanced Research Resources Organization (ARRO)
ARS-Research Systems Corp., 272, 276
ASI/IDC Sevice, 302
ASI Market Research, Inc., 220, 222, 235, 270, 272, 276
ASSESSOR (IRI), 242, 257–258
AT&T, 78, 80, 188
AT&T Long Lines, 277
Audience Research, Inc., 205, 208, 262

Audimeter (ACN), 180
Audits & Surveys, Inc., 141, 187, 215, 218
Australian Tourist Commission, 75, 80
Axiom Market Research Bureau, 237
Ayer, N. W., & Son, 73–89, 173, 281

B

Bahamas Government Ministry to Tourism, 75, 78, 80
BAI. *See* Behavioral Analysis, Inc., 15
BASES (BMSI), 227, 257
Bates, Ted, & Co., 55–56, 57, 75, 185, 263, 283, 285, 291–292, 311
Bayer aspirin, 125
BBDO, 267, 268, 283, 287–288
BECKET, 188
Beetle (Volkswagen), 137, 146
Behavioral Analysis, Inc. (BAI), 15, 123, 124
BehaviorScan (IRI), 22, 103–104, 106, 107, 109, 229–230
Benson & Benson, Inc., 139, 209–210
Benton & Bowles, 94, 98, 293, 294
Berelson, D. B., & Co., 4, 5
Berlinger TageBlatt, 191
Beta Research Corp., 188
Betty Crocker (General Mills), 2
Birch Research Corp., 248, 262
Birds Eye (General Foods), 4, 8, 9, 21
Block Drug, 122, 246
BMSI. *See* Burke Marketing Services, Inc. (BMSI)
BOAC, 75, 80
Boehringer Ingelheim, 187
Boise-Cascade, 12, 19
Booz Allen & Hamilton, Inc., 20, 99, 223, 241, 302, 305
Bowdren, Don, Associates, 186
Boyle-Midway (American Home Products), 118, 122
Bringham Young University Survey Research Center, 47
Bristol-Meyers Co., 185, 200
British American Tobacco Co., 195
Brown and Williamson Tobacco Company, 11, 195
Bruskin, R. H., Associates, Inc., 187, 188
Buick (GM), 138, 278
Bunte, 84

Bureau of Business Research at Harvard Graduate School of Business, 174
Bureau of Social Science Research, 264
Burger Chef Systems, 100
Burger King, 2, 12
Burgoyne, Inc., 15, 262
Burke Institute, 227, 257
Burke International, 227, 256
Burke Marketing Services, Inc. (BMSI), 105, 155, 219, 220, 222, 226–228, 254, 257, 259, 268, 272–275, 279–280, 300, 302
Burnett, Leo, Co., 56, 263, 267, 283, 285, 288–289, 292
Burpee, W. Atlee, Company, 100
Busch Entertainment Corp., 78
Business and the Media Survey (ORC), 236
Business Bourse, 174, 178
Business Trends Analysis, 263

C

Cadet (GM), 138
California Home Brands, 134
Calle and Company, 247
Cambridge Opinion Studies, Inc., 187
Cambridge Reports, 49
Cambridge Survey Research, 49
Campbell-Mithun, 291
Campbell Soups, 1, 2, 14, 92, 276
Caravan Omnibus Surveys (ORC), 236
Cardinal (Ford), 139, 146
Carnation, 8, 9, 11, 12, 21
CBS News/*New York Times* polls, 42
Central Location Testing, 223, 238
Challenger (Chrysler), 144
Chase Manhattan Bank, 188
Cheddar Browns (Ore-Ida), 15
Chef-Reddy, 12
Chesebrough-Pond's, 188
Chevette (GM), 144, 145, 154, 162
Chevy II (GM), 139
Chicago Tribune, 174
Chilton Research Services, 220, 234-235, 265, 302
Christian Herald, 174
Chrysler Corp., 136, 138, 142, 143–144, 147–149, 152, 154, 195
Chuohchosasha (Central Research Service), 254

Company/Product/Service Index 323

Church & Dwight Company, 117–134
Civic (Honda), 154, 156
Clairol, Inc., 188
Claritas Corp., 238, 263, 304
Claritas GeoBase, 248
Claritas L. P., 247, 248
Clorox, 14
ClusterPlus (SMRB), 238
Coca-Cola Co., 185, 187, 195, 246, 278
Coding Enterprise, 189
Colgate-Palmolive, 119, 122, 189, 195
Columbia Pictures Industries, 300
Comet (Mercury), 137
Compton Advertising, Inc., 152, 156–157, 192, 212, 275, 276
Computer Science Corporation (CSC), 201
COMTEC (BMSI and Gartner), 227
Concord (AMC), 152
Connaghan & May Ayer (Australia), 80
Consumer Interviews, Inc., 240
Consumer Mail Panel (MF), 229, 258
Consumer Opinion Forums (MF), 229, 258
Consumer Research Division, Management Decision Systems, Inc., 242
Contemporary Research Center, 212
CONTEST (DDB), 293
Continuing Automotive Market Information Program (CAMIP), 139
Control Data Corp., 223, 226, 227, 256, 300–302, 305
Copartner Ayer, 79
Corolla (Toyota), 154
Corporate Reputation Survey (ORC), 236
Corvair Monza (GM), 139, 140
Cosmopolotian, 174
Council of American Survey Research Organizations (CASRO), 218, 223, 262
Country Style Dinner Fries (Ore-Ida), 8
CREST service (NPD Research), 2
Crinkle Cuts (Ore-Ida), 8
CRISPERS! (Ore-Ida), 11
Crisp Whips! (Ore-Ida), 15
Crispy Crowns! (Ore-Ida), 15
Crossley Surveys, Inc., 175, 232, 260
Crossley Youth-Student Surveys, Inc., 188

CSMI (Compton Sales Message Index), 275
Curtis, Helene, Industries, Inc., 124
Curtis Publishing Co., 174
Custom Research, Inc., 220, 240–241, 303
Cycle Dog Food, 91–100

D

Dai-Ichi Kitaku, 16
Dailey & Associates, 189
DAR (Burke), 268, 274, 275
D'Arcy Advertising, 188
D'Arcy MacManus Masius, 13, 295-296
D'Arcy-MacManus & Masius/de Garmo, 270
Dasher (Volkswagen), 146
Data + Medics (HSR), 214
Data Development Corp., 187, 188, 220, 223, 238, 263, 293, 303
Data Market Service (ACN), 103
Data Resources, Inc., 247
Datsun, 142
Dauphine (Renault), 153
DCI International, 238
DDB. *See* Doyle Dane Bernbach (DDB)
De Beers, 78
Decision/Making Information (DMI), 27, 29, 30, 33, 35–36, 38–41, 44, 46, 47–48, 54, 55, 58–65, 218, 220, 241–242, 303
Decision Research Corp., 218, 220, 246, 302
Decisions Center, Inc., 188, 220, 238-239, 303
Deep Fries (Heinz), 1, 10, 15, 20
DEFENDER (CRD), 242
de Kadt Marketing and Research, Inc., 187, 189
Demographic Survey Division of the Bureau of the Census, 265
Dentsu, 254
Der Spiegel, 84
DFS, 276
Diagnostic Copy Test (FCB), 290
Dialogue Canada, 301
Dinner Fries (Ore-Ida), 9
Directions for Decisions, Inc., 186
DKG Advertising, 267
DMI. *See* Decision/Making/Information
Dodge Colt (Chrysler), 144

Donnelley Marketing Information Services, 54, 247
Donnelley, Reuben H., Corp., 187
Dow Chemical Co., 190
Doyle Dane, 2, 10, 25
Doyle Dane Bernbach (DDB), Inc., 6, 10, 25, 141, 186, 188, 189, 268, 283, 292-293
Duetsch, Shea & Evans, 289
Dun & Bradstreet, 54, 110, 222, 223, 224, 255, 300-302
duPont, E.I., de Nemours, 195

E
Eastman Kodak Company, 47
Eastman Research Bureau, 174, 178
EASYTRAC (MDS), 251
E-B Custom Research (E-B Group), 236-237
Econo-Net Interviewing (Maritz), 232
Educational Testing Service, 204
Ehrhart-Babic Group (E-B Group), Inc., 220, 236-237, 303
Electronic Research for Insights into Marketing Information Services (ERIM), 102, 106, 108, 110, 224
Elliot Music Co., Inc., 83
Elrick and Lavidge, Inc., 220, 233, 302
English Ford (Ford), 138
EPSILON, 247 248-249
Epstein, Edward, & Associates, Inc., 187, 188
Equifax, Inc., 223, 233, 301, 302
ERIM. *See* Electronic Research for Insights into Marketing Information Services
ERIM-France, 106
Escourt (Ford), 147, 154, 156, 161-162
ESP (NPD Group), 231
European Viewpoint (YSW), 234
Evaluative Criteria, Inc., 189
Executive Corporate Image Survey (ORC), 236
EXPRESS EASYCAST (MDS), 251
EXPRESS EASYTRAC (MDS), 250
Exxon Office Systems, 204

F
Falcon (Ford), 137, 139, 142
FASTRAC (IRI), 230
Field Research Corp., 215

Fiesta (Ford), 145
Financial Relations Image Assessment Program (ORC), 236
Finkelstein, Arthur J., & Associates, 262
Firmenich, 204
Fit 'n Trim (Ralston Purina), 98
Florida Citrus Commission, 195
FMC, 204
Foodways National, Inc., 2, 24
Foote, Cone & Belding, 263, 279, 283, 286, 289-290
Foote, Cone & Belding/Honig, 10
Ford Motor Co., 136-139, 142, 144, 147, 148, 152, 154
French Fries (Ore-Ida), 8
Frost & Sullivan, 263

G
Gagliardi Bros., 11
Gaines Supreme (General Foods), 92, 93
Gallup International Research Institute, 82, 208
Gallup Opinion Index, 208
Gallup Organization, 171, 173, 205, 208-209, 211, 212, 215, 217, 220, 242-243, 303
Gallup Poll, 174-175, 208
Gallup & Robinson, 205, 210, 212, 272, 274-276
Gallup Social Science Research Group, 208
Gallup *Wall Street Journal*, 208
Gallup Youth Survey, 208
Gannett Co., 223, 235, 301
Gartner Group, Inc., 227
Gas-Oil Recordimeter (ACN), 180
GDR/CREST Enterprises (NPD Group), 231
Gelco Marketing Services Div. of Gelco Corp., 251
General Electric, 174
General Foods, 4, 8, 9, 14, 91-100, 102, 122, 187, 188, 263, 269
General Mills, 1, 14, 102, 109, 263, 277
General Motors (GM), 136, 138, 139, 140-144, 149, 152
Geo, 84
GFK Nurnberg Gesellschaft F Konsum und Absatzforschung & V, 254, 259
Gillette, 109

Company/Product/Service Index   **325**

GLC (Mazda), 156
Glendinning Associates, 6, 17, 24
GOALS (DDB), 293
Golden Patties (Ore-Ida), 15
Gravy Train (General Foods), 99
Gremlin (AMC), 140, 152
Grey Advertising, Inc., 94, 96, 98, 152, 156–157, 190, 263, 283, 293–294
Greyhound Lines, Inc., 78

H
Hambrecht & Quist, 104
Hardees, 12
Harrah's Hotel and Casino, 75
Harris, Louis, and Associates, Inc., 217, 220, 235–236, 301
Harris, Louis, France, 235
Harris, Louis, International, 235
Harris, Louis, International Medical Surveys, 235
Harte-Hanks Communications, 223, 231, 239, 250, 301
Harte-Hanks Marketing Services Group, 220, 222, 239, 302
Hart, Peter D., Research Associates, Inc., 48, 262
Hase-Schannen Research Associates, (HSR), 214
Hash Browns (Ore-Ida), 4, 9, 19
HBM/Creamer, 106
Heinz, H. J., 1, 4, 5, 6, 8, 10, 16, 18, 24
Hewlett Packard, 12
High Technology Market Research (TRC), 211
Hill & Knowlton, 263, 290
Hilton Corp., 75, 76, 85
Hispanic Viewpoint (YSW), 234
Hoagland & MacLachlan, 153
Holiday Inns, 75
Hollander, Kenneth, Associates, 214
Home Style (Ore-Ida), 15
Home Testing Institute (NPD), 231, 248, 259
Honda, 142, 145, 154
Hooper, C. E., Inc., 173, 175
Hooper Telephone Interviewing Service, 243
Horizon (Chrysler), 147, 154, 156
Hornet (AMC), 152
Hotline (BBDO), 288

Household Products Div. of Colgate-Palmolive, 122
HTI (NPD Group), 231
Hudson Motor Car Co., 159

I
ICOM, 108
Idaho Frozen Foods, 12
Idaho Potato Commission, 13
IDC Services, 223, 235, 301
IMS America, 223, 255
IMS International, 205, 219, 220, 225, 253–256, 302
India Government Tourist Office, 75
Information & Analysis, 256
Information Resources, Inc. (IRI), 103, 219, 220, 223, 229–230, 242, 254, 257–258, 302, 305
Infratest Forschung GMBH & Co., 253, 254, 259
INMARCO, 300
Institue for Advanced Study, 204
Integrated New Product Development (TRC), 212
Interactive Market Systems (IMSI), 247, 249, 304
International Playtex, 6, 11, 17
IRI. *See* Information Resources, Inc.
IRI-MDS, 305

J
Jack in the Box, 12
Japan Marketing Research Association, 254
Jaguar, 153
Jeep (AMC), 149, 152–153
Jeffery, Thomas B., Co., 158
Jewelry Tracking Service (NPD Group), 231
Johnson & Johnson, 214
Johnson, S. C., & Son, 14, 267
JWT Group, 223, 237, 270

K
Kal Kan, 92, 96, 97, 98
Kapuler Marketing Research, Inc., 218, 220, 244–245, 303
Kellogg Co., 14, 174
Kelly, Nason, 119, 121
Kennecott Copper, 6
Kentucky Fried Chicken, 16

Kidder, Peabody, 11
Kilduff Motors, Inc., 161
Kimberly-Clark, Corp., 185, 195
Knobler, William, Co., Inc., 188
Kohner Bros., 100

L
Laboratory Test Market Service. *See* LTM
Lamb-Weston (AMFAC), 12
Landor Associates, 7
LeCar (Renault), 153
Leggett & Lustig Research, Inc., 188
Lever Bros., 195
Life cereal, 268
Life Savers, Inc., 187
Lifestyle (Burnett), 289, 304
Lites (Ore-Ida), 15, 22, 23–24
Little, Arthur D., Inc., 209, 220, 223, 236, 302, 305
LNA/BAR multimedia expenditure report, 249
LTM (Laboratory Test Market) (YSW), 15, 24, 234
Lynch Research, 51
Lynx (Ford), 161–162

M
Magid, Frank N., Associates, 262
Mahin's Advertising Agency, 173–174
MAJERS Corp., 15, 222, 247, 250, 263, 304
Major Market Service (ACN), 103
Management Decision Systems, Inc., 223, 230, 242, 247, 250–251, 257, 263, 304, 305
Mapes and Ross, Inc., 15, 212, 272, 276
MAPPS (Maritz), 232
M/A/R/C, Inc., 219, 220, 228–229, 254, 258, 302
Maritz Market Research, Inc., 219, 220, 223, 232, 254, 259–260, 301, 302
Market Analysis Division of C.A.C.I., Inc., 247, 304
Market Audits (BMSI), 227
Marketest (MF), 229, 258
Market Facts, Inc., 56, 219, 220, 229, 248, 254, 258, 302, 305
Market Facts of Canada, Ltd., 229, 258
Marketing Fact Book (IRI), 230, 257
Marketing Index (ORC), 209

Marketing Information Systems, Inc., 186
Marketing Intelligence Service, Ltd., 247
Marketing Research Workshop, 190
Marketing Strategy, Inc., 160
Marketmath, Inc., 187, 189
Market Opinion Research (MOR), 30, 36, 46, 47, 51, 54, 220, 244, 303
Market Probe International, Inc., 189
MarketPULSE Measuring Systems (Walker), 233
MARKETRAX (NPD Group), 222, 231
Market Research Corp. of America (MRCA), 15, 174, 178, 213, 262, 305
Market Statistics, 189
Market Trends, Inc., 240
Marplan, 278, 294
Marriott Hotel, 12
Marschalk, Inc., 188
Marsteller, Inc., 286–287
Marylander Market Research, Inc., 15
Mastertrack (MAJERS), 250
Mathematica Policy Research (MPR), 213
Maxwell House (General Foods), 95
Mazda, 142, 153, 156
MCAs, 24
McBer & Company, 234
McCann Erickson, preface 1, 75, 278
McCollum/Spielman & Co., Inc., 220, 239–240, 272, 276, 303
McDonald's, 2, 12, 16
McGraw-Hill, 209, 263
McHugh & Hoffman, 262
McKim Advertising (Canada), 80
McKinsey & Co., 4, 5
McKinsey & Co.—Japan, 16
Mealtime (Kal Kan), 98
Measurement of Trade Cooperation (MTC) (E-B group), 237
MediamarkMills, 302
Mediamark Research, Inc., 220, 243–244
Mercedes-Benz, 168
Merian, 84
METER (DDB), 293
MF. *See* Market Facts, Inc.
Mid-America Research, 295
Miles Laboratories, 277, 278
Miller & Kops, Inc., 188
Mills & Allen International, 223, 301

Mills & Allen International PLC, 243
Minute Maid, 1
Mitsubishi, 144
MIVIS (Maritz), 232
MMSL, 231
Mobil Corp., 185, 192, 195, 204
Mobil division of Socony-Vacuum Oil Co., 185
Monitor (YSW), 234
MOR. *See* Market Opinion Research (MOR)
Morrison-Knudsen, 12
Motorola, 113–114
MPR. *See* Mathematica Policy Research (MPR)
MRCA Information Services, 262, 305
MRCA. *See* Market Research Corporation of America, 15
Multivariance Data Analysts, 203

N

Nabisco Brands, 92, 188
NABSCAN USA, 262
Nash-Kelvinator, 158
Nash Motors, 158
National Analysts, 174, 220, 241, 265, 302, 305
National Association of Political Pollsters, 50
National Center for Health Statistics, 265
National Decision Systems, 247, 263
National Demographics & Lifestyles, 247, 304
National Liquor, Wine & Beer Index (E-B group), 237
National Marketing Studies, Inc., 187, 188, 189
National Pet Food, 92
National Quality Interviewing, 210
National Retail Tracking Index (NRTI) (E-B group), 237
National WATS Service (Harte-Hanks), 239
NDI (Nielsen Drug Index), 178–179
Needham, Harpers & Steers, 93, 105, 282, 283, 294–295
Newman-Stein, Inc., 188
New Product Scan (Bates), 292
Newsweek Poll, 208
New York Convention and Visitors Bureau, 75

New Yorker, 189
New York Times/CBS News poll, 60, 68
NFI (Nielsen Food Index), 179
NFO International Research, 231
NFO Research, Inc., 219, 220, 230–231
Nichols-Shepard Co., 173, 281
Nielsen, A.C., Co. (ACN), 101–115, 171, 173, 175, 177–181, 205, 219, 220, 222, 224–225, 253, 254, 255, 260, 300, 302, 308
Nissan, 136
Nomura Research Institute, 254–255
Northwest Orient Airlines, 78
Nova (GM), 139, 149
NPD Group, 219, 220, 222, 231–232, 248, 254, 259, 303
NPD Research, Inc., 2, 231, 240
NRI (Nielsen Radio Index), 179
Nutritional Segmentation System (NPD Group), 231

O

O'Briens (Ore-Ida), 8
Ogilvy Group, 305, 307
Ogilvy & Mather, Inc., 75, 93, 210, 279, 282, 283
Ogilvy & Mather Worldwide, 305, 307
Omni (Chrysler), 147, 153
Omni-Horizon (Chrysler), 143
18i (Renault), 153
On-Site Testing, Inc., 188
Opel (GM), 138
Opinion, Inc., 205, 209
Opinion Research Corp. (ORC), 46, 175, 205, 209, 211, 212, 214, 236, 302, 305
ORC. *See* Opinion Research Corp.
ORC Public Opinion Index, 209
Oregon Frozen Foods, Inc., 4
Ore-Ida Foods, Inc., 1–26
Oxtoby-Smith, Inc., 154, 156, 157, 161, 218, 220, 246, 276, 303

P

PACT report, 286
Pan American World Airways, 74, 75, 78
Pan Eval, 251
Pegatex, Inc., 301
Penney, J. C., Co., 80, 187

Pensar, 108
People Meter (Arbitron), 257
PepsiCo, 186, 253, 268
Perception Research Services, Inc., 278
Performance Measurement Systems (Walker), 233
PERQ Medical Industries Service (IMS), 249
Pet Foods Division of General Foods Corporation, 91–100
Peugeot, 136, 145, 168
Pinto (Ford), 140
Pipeline Research, 223, 225, 255
Pixie Crinkles (Ore-Ida), 8
Plymouth Arrow (Chrysler), 144
Polaris Research Associates, Inc., 187, 190
Politz, Alfred, Research, Inc., 171, 183–202, 300
Politz, Alfred, Weberberatung, 191
Pontiac (GM), 138
Port Authority of New York and New Jersey, 189
Post (General Foods), 96
Potato Services, 9
Power, J.D., & Associates, 143, 168, 262
Premium House, 13
Princeton Research & Consulting Center (PRCC), 214–215
PRIZM (Claritas), 238, 248
Procter & Gamble, 102, 122, 130, 162, 263, 275
Product Image and Awareness Study (PIAS) (GM), 140–141
PROMOTER (MDS), 251
Promotion Test Lab, 228
PSA (NPD Group), 231
Psychological Corp., 175
Psychophysiological Research Management Co., 278
Public Opinion Index (ORC), 209, 236
Publishers Information Bureau Advertising Expenditure Services, 249

Q
Q.E.D. Research, Inc., 262
Quaker Oats Co., 98, 100, 102, 179, 263, 268

Qualitative Consultancy, Inc., 56
Qualitative Decisions Center, 238
Quantitative Communications Test (QCT), 214
QUIP—Arbuckle, Cohen & Trewhella, Inc., 189

R
Rabbit (Volkswagen), 146
RAC. *See* Response Analysis Corp. (RAC)
Ralston Purina, 98
Rambler (AMC), 135, 136, 139, 140
RAM (DM&M), 295
Rand Survey Research Institute, 264
RCA, 204
Reader's Digest Association, Canada, 301
Recall Plus (ASI), 276
Recipe Balanced Dinners (Campbell), 92
Reeder, Frank, Marketing Research, 212
Reklame-Adviesburo BS Marketwinning-Ayer Wierden Holland, 80
Reliant (Chrysler), 147
Remington Rand, 204
Renault, 145, 151–168
Research 100, 209, 212
Research Information Center, Inc. (RICI), 186
Research International (RI), 253, 254, 258
Research/Strategy/Management, 47
Research Systems Corp., 262, 273
Response Analysis Corp. (RAC), 209, 211, 218, 220, 245–246, 265, 303
Reymer & Gersin Associates, 262
Rhinegold Beer, 195
RI. *See* Research International (RI)
RICI. *See* Research Information Center, Inc. (RICI)
Rival Task Chuck Dinners (Nabisco), 92
R L Associates (RLA), 213
RMH Research, Inc., 239
Rockwell, John, & Associates, 93
Rogers National Research, Inc., 144–145
Rome Report (IMS), 249
Roper Organization, 173, 243

Roper Research Associates, 192
Ross-Cooper Associates, Inc., 188
Ross, J., Associates, Inc., 188, 214
Rothstein-Tauber, Inc., 188, 189
Royal Bank of Canada, 187
Roy Rogers, 12
Ruder & Finn, 263

S
Saatchi & Saatchi, 223, 234, 301, 302
Salmon, Kurt, Associates, 231
SAMI. *See* Selling Areas—Marketing Inc., (SAMI)
SAMSCAN (SAMI), 226, 227, 256
San Francisco Chronicle, 188
SA Shapiro Research Corp., 189
Saturn (GM), 149
SBRA. *See* Spencer Bruno Research Associates (SBRA)
ScanAmerica (Arbitron and Burke), 227–228, 256, 257
Scantrack (ACN), 103
Scarborough/LNR, 248
Scarborough Research Corp., 238
Scherwin Research Corp., 276
Schiller, Nathan, Marketing Research and Consulting, 189
Schmidt Products, Inc., 187
Schoenfeld, Gerald, Inc., 120–121
Scholastic Achievement Tests, 204
Schrader Research & Rating Service (SRRS), 210–211
Scott Paper, 14
Seagram Distillers Company, 185, 189, 195
Sears-Roebuck, 195
Selling Areas-Marketing, Inc. (SAMI), 15, 219, 220, 226, 227, 254, 256, 301, 302, 308
SE Surveys, Inc., 187
7-Up, 80
Seventeen Magazine, 187
Sheraton, 75
Sherman Group, 272
Shoestrings (Ore-Ida), 8
Silbermann, Jon, Music, 82
Simca, Inc., 138
Simmons Market Research Bureau, 189, 220, 237–238, 248, 290, 302
Simmons, W. R., & Associates Research, Inc., 187, 189, 195, 237
Simplot Corp., 9, 12, 13

Skippy Dog Food, 134
Skippy Premium (National Pet Food), 92
Skyline Farms, 5, 10
Slurzberg, Lee, Research, Inc., 189
Small Business Viewpoint (YSW), 234
Small Whole Peeled (Ore-Ida), 8
Smith, Harry, Research Associates, 189
Socony-Vacuum Co., 192
SOFRES, 254
Somerset Importers, Inc., 188
Southern Hash Browns (Ore-Ida), 8
SPAR, Inc., 247, 251, 263
SPARBASE, 251
SPARLINE, 251
SPARTRAC, 251
Spencer Bruno Research Associates (SBRA), 212
Spirit, 152
Split Tablet, 191
Sprigg Lane Investment Co., 223, 302
Springs Industries, 168
Squibb, 204
SRI/Financial, 248
SRI Research Center, Inc., 243
SRI/VALS, 248
SSC&B, 187
Starch Ad Readership, 243
Starch, Daniel, & Staff, 175
Starch INRA Hooper, Inc., 173, 175, 220, 243, 253, 302
Star-Kist Foods, 4
STARS (Starch Travel Agent Readership Study), 243
Statistical Policy Division of the Office of Management and Budget (OMB), 264–265
STEP ONE (McCollum/Spielman), 240
Stern, 84
Stewart, Dougall & Associates, 175
Store Audits, 262
Stouffer, 1
STP Corp., 162
Stratplan (TRC), 211
Subaru, 142
Summa Consulting Group, 250
Survey Research Center at the University of California, 213
Survey Research Center at the University of Michigan, 175
Survey Research International, 257

Survey Research Laboratory at University of Illinois, 264
Swift & Co., 174

T
Tappan Motors, 151
Target Planning System (JWT), 291
Tarrance, Lance, & Associates, 54, 262
Tasty Fries (American Kitchen Foods), 8
Tater Pops (Carnation), 11
Tater Tots (Ore-Ida), 4, 8, 11, 19
Teaman/Lehman Associates, 222, 235
Technomic Consultants, 263
Telcom Research, Inc., 189, 278
Telemeter (ACN), 107–108
Tele-Research (Harte-Hanks), 239
Teleservice Research, 190
Telmar, 247, 263
TELSAM/PULSE (E & L), 233
Temple, Barker & Sloane, Inc., 223, 246, 302
Tender Chunks (Quaker), 98
TestSight (ACN), 101–115, 224
Texas Co., 174
Thompson, J. Walter, Co., 137, 178, 263, 267, 271, 283, 290–291, 301, 302
Three Sigma Research Center, Inc., 189
Time, Inc., 185, 189, 220, 223, 256, 301, 302
TMQ, Inc., 108
Topline Research Corp., 190
Total Research Corporation (TRC), 209, 212
Toyo Kogyo, 147
Toyota, 136, 142, 149, 154
Toy POS Data Base (NPD Group), 231
TRACE (MF), 56, 229
TRAC Forecasting (YSW), 234
Tracy-Locke, 287
Trade Magazine Total Audience Studies (SMRB), 238
Travel Industry Association of America, 76, 82
Traveller's World, 84
Travel Pulse (ORC), 209
Travel Tourism Research Association, 75
Trig (Bristol-Meyers), 200

TRIM (Harte-Hanks), 222, 239
TRIM, Inc. (MAJERS), 222, 250, 262
TRW, 248
TV Buying Guide (IRI), 230

U
UniFocus (Kapuler), 245
Unilever, 258
United Fruit Co., 195
U.S. Army Recruiting Command, 78, 80
U.S. Rubber Co., 174
U.S. Steel, 195
U.S. Travel and Tourism Administration (USTTA), 73–89
Universal Marketing Research, 195
University Resources (University of Hartford), 264
Urban Data Processing, 239
Urban Decision Systems, 247
Urban Opinion Surveys (MPR), 213

V
Valiant (Chrysler), 140
Valley Forge Information Service, 188
Values and Lifestyles Research Program (Bates), 292
Vancar (Chrysler), 149
Vauxhall (GM), 138
Vega (GM), 140
Video-Audience Research, 254
Video Storyboard Tests, 269
Viewer Response Profile, 56
Viewpoint (YSW), 234
VNU Amvest, 248, 249
VNU (United Dutch Publishing Co.), 248, 249
Volkswagen, 136, 137, 139, 141, 142, 146
Vopan Marketing Research, 278

W
Walker Research, Inc., 172, 220, 233–234, 303
Ward, J. A., Inc., 212
Wegman Grocery Stores, 105
Weight Watchers, 2, 24